FROM PROTEST TO PART

FROM PROTEST TO PARTIES

Party-Building and Democratization in Africa

ADRIENNE LEBAS

OXFORD
UNIVERSITY PRESS

OXFORD

UNIVERSITY PRESS

Great Clarendon Street, Oxford OX2 6DP

Oxford University Press is a department of the University of Oxford.
It furthers the University's objective of excellence in research, scholarship,
and education by publishing worldwide. Oxford is a registered trade mark of
Oxford University Press in the UK and in certain other countries

© Adrienne LeBas 2011

British Library Cataloguing in Publication Data
Data available

Library of Congress Cataloging in Publication Data
Data available

ISBN 978-0-19-954686-2 (Hbk)
ISBN 978-0-19-967300-1 (Pbk)

For my parents

The progress of human liberty shows that all concessions yet made to her august claims have been born of earnest struggle. The conflict has been exciting, agitating, all-absorbing, and for the time being, putting all other tumults to silence. It must do this or it does nothing.

Frederick Douglass

Citizens who are individually powerless do not very clearly anticipate the strength which they may acquire by uniting together. It must be shown to them in order to be understood.

Alexis de Tocqueville

Acknowledgments

In the course of writing a book, one accumulates many debts. This is especially true in my case, as fieldwork in Zimbabwe in 2002–6 was complicated by political crisis and economic collapse. I am grateful to the many individuals who agreed to talk to me, sometimes at personal risk. I am indebted to the many others who vouched for my trustworthiness, eased my movement within and across Zimbabwe's borders, and "sorted" my petrol and forex, despite what was doubtless an annoying over-usage of the phrase "now now." Finally, to the many Zimbabweans who had to remain nameless or uncited in these pages, your help is gratefully remembered here.

This book began as a dissertation, and I must thank my teachers who shaped the arguments here and did so much to point the way. Jack Snyder, Charles Tilly, and Mahmood Mamdani were excellent advisors during the writing, and Anthony Marx bears a good bit of responsibility for it being written in the first place. Jack's enthusiasm for the project has never flagged, and I thank him for pushing me in the direction of broader comparisons and bigger claims. It is a great sadness that Chuck did not live to see this book sitting on his shelf, but it heartens me to know that he would find his fingerprints all over the pages that follow. I am certain that, given a few more hours and a whiteboard, he and I could have come up with a still stronger, simpler, and more compelling way of presenting the arguments here.

In addition to my luck with mentors, I have been lucky with institutions. After funders expressed doubts about the feasibility of research on political opposition in Zimbabwe, a number of institutes at Columbia University made the fieldwork possible. The Institute for Historical Social Science provided the fellowship that allowed me to start fieldwork, and smaller grants from the Institute of African Studies and the Saltzman Institute of War and Peace Studies allowed me to stay in the field for longer than I had planned. The Woodrow Wilson International Center for Scholars in Washington, DC and the Institute for Social and Economic Research and Policy at Columbia provided office space and other support during the research and writing of the dissertation. I thank the following for access to their archives: the National Archives of Kenya; the National Archives of Zambia; the National Archives of Zimbabwe; the Zambian Consolidated Copper Mines; the Zambian Congress of Trade Unions; the Zimbabwean Congress of Trade Unions; the National Constitutional Assembly in Zimbabwe; the special collections of the University of Zambia; and the French Institute for Research in Africa (IFRA) in Nairobi. In Kenya, the Congress of Trade Unions and the Kenya Human

Rights Commission also provided access to materials. In the United States, I thank the United States Library of Congress and the New York Public Library's Schomberg Center for Research in Black Culture for access to their collections. In the United Kingdom, I benefited from the newspaper collections of the British Library. Portions of Chapters 5 and 7 draw on material initially published in Comparative Politics 38:4 (2006). This material is reprinted with permission.

After leaving Columbia, Nuffield College at the University of Oxford provided a stable home over the course of several years. Nuffield supported additional fieldwork for the project, as well as for new research that has informed the arguments that I make here. I thank Christel Kesler, Maria Sobolewska, and the community of Nuffield post-doc fellows, too large to mention individually here. The Department of Political Science at Michigan State University and the Department of Government at American University's School of Public Affairs also provided collegial environments in which to write. Michigan State provided funding for field research in Kenya. I thank both universities for their support.

In Zimbabwe, I owe special thanks to the Movement for Democratic Change, especially Nelson Chamisa, Last Maengehama, and Dennis Murira. My colleagues at the University of Zimbabwe and in the Department of Economic History were a source of support and advice. I am especially grateful to Eira Kramer, John Makumbe, and Joseph Mtisi. I must also thank, among so many others, Chen Chimutengwende, Godfrey Kanyenze, Timothy Kondo, Chris Kuruneri, Andrew Mudharara, Ralph Nkomo, Lucia Matibenga, Sam Moyo, and Sikhululekile Mkandla. I am grateful to friends David and Melanie McDermott Hughes, Erin McCandless, and Ezekiel Pajibo, who were in Zimbabwe during portions of the fieldwork. In Zambia, Marja Hineflaar and Opa Kapijimpanga extended hospitality and guidance. In Kenya, Otieno Aluoka has been an excellent friend and facilitator, and Jacob Achieng, Ejidiah Gachika, Patricia Kubai, and Eunice Ndomo provided research assistance at different points.

As I presented pieces of this project over the years, it was strengthened by questions and criticism from many individuals. Though this is almost certainly a woefully incomplete list, I am grateful for comments from: Jocelyn Alexander, David Anderson, Nancy Bermeo, Scott Blinder, Cristina Bodea, Michael Bratton, Kanchan Chandra, Nic Cheeseman, Daniel Compagnon, Tyler Dickovick, Geoff Evans, Julia Gallagher, Macartan Humphreys, Elisabeth Ivarsflaten, James Jasper, Laleh Khalili, Desmond King, Jackie Klopp, Norma Kriger, Miles Larmer, Johannes Lindvall, Carolyn Logan, Anthony Marx, Sam Moyo, Ngonidzashe Munemo, Dan Nexon, Brian Raftopoulos, Philipp Rehm, Rachel Beatty Riedl, Phil Roessler, Antoine Roger, Meredith Rolfe, Alexandra Scacco, Gilles Serra, Dan Slater, David Soskice, Sidney Tarrow, Scott Taylor, Nick Toloudis, Nicolas Van de Walle, and two anonymous reviewers for Oxford University Press. Diego Gambetta offered insights and encouragement at several points, as did Michael Bratton, who was my down-the-hall colleague for far too short a time. Eric Little, Richard Norrie, and Jennifer Yelle provided excellent research assistance. I appreciate the feedback provided by the Contentious Politics Workshop at Columbia University, the Junior Faculty Workshop at Michigan State, and the Nuffield College Politics and Sociology Post-Doc Seminar, as well as audiences at several universities and conferences. Finally, I thank Dominic Byatt, Jennifer Lunsford, Lizzy Suffling, and the rest of the OUP production staff for their patient help in bringing this book to press.

I am grateful to the many friends who saw me through the highs and lows of the decade-long process of writing this book, especially Cristina Bodea, Katie Cecil, Thomas Kenyon, Laleh Khalili, Denis Maslov, Cristian Meghea, Meredith Rolfe, Jennifer Tennant, Phil Tsui, and Robert Trager. I am also deeply thankful for the friendship and care of Patricia Kasiamhuru, whose generosity and sense of humor lightened many loads. Without her, Zimbabwe would have remained a foreign place, and I might not miss it as much as I do. The largest share of my gratitude must go to my family – my parents, my brothers Joe and Will, and my sister-in-law Lauren – for their constant love, support, and encouragement. This book is dedicated to my parents, Joe and Edie LeBas, who taught me the value of integrity, social justice, and a well-phrased argument. I hope they see some of that in the pages that follow.

Table of Contents

List of Figures and Tables

FIGURES

TABLES

List of Abbreviations

AWC	Association of Women's Clubs (Zimbabwe)
CCJP	Catholic Commission for Justice and Peace (separate organizations in Zimbabwe and Zambia)
CJPC	Catholic Justice and Peace Committee (Kenya)
CCZ	Christian Council of Zambia
COTU	Central Organization of Trade Unions (Kenya)
DC	District Committee of the ZCTU, Zambia
DP	Democratic Party (Kenya)
ESAP	Economic Structural Adjustment Program
FORD	Forum for the Restoration of Democracy (Kenya)
GEMA	Gikuyu Embu Meru Association (Kenya)
ICFTU	International Confederation of Free Trade Unions
IMF	International Monetary Fund
IRA	Industrial Relations Act (Zambia)
KANU	Kenya African National Union
KAWC	Kenya African Workers Congress
KFL	Kenyan Federation of Labour
LRA	Labor Relations Act (Zimbabwe)
LRF	Legal Resources Foundation (Zimbabwe)
MDC	Movement for Democratic Change (Zimbabwe)
MMD	Movement for Multiparty Democracy (Zambia)
MUZ	Mineworkers Union of Zambia
NARC	National Rainbow Coalition (Kenya)
NCA	National Constitutional Assembly (Zimbabwe)
NCCK	National Council of Churches of Kenya
NEC	National Executive Council of the MMD in Zambia and of the MDC in Zimbabwe
NERP	National Economic Recovery Program (Zambia)
NGO	Non-Governmental Organization
ORAP	Organisation of Rural Associations for Progress (Zimbabwe)
PF	Patriotic Front (Zambia)
SCCs	Small Christian Communities (Zambia)
SDF	Social Dimensions Fund (Zimbabwe)

UDI	Unilateral Declaration of Independence (Zimbabwe)
UNIP	United National Independence Party (Zambia)
ZANU	Zimbabwe African National Union (before 1987)
ZANU-PF	Zimbabwe African National Union – Patriotic Front (after 1987)
ZCC	Zimbabwe Council of Churches
ZCCM	Zambia Consolidated Copper Mines
ZCTU	Zambian Congress of Trade Unions
ZCTU	Zimbabwe Congress of Trade Unions
ZEC	Zambian Episcopal Conference (Catholic)
ZNUT	Zambian National Union of Teachers

Part One

Introduction

One

Opposition Parties and Democratization in Africa

In August of 1999, the Friedrich Ebert Stiftung, a German party organization that supports party and trade union development overseas, hosted a training workshop for opposition political party leaders in Harare, Zimbabwe. At the time, Zimbabwe's ruling party seemed assured of a landslide victory in upcoming parliamentary elections, then only ten months away. Surveying the parties gathered at the Harare Holiday Inn, no observer would have predicted the emergence of an effective opposition challenger. The existing opposition parties in Zimbabwe were weak: they lacked both grassroots structures and the resources to run campaigns in more than a handful of constituencies. Given this state of affairs, the prevailing sentiment at the workshop was one of frustration.[1] Opposition party leaders pointed to the lack of an independent electoral commission, irregularities in the voters' roll, and restrictions on public funding for opposition parties. They accused the ruling party of vote-buying, gerrymandering, and campaign interference. The more radical blamed civil society, arguing that intellectuals and activists refused to "take off the veils" and undertake any actions that could be construed as political. There was good reason for party leaders' pessimism about the state of opposition politics in Zimbabwe. Fueled by economic decline and rising prices, the 1990s had been a decade of vibrant protest, but protest and discontent had not translated into electoral success for opposition parties. The opposition had performed badly in the 1995 parliamentary elections. No opposition party won more than 7 percent of the national vote, and opposition and independent candidates captured only two of Zimbabwe's 120 popularly elected parliamentary seats. The ruling party improved its vote share in both urban and rural areas, and ruling party candidates were reelected unopposed in forty–five constituencies.

---

[1] Field notes, August 1999; also, interviews with Margaret Dongo, July 27, 1999; with W. Zembe, July 16, 1999; and with Clark Mpofu, June 1999.

The June 2000 parliamentary elections upturned observers' expectations of continued ruling party dominance in Zimbabwe. An opposition party formed after the Harare workshop won 47 percent of the popular vote and 57 of the 120 parlimentary seats. In contrast to the small opposition parties that had run in past elections, the Movement for Democratic Change (MDC) fielded candidates in all 120 constituencies, and it won support across ethnic lines and in both rural and urban areas. Even though its support was concentrated in urban areas and western Zimbabwe, the party was also competitive in regions that were considered the ruling party's heartland. In the Mashonaland provinces, where both ruling party support and state-sponsored violence were greatest, the MDC won more than 30 percent of the vote in eleven of thirty-four constituencies. In Midlands and Masvingo provinces, the party won more than 30 percent of the provincial vote, and it won nearly 50 percent in Manicaland province. Significantly, the MDC was able to coordinate anti-incumbent voters. The party won 91 percent of all votes cast for the opposition, and older opposition parties received even less support than they had in past elections.[2] The party built this base of support in a violent political environment that was not amenable to opposition success. Invasions of white-owned commercial farms began in March 2000, and the farms served as base camps for campaigns of violence by ruling party youth militia and war veterans.[3] Nor was repression limited to commercial farms. The police refused to license MDC rallies, and they periodically arrested MDC officials and candidates, only to release them days later without charge. Ruling party militia created "no-go" zones in rural areas where the opposition party could neither campaign nor maintain a presence. Those perceived to be MDC supporters, notably teachers, were beaten and driven from their homes. By the elections in late June, over 10,000 MDC supporters and activists had been displaced by state-sponsored violence.[4]

State repression in Zimbabwe intensified in subsequent years, but the MDC survived and continued to win elections. How do we explain this remarkable change? Out of Zimbabwe's fragmented opposition landscape, how did a single party emerge? And how was this party able to both mount an effective electoral challenge and withstand a concerted campaign of targeted repression? This book addresses the causes of opposition party strength and weakness. More specifically, I examine why some opposition parties are able to build strong organizations and mobilize large cross-ethnic constituencies, as the MDC did, while other African opposition parties tend toward

---

[2] ZANU-Ndonga, which had been the sole opposition seat in Parliament prior to the elections, retained the Chipinge South seat. It subsequently lost the seat to the MDC in the 2005 parliamentary elections.

[3] For more on repression on the farms, see Rutherford (2008); also HRW (2002).

[4] The best synopsis of the violence during this period remains ZHRNF (2001). The estimate for the number displaced from interview with an Amani Trust official, March 2003.

organizational weakness and fragmentation on ethnic lines. Though the book's empirical terrain is sub-Saharan Africa, the argument is generalizable to other late Third Wave democratizers, which share similar characteristics and pose similar challenges for opposition.

The book is built around a comparison of opposition parties in three countries: Zimbabwe, Zambia, and Kenya. The organizational strength of opposition parties varies across these countries, as well as within each country over time. This is not an account of political party formation in democratic contexts, as my interest is restricted to those mixed semi-democratic, semi-authoritarian settings known as "hybrid regimes."[5] In these regimes, the degree of political opening and the rules of the game remain uncertain, contested both by incumbents and by their challengers. The strength of opposition parties obviously influences this contest but does not determine its outcome. Negotiations over rules and practice are protracted and necessarily contingent, and reversals at one point can often lay the groundwork for more lasting changes at another. To be as clear as possible, the cases discussed here cannot be termed democratizing regimes, as that would misleadingly imply movement in the direction of greater democracy. But neither should competitive authoritarian regimes be viewed as static or "stuck." As this book hopes to suggest, the building blocks of democracy can be put in place during periods of political closure, but progress in one area of institution-building need not have immediate effects on the overall political system. Thus, rather than offering a deterministic model that links party development and successful (or failed) democratization, I suggest instead a set of mechanisms that together produce more cohesive and more socially rooted political party organizations. The book also provides some reasons that these mechanisms can lead to violence and conflict *as well as* to more competitive elections.

In order to explain the differential strength of opposition parties, I argue for the importance of two factors. First, strong parties are, at least in the initial stages of democratization, likely to be those that borrow the resources and organization of pre-existing institutional structures, especially those that span ethnic and regional cleavages. Secondly, opposition elites are more likely to maintain the cohesion of their parties and the commitment of activists when they use strategies and appeals that escalate conflict and reorient social boundaries around the lines of partisan affiliation. The first of these factors, the presence or absence of mobilizing structures, is a legacy of past periods of authoritarian rule. In sub-Saharan Africa, some authoritarian states pursued alliances with corporate actors, such as trade unions, in order to establish

---

[5] Hybrid regimes are also known as semi-authoritarian regimes or electoral autocracies. Literature defining this category of regimes includes Diamond (2002), Levitsky and Way (2002), Schedler (2006). The most comprehensive discussion of the character and diversity of competitive authoritarian regimes is found in Levitsky and Way (2010).

greater control over society. As political opening increased, labor movements in these countries had the organizational heft and political visibility to serve as focal points for opposition and, eventually, the mobilizing structures of new parties. In Zimbabwe and Zambia, we will see how labor-led opposition parties were able to mobilize diverse constituencies due to the geographical reach of the institutional structures they borrowed from previously state-allied labor movements. In contrast, where authoritarian state rule repressed organized labor, as in Kenya, opposition parties lacked mobilizing structures that spanned constituencies and regions. Opposition parties in these contexts were more likely to fragment on ethnic lines, organize themselves around personalized or otherwise limited networks, and fail to institutionalize over multiple election rounds. Where entrepreneurs attempted to build cross-ethnic parties in these countries, they usually failed, as they were unable to tap into organizational structures that spanned geographic and other network barriers. To put this point most simply, the choices of states matter. Forms of authoritarian rule that relied on semi-corporatist alliances unintentionally armed their allies, providing them with structures and resources that could later be used to effectively challenge the state. Authoritarian states that were instead built on ethnic brokerage yielded opposition parties mirroring this form of linkage. In these settings, party fragmentation and volatility have been the typical results.

History therefore endows opposition elites with more or fewer opportunities and resources. As time passes, however, these advantages become more diffuse, and the choices of elites and organizations drive party-building. The tasks of opposition parties similarly shift over time. If the first phase of party formation is concerned largely with mobilization and how to create a mass base, the second phase of party development is concerned with how to preserve and institutionalize links between elites and constituencies. Opposition parties are more successful at sustaining mobilization and preventing fragmentation when they pursue strategies that increase the distance between themselves and incumbents, limit inter-party negotiation, and forge new social boundaries that make cross-partisan interaction more difficult. Political polarization is, in other words, an effective party-building strategy. By reinforcing conflict with other parties or with incumbents, opposition elites are sometimes able to recraft existing (and occasionally cross-cutting) social identities around the single cleavage of political partisanship.[6] In sharply polarized settings, activists and constituents derive meaning from party affiliation, and solidarity serves as a side-benefit that may compensate for an opposition party's failure to win or distribute patronage. As polarization

---

[6] An earlier version of this argument is advanced in LeBas (2006). For other perspectives on "boundary work", see Benford, Gamson (1995), Gould (1995), Hunt, and Snow (1994), McAdam et al. (2001), Tilly (2004*b*).

empties out the middle ground between the incumbent party and its primary challenger, defection and the formation of third parties are also rendered more difficult. But strategies that increase social distance between parties also increase incumbent perceptions of threat. At the heart of the book's argument, therefore, lies a paradox: the tools that build stronger and more effective party organizations can also trigger conflict and violence. Party polarization raises the stakes of political competition, making authoritarian retrenchment an appealing option for incumbents. It can also lead to organizational changes within parties, changes that make conflict and deadlock more likely. Democratization requires strong parties, but party-building strategies slip out of the control of political actors, generating unintended consequences that can further lower the likelihood of successful democratization, at least in the short run.

I will lay out the mechanics of this argument in greater detail in Chapter 2. This chapter provides an answer for why opposition parties in these contexts "matter," even though their activities and their abilities to effect change via the ballot box may be limited. The rest of the book will then examine how parties are built in contexts where they are required to act as both electoral challengers and popular movements for reform. Why are strong opposition parties necessary in newly democratizing states? Opposition parties play two roles in the "hybrid" or semi-democratic regimes that have become prevalent in the late Third Wave of democracy. They compete in elections, but they also coordinate the popular mobilization and protests that push political change forward. Strong party organizations are necessary to push reluctant incumbents toward reform and political opening in semi-democratic or in competitive authoritarian regimes. Without strong opposition, elections in these contexts are unlikely to become competitive, and representative links between governments and citizens will remain weak. Democratization in these regimes operates differently, therefore, than in the pacted or negotiated transitions of the early Third Wave. It is more protracted, and it is ultimately more contentious than the transitions that have served as the empirical base for the transitology theory of past decades. By contentious, I mean that the shape and extent of transition is shaped to a large extent by the extent and durability of popular mobilization.

PROTEST IN HYBRID REGIMES

Understanding variation in the character of opposition parties is an interesting puzzle in and of itself, but it is also important because these parties affect the quality of governance in new democracies. As suggested above, the organizational strength and durability of opposition parties are partial determinants of how far political liberalization progresses. Where opposition parties are weak or unable to coordinate their actions, they place little pressure on reluctantly democratizing incumbents. Small party splinters, particularly when organized around a single leader, are easy for incumbents to co-opt via patronage or selective incorporation. Where parties are weak in these ways, incumbents retain control over the pace and extent of democratization, leading in many cases to a stable "halfway house" of semi-authoritarianism.[7] I argue that the weakness of opposition party mobilization – not the resources or cohesiveness of ruling party – is the primary cause of this kind of authoritarian persistence.[8] This weakness is in turn determined by the choices of parties themselves, as well as by the set of resources that history has handed them. This book suggests that differences in opposition strength are not primarily a reflection of the skills or short-run strategies of incumbents, as suggested in work by Lust-Okar and others (Bellin 2000, 2002; Lust-Okar 2004). Nor should we see the deficiencies of opposition as the result of a lack of political opening. State-level factors shape the environment in which opposition movements maneuver, but a focus on top-down instruments of control can occlude the ways in which popular contention can sidestep and even undermine these controls. The starting point for this book, therefore, is a somewhat different presumption. Political change is driven forward by popular mobilization. Explanations for the differential strength and durability of mobilization are best found through an examination of protest and its interaction with party formation.

From the 1980s to the present, the number of countries that have experimented with some degree of political liberalization and party competition has dramatically increased. In 1989, only sixty-nine countries held contested and minimally free multiparty elections; today, over 120 do (Freedom_House 2008). Nowhere has this change been more striking than in sub-Saharan Africa. In the early 1990s, pressures for democracy resulted in political change in nearly all of the continent's countries: the majority of African states legalized opposition and instituted other political reforms, and more than thirty African states had held multiparty elections, of highly variable quality, by 1995. There have been reversals of this progress in some countries, but political change in several countries has proven lasting. Twenty-two African states have held between three and five uninterrupted rounds of multiparty elections; if one adds countries in which brief interruptions of constitutional

---

[7] In the early 1990s, Samuel Huntington and others argued that liberalized authoritarianism was a "halfway house [that] cannot stand" (Huntington 1991: 598). Two decades of intervening experience shows that semi-authoritarianism can sometimes be "not a way station, but a way of life," as Jason Brownlee elegantly suggests. See the discussion in Brownlee (2007), chapter 1, especially pp. 16–17.

[8] I will return to this point briefly in chapter 2. Work that instead stresses the strength and resources of state institutions, particularly the ruling party, includes McFaul (2002); Smith (2005); Way (2005); Brownlee (2007).

rule were followed by the restoration of democracy, the tally increases to twenty-six.[9] When one includes countries that have held founding elections in the past five years, the strength of the trend toward multipartyism is staggering. In 2009, over 85 percent of Africa's 1 billion people lived in multiparty electoral regimes.[10]

Though the numbers tell an optimistic tale, the quality of democracy practiced in these countries varies widely. Freedom House names only eleven African countries as fully free,[11] but, even in this limited group, commitment to democratic norms is shaky. In 2005, a high-profile journalist in Mali was beaten and left for dead after criticizing politicians for corruption and abuses of power on his radio show. The Namibian state is widely believed to have been involved in the 2003 assassination of civil society activist Bernard Shevanyenga, and opposition parties are a regular target of state harassment. In South Africa, the privatization of security and evidence of systemic corruption in the police force raise questions about the extent to which the rule of law extends equally to all citizens. The majority of multiparty regimes in Africa depart even more sharply from the standards associated with democracy in other parts of the world (Kirschke 2000; Van de Walle 2002; Gyimah-Boadi 2004; Tripp 2004; Roessler 2005; Bratton and Mattes 2009). Violations of democratic norms are not an occasional occurrence; instead, they are regular enough to create uncertainty over the degree to which democracy governs the rules of the game. In these hybrid regimes, multiparty elections have been grafted onto state institutions and political cultures that remain stubbornly authoritarian. Thus, in the Gambia, parliamentary elections are held in one year, while the President publicly threatens human rights activists with death in the next. The Nigerian state shows greater respect for civil and political rights, at least in some parts of the country, but party-linked militia are responsible for hundreds of deaths during each election cycle. Even in Malawi, a markedly better democratic performer, opposition politicians have been detained and charged with treason, and press freedom is only sporadically respected.

The disappointments of democratization are not limited to Africa alone. Flawed or partial democratization in Asia and Eastern Europe has also resulted in "illiberal democracies" and "electoral autocracies" that fall far short of the pluralism and respect for human rights that democracy is meant to deliver (Gills et al. 1993; Zakaria 1997; Schedler 2006). At times, the third

---

[9] This includes a handful countries that held multiparty elections even prior to the transitions of the early 1990s, such as Botswana, Senegal, and Zimbabwe.

[10] If we place North Africa outside the region, as Africanists and Middle East specialists often do, the percentage of Africans living in multiparty regimes increases to 90 percent.

[11] These countries are Benin, Botswana, Cape Verde, Ghana, Lesotho, Mali, Mauritius, Namibia, Sao Tome and Principe, Senegal, and South Africa. Notably, three of these countries are island nations with small populations, two of which have less than half a million people.

wave of democratization seems to have brought with it increased political violence, state repression, and instability (Fein 1995; Snyder and Ballentine 1996; Snyder 2000; Regan and Henderson 2002; Villarreal 2002; Davenport 2004; Davenport and Armstrong 2004).[12] In a number of countries, electoral competition has generated incentives for the politicization of ascriptive identities and has even served as a trigger for ethnic and communal violence (De Nevers 1993; Snyder 2000; Klopp and Zuern 2007). Rwanda is perhaps the most commonly cited example of the destructive potential of democratization, but electoral mobilization has led to lower-level violence in a number of other countries. It could be that democratization leads to an initial uncertainty over the boundaries of the political community that only violence can solve, as Michael Mann argues (Mann 2005). But violence has not only been a feature of the first stages of regime transition. In India, "institutionalized riot systems" exist comfortably alongside party competition (Brass 1997; Varshney 2003). In Venezuela and Colombia, violence has been a similarly durable feature of inter-party competition, even though these countries are not sharply divided on ethnic, regional, or class lines (Coppedge 1994; Green 2005). In still other democracies, elected leaders have used unwarranted violence to repress strikes and protests or to enforce "law and order" (e.g., Gledhill 2005; HRW 2009).

It is important to assess whether the distinct qualities of these regimes yield patterns of party competition and organizational development that differ substantially from what we currently believe about these processes. Is party formation governed by a different set of rules in hybrid regimes? Is it possible for parties to build stable linkages with mass constituencies when institutional rules remain in flux? In what ways does the weakness of rights regimes or the routinization of violence affect the organizational forms that parties take? In terms of definitions, hybrid regimes are not so much incompletely democratized regimes as those in which democratic and authoritarian characteristics *coexist* – with varying degrees of stability. Multiparty elections are held, but incumbents retain control over the extent of political opening and may use undemocratic means, including violence, to retain power. Incumbents allow some space for the expression of popular demands, notably through multiparty elections, but they consistently deny the

---

[12] The exact shape of the relationship between democracy and repression remains unclear, but the most recent statistical work does not contradict the U-shaped "more murder in the middle" thesis advanced in Fein. However, in a careful statistical analysis, Davenport and Armstrong (2004) conclude that repression decreases when the level of democracy approaches a critical threshold level – but does not necessarily increase at intermediate values of democracy. This does not contradict the basic claim that democratization and violence can coexist, and I am concerned that the five-point terror scale used as the dependent variable in the article may wash out variation that could prove important in understanding differences between autocracies and partially democratized countries.

"protected consultation" between the state and its citizens that Tilly identifies as the hallmark of democracy (Tilly 2004*a*). Political opening allows for new collective actors and new forms of collective action, but the products of this increased space are often met with harassment or renewed repression. Uncertainty over the rules of the game is characteristic of hybrid regimes, and it stems from the different motivations of incumbents and their challengers. Mobilization by opposition parties in hybrid regimes is, by its nature, transformational. At least initially, challengers organize their campaigns around demands for greater political opening, deconcentration of state power, increased transparency, and other reforms that increase the number of individuals with access to power. Incumbents, on the other hand, resist change to the status quo. They are pressured to undertake reforms, by domestic actors and by the international community, but they find means of retaining control over the process (Ake 1994; Joseph 1999). Reluctant democratizers use a variety of means to undercut competition, including restrictions on rights to assembly and association, inconsistent application of the rule of law, harassment of activists and opposition politicians, misuse of public resources for electoral purposes, and manipulation of the media.[13]

During democratization, therefore, opposition political parties straddle two realms. On the one hand, they compete in elections and are the means by which political elites win office. Like their counterparts in consolidated democracies, parties in democratizing countries are the crucial institutions of democracy: they structure political competition, aggregate societal interests, serve as the primary link between elites and masses, and may even build trust in democratic institutions (Schattschneider 1942; Sartori 1976; Aldrich 1995; Coleman 1996; Caillaud and Tirole 2002). But parties in hybrid regimes are also protagonists in battles over political opening and institutional reform. This is perhaps more true in sub-Saharan Africa and other parts of the late Third Wave, which have lacked the political pacts and consensual leveling of the playing field that characterized transitions in Latin America and Southern Europe. Political parties in these countries are engaged in what Andreas Schedler terms a "nested game," in which elections are merely one means of advancing larger aims (Schedler 2002*b*). An uneven playing ground may render electoral victory impossible, but elections are the key sites of struggle and negotiation for opposition parties. As Schedler notes:

> accumulating strength in the electoral arena, [opposition parties] improve their chances to extract institutional reforms from the ruling party.... Rather than establishing a "self-enforcing" equilibrium, ambivalent elections thus trigger a

---

[13] For an overview of tactics, see Schedler (2002*a*), Ottaway (2003). Excellent case studies include Lehoucq and Molina (2002), Tronvoll (2001), Agbese (1999), Wiktorowicz (2000).

"self-subversive" spiral that over time undermines both the institutional and the electoral bases of the authoritarian incumbent (10).

According to Schedler, it is the threat of electoral loss that pushes incumbents to implement substantive reform. Where incumbents can secure consistent, convincing electoral margins, regimes are unlikely to shed more than the most superficial trappings of authoritarianism.

The relationship between opposition weakness and preservation of a semi-authoritarian status quo is even stronger in the strongly majoritarian electoral systems that characterize much of sub-Saharan Africa. Nearly all Anglophone African countries have single-member district systems, and presidential elections are typically single-round, which allows them to be won with a plurality of votes.[14] Francophone African countries typically have multimember districts, but these systems are also strongly majoritarian with fairly high thresholds for party entry. When the anti-incumbent vote is split across two or more opposition challengers, ruling parties can win parliamentary elections with small pluralities of the popular vote. Kenya's 1992 and Lesotho's 1998 elections are the most oft-cited examples of this outcome. The ruling party in Kenya held onto a parliamentary majority in 1992 with just under 30 percent of the total vote, and Daniel arap Moi retained the presidency with 36 percent. In Lesotho, opposition parties received 40 percent of the popular vote but captured only one parliamentary seat, a result that led to rioting, political crisis, and, eventually, military intervention by South African and Botswanan troops (Southall and Fox 1999). The adoption of a system of proportional representation was one of the components of the resolution to the Lesotho crisis. Lesotho, however, is the exception. More commonly, opposition party fragmentation has effects on neither political stability nor the behavior of the ruling party. Ruling parties in Cameroon and Ethiopia, for instance, have maintained political control easily, despite deep political cleavages, widespread dissent, and a series of deeply flawed elections. In both countries, coercion is certainly part of the story, but ruling parties also manipulate and benefit from fragmentation in the opposition, which is split on communal lines (Engedayehu 1993; Lyons 1996; Joireman 1997; Menthong 1998; Takou-gang 2003).[15] African countries also typically possess powerful presidencies, which undermine party development, amplify the effect of opposition

---

[14] For more on the disproportionality of electoral systems in sub-Saharan Africa, see Reynolds (1999), Barkan et al. (2006); for related analysis of a different set of countries, see Reilly (2001).

[15] The Ethiopian elections in 2005 mark a departure from this pattern, with a strong showing from new cross-ethnic opposition parties. Abbink notes, however, that these parties struggled with internal divisions and feared government "moles" who were bent on manufacturing party splits (Abbink 2006).

party fragmentation, and increase the power that can potentially accrue to winners of small pluralities of the vote.[16]

The absence of competitive elections allows for the preservation of authoritarian practices and reserve realms of state power. It also frees incumbents to engage in corruption and other practices that undermine state authority (Coppedge 1993; Corrales 2001; Grzymala-Busse 2003). Competition, on the other hand, imposes constraints and some degree of accountability on ruling parties (Schumpeter 1976; Key 1977). The building of strong party organizations delivers other additional benefits. The mass party organizations built to fight elections can tip the balance of power in favor of popular constituencies, creating incentives for elites to incorporate and respond to the demands of the grassroots (Mainwaring 1988; Coppedge 1993). Though competitive party systems do not immunize countries from political violence or from popular distrust of government, these systems allow citizens a means of engaging with government and effecting political change. Countries faced with a persistent "party deficit" are more likely to experience low levels of popular support and engagement – and they may even fall prey to anti-system movements and democratic breakdown (Mainwaring 1999; Corrales 2001; see also, Linz and Stepan 1996).

In sum, strong electoral competition is necessary for rooted and accountable government, and strong opposition parties are necessary for competitive elections. This point is fairly uncontroversial. There is a much weaker consensus, however, regarding the contributions of contention to the building of these kinds of parties and these kinds of elections. In order to place pressure on incumbents to institute political reform, pro-democracy movements and opposition parties may draw on popular mobilization, street protests, and the other forms of non-routine politics regularly called "contentious politics." This book is primarily interested in explaining how opposition parties organize and discipline dissent, but it also engages with a larger debate about the relationship between protest and political change.

DEMOCRATIZATION AND POPULAR MOBILIZATION

Does sustained popular mobilization assist democratization, or does it hinder it? Are popular movements necessary for pushing authoritarian governments toward reform, or must their demands be moderated in order for incumbents to accept democracy? To a large extent, scholars have viewed sustained popular mobilization as an impediment to democratization. In work

---

[16] For a review of the problems that presidential systems can create for party development, see Mainwaring (1993); Stepan and Skach (1993); Linz and Valenzuela (1994); Shugart (1998); Stoner-Weiss (2001); Samuels (2002); and Hale (2005).

stretching back to Samuel Huntington, popular mobilization is viewed as destabilizing, especially in contexts where institutions and state authority are weak. Popular demands can "overwhelm" political institutions, particularly political parties, if these are not strong enough to absorb and channel demands into the realm of routine politics (Huntington 1968). The subsequent break-down of public order results in reversion to authoritarianism. Similar arguments have been made in more recent work on democratic transition. Popular mobilization and protest are presumed to reduce the flexibility of the actors who have the power to form pacts and make compromises. According to this logic, strong demands from below make coalitions of moderates unlikely, as neither side is able to make credible claims about its end goals or about its ability to control hardliners (O'Donnell and Schmitter 1986; Przeworski 1991). Strong popular mobilization and visible protest raise the perceived "costs of toleration" for incumbents and for those who benefit from the status quo (Dahl 1971). In countries where inequality is high or there exist demands for redistribution, strong popular movements are likely to trigger authoritarian retrenchment (Boix 2003; Acemoglu and Robinson 2005). Even for those who believe that protest weakens authoritarian control, there is a widespread presumption that early mobilization must be dampened at some point to prevent a backlash from hardliners (Valenzuela 1989; Ekiert and Kubik 1999; Zielinski 1999). Mobilization may be required to unsettle the status quo, but the balance between mobilization and moderation rests on a knife-edge. To use Dahl's felicitous phrasing, "one perennial problem of opposition is that there is either too much or too little" (quoted in Rustow 1970: 354).

There are, of course, challenges to this point of view. Charles Tilly has consistently argued that sustained popular contention transforms the nature of authoritarian states and the character of state–society relations, changes that foster greater democracy in the long run (Tilly 1995, 2004a). Other social movement scholars similarly view democratization as an extended process forged by challenge and by "cycles of contention" (Tarrow 1994; McAdam et al. 2001). The creation and mobilization of strong working class movements play a central role in many historical institutionalist accounts of democratization (Rueschemeyer et al. 1992; Collier 1999). For scholars working with shorter time horizons, disruptive and even "dangerous" protest often plays a prominent role in the destabilization of authoritarian rule and its transformation into new forms of politics (Alves 1984; Keck 1992; Adler and Webster 1995; Collier and Mahoney 1997; Wood 2000; Bunce 2003).[17]

---

[17] It may also be that mass mobilization-led transitions result in regimes with higher levels of freedom than those that result from incumbent-managed political openings, as Freedom House argues (Karatnycky and Ackerman 2005); also, Stephan and Chenoweth (2008). As others point out, pacted transitions often preserve the power of authoritarian coalitions and prevent the

In Eastern Europe, street protests contributed to the erosion of authoritarian regimes and the beginnings of democratic transition (Lohmann 1994; Ekiert and Kubik 1998, 1999). In sub-Saharan Africa, authoritarian states were similarly pushed toward political liberalization by strong waves of popular protest (Bratton and Van de Walle 1997). Drawing on the same cases that inform O'Donnell and Schmitter, Nancy Bermeo challenges the assumption that pacts occur only through the moderation of protest (Bermeo 1997). She points out that extremist mobilization, including physical attacks on moderates, continued throughout transition periods in Portugal, Spain, and elsewhere. Rather than hardening incumbents against democratization, popular mobilization may increase its appeal. Threatened elites may simply conclude that democracy is the best solution to the "problem" of extremist mobilization (Bermeo 1997: 316–19).

To a large extent, both of these perspectives are correct. Popular mobilization is destabilizing. It creates uncertainty over incumbents' ability to retain power, and it may open up space for further challenges to the status quo. But increased uncertainly has ambiguous effects on democratization. In some settings, authoritarian elites may choose to resist popular demands via repression. In others, they may attempt to accommodate, co-opt, or recast popular demands, an outcome that we would generally see as increasing the likelihood of democratization. But popular mobilization has deeper effects as well, making its effect on long-run political development even harder to ascertain. Protest is not simply a weapon used to extract concessions; instead, the organizations built in order to coordinate and sustain protest can change the character of state-society bargaining, channeling it in directions that favor the escalation of conflict. When we see increases in the scale and organization of protest in closed regimes – a shift that I argue is necessary for the opening-up of competitive authoritarian regimes – we are witnessing a solution to the problem of high-risk collective action. I argue that movements are often most effective in encouraging collective action where they abandon the politics of moderation and compromise.

To put this point more clearly, opposition parties are fractious coalitions that face a constant threat of organizational fragmentation and mobilizational decline. Strong parties hold these coalitions together by constructing social boundaries that both make defection difficult and provide meaning to activists and supporters. Where parties use polarizing tactics and exclusionary campaigns, they are more likely to maintain control over party structures and popular constituencies. Where opposition parties of this type face incumbents that retain a similar capacity to mobilize, conflict ensues.

democratization of state institutions (Karl 1986; Hagopian 1990; Przeworski 1991; Linz and Stepan 1996; Jones Luong 2002; Encarnacion 2005).

Democracy requires strong, competitive, and socially rooted parties, but the building of the rooted and durable parties that we desire can increase conflict and the potential for violence. This argument challenges the sunnier models of transition that underlie the enthusiasm for democracy promotion and democratic "enlargement" in policy circles. It hearkens back, however, to older ideas about how democracy is forged. Rustow suggests that democracy is the space that lies between enforced unanimity and "implacable hostility"; in order to get there, "what infant democracy requires is not a lukewarm struggle but a hot family feud" (Rustow 1970: 363, 355). Just as intractable conflict may be the only route to democracy, mobilization that intensifies conflict and erects sharp social boundaries may be the only means of effective party-building in hybrid regimes. Strong opposition parties are necessary for democracy, but the tools and tactics needed to forge them increase the likelihood of conflict.

THE PLAN

The book is centered on the close analysis of three cases in sub-Saharan Africa: Zimbabwe, Zambia, and Kenya. The time horizon spans the entirety of each country's immediate pre- and post-independence history, but analysis privileges particular moments or "critical junctures" that had far-reaching effects on subsequent political developments (Collier and Collier 1991; Mahoney 2000; Pierson 2004). Attention is first focused on the immediate post-independence period and, especially, the critical choices that states made in response to post-independence strike waves that occurred in these – as well as in most other – African countries. I argue that the choices made by states at this juncture were both contingent and had lasting effects on political development. Where states chose to use organized labor to discipline protest, trade unions were available to serve as a base for opposition in subsequent periods. Where states chose instead to repress or fragment trade unions, mobilizing structures based on organized labor were absent. The second critical juncture is when protest turns into parties, a period that might be described as the beginnings of "democratic transition" by others. Once again, there was a moment of contingency: movements made choices about how to link themselves to other social actors who were involved in popular protest, and they made choices about party strategy and internal party organization. These choices had medium-run effects on opposition parties' connections to popular constituencies, their success at boundary creation and manipulation, and their internal decision-making and cohesion.

The three cases examined in the book are selected because they share institutional settings that are roughly comparable. Compared to many other African countries, state capacity was strong in these three countries, and authoritarian regimes were both more stable and less repressive than elsewhere on the continent. None of the cases experienced a successful military coup or other extraconstitutional transfer of power. Ruling parties in all three countries relied on popular mobilization and held regular elections, though opposition parties were often barred from participation.[18] Associational life was constrained, but it was never as circumscribed as in communist Eastern Europe or elsewhere in Africa. Put simply, these are settings in which we would expect opposition parties to be more successful. By the time opposition parties were launched in the early or late 1990s, citizens in all three countries had had extensive experience of elections, and they had previously voted against candidates preferred by those in power. During authoritarian periods, intra-party primaries were sharply contested in all three countries. Even though ruling parties banned or placed constraints on opposition parties, turnover rates in these countries' parliaments remained high, and MPs favored by party leadership were periodically voted out of office. In terms of institutional rules, electoral rules also favor opposition party coordination. All three countries currently operate first-past-the-post (FPTP) systems with single-member districts. Parties are required to register, but there is little legislation in place to govern their operations or internal governance. Though party registration is sometimes manipulated by ruling parties, it does not create differential barriers to party fragmentation. In all three countries, at various points, more than fifteen opposition parties have been registered.

Despite this backdrop of contextual similarity, political outcomes in Zimbabwe, Zambia, and Kenya differ from one another markedly. In Zimbabwe, as suggested above, protest united around a single party, which has monopolized the opposition vote over multiple electoral rounds. In Zambia, a similarly labor-based opposition party won multiparty elections in 1992. Defections from this party initially fueled a fragmented opposition landscape, which often took on an ethnic cast, but recent elections may suggest some reconsolidation of the party landscape. Finally, in Kenya, opposition parties have been consistently marked by high volatility, severe fragmentation, and highly ethnicized linkages between parties and constituencies. Vote fragmentation, at both the national and the constituency level, has increased over time.

---

[18] Zambia and Kenya experimented with competitive multiparty politics immediately after independence, but ruling parties in the two countries quickly established monopolies on political representation. Zambia was a de jure single-party state from 1971 to 1990; Kenya became a de jure single-party state in 1982, though opposition parties had been banned since 1969. In contrast to these two, Zimbabwe never formally adopted single-party rule. After independence in 1980, the ruling party brutally suppressed its major party rival, eventually forcing its merger into the ruling party in 1987. For the 1980s and the 1990s, Zimbabwe functioned as a de facto single-party state. The Marxist–Leninist ruling party redirected many state powers to the party, it suppressed opposition parties, and the state seriously contemplated the formal institution of single-party rule in 1989–90. At the beginning of the opposition movements I consider here, all three countries could be safely termed "party-states."

The case selection strategy used in the book makes an argument based on small perturbations and political choices more convincing. At independence, structural conditions were broadly similar, but, as I will signal in the pages that follow, the choices of state elites and other political actors set popular mobilization and party organization on different paths. States, politicians, and popular movements move creatively within the structures they have built, but they are also products of those structures. New opposition parties are shaped by the mobilizing structures they inherit and the set of strategies that seem reasonable or possible in a given political environment. They can improvise on the margins, but it is difficult to stray too far from established scripts.

The argument advanced here borrows heavily from notions of path dependency (David 1985; Pierson 2000; Mahoney 2004). Small perturbations result in quickly divergent pathways, pathways that both constrain and create opportunities for popular mobilization at later points in time. Party organizations retain agency within this structure of opportunity and constraint. The internal structure of parties is shaped by the choices of elites and grassroots, and party strategies create political landscapes that make the defection of supporters and elites more or less difficult. Chapter 2 introduces these dynamics in greater detail. The definition of party strength in Chapter 2 is derived from the classic literature on party organization and internal party structure. Strong parties vary in terms of organizational forms and in their adaptability, but they all provide resources to candidates and to constituents that make defection difficult or costly.

The remainder of the book is organized into three sets of paired chapters. Each pair consists of one chapter that is focused on Zimbabwe and another that broadens the lens to examine similarities and differences in Zambia and Kenya. Chapters 3 and 4 examine authoritarian labor control in the three countries, focusing especially on the degree to which trade union structures were centralized, autonomous from the direct control of the state, and had control over the actions of union members. These chapters trace the process by which authoritarian states instituted control over labor in the immediate post-independence period, and they also chart the ways that labor movements struggled to liberate themselves from authoritarian state control. In Zimbabwe and Zambia, state corporatism facilitated the construction of strong, centralized labor movements that connected workers across the lines of ethnicity and region. In these two countries, organized labor liberated itself from state control prior to the emergence of political protest, and trade unions served as powerful mobilizing structures. In Kenya, on the other hand, state labor control stifled the autonomy and organizational capacity of trade unions. By the time that popular protest emerged, organized labor was not a significant political actor.

In Chapters 5 and 6, I examine how the implementation of economic structural adjustment broke the alliances that had previously played a role in legitimating authoritarian rule. Economic crisis and reform triggered waves of popular protest across sub-Saharan Africa. During this period, labor movements in Zimbabwe and Zambia built links with larger constituencies and took more confrontational stances vis-à-vis the state, while the lack of a strong labor movement in Kenya led to very different developments there. What was notable about this period of civil society "rebirth" was the shift in the character of protest from limited economic demands to transformational political ones. In this pair of chapters, I suggest that opposition movements had different degrees of organizational capacity at the time that the shift from limited to transformational demands occurred. Movements differed markedly in the density of their networks and the degree to which followers saw themselves as sharing a common identity. These differences had significant effects on the parties that emerged from social movements.

The final set of paired chapters addresses party-building outcomes. Chapters 7 and 8 examine differences in how opposition parties structured their internal decision-making and managed their links to popular constituencies. In only one of the three cases, Zimbabwe, were party elites able to manage tendencies toward organizational fragmentation, and the MDC's vote bloc remained fairly stable over multiple election rounds. This was partly due to the strength of cooperative ties connecting elites and activists when the party was still a movement, but cohesion was also due to the solidarity-boosting effects of political polarization. In Zambia and Kenya, neither incumbent nor opposition parties made attempts to restructure political cleavages or create sharp boundaries that polarized voters. Party vote shares were instead marked by fluidity and the periodic defection of voting blocks. Chapters 7 and 8, therefore, shed light on how the choices of political elites can forge polarization and adversarial partisanship – or the opposite.

In the book's final pages, I pull back from the specifics of individual cases to briefly examine broader implications for theories of opposition party formation. The conclusion argues that we would expect to find similar factors at play and causal mechanisms at work in other late Third Wave democratizers, both within and beyond sub-Saharan Africa. The chapter also reflects, briefly, on democracy promotion policies. But before we turn to the complexities of individual countries and how best to influence their politics, we must first build a model that might explain opposition party formation in a diverse set of hybrid regimes.

Two

The Sources of Opposition Party Strength

Opposition parties in sub-Saharan Africa are presumed to be weak. Scholars argue that African parties lack structures, disappear in the periods between elections, and have little to no connection to civil society organizations and popular constituencies (Widner 1997; Olukoshi 1998; Manning 2005; Erdmann 2007). The track records of parties in a number of countries often seem to confirm the early assessment of African opposition parties as "[constituting] little more than an ambitious politician, a handful of acolytes, and a nonexistent base of members and finances" (Bratton and Van de Walle 1997: 115). Many parties do look like little more than the personalized vehicles of "recycled elites" (Chabal and Daloz 1999). Partly, the general weakness of parties reflects the primacy of personalized clientelism in structuring elite–mass ties in sub-Saharan Africa. There are consistent patterns across African states in terms of the personalization of power, the use of state resources to serve clientelistic ends, and the suffusion of formal institutions with practices and logics derived from the private or communal sphere. Collectively, this set of practices produce regimes that are often termed neopatrimonial (Bratton and Van de Walle 1997: ch. 2). In neopatrimonial settings, the maximization of clientelistic rewards is the primary driver of individual and collective decision-making, and individuals are presumed to act in order to strengthen their ties with those already possessing access to power. New parties face particular obstacles in these environments. Where informal institutions or charismatic linkages govern the bulk of political practice, neither elites nor political aspirants have incentives to invest in formal party structures or programmatic appeals (Shefter 1994; Kitschelt 2000; Helmke and Levitsky 2004; Kitschelt and Wilkinson 2006). Clientelism strengthens incumbent control over elections (Van de Walle 2003); it reinforces ethnic voting (Horowitz 1985; Wantchekon 2003); and it commercializes elections, meaning that outcomes tend to reflect the existing distributions of power within a system (Lindberg 2003; Schaffer and Schedler 2007). In these settings, the building of institutionalized, programmatic parties seems particularly problematic. But is party development in Africa really as uniform as this depiction would suggest? Or might there exist some variation in the strength and the organizational character of opposition parties?

Many African countries have volatile party systems and poorly rooted parties. The region's mean electoral volatility is higher than in other regions (Kuenzi and Lambridght 2005: 431),[1] and, in several countries, there is a remarkable degree of party-switching by candidates from one election to the next. Looking at election data through 2000 alone, Van de Walle suggested that the typical African party system is characterized by a single dominant presidential party, typically the one that gained power in the first multiparty election, surrounded by a large number of splintered and transient opposition parties (Van de Walle 2003: 298). In some countries, voting patterns since 2000 either support Van de Walle's characterization or suggest an even more fluid and less party-governed political landscape. For instance, in the 2004 elections in Malawi, 20 percent of the electorate voted for independent candidates who were not associated with any party. Nor has Malawian voters' retreat from parties proven short-lived: in 2008, independent candidates received 400,000 more votes than they had in 2004, and independents currently hold 17 percent of the seats in parliament. In several other countries, including those with plurality electoral systems, opposition party fragmentation remains high or has increased over multiple election rounds in the last decade. Opposition parties are also viewed with considerable degrees of distrust by African voters: across the eighteen countries included in the Afrobarometer, only 36 percent of respondents say that they trust opposition parties, and no other government institutions score lower levels of trust (Logan 2008: 13–15).

But the presumption of weak parties obscures variation in the organizational strength, support bases, and electoral performance of opposition parties across countries and over time. In many countries, large majorities express partisan attachments: 79 percent of Tanzanians "feel close" to a party, and rates of partisanship are similarly high in Botswana, Namibia, and Ghana (Bratton et al. 2005: 258). Opposition parties have engineered electoral turnovers in a number of countries, including Benin, Cape Verde, Ghana, Senegal, and Zambia. In Botswana and Mozambique, opposition parties receive fairly stable shares of the popular vote over election rounds, though their support is not sufficient to force a turnover. In several countries, there is a high premium placed on party nominations, within both opposition and incumbent parties, to the extent that candidates and party leaders will devote significant resources to swinging the outcomes of nomination processes.[2] This suggests that party nominations are an electorally valuable commodity. We also know that

---

[1] Bogaards suggests that volatility is only higher in comparison to Western Europe but is relatively similar to volatility in Eastern Europe and Latin America (Bogaards 2008: 122).
[2] In both Kenya and Nigeria, in particular, violence, bribery, and fraud are often heavily associated with intra-party primaries. See Ibrahim (2007) and Bratton (2008).

internal party rules and procedures differ, although there is still very little research on the forms or causes of these differences. Party quotas for women's representation have been adopted in Namibia, Rwanda, and other countries, while they remain absent elsewhere (Geisler 2000; Bauer 2004).

There is enough variation in electoral success and internal governance to make an analysis of African party organization valuable. But even if we did find a puzzling similarity and formlessness to parties across the continent, party organization remains an important object to be explained. A lack of attention to parties – and the belief that what they say and do has little effect on political outcomes – can lead to dramatic simplifications of what are in reality very complex processes. If parties' appeals are immaterial, for instance, then vote choice can be reduced to the size of a voter's ethnic group or her susceptibility to patronage. If party strategies have slight and temporally dwindling effects on individual and group behavior, then elections in a single country can more reasonably be treated as independent events. But we do observe substantial differences. Parties are not uniformly weak, nor can ethnicity alone explain vote choice (Cheeseman and Ford 2007; Dunning and Harrison 2010; Keefer 2010). The strength of party organization and party control over patronage varies not only across countries but also within countries over time.

I begin this chapter with a simple question: what is party strength? Scholars have consistently linked party strength to both representation and political stability, but strong parties can take on a diversity of forms. Absent a single hallmark of party strength to serve as a guide, we must instead rely on close observation of decision-making, organization, and ties to constituencies. These characteristics cannot be captured by the fragmentation measures used in growing body of quantitative work on African party systems (Mozaffar et al. 2003; Van de Walle 2003; Brambor et al. 2007; Mylonas and Roussias 2008). After defining party strength, the chapter turns to a brief discussion of why existing theories of African party system development, particularly those that emphasize electoral institutions and ethnic diversity, do not help us understand differences in party organization or party strength. I have developed some of these ideas in greater detail elsewhere (LeBas 2010), but readers should take away a single basic point: explanations pitched at the level of the party system have trouble explaining differences in political outcomes. Party systems in Africa take unexpected paths, and structural factors are not sufficient to explain these outcomes.

The second half of the chapter lays out a framework for how variation in paths of party development and political outcomes can be explained. As I will point out in greater detail below, we should see party development as a function of both legacy and choice. Authoritarian rule orders social relations in different ways, which can either encourage or hinder large-scale mobilization. Opposition parties are, therefore, influenced by historical legacies, but strong parties also have the capacity to reshape how people are connected and how power is distributed within a particular political system. Opposition parties' own strategies and choices – like those of authoritarian states in the past – can reshape social relations and create new forms of identity for diverse populations. Strength lies in a party's ability to shape and manage *relations*: relations with mass constituencies, with activists and other "specialists," and with other parties. Historical patterns of state rule provide opposition parties with resources to mobilize constituencies, but the strength of party organization is dependent on how well parties are able to leverage those resources.

DEFINING PARTY STRENGTH

How do we differentiate strong party organizations from weak? Party strength is, quite simply, the ability to effectively organize and represent societal interests. This understanding of party strength underlies the substantial work on the regime-stabilizing effects of political parties. Huntington draws a clear line between political stability and the ability of parties to represent – indeed, to monopolize the representation of – interests (Huntington 1968: esp. ch. 7). Where parties fail at this task, "anomic or revolutionary political activity" ensues. For Huntington, the moderation of popular demands is critical for political stability. Parties domesticate popular mobilization, channeling it away from dangerously transgressive forms into the realm of routine politics. In strikingly similar language, Morlino argues that strong links between parties and constituencies allow parties to "constrain the behaviour of individuals and groups in civil society, channelling that behavior into democratic institutionalized arenas that eventually contain conflict" (Morlino 2005: 758). Highly competitive elections drive parties to build strong party structures and attempt to locate or shift new blocks of voters. Where they are successful, parties pull previously unrepresented groups into the public sphere and alter the way in which grievances are expressed. Absent the disciplining effect of a competitive struggle for the vote, elites have little incentive to represent or respond to the interests of large portions of the population, especially the poor (Mainwaring 1988). Finally, weak parties cannot build stable bonds of attachment between citizens and governments, nor can they secure the interests of the groups they ostensibly represent. Both democratic consolidation and survival are more difficult where parties have few "roots" in society, lack autonomy from the executive and from individual leaders, or are highly volatile (Mainwaring 1988; Mainwaring and Scully 1995b; Linz and Stepan 1996; McGuire 1997; Stoner-Weiss 2001; Levitsky 2003a; Levitsky and Cameron 2003). The characteristics of individual parties – as well as the overall level of competition in the electoral system – have significant effects on political development.

This substantial literature is united by a common presumption that strong parties build independent organizational capacity and sustain it over time. A party's ability to express and channel mass demands is directly related to its organizational reach and cohesion. It is not enough for parties to win mass support. In order to be effective over time, they must develop means of resolving conflict within their organizations, preventing party fragmentation, and keeping local party cadres "on message" (or disciplining them when they act contrary to leadership decisions). A balance must be struck, therefore, between maintaining channels through which demands can be expressed and building means of exercising directive control over activists and constituencies. As discussed in Chapter 1, opposition parties in democratizing countries may need to coordinate mass protest or organize other demonstrations of mobilizing ability, especially if they are facing entrenched authoritarian rivals. Parties solve these problems of organization-building and mobilization in different ways. A heavily ideological party with highly committed cadres might structure itself in a more top-down and centralized fashion than would a more heterogeneous, catch-all party, which would have to provide different selective benefits to its cadres. Rather than seeing party strength as a characteristic that can be captured with a single measure or demonstrated by a set bundle of organizational features, we can speak of strong parties sharing particular "family resemblances." Scholars have identified a wide range of resources, organizational qualities, and outcomes that we would expect to be associated with strong parties. Table 2.1 is suggestive of the wide set of defining characteristics used in the literature.

Some of these features may be common to all parties that we would classify as strong or effective; others may be better suited to describing institutionalized parties (e.g., stable mass membership, stable dues-paying membership) or institutionalized party systems (e.g., high levels of partisanship in electorate). Others may not be fully applicable to parties that we *would* classify as strong in sub-Saharan Africa (e.g., ideological coherence, stable position on left–right continuum). So, if we believe that party strength is linked to party organization, how do we determine which parties meet a threshold for classification as "strong parties"? Are there particular characteristics that all strong parties *must* share?

At the most basic, we would expect strong parties to possess roots into society, to be able to run national campaigns, and to have basic procedures (even if inconsistently applied) for resolving internal conflicts and formulating party policies. In hybrid regimes, mass mobilization may be a particularly important aspect of party-building and party durability. In these settings, opposition parties are stronger where they can control the extent and timing of popular protest: parties with rooted and well-disciplined structures can call constituencies out onto the streets, and they can call them back off again. Readers will note that I particularly emphasize the importance of two factors

Table 2.1. Attributes of Strong Parties

Resources	Financial resources
	Permanent staff, skilled party organizers
	Party newspaper, means of communication with electorate
	Local branches, party presence at grassroots
	Dues-paying membership
Organization	Communication and coherence across different levels of party organization (Panebianco 1988; Chhibber 1999)
	Internal democracy, means of resolving intra-organizational conflict (Panebianco 1988; Keck 1992)
	Penetration of national party to local level
	Societal "rootedness" (Mainwaring 1995)
	Organizational complexity, linkage between party and other socioeconomic organizations (Huntington 1968)
	Autonomy from other societal organizations (Panebianco 1988; Kalyvas 1998)
	Party penetration of civic associations, trade unions (Coppedge 1994)
	Authority resides in party rather than leader (Huntington 1968; Panebianco 1988)
	Ideological coherence, stable position on left–right continuum
Outcomes	Mass membership (Coppedge 1994; Levitsky 2003a)
	Electoral success
	Development of "diffuse organizational loyalties," loyalty to party on part of cadres (Huntington 1968; Panebianco 1988)
	High levels of partisanship in electorate
	Lack of antiparty sentiment in electorate
	Adaptability, survival over time (Dix 1992; Levitsky 2003)
	Ability to prevent protest by associated groups (Coppedge 1994)

in differentiating opposition party organizations: the way that information is structured within organizations (i.e., the ease with which information can be conveyed both from the bottom up and from the top down), and the ability of organizations to prevent fragmentation or resolve intra-organizational conflicts that could lead to fragmentation. Certainly, strong parties will possess many of the characteristics listed in Table 2.1, but many of these attributes are reflections rather than causes of party strength.

To stake my claims in the clearest language possible, I argue that strong parties are distinguished by having: (*a*) formal structures that are used to convey information across levels of the organization; (*b*) decision-making procedures that manage conflict and create consensus within the party; and (*c*) ties with popular constituencies that are based on common understandings and, to some extent, a shared identity. Where parties lack these attributes, they may be able to mobilize mass constituencies and even win elections, but they are likely to, eventually, fall prey to the collapse of mobilization or the fragmentation of the party at the elite level. This definition in no way excludes ethnically based parties from being strong party *organizations*. In hybrid regimes, however, for the reasons outlined in Chapter 1, opposition parties are politically effective only when they mobilize across ethnic lines, and it is only these parties that contribute to the construction of competitive party systems. In hybrid regimes and majoritarian electoral systems alike, narrowly ethnic parties are unlikely to succeed. The tendency of parties in Africa to organize themselves as multiparty coalitions merely underlines this fact.

Why not use electoral success, which is much more easily measured, as an indicator of party strength? In both consolidated democracies and other electoral regimes, the effective number of parties is often used to describe the character or degree of competition in an electoral system (Laakso and Taagepera 1979; Taagepera and Shugart 1989; Lijphart 1994; Ordeshook and Shvetsova 1994; Cox 1996; Neto and Cox 1997; Moser 1999; Chhibber and Nooruddin 2004; Madrid 2005; for applications to Africa, see Kuenzi and Lambridght 2001; Van de Walle 2003; Mozaffar and Scarritt 2005; Brambor, Clark and Golder 2007; Mylonas and Roussias 2008). The measure is simply the inverse of the sum of squares of each party's share of the vote or of seats in the primary legislative body. It and other measures based on voting patterns are easily calculable and widely used, but they have their limitations. Several scholars have noted the problems associated with standard fragmentation measures, which can collapse variation, mask change or volatility, and lead to mistaken conclusions about the similarity of cases (Pedersen 1980; Molinar 1991; Bogaards 2004). Nor does fragmentation allow us to effectively distinguish cases from one another: nearly half of African elections from 1990 to 2002 produced effective numbers of parties of around 2.0, a score that can indicate the presence of two strong parties, as in Ghana, or one dominant party with several small parties, as in Gabon (Bogaards 2004: 185–8). More troubling, scholars occasionally extrapolate from party system fragmentation and volatility to draw conclusions about the strength or weakness of individual parties within the system. Vote and parliamentary fragmentation is useful in describing general trends or attributes of party systems, as I do below, but the effective number of parties cannot be used to assess the character of party organizations within a system. Measures based on electoral success or failure cannot capture differences in party organization because there is no means of separating consequences of party organization from consequences of other factors.[3] Electoral success could indicate that an opposition party has strong links to society and is effective in mobilizing the vote, or it may merely indicate high levels of discontent and a strong "protest vote" that had little to do with the actions of a particular party. Conversely, electoral failure could be due to the weakness of opposition parties, or it might reflect high levels of state violence, insufficient institutional reform, or other formal and informal constraints that prevented strong parties from capitalizing on their effectiveness as organizations.

---

[3] For a much more general critique of defining parties in terms of their effects or functions, see Schonfeld (1983).

If vote and parliamentary fragmentation are not sound measures of party strength, are there other ways of using election returns to capture differences? We could, for instance, view the following as proxies for opposition party strength: (*a*) strong opposition parties are those that engineer electoral turnovers; (*b*) strong parties are those that monopolize the opposition vote; (*c*) strong parties are those that show stability in their vote share in successive elections. Of these, I find the latter two more convincing. Where an opposition party monopolizes the "protest vote," it demonstrates some ability to reach across geographic and, possibly, other political divisions in order to coordinate the actions of voters. This may indicate strong party organization across a range of contexts, or it may indicate that a structurally weak party has been able to serve as a focal point for opposition. In the chapters that follow, I sometimes use the stability of vote share to suggest that a party serves as a stable referent for some portion of the electorate. Stability of vote share is a particularly convincing indicator of strength where there is reason to expect party fragmentation, as, for instance, when the party is a target of state repression. Though suggestive, these indicators cannot be used as stand-alone measures; at best, they supplement and increase our confidence in conclusions derived from more direct observation of party structures and behavior. Other proxies for party strength, notably those relying on the age of parties (Dix 1992; Kuenzi and Lambright 2001: 446–7), have similar drawbacks.

Electorally successful parties may be fairly weak from an organizational perspective. Among our cases, for instance, this is best illustrated by the party coalitions that have been formed from time to time in Kenya. In 2002, the National Rainbow Coalition (NARC) won just over 50 percent of the popular vote in the parliamentary polls, and its presidential candidate won 62 percent of the presidential vote. NARC did not have party structures, and it did not aim to build a lasting party identity or stable partisan attachments with voters. A coalition of the country's major opposition parties, NARC's campaign was managed through its component parts, and it never made attempts to build organizational capacity that was autonomous from alliance members. After the withdrawal of several ministers from the NARC government, the "party" split apart, largely on the lines of its constituent parties, and voting in a subsequent constitutional referendum reflected pre-coalition divisions and ethnic camps. Subsequent coalitional behavior in the 2007 Kenyan elections was, from the standpoint of party-building, even more bizarre. President Mwai Kibaki's party, the Party of National Unity (PNU), was a coalition of several parties, all of which had agreed to back common candidates in presidential, legislative, and civic elections. After losses in PNU primaries, several candidates announced that they would contest seats under other party labels. The PNU subsequently agreed to finance the campaigns of these other candidates in an attempt to hold together the PNU coalition at the presidential level.[4] As a result, the PNU funded multiple candidates in several constituencies, effectively fueling party fragmentation and leading to the loss of several seats to the opposition Orange Democratic Movement (ODM). The experiences of NARC and PNU suggest that coalitions can perform well in elections with only the most minimal investment in party-building. But coalitions should be treated as analytically distinct from the party organizations addressed here.

In a world of small number of cases and few ways of measuring all potentially confounding factors, it is impossible to assess the relationship between structural conditions and party system outcomes in democratizing countries without looking more deeply at party organizations themselves. Even if we were to accept electoral returns as acceptable proxies for party strength, this gives us little understanding of how party organizations are formed or how they develop in different political contexts. An organizational definition of party strength makes measurement more difficult, but it comes closer to what we would like to capture about party differences than do measures premised on electoral outcomes. If we believe that party systems are built by party organizations – and are only contingently shaped by electoral institutions or societal cleavages – then there is a need for greater scholarly attention to differences in party formation and organizational choice.

POLITICAL PARTIES IN DEMOCRATIZING AFRICA

Party organization in sub-Saharan Africa is not well understood. Particularly when compared with the state of party research in other regions, such as Latin America and Eastern Europe, those interested in African party organization have few materials with which to build comparisons and general theories. This is partly because there has been little sustained academic attention to party organizations in sub-Saharan Africa since the 1970s. Soon after independence, the study of parties had a central place in Africanist political science. Scholars saw the nationalist parties as the institutions that would structure newly independent states: they were to function as instruments of governance and communication between elites and masses, as well as tools for social integration and the construction of new national identities

---

[4] Candidates contesting on nineteen different party affiliate tickets each received KSh 250,000 (approximately US$3,850) from the PNU, half the amount given to PNU candidates. *Daily Nation*, December 4, 2007. Subsequent attempts to turn the PNU into a membership-based organization, like its ODM rival, were strongly resisted by constituent parties. *Daily Nation*, July 23, 2008.

(Coleman 1954; Apter 1955, 1962; Ashford 1965; Zolberg 1966). In much of the earlier literature, the study of popular mobilization was the study of African political parties (e.g., Schachter 1961: 303–6). Several scholars built schemes for the categorization of regimes, based to some extent on differences in the organization and ideology of ruling parties (Morgenthau 1964; Collier 1982). However, as a number of scholars noted, the nationalist parties that won independence more closely resembled social movements than they did party organizations, and they did not prove durable (Wallerstein 1966; Zolberg 1966; Bienen 1967; Bratton 1980).

These parties' initial organizational weakness partly explains their actions in the immediate post-independence period. In many countries, ruling parties borrowed state resources and institutions to serve party aims, and they outlawed opposition parties when they found themselves facing powerful challengers. As the brief post-independence spell of "open politics" came to an end, ruling parties abandoned their role in popular mobilization, and participation came to play very little role in new authoritarian regimes (Kasfir 1974). In the single-party states of Southern and East Africa, parties remained vibrant political machines for a longer period of time, but popular mobilization became less important as time passed. In many cases, it came to take on largely ceremonial or performative aspects (Haugerud 1993: ch. 3). Even in those countries where the party progressively expanded its reach and the powers allocated to it, as in Zambia, for instance, popular alienation increased. As parties waned in importance, Africanist scholars turned their attention to informal institutions, especially ethnicity, in order to explain the character of African political systems. The return to multiparty electoral competition has done little to reverse this trend. African party organization remains a neglected topic.

Given this relatively blank slate, there is an unsurprising tendency to import theories of party system development from elsewhere to explain variation in African political outcomes. The fit is imperfect, however, between models derived from the experience of Western Europe and other advanced democracies and the realities of party systems in emerging democracies. Traditional theories of party system development emphasize electoral institutions and ethnic cleavages as the primary drivers of party behavior and party system development (Duverger 1964; Lipset and Rokkan 1967; Cox 1996). Where electoral systems are permissive, as in proportional representation systems, we expect greater party system fragmentation; where institutions are restrictive, as in plurality or first-past-the-post (FPTP) systems, both voters and parties have incentives to coordinate, and we expect relatively low levels of fragmentation. In terms of the effect of societal cleavages, greater degrees of ethnic diversity – or, alternatively, the presence of a few strong ethnic cleavages – are expected to produce higher levels of party system fragmentation. The motivations of parties are narrow in these models: parties are formed to pursue political office, and their choices of strategy are driven by a vote-maximizing logic (e.g., Downs 1957).[5]

So, do we see the patterns we would expect in new party systems in sub-Saharan Africa? Do electoral institutions discipline voters' choices, and do different levels of ethnic diversity lead to predictable patterns of party system fragmentation? There is a body of work that has addressed itself to these questions, but the conclusions remain unclear. In a widely cited 2003 article, Mozaffar, Scarritt, and Galaich argue that electoral institutions do not have the expected effects on the number of parties in sub-Saharan Africa (Mozaffar et al. 2003). They find that more proportional systems are *negatively* associated with the number of electoral and legislative parties, and ethnopolitical fragmentation is, surprisingly, also negatively associated with party system fragmentation. The second effect is offset where ethnopolitical fragmentation coexists with moderate or high levels of ethnic group geographic concentration, which increases the number of parties, as Lipset and Rokkan would expect. These surprising findings have been challenged: others have argued that, after corrections of methods or restrictions on the universe of cases, ethnic diversity and electoral institutions produce effects on party system fragmentation in the expected directions (Brambor et al. 2007; Mylonas and Roussias 2008). All these authors rely on the same dataset as Mozaffar and his co-authors. It is difficult to have great confidence in any of these findings, as this dataset covers a very short time span, includes a number of elections that should probably be excluded, and contains factual inaccuracies (Lindberg 2007: 219–21).

In his provocative and meticulously researched *Institutions and Ethnic Politics in Africa*, Daniel Posner makes a more sophisticated argument about the interaction between electoral institutions and ethnicity (Posner 2006). According to Posner, voters choose from a variety of political identities, only one of which is ethnicity. As he argues in the book and several related articles, the political salience of ethnicity or ethnoregional identity varies according to the demographic structure of countries, the historically determined stable of political identities from which individuals can choose, and the electoral rules that govern political competition (Posner 2003, 2004a, 2004b, 2006). Posner makes clear predictions about how the transition from single-party to multiparty elections will affect ethnicity and voting. The two systems result in differently sized political arenas: "a shift from multi-party to one-party competition will shrink the arena from the nation as a whole to the level of the electoral constituency, and a shift from one-party to multi-party competition will expand it from the electoral constituency to the nation as a whole"

---

[5] There have been numerous critiques of Downsian spatial models of voting, and many have suggested that parties can pursue aims other than vote maximization. See the overview in Strom (1990), as well as the interesting discussion of the motivations and behavior of parties in Aldrich (1995).

(Posner 2006: 145). In Zambia, where Posner builds his model, party labels are presumed to convey either ethnic or language group information in multiparty elections, and individuals make voting decisions in order to maximize their group's share of the national cake. We would, therefore, expect to see a "simplification" of electoral competition at the local level in multiparty elections. Orienting themselves toward the national political arena, voters will disregard localized concerns and, possibly, depending on the size of their own ethnic group, ethnicity as well. They will instead coordinate their votes behind the candidate of the party most likely to win political office *and* represent group interests. The model is a flexible representation of how national context and individual identity might interact, but parties remain thin actors for Posner. Voters see parties simply as informational cues; party campaigns and strategies are responses to ethnic or language-group demography; and institutional rules, once again, are the primary shapers of party systems. More problematically, vote coordination emerges naturally from individual incentives and institutional setting. This assumption does not seem borne out by voting behavior at the local level in a number of African countries.

There are clear empirical implications that emerge from the research discussed above. I will not undertake systematic analysis here, but let me note a few empirical trends that cast some doubt on structural approaches to party system development. Institutions cannot be expected to discipline parties and voters immediately; however, if electoral institutions are determinative, we would expect party system fragmentation to decline over time, especially in plurality or FPTP systems. In the early stages of multiparty elections, electoral institutions may have weaker effects on outcomes due to "political actors' limited knowledge and understanding of institutional incentives" (Mozaffar et al. 2003: 387). Similarly, political restrictions in authoritarian and hybrid regimes may create an informational deficit that initially impedes the communication of institutional incentives to parties and voters (Mozaffar and Scarritt 2005: 408-9).[6] But party coordination should increase over election rounds, as election results provide informational cues to voters and candidates. Voters, hesitant to "throw away" their votes, would not vote for candidates who were unlikely to win, and votes would tend to shift to candidates running on the tickets of known parties.

For the most part, strategic voting does not seem to be occurring – or, at the very least, is not occurring uniformly – in multi-party electoral systems in Africa. The failure of electoral coordination is particularly noticeable in those countries with the most restrictive electoral systems. In the plurality systems of

---

[6] African parties operate in strikingly information-poor environments. Large percentages of the population have restricted access to newspapers, radio, or television (Mattes and Shenga 2007), and we know that political knowledge and access to media have striking effects on citizens' attitudes toward democracy and reform (Bratton et al. 2005: ch. 8).

Anglophone Africa, a small number of countries, such as Botswana, Namibia, and Zimbabwe, show fairly low levels of party system fragmentation across multiple election rounds. A far larger number of countries, however, show either a great deal of volatility in the degree of party system fragmentation or a dramatically increasing pattern of fragmentation over time. Malawi, already mentioned above, is one of the exemplars of this trend, as is Kenya. In Malawi's founding multiparty elections in 1994, parties representing Malawi's three main ethno-regional blocs split the vote fairly cleanly, which some saw as a result of the ethnic balancing politics that had prevailed in the authoritarian period (Kaspin 1995). Subsequent elections have, however, been marked by a slow disordering of the electoral landscape and sharp increases in overall party system fragmentation. By 2004, Malawi's third multiparty election, the effective number of electoral parties exceeded seven, and vote fragmentation lessened only marginally in the 2009 elections. Much of this fragmentation was driven by Malawians' eschewal of established parties in favor of independent candidates. Independents won 26 and 30 percent of the popular vote in 2004 and 2009, respectively, as well as 20 and 17 percent of the parliamentary seats. Kenya, another FPTP system, showed a similar sharp increase in party system fragmentation in its fourth multiparty election in 2007, as the effective number of electoral parties rose to 6.5.

Kenya and Malawi are extreme examples, but they are not the only places where electoral institutions fail to effectively discipline voting. If we look at regional averages, sub-Saharan Africa seems to have fairly low party fragmentation overall, as Mozaffar and Scarritt suggest (Mozaffar and Scarritt 2005). For instance, for the period 1991–2008, the average effective number of legislative parties (ENLP) was 2.30, while the average effective number of electoral parties (ENEP) was 2.80. Means, however, obscure significant variation across countries and over time. For the 114 legislative elections for which I have data, fifteen of thirty-eight countries registered ENLP scores of more than 3.0 in at least one election, and five had an ENLP of more than 4.0 at least once.[7] A high level of vote fragmentation was also more common than the mean might suggest: thirteen of the countries had at least one ENEP score of over 3.0, and six had an ENEP of more than 5.0 at least once. The bulk of these systems have strong majoritarian elements: thirteen are pure plurality or FPTP systems; several of the others have mixed systems in which the majority of seats are allocated in single-member districts, as in Mauritania and Mali. This

---

[7] I have not collected data for founding elections that resulted in civil war, military coup, or indefinite suspension of elections; similarly, countries that have not yet held a second round of elections are excluded. This leaves the following countries: Benin, Burkina Faso, Cameroon, Cape Verde, Chad, Equatorial Guinea, Ethiopia, Gabon, Gambia, Ghana, Kenya, Lesotho, Madagascar, Malawi, Mali, Mauritania, Mauritius, Mozambique, Nigeria, Sao Tome, Senegal, Seychelles, South Africa, Tanzania, Zambia, and Zimbabwe. Of these, electoral regimes in Mauritania and Chad collapsed after three and two rounds of elections, respectively.

is a context in which we would expect coordination, if voting were shaped strongly by electoral rules. The least permissive electoral systems also produced highly fragmented legislatures. Kenya, Malawi, and Zambia have all had ENLP values of 3.0 or higher at least once, which compare to Venezuela, Uruguay, and Peru in terms of legislative fragmentation (Mainwaring and Scully 1995*a*: 30).

Levels of fragmentation in African party systems are highly unusual from a comparative perspective. In the highly diverse set of forty-eight older democracies examined by Taagepera and Shugart, the authors find that the median difference between ENEP and ENLP was 0.4, and only in India did the gap exceed 1.4 (Taagepera and Shugart 1989: 81–5). This gap indicates the proportionality of the system, but one might also see it as a measure of the degree to which vote choice is disciplined by electoral institutions. We know that FPTP systems are more disproportional than proportional representation systems, but well-disciplined party systems should provide a constraint on disproportionality, as voters shift their votes to candidates who are likely to win. In the established democracies examined by Taagepera and Shugart, countries in the sample with plurality systems did tend to have larger gaps between the two measures, but electoral systems consistently provided a constraint on vote fragmentation. No plurality systems in the sample had ENEP values higher than 3.1 at any point, other than India. Party systems in Africa are simply more fragmented than institutional models and the empirical patterns found in older democracies would predict.

Might high levels of fragmentation be explained by ethnic diversity? In countries where ethnic groups are concentrated geographically, national-level fragmentation might result from the concentration of different parties' support bases in ethnic zones. Party system fragmentation would indicate that party systems are not nationalized, not that parties and elites are incapable of building stable and cohesive voting constituencies in particular areas. Elsewhere, for instance, FPTP systems have produced small, regionalized opposition party enclaves (Caramani 2004; Birch 2005). This does not seem to be the case in sub-Saharan Africa. Instead, parliamentary election results indicate that party systems at the local level are often more various and more fragmented that national-level party systems would suggest (e.g., Morrison and Hong 2006). In the countries for which I have constituency-level electoral data, high party fragmentation at the national level is often mirrored by high fragmentation at the constituency level, including in more ethnically homogenous constituencies.[8] To flesh out this proposition, let us look at Kenya, one of the book's core cases.

---

[8] For drawing my attention to constituency-level vote fragmentation, I am indebted to Chhibber and Kollman (1998) and Chhibber and Nooruddin (2004), who use state-level vote

Kenya is a most-likely case for vote coordination within ethnic blocks. Parties mobilize on the basis of ethnic cleavages and use heavily ethnicized campaigns; ethnic groups are geographically concentrated, to differing extents; and politics is structured around the distribution of patronage. The country is characterized by high levels of vote fragmentation at the constituency level, and furthermore, constituency-level vote fragmentation increases over election rounds. Ethnic homogeneity does not seem associated with lower levels of constituency-level fragmentation. Constituencies that are overwhelmingly Kamba, for instance, show high levels of fragmentation; similarly, one of the most ethnically homogenous constituencies in the country, Turkana South, had a fragmentation index of 3.76 in 2007. Historically, the Kamba and Turkana have been under-represented at the national level, and these areas have received correspondingly less state investment than others. Despite this, Kamba and Turkana do not seem engaged in "ethnic head-counts" (Chandra 2004), and, contrary to Posner, voters in these areas still seem divided by local concerns and sub-ethnic cleavages. Secondly, if we look at changes in local-level fragmentation across election rounds, constituency-level fragmentation is not moving in the expected direction. In 1997 and 2002, the mean constituency ENEPs were 2.27 and 2.40, respectively; in 2007, the mean constituency ENEP jumped to 3.83. In 1997, only 21 of 200 constituencies had ENEP values of more than 3.0, and the highest value was 5.03; in 2002, the proportion of high-fragmentation constituencies was roughly similar, but scores in these constituencies were marginally higher. The 2007 election results showed a sharp uptick in local vote fragmentation: 99 of 210 constituencies had ENEP values that were higher than 3.0, and 31 had values above 5.0. In two constituencies, the ENEP exceeded 10.0: in Kitutu Masaba, the ENEP was 11.34, and, in Emuhaya, it was 12.13. Remarkably, neither of these is particularly diverse ethnically, and they are not urban constituencies.

This evidence suggests that vote coordination is difficult, and structural factors do not produce ordered party systems on their own. If FPTP electoral rules do not produce lower levels of party system fragmentation over multiple election rounds, then institutional incentives alone are too weak to push parties and voters toward coordination. And if party systems in ethnically homogenous constituencies are as fragmented as those at the national level, then group cleavages do not structure voting as cleanly as Lipset and Rokkan, or Posner, might suggest. The differential strength of political party organization is the crucial intervening variable. Party organization mediates the effects of electoral rules and ethnic diversity on overall political outcomes. In some countries, political parties may

---

fragmentation to examine variation in patronage distribution and the nationalization of party systems.

structure voting choice in the ways that we would expect; in others, parties do not serve as strong informational signals and are not the basis for stable political alignments. Country specific patterns of party formation matter. Though clientelism permeates electoral processes in Africa, but it is rarely channeled through the local party machines through which it operates in other contexts (e.g., Scott 1969; James 2005; Stokes 2005). As Kitschelt and Wilkinson note, machine or party clientelism requires significant investments in building networks and linkage structures (Kitschelt and Wilkinson 2006). In Africa, where this investment has been absent, clientelism is volatile, and access to state resources does not ensure stable support for the ruling party. Clientelistic mobilization seems to further disincentivize party-building.

A closer examination of party behavior in Africa also casts doubt on whether vote maximization serves as the primary aim of party elites. Opposition parties in Africa are under-resourced and often struggle to establish a presence nationwide, but they also seem motivated by a more diverse set of party aims than has been traditionally presumed for parties. Parties do not exist merely to capture power; instead, Africa's peculiar patterns of party fragmentation suggest that benefits and resources can accrue even to small parties that do not win office (Van de Walle and Smiddy Butler 1999: 23). In these contexts, the emergence of strong, cohesive opposition parties that can coordinate opposition voters is even less likely. In order to understand how parties and voters behave in sub-Saharan Africa, there is a greater need to look at party organization and the patterns of mobilization and linkage that emerge during party formation. As Aldrich (1995) points out, party organizations must be treated as endogenous institutions, products of a diverse set of aims and processes. In the following section, I emphasize two processes that have resulted in differences in the character and durability of party organization.

THE ARGUMENT

Party organization is not simply an effect of electoral rules, socioeconomic and ethnic cleavages, or the incentives that differences in these factors create for political actors. In order to understand differences in party organization and party system development, starting conditions matter. In democratizing countries, different forms of authoritarian state rule provide new parties with different resources and mobilizing structures, biasing one path of party development toward greater opposition coordination and another toward more fragmented, ethnically inscribed opposition party politics. But starting points are not determinative. Social actors, including parties, maneuver creatively within the structures in which they are placed. The strategies implemented by a social movement and party can increase the strength of ties between elites and mass constituencies, and they can make the defections of activists and supporters more costly. Put simply, paths of opposition party development are shaped by the interplay of structure and agency. In authoritarian settings, the state limits popular participation to certain sanctioned fora, but individuals and groups find ways to transform those institutions into staging grounds for popular opposition. During periods of political change, opposition parties reflect past patterns of political mobilization, but they can also alter the structure of salient political cleavages in a given society. There is a fundamental contingency built into this model of party development, despite its historical institutionalist underpinnings. It is not semi-fixed social cleavages that structure political mobilization; instead, it is party mobilization that determines which cleavages will be activated and which identities become politically salient (Kalyvas 1996; Chhibber 1999). I will turn first to the ways that the choices of authoritarian states produce different kinds of mobilizing structures, which then become available for use by opposition parties during democratization. Secondly, I will turn to the tools used by political parties to manipulate relations with mass constituencies, activists, and other parties. I argue that strong parties often use strategies that escalate conflict and limit interactions across partisan lines. By fostering polarization, political parties increase organizational cohesion and control over mass constituencies.

THE ORIGINS OF PARTY MOBILIZING STRUCTURES

Pre-existing informal networks, and the formal organizations to which they are sometimes attached, serve as paths through which information can be shared and individuals can be recruited to participate in collective action (McAdam 1982; Gould 1991). The role of these mobilizing structures in facilitating protest is especially important in closed political environments, where information flow is sharply constricted (Osa 2003). Where opposition movements lack a strong organizational base, popular resistance tends to either splinter or fade. I argue that the differential ability of opposition social movements and political parties to channel, discipline, and sustain mobilization is partly a result of historical legacies. Past strategies of authoritarian states structure what organizational resources are available to social movements, which group identities are salient, and what kinds of coalitions of non-state actors are possible. In many countries in sub-Saharan Africa, authoritarian rule flattened the associational landscape, channeling social ties and interaction into sharply delimited local networks. This impeded popular coordination and large-scale collective action (Bayart 1986; Azarya 1988). Other state practices often reinforced the weakness of associations, as many governments relied on clientelism and ethnic brokerage to extend shaky control over their territories. But the lack of building blocks was not universal: in a handful of countries, authoritarian states relied on alliances with corporate actors, notably trade unions, in order to expand their reach into society, enhance control over potentially disruptive mass constituencies, and implement economic and social policy. State–labor alliances initially stabilized authoritarian rule and extended state control over workers, but they also produced trade union structures with autonomy from the state, organizational resources, independent ties to mass constituencies, and a great deal of political visibility. These mobilizing structures could later be co-opted by opposition parties, giving these parties a greater ability to mobilize voters across the lines of ethnicity and geographic space. Where authoritarian rule instead relied on societal control via patronage and networks of ethnic brokers, there were much larger obstacles to cross-ethnic and cross-regional mobilization by opposition parties. Opposition parties were instead more likely to be based on personal networks, and they were characterized by fragmentation and more tennous ties to popular constituencies.

The strategic choices of African states in the immediate post-independence period explain the presence or absence of cross-ethnic mobilizing structures. African states came to independence with limited means of exerting control over their territories.[9] Party-states often had stronger institutions and higher degrees of state capacity than military or personal dictatorships; however, even in these systems, ruling parties often piggybacked on the organization and legitimacy of other institutions in order to exercise control. Differences in state strategy toward collective actors, such as trade unions, can be traced to the early days of independence. At independence, new states were faced with a crisis of expectations: many Africans presumed that independence would quickly bring economic benefits, such as higher wages, cheaper food, the provision of shelter, and the expansion of schooling and health care. One of the most visible manifestations of these expectations was a series of strike waves, typically fueled by shopfloor labor militancy, in the first years after independence. Forced to focus attention on labor policy relatively quickly, states answered the labor question in strikingly different ways. At one end of the spectrum, some states responded with direct repression of strikes and unions. In hopes of restraining labor militancy, labor-repressive states either banned trade unions or manipulated their internal politics in order to fragment affiliates and undermine national trade union centers. In labor-repressive states, trade unions were either too weak or too fragmented to serve as national-level mobilizing structures for the coordination of protest and organization of

---

[9] The literature on state weakness in sub-Saharan Africa is vast. Major works include Jackson and Rosberg (1982), Young and Turner (1985), Bayart (1993), Mamdani (1996), and Herbst (2000).

demands. Working with the materials at hand, opposition leaders built the organizations that were possible. As countries instituted multiparty electoral competition, opposition parties were built around fairly localized ethnoclientelist networks, and the electoral appeal of these parties was often tied to the fortunes of local and regional "big men." Opposition parties tended to proliferate and fragment quickly, leading to a crowded opposition landscape and a splintered opposition vote.

In a handful of countries, labor control regimes were based instead on corporatist alliances between ruling parties and labor movements. In these states, trade unions were formally integrated into state decision-making processes, though their input and influence were often limited. Corporatism seldom provided African trade unions with power or influence, but it did deliver concrete benefits. In exchange for assistance in enforcing wage restraint and limiting strike activity, governments passed labor legislation that centralized and expanded the organizational reach of organized labor. Governments implemented check-off systems of union dues collection, and they made union membership mandatory for the majority of formal sector workers. Affiliate unions were organized on the basis of "one union, one industry"; governments were often actively involved in the establishment and strengthening of overarching trade union federations; and organized labor was given a formal role in policy discussions. State–labor alliances initially stabilized authoritarian rule. Alliances strengthened state control over workers, the number and duration of strikes initially declined, and formal sector wages remained relatively stagnant during the first decades of independence. There has been some resistance to applying corporatist frameworks to regimes in sub-Saharan Africa (e.g., Mozzaffar 1989), but corporatism as practiced in Zimbabwe, Zambia, Tanzania, Sierra Leone, and other countries included all the hallmarks of corporatist systems elsewhere. Schmitter, for instance, defines corporatism as: "a system of interest representation in which the constituent units are organized into a limited number of singular, compulsory, noncompetitive, hierarchically ordered and functionally differentiated categories, recognized and licensed (if not created) by the state and granted a deliberate representational monopoly ... in exchange for certain controls on selection of leadership and expression of demands" (Schmitter 1974: 93–4; also, Collier and Collier 1991: 51–4). This quite accurately describes the centralized trade union structures characteristic of Zimbabwe and Zambia, as Chapters 3 and 4 will detail. In addition to the mixture of inducements and constraints characteristic of these systems (Collier and Collier 1979), corporatist bargains also rely on a particular ideology and discourse about which interests will be represented (Schmitter 1974: 121–3). Thus, corporatist trade unions are to be oriented toward the interests of the "nation" as a whole rather than the narrow interests and demands of a particular constituency. In corporatist systems in Africa, once again, this is the case. In the early period of state–labor alliances, trade unions eschewed the representation of workers' interests in order to demonstrate support for state development policies (e.g., Bates 1971).

When African states adopted neoliberal reforms in the 1980s and 1990s, state–labor alliances began to fray. Labor quiescence had been based on the delivery of political goods, such as privileged access to the state, and material benefits, notably subsidies on food and other living expenses. As was the case with party–union alliances in Latin America, economic decline and the removal of subsidies eroded the loyalty of union leadership to the ruling party, and unions became more vulnerable to pressures from the grassroots (Burgess 1999). Trade unions began to play an active role in coordinating economic protest and, eventually, became effective mobilizing structures for pro-democracy movements and opposition parties. Previously state-allied labor movements had ready-made memberships, established organizational structures and physical resources that compensated for some of the advantages of ruling parties. In addition, trade unions in corporatist settings were prominent political actors even before they moved into active opposition. They were allocated a degree of public visibility that made them "serious" actors in the public mind when they did voice dissent, and the role that the state assigned these organizations in the legitimation and implementation of state policies reaffirmed their public credibility. As economic decline and the removal of state subsidies increased popular disaffection with incumbents, the opposition parties built by organized labor served as somewhat natural focal points for popular discontent. Because of the mobilizing structures provided by organized labor, labor-based opposition parties were more effective in launching nationwide election campaigns, resisting tendencies toward fragmentation, and coordinating opposition voters.

Several scholars have expressed skepticism about the ability of state-allied labor to play this kind of transformational role. For much of the post-independence period, African organized labor was depicted as a small, privileged "labor aristocracy," which lacked ties to other constituencies and had an interest in maintaining the status quo (e.g., Arrighi and Saul 1968). Even before African workers became involved in oppositional politics, labor aristocracy theories rested on a weak empirical base. African workers had strong social ties to rural constituencies and the urban poor, and workers often protested and criticized state policy during the authoritarian period (Jeffries 1978; Nelson 1979; Crisp 1984; Wiseman 1986; Mamdani and Wamba-dia-Wamba 1995; Chikhi 1995; Ferguson 1999; also, Sandbrook 1977).

A good deal of scholarship, however, still expresses skepticism about the ability of state allies and coopted actors to work themselves free of state control. Lust-Okar, for instance, argues that state-sanctioned opposition parties will not support action that endangers the current regime (i.e., will

not collaborate with protest movements) for fear of losing the bounded
privileges they possess in that system (Lust-Okar 2004). This argument
could be applied to unions as well. In cases in North Africa and elsewhere,
state corporatism is presumed to create ties of dependency between the state
and organized labor, which trade unions have little capacity to disavow,
even in contexts of economic crisis and political change (Bianchi 1989; Bellin
2000, 2002). This literature overstates the stability of state control over
labor movements, both during periods of stability and, especially, during
periods of change. Authoritarian governments may be involved in the creation
of structures for labor control. This does not translate, however, into stable
control over labor leaders or trade union structures. Where allied trade
unions possess autonomy from the state and the ruling party, their institutions
can be subverted from within (LeBas 2007). Internal union elections
may elevate more radical union leaders than those preferred by the state,
and the union leadership's difficulty in controlling wildcat strikes may
make unions more responsive to grassroots demands than state dictates.
The result is the gradual transformation of a state ally into an oppositional
actor.

In terms of how this works in the book's three main cases, corporatism in
Zimbabwe and Zambia led to the emergence of oppositional labor before and
during political opening, while repressive labor control in Kenya resulted in
weak, fragmented, and apolitical union structures. It is important to underline
that the strength of organized labor at independence did not determine these
countries' subsequent trajectories. Kenyan trade unions were much better
organized and politically influential than were Zimbabwean trade unions at
independence, for instance. Nor do the sizes of labor forces account for the
differential strength of labor across the three countries. The size and concentration of the mining sector in Zambia does mark it off as distinct from the
other two cases, but, as I will show somewhat exhaustively in Chapters 4 and 6,
the Zambian labor movement's strength and mobilizing reach was a reflection
of the national reach of a number of other unions, not the mineworkers union
alone.

Table 2.2 separates the three cases by both the form of authoritarian
labor control and also the mobilization strategies pursued by opposition
parties as countries began to turn toward political liberalization and more
open electoral competition. Mobilization strategies and boundary construction will be discussed shortly, but let me underline one important dimension
that is not apparent in this matrix. The corporatist labor regimes in Zimbabwe
and Zambia both accorded significant degrees of autonomy to labor movements. Thus, trade unions retained control over their internal governance,
and union members had the ability to elect more radical union leadership
over time. This was not necessarily the case in other countries that relied
on corporatist alliances. As in Zimbabwe and Zambia, the Tanzanian state

Table 2.2. Labor Legacies and Opposition Mobilizing Strategies in Kenya, Zambia, and Zimbabwe

	Boundary construction	Minimal boundary work
Labor autonomy (semi-corporatism)	Trade unions provide mobilizing structures	Trade unions provide mobilizing structures
	Labor provides focal point for voters	Labor provides focal point for voters
	Coalition reinforces difference, builds "us" identity	Coalition is pro-change but does not build "us" identity
	Uses polarizing discourse, defectors disallowed	Polarization absent, opposition accepts defectors
	Able to discipline candidates and activists	Candidates pursue own interests
	Cases: Zimbabwean Movement for Democratic Change	*Cases*: Zambian Movement for Multiparty Democracy
No labor autonomy (repressive labor control)	Particularistic identities provide mobilizing structures	Particularistic identities provide mobilizing structures
	Absence of focal point; vote coordination weak	Absence of focal point; vote coordination weak
	Coalition uses polarizing discourse	Coalition lacks coherent agenda, "us" identity
	Some disciplining of candidates but unity fragile and short-lived	Candidates pursue own interests
	Cases: Kenyan National Rainbow Coalition (2002)	*Cases*: Kenyan parties. Standard party form in sub-Saharan Africa

responded to strike waves by strengthening union structures and establishing the National Union of Tanganyika Workers (NUTA). Organized labor, however, had little to no autonomy from the state (Bienefeld 1979; Nyang'oro 1989). In 1977, NUTA was formally folded into the ruling party as a mass organization. Unions were not available, therefore, for use as opposition mobilizing structures when Tanzania returned to multi-party electoral competition in 1994.

Why were labor movements in Zimbabwe and Zambia able to effectively coordinate protest and voting? And why do we see differences in the abilities of Zimbabwe and Zambian trade unions to sustain opposition cohesion over time? On the one hand, the legacies of semi-corporatist rule made labor movements focal points for opposition. As Boix points out, in nineteenth century party systems in Western Europe, new parties had success only where they could draw on "a strong organizational base or, more often, on some parallel, 'pre-partisan' organization that could convince all their members that (given the context of majoritarian rules) everyone else in that organization would vote for that new party simultaneously" (Boix 2007: 516). Kalyvas's account of the rise of Christian Democratic parties in Western Europe similarly stresses the importance of pre-existing mobilizing structures in coordinating the choices of voters (Kalyvas 1996). But trade unions in Zimbabwe and Zambia did not just convince union members to vote for new labor-backed political parties: given the relatively small size of the formal sector labor force in these countries and elsewhere in Africa, labor movements needed to serve as focal points for much larger constituencies. Economic protests – and the visibility of trade unions during these protests – played an important role in coordinating the support of more diverse constituencies behind a single opposition party. Because of organized labor's ability to disrupt the economy, protests involving trade unions often won concessions, at least in the early stages of confrontation with the state. The success of early protests drew diverse constituencies toward participation, protests became larger and more numerous, and the scope of protesters' demands widened as protests began to cohere into "cycles of contention" (Tarrow 1994). Elections held in the midst of these protest cycles turned into referenda on political change. Where a single organization was the most visible proponent of change, and where this information was effectively conveyed across the population, it is not surprising that those protesting the status quo would tend to vote for that organization's candidates.

Vote coordination is distinct, however, from the development of strong affective ties between parties and constituencies. Semi-corporatism in Zimbabwe and Zambia provided organizational networks that facilitated mobilization. Labor-led opposition parties served as natural focal points for disgruntled voters. But focal points are inherently unstable: in order to build durable party organization and popular support, parties must find means of maintaining mobilization and resisting tendencies toward organizational fragmentation. This is where party strategy and, especially, the ability to shape or manipulate social boundaries come into play. In Zimbabwe, the labor-backed Movement for Democratic Change (MDC) was not merely a focal point. Through cooperation with other social actors, through a series of grassroots campaigns, and through the decisions that the party made about internal decision-making, the MDC created affective ties that knit together activists, elites, and mass constituencies. In Zambia, on the other hand, the labor-backed opposition party also benefited from the resources and networks of organized labor, but it did not use those resources to build a party identity that could be sustained beyond the first period of mobilization. The next section will address how parties manage diversity and disagreement within their organizations and how they build solidarity and shared identity among party activists and supporters. As suggested above, I particularly emphasize the role played in party-building by the strategic or instrumental use of polarization and the escalation of party-based conflict.

COLLECTIVE IDENTITIES, POLARIZATION, AND PARTY CRAFT

Opposition parties have greater negotiating power when they possess large, all-encompassing constituencies. In most contexts, pro-democracy movements try to incorporate all actors outside the state, a strategy that both strengthens and weakens. Inclusion gives these movements their moral force, but it also creates strong tendencies toward fragmentation. For the opposition parties that succeed movements, the challenge is how to manage the diverse interests that make up the party while preventing the defection of elites and constituencies. During the first stages of party-building, mobilization is the primary concern; subsequently, the differential success of new parties is determined by how effectively they can bend this initial wave of mobilization to suit their purposes. Discipline, therefore, becomes the primary concern of party organizations as they age. How do parties retain control over their activists and followers? Can they prevent segments of their membership from defecting to key rivals, and can they enforce compliance with the strategies or policies adopted by party leadership? As suggested above, a party's initial success with mobilization is strongly shaped by historical legacies, while its facility with discipline and cohesion is determined by choices about strategy and party governance. The use of exclusionary appeals and the intensification of conflict with other parties can play important roles in knitting a party together while allowing it to maintain its mobilizational reach.

Parties, like social movements, are more effective when their supporters and leaders are united by a common identity. Shared identities and affective loyalties facilitate collective action, and they can also maintain mobilization over time, even if participation delivers little in the way of concrete benefits. In social movements and other risky forms of collective action, recruitment and mobilization typically occurs through existing social networks, and free riding is dissuaded by norms of mutual dependence and group enforcement (Tilly 1978; McAdam 1982; Gould 1991). We know that increased network density – or a greater number of shared and overlapping ties – results in stronger and more durable individual commitments to movements (McAdam 1986). Indeed, where group solidarity is very strong, individual interests and assessments may cease to be the primary determinants of participation; instead, "the decision to participate is made by groups of individuals, who were already part of formal or informal groups, and who therefore deliberated and decided to act jointly, as a group" (Goldstone 1994: 142).

To return to the puzzle mentioned above, opposition parties in Zimbabwe and Zambia were equally well endowed with organizational resources, and labor movements had served as sources of identity and belonging for unionized workers in both countries. But opposition parties in the two countries diverged. The MDC in Zimbabwe maintained its cohesion and the commitment of its members, despite severe political repression. In contrast, the MMD in Zambia was not able to prevent organizational fragmentation and the disintegration of its popular base, despite its access to patronage resources. I argue that the two parties' differential success was due to their differential attention to the construction of social boundaries. In Zimbabwe, the MDC and its movement predecessors devoted time and resources to a series of linked campaigns that built the density and intensity of ties across several more localized networks. Movement and party elites in Zimbabwe also selected strategies that escalated conflict between the opposition and the ruling party. These strategies contributed to the creation of a strong and durable political cleavage, built around partisanship, which maintained individual commitment to the party over time. In Zambia, on the other hand, the trade union congress and its successor party could count on the loyalty of workers, but it devoted few resources to building ties between union structures and broader civil society networks. In both Zambia and Kenya, opposition party-building did not touch existing social cleavages. Opposition parties in both countries have remained characterized by weak ties between leaders and voters, resulting in marked tendencies toward organizational fragmentation.

Polarizing or conflictual strategies are chosen because they are in the instrumental interests of party-building elites. When these strategies are mirrored by actors on both sides of a political divide, the larger process of polarization is the result. Polarization is not due to the divergent interests or identities of actors at the beginning of a period of negotiation. Instead, it is a dynamic process that both generates new collective identities and reinforces the internal solidarity of groups that already exist, thereby increasing the space or divide between those groups. The construction of political identities is typically seen as a long-term process, but parties can, in some contexts, quickly swing the cleavages that are considered politically salient in a given society (Brass 1997; Chhibber 1999; LeBas 2006). "Groupness" facilitates collective action, but it is also systematically built through the process of mobilization and party-building. Movements create community, a set of shared understandings, and collective identity for their participants (Gamson 1991; Poletta and Jasper 2001). Polarization may be facilitated by network segregation and by existing group stereotypes and differences, but choices and actions can also prove consequential. Elite entrepreneurs fashion "us–them" distinctions to mobilize constituencies, and interactions between groups produce narratives and stories that justify these group boundaries (Malkki 1995; Tilly 2003a, 2004b; Poletta 2006; Fujii 2009).

Across our cases, movements and parties approached political strategy and aims differently. In both Zambia and Kenya, pro-democracy movements had different levels of organization but a similar lack of interest in organizing campaigns that would shift existing social boundaries. Parties did not invest in building a common identity or common values among their supporters, nor did they attempt to train or bring together party activists from different parts of the country. The discourses used in party campaigns were built around delivery of political goods, not the transformation of society. In contrast, Zimbabwe's pro-democracy movement devoted energy to developing ties and collaboration across civil society organizations at the elite level, and it used rallies and public meetings as opportunities for civic education. By the time the MDC was formally launched, its activists and many of its supporters shared a common vocabulary and set of political understandings. Party campaigns emphasized these commonalities, and they framed electoral competition as a struggle over values and identity as much as a struggle over political power. As campaigns of state-sponsored violence displaced MDC activists and supporters, opposition party cohesion increased. State violence in Kenya produced the opposite result, as violence further ethnicized politics and magnified divisions within the opposition coalition.

Why would we expect polarization to prevent fragmentation? Common values do not necessarily produce solidarity in other contexts, so why would the construction of new social boundaries strengthen opposition parties in hybrid regimes? In order to answer this question, let us consider the process of boundary construction. Tilly suggests that a social boundary is characterized by three elements: a degree of solidarity within groups on either side of the boundary, an established form of interaction across the boundary, and a legitimizing discourse that makes maintenance of the boundary seem vital to those involved (Tilly 2004b: 214). Boundaries can be constructed of a variety of materials, but they can quickly become social facts that shape behavior. Once mobilization and counter-mobilization is organized primarily around a single boundary, interactions between rivals reinforce the salience of that boundary and deactivate rival cleavages as bases for group mobilization. Political entrepreneurs find it difficult to lessen the distance between groups or activate other cleavages. In polarized settings, individuals and groups cannot credibly claim neutrality, and actors who attempt to position themselves in an intermediate position are instead pushed toward one of the poles. This "hollowing out" of middle ground is often built into definitions of polarization, and it is one of the core reasons that polarized conflicts are less amenable to negotiation or resolution (McAdam et al. 2001: 322). Groups define themselves in opposition to one another, they limit interaction to conflict or violence, they silence moderates by accusing them of disloyalty. Each of these mechanisms reinforces the others, yielding a cycle of boundary hardening and distancing between groups.

Conflict and polarization are useful to parties because of their effects on internal party solidarity and discipline. There has been a common presumption that violence and exclusionary appeals are used to split or reshape constituencies, to rally the base, or to communicate group commitment to political rivals. The internal organizational consequences of polarization and conflict are less often examined. I argue that boundaries are created and hardened by new parties in order to discipline the behavior of those who are located on their own side of the political divide, not to affect the behavior of parties and individuals who reside on the other. For instance, when discussing the early days of political mobilization and party formation in Zimbabwe, opposition elites consistently mentioned the fear that their party would be "eaten" by the ruling party. Early party strategies were aimed at preventing the ruling party from nibbling away at what was considered the MDC's natural constituency. Trade unions and their movement allies wished to build a large and diverse popular base for the party, but the party needed to find ways of building walls around that base. A similar process was at work within the ruling party. Ultimately, confrontational tactics and the resulting intensification of party-based polarization assisted both opposition and ruling party leaders. Constituencies and candidates had few options for defection, and a surprisingly stable distribution of party support emerged over the course of three election cycles. In order for conflict to have these solidarity-boosting effects, party leaders had to reinforce partisan identity as the key political boundary. They did so through both discursive and more direct means, as I will discuss in Chapters 5 and 7.

The creation and intensification of a partisanship-based social boundary prevents defections and also shifts power within party organizations. Where party competition is polarized, independent and third-party candidates are significantly less likely to win election battles, and political aspirants are therefore unlikely to form new parties, even if they lose nomination battles. Polarization creates intra-party cohesion by "trapping" potential defectors within the party. But polarization can also strengthen party cohesion and individual commitment to the party through more complicated pathways. Where party polarization is coupled with state repression or violence, as it was in Zimbabwe, party followers and, especially, activists perceive their own interests as linked to the success or failure of the party. This perception of a "linked fate" reduces individuals' focus on their own self-interest and makes collective action easier to maintain (cf., Dawson 1994). Party supporters and activists are less likely to recognize the possibility of alternative forms of political organization in climates of severe party polarization. They are less likely to leave parties, even if they disagree with party tactics or feel that party leaders do not reflect their interests.

Individual decision-making in these kinds of environments differs substantially from what rationalist scholars would expect. Many individuals involve themselves in opposition not only because they hope for or expect success but also because involvement is in itself *meaningful* to them. My Zimbabwean informants, for instance, consistently explained the movements and parties of which they were members in moral terms. As assessments of likely success shifted, informants underlined the moral necessity of resistance, even if such resistance was doomed. In her work on Holocaust-era rescuers of Jews, Kristen Renwick Monroe argues that actions that are morally loaded cannot be explained with reference to rational calculation or cost–benefit analysis (Monroe 2001, 2004). Renwick Monroe's key insight is that individuals often refuse to recognize that they might have acted differently than they did, which she terms the "lack of a language of choice." Actions are instead filtered through an individual's understanding of her own identity or morality, rendering actions that are inconsistent with that understanding inconceivable. By framing demands and "we" statements in moral terms, pro-democracy and human rights movements may be able to similarly muddy the water between morality, identity, and action. Particularly where the risk associated with movement participation is very high, as it was in Zimbabwe in the early 2000s, activists and supporters may find themselves bound to an ethics of participation and solidarity. In Zimbabwe and perhaps elsewhere, the fear of being labeled a "sell-out" or a traitor limits the "language of choice" in ways similar to those Renwick Monroe describes.

New parties navigate a complex relational terrain: they are engaged in conversation and interaction with potential voters, with their own activists, with other allied organizations, and, perhaps most importantly, with the parties they seek to displace. The construction of social boundaries simplifies internal decision-making and reinforces the commitment of elites, activists, and supporters. But the strategies adopted by a party to alter one set of relations have unintended effects on other relationships as well. For instance, an opposition party's adoption of confrontational tactics and appeals can increase incumbents' perception of threat, leading them to believe that power must be retained at all costs. This belief may be driven by a variety of motivations: in Zimbabwe, some ruling party members felt that the opposition party attacked core values of the nation, others believed that electoral turnover would lead to appropriation of property and wealth, and still others simply feared prosecution. Regardless of motivations, polarizing tactics on one side of the political divide are likely to be mirrored by similar tactics and choices on the other. Seemingly rational strategies of party-building can therefore backfire, leading to polarization and the empowerment of hardliners on both sides of the political divide. Political violence is, obviously, one potential outcome.

SUMMARY

To summarize the arguments of the chapter in the clearest language, I define party strength with reference to organizational qualities. Strong parties are those that develop stable and institutionalized linkages with their constituencies. Ties may be mediated by grassroots party branches, or they can be maintained through the structures of party-affiliated associations. But strong parties, regardless of their exact form, have roots. In order to explain variation in organizational strength, I emphasize the importance of two factors. First of all, authoritarian legacies determine the resources and organizational networks that are available to opposition movements and parties as political opening increases. In particular, where authoritarian states pursued corporatist strategies of social control, strong and centralized labor movements were available to provide mobilizing structures and a skeletal collective identity to new opposition parties. Where authoritarian governments ruled through ethnic brokers instead of formal institutions, opposition parties lacked the structures to mobilize large constituencies across the lines of ethnicity or geographical distance. Secondly, I argue that choices of party strategy in the early days of democratization can reinforce internal solidarity and popular commitment to the party, or it can spur defections and the erosion of parties' popular bases. In this chapter, I have focused particularly on how opposition parties use polarizing or confrontational tactics in order to forge social boundaries. This process generates internal solidarity and makes defection more difficult, but it also fosters inter-party conflict and may radicalize party activists. While polarization forges stronger party organizations, it also makes violence and authoritarian retrenchment more likely. This chapter has argued that differences in party organization might explain various puzzling aspects of African party systems. Different patterns of party-building may cause some party systems to become ethnicized, while other paths leave greater space for cross-ethnic mobilization. Some strategies of party-building create fluid and volatile forms of linkage between elites and mass constituencies, while others forge more stable political ties. We will see the mechanisms underlying these processes more fully in the chapters that follow.

Part Two

Historical Legacies

✱

────────

ORGANIZED LABOR IN AUTHORITARIAN SETTINGS

"We, the workers, pledge that we will put the interests of Zambia before our own interests, either as individuals or as members of trade unions; [and] we will work hard to play our part in the National Development Plan."

— Declaration signed by Zambian trade unionists at the Livingstone Labour Conference, 1967.[1]

"It was we who created the trade unions, it was we who thought of the workers. But we didn't know then what kind of monster we were creating."

— Chen Chimutengwende, former member of ZANU-PF Politburo.[2]

In the late 1970s and early 1980s, the Zambian Congress of Trade Unions (ZCTU) started to take positions that were increasingly critical of the Zambian government on matters as wide-ranging as wage policy, corruption within the ruling elite, the price of basic commodities, the treatment of university students, and the decentralization of local government. In the mid-1990s, the labor movement in Zimbabwe similarly moved toward a more critical and confrontational attitude toward the government. These public positions marked a change from past practice. Previously, labor movements in the two countries had served as allies of ruling parties. Trade unions had supported government development policy, they had assisted the government in enforcing wage restraint, and they had occasionally played political roles as well. What changed? The implementation of economic austerity measures under the direction of the International Monetary Fund (IMF) undermined many of the commitments that had structured state–labor relations since independence, but labor movements in Zimbabwe and Zambia had changed internally as well. In both countries, ruling parties had given trade unions autonomy over their internal governance, and workers had used that autonomy to gradually push their leadership toward

---

[1] Quoted in Simutanyi (1987: 33).
[2] Interview, Harare, November 2002.

greater independence from the state. Eventually, trade unions formed opposition parties, the success of which derived from the organizational and political resources unions had been granted in the corporatist period.

Both Zambia and Zimbabwe tell a classic story about the unintended consequences of what might be termed incorporative control. Zimbabwean and Zambian unions were intended to implement the ruling party's economic policies, and they were provided with resources, organizational assistance, and supportive labor legislation. But in both countries, corporatist state strategies not only failed to contain dissent but actively contributed to the construction of new mobilizing structures for its expression. The consolidation of state rule in Africa, both colonial and post-colonial, abounds with examples of this story of unintended consequences. For example, in Transkei, South Africa, in the early 1950s, the apartheid state introduced institutions that allowed local communities some role in decision-making. Govan Mbeki argues that the *limited* popular participation allowed by these district councils spurred rather than sated popular demands for greater voice. He writes:

> In the beginning the White rulers had trusted these institutions to turn discontent and aspiration inwards. They had hopes that the Africans would become so absorbed in the settlement of petty disputes, in the issues within and between the tribes, that they would cease to require a place in the political sun. But contrary to expectations, the annual sessions of these Councils served merely to bring the peoples' representatives from different parts of the country close together, so that together they could hammer out common demands. (Mbeki 1984: 37)

The state, of course, learned from such experiences and quickly moved to dismantle structures that had become fora for organization and dissent. Until 1994, the administration of Transkei and the other "homelands" would rely on authoritarian local rule that cloaked a lack of any participatory channels in the language of the "customary" or the traditional (Ranger 1983; Mamdani 1996).

Mbeki's description of the learning process that took place within the Councils is an eloquent description of the way in which actors gradually transform captive or constrained institutions into focal points for opposition in authoritarian regimes. This process is not without antagonism, conflicts, and setbacks. The creation of limited or localized channels for voice does often turn "discontent and aspiration inwards," and the early days of the Councils in Transkei were largely consumed by the "petty disputes" that the apartheid state foresaw. African labor movements in the postcolonial period were similarly troubled by internal disagreement over strategy, division of power, and other issues. Even where state policy was supportive, the forging of strong and autonomous labor movements took time. In Zimbabwe, labor was characterized by organizational fragmentation and lack of a coherent mission for several years before it was able to make demands and win concessions from government. This unification of the labor movement occurred through the strengthening of the national center, through workshops and training sessions, and through center and affiliate cooperation in collective bargaining negotiations. By the mid- to late 1990s, when the trade union congress began to organize strikes and large-scale demonstrations, the Zimbabwean labor movement was well organized and disciplined. In Zambia, development of an opposition labor movement took a different course. Trade union leadership consistently faced challenges from below, and national unions had but tenuous control over militant and often strike-prone shopfloor structures. Protest and contentious action therefore served a more important role in knitting together organized labor than it had in Zimbabwe, and the Zambian Congress of Trade Unions gained its political influence less through its own actions than through its ability to serve as a focal point or symbolic center.

What occurred where state policy was not supportive of strong labor centralization? In most African countries, including Kenya, authoritarian states did not choose to rule through alliances with corporate actors like labor. Labor control in these countries relied on repression, and trade unions were allowed much smaller degrees of autonomy from the state. In Kenya, restrictive legislation, an intrusive Registrar of Trade Unions, and state interventions in internal union affairs fostered splintering and disorganization within affiliate unions. Trade unions that had been vibrant at independence gradually lost their ability to express workers' demands or resist state encroachment. By the late 1980s, when other social actors were increasing their opposition to the Kenyan state, the labor movement was divided, permeated with ruling party influence, and insignificant as a political actor. After the reintroduction of multiparty politics, trade unions made scattered statements in support of the ruling party, but they played no role in party mobilization or opposition politics.

The two chapters that follow describe how authoritarian policies put in place immediately after independence shaped labor movements in Zimbabwe, Zambia, and Kenya. They shed light on why trade unions in two of these countries had the resources and the ability to mobilize large constituencies as protest turned into parties, while organized labor in the other had faded into political obsolescence by the beginnings of political opening in the 1990s. The chapters also aim to underline the contingency of authoritarian state control in these three countries. Though formal institutions set bounds on the choices available to actors, these two chapters also tell a story of agency on the part of both union leaders and rank-and-file members. From independence to the emergence of oppositional unionism, workers moved creatively within structures of labor control that were meant to channel their actions in predictable ways. In the cases of Zimbabwe and Zambia, workers adapted institutions formed for one purpose to better suit their needs, and they gradually changed their minds about the role that they thought unions should play in economic and political life. Kenya plays a rather different role in this set of chapters: at particular points in time, union leaders may have had choices, but the strategies of the state left them with considerably fewer resources and a sharply delimited political space. Though economic grievances and popular discontent increased over the course of the 1980s in Kenya, organized labor remained marginal in battles over economic reform and political opening. In Zimbabwe and Zambia, unions were the central actors in the formation and mobilization of opposition political parties. In Kenya, on the other hand, organized labor remained loyal to the ruling party and played no role in organizing popular protest. Despite these differences in labor outcomes, all three of the cases suggest that democratization is shaped by processes that emerge long before the visible drama of the transition period.

Three

Corporatism in Zimbabwe

In Zimbabwe, organized labor was weak at independence in 1980. The post-independence state did involve itself in strengthening and centralizing the trade union movement, but state–labor relations remained characterized by a kind of neglect throughout the 1980s. The political base of the ruling party in Zimbabwe, the Zimbabwe African National Union – Patriotic Front (ZANU-PF), lay in the rural areas, and ZANU-PF never expressed a strong interest in using trade unions as a means of political mobilization, as the ruling party had in Zambia. The labor control regime was a form of state corporatism, but state rhetoric was significantly milder in Zimbabwe than in its northern neighbor. Unions were expected to restrict strike activity, but they did not play a prominent political role in Zimbabwe. Notably, relatively few unionists vied for ZANU-PF parliamentary nominations, nor did sitting trade union leaders serve as Members of Parliament (MPs) or in the decision-making structures of the ruling party. The marginal position to which labor was consigned was a blessing in disguise: during the 1980s and early 1990s, organized labor in Zimbabwe transformed itself from a weak and fragmented collection of elites into a strongly rooted, membership-led organization.

As economic liberalization and hardship increased Zimbabweans' dissatisfaction with their government, the labor movement used its zone of autonomy to expand its organizational reach and its ability to speak for constituencies much larger than unionized formal sector workers. The trade union center, the Zimbabwe Congress of Trade Unions (ZCTU), undertook campaigns to unionize an ever-increasing number of workers, and, in the 1990s, its attempts to bring civil service workers, previously excluded from union representation, under its umbrella brought it into direct conflict with the state. By the mid-1990s, the ZCTU was one of the ruling party's most consistent critics: at several points, it was accused of serving as an "unofficial opposition." This more confrontational stance versus the state was coupled with stronger links between the ZCTU and rank-and-file workers. During the 1990s, the ZCTU supported and offered technical advice to affiliates that went on strike, and it organized demonstrations of its own. In contrast to the situation in Zambia in the 1980s, ZCTU and affiliate leaders in Zimbabwe were capable of disciplining their grassroots, and the unions' decision-making procedures allowed for the expression of worker grievances and demands. When the ZCTU moved into opposition in the late 1990s, it did so at the head of a disciplined and unified labor movement.

ORGANIZED LABOR PRIOR TO INDEPENDENCE

In order to understand the sources and impact of state policy after independence, we must briefly consider the origins of organized labor in Zimbabwe. There is a history of strong labor militancy in Zimbabwe, which was especially marked in the colonial period preceding the Rhodesian white settler regime's Unilateral Declaration of Independence (UDI) in 1965. Militancy was, however, built on a fairly tenuous organizational base, which obviously had effects on the shape of trade unionism at independence. Accounts of organized labor typically begin with the December 1945 strike organized by the Rhodesian Railways African Employees Association (RRAEA), one of the first unions to be formed in the territory. The 1945 railways strike began as a protest of 2,708 Bulawayo-based railway workers over an announced change in the overtime pay scheme. The strike quickly spread from Bulawayo along the line of rail to the rest of the country and on to Northern Rhodesia (Zambia), eventually involving as many as 10,000 workers (Vickery 1998). In the two years following the railways strike, two African labor confederations were launched in Bulawayo, Zimbabwe's second largest city, while another was formed in Harare (Raftopoulos 1997; Lunn 1999). Individual workplaces formed their own unions, which sometimes affiliated to one of the three federations. By the end of 1947, the Bulawayo-based organizations were organizing meetings that attracted large audiences of unionized and non-unionized workers. In early 1948, Bulawayo municipal workers went on strike over rising food prices. They constructed barricades on roads leading from the high-density townships to the industrial areas, and strike activists also traveled to other parts of town to convince others to join the strike. Within three or four hours, the majority of workers in Bulawayo had joined the strike; within a week, municipal workers in six other cities staged similar protests. By the end of the strike in late April, strike observance had spread to most sectors of the African workforce and grown to perhaps 100,000 participants, by far the largest act of collective protest in Zimbabwe's history to that point (Phimister 1988: 273).

Up to the present, these events continue to serve as touchstones for Zimbabweans active in the trade unions and civil society. Photos of the 1948 strike rallies hang on the walls of union offices in Bulawayo, and trade unionists often reference it as an example of successful popular mobilization. Indeed, in the tactics of labor-led mass stayaways in 1997 and 2002, one often sees echoes of the urban protest of 1948. When one looks more closely at the organization of the 1948 strike, however, union structures played a marginal role. Lunn reports that the Bulawayo union leadership, including the supposedly militant Benjamin Burombo, was repeatedly forced from platforms or shouted down in the public meetings that preceded the strike (Lunn 1999: 165–6). Raftopoulos notes that the 1948 strike and other protests were organized by "shadowy figures" who "stood at the opposite end of the economic and political spectrum from the petty-bourgeois leadership of the formal trade union movement" (Raftopoulos 1997: 290).

Despite dramatic episodes of labor protest, trade unionism was much weaker in Zimbabwe than in Zambia or Kenya. With the notable exception of the railways union, unions were denied legal recognition throughout the 1940s, 1950s, and 1960s, and the 1948 general strike resulted in the passage of legislation that increased state monitoring and regulation of African associations. Unlike the colonial administration in Northern Rhodesia (Zambia), the colonial government actively discouraged African union organization in Southern Rhodesia (Zimbabwe), and African union organizers faced constant harassment from employers and from the government. Repression intensified following UDI and the formation of a minority white government based on "socialism for the whites." The Industrial Conciliation Act, which governed labor relations in this period, legalized only white unions that had been formed prior to 1959 and multiracial unions formed thereafter (Dhlakama and Sachikonye 1994). The law allowed formation of skill-based, not general, unions, which effectively excluded the bulk of the African labor force from union representation. In addition, voting within unions was weighted by skill level, thereby ensuring that decision-making in recognized unions would be determined by whites (Brittain and Raftopoulos 1997: 97; Raftopoulos 1997: 57).

After the declaration of UDI in 1965, the war between the Rhodesian white-minority regime and Zimbabwean nationalist movements steadily intensified. The fortunes of African workers declined precipitously during the UDI period, which may have been due in part to the restrictions on union representation mentioned above. From 1963 to 1972, African industrial workers received increases in wages that only slightly outstripped the rising cost of living. The Rhodesian state restricted the advancement of blacks into more skilled and middle-level positions and instead recruited new white immigrants to fill these positions (Harris 1972: 144–5). In addition to the widening of income inequality on racial lines, the period stunted the growth of the previously expanding black middle class. By 1973, the wage differential in Rhodesia between whites and blacks was 10 to 1, and 89.8 percent of black wage-earners earned less than $50, even though the poverty datum line (PDL) was estimated at $60 a month (Good 1974: 17–18). By the time the liberation war reached its height in the 1970s, Harris observed that "a substantial majority of industrial workers live under a regime of constant want, in which their wages do not enable them to rise above a poverty-striken state" (Harris 1975: 150). High levels of discontent were tamped down by increasingly authoritarian state policies toward unions and other formal associations. In the 1960s and 1970s, Zimbabwe's incipient union structures were largely dismantled. Over the course of 1966, for instance, the number of trade unionists detained by the new Rhodesian government reached 138. Other labor leaders went into exile, including the bulk of the leadership of the country's two main union confederations (Brittain and Raftopoulos 1997: 92).

Economic sanctions were placed on Rhodesia in the 1970s, and the economic situation worsened precipitously. Employers demanded that the government restrict wage growth, and they became hostile to grassroots labor-organizing efforts that had previously been tolerated.[1] Therefore, in addition to the formal legal obstacles black unions faced in registering, unions found it more difficult to hold meetings, even small meetings of the union executive, and communication with membership became near-impossible. Some unionists were able to creatively circumvent this repression, holding, for instance, union meetings in hired busses that would drive around town until union business was concluded.[2] Most unionists remember the period as one of increasing labor repression, greater surveillance, and a generalized feeling of wariness on the part of organized labor. One trade unionist, who had been detained after attending a labor education course in Kampala during this period, summed it up: "the Rhodesian state could not see the difference between trade unions and politics."[3]

Repression lessened unions' ability to organize the grassroots, but it also led to few linkages between union structures and nationalist movements, a disconnect that would color state–labor relations in the immediate post-independence period. As in Zambia, some segments of the labor movement were committed to economistic or strictly apolitical unionism. But former trade unionists also made up large proportions of the leadership of the two main nationalist parties. When both these parties – the Zimbabwe African Patriotic Front (ZAPU) and the Zimbabwe African National Union (ZANU) – were banned in 1962, the debate over whether the labor movement should take on a political role led to a split in the country's main trade union congress.[4] Successive splintering yielded five rival federations by the end of

---

[1] For instance, Ignatius Chigwendere, at that time the organizing secretary for the Textile and Garment Workers Union, remembers illegally organizing through the mesh fences at worksites in 1961. Later, this organizing became difficult. Interview with Ignatius Chigwedere by Brian Willan, May 24, 1974. Filed with Oral Histories, National Archives of Zimbabwe. For an analysis of the reasons that Rhodesian industry became increasingly worried about wage expansion, see Riddell (1990).

[2] Interview with Isdore Zindoga, July 16, 2004.

[3] Interview with Sylvester Rusike, July 28, 2003.

[4] Interview with Ignatius Chigwedere (1974), op. cit.

the 1960s. Some of these unions left Zimbabwe and relocated to the Frontline states from which the nationalist parties were staging military operations (Ndhlovu 1978). Those that remained within Zimbabwe resisted taking political stands for fear that any politicization of unionism would lead to government repression and union dissolution (Brand 1971).

Because of their ambivalent attitude toward politics, Zimbabwean unions played little role in the organization of protest during the 1960s and 1970s. Rather than work stayaways or strikes, rent and beer boycotts became the major expression of resistance in high-density townships of Harare (Salisbury) and Bulawayo. These boycotts were organized again by "shadowy figures": flyers were distributed that threatened those who paid rents with "elimination" by the "underground army of General Chedu," and vandalism and property destruction were integral parts of these campaigns (Kaarsholm 1999). Government documents of this period reported that "pressure [to comply with the boycotts] is exercised by veiled rumours and threats of violence spread by posses of young men, by smears on walls or notices slipped under doors at night, and by actual violence" (quoted in Kaarsholm 1999: 244). The contrast with Zambia is stark. There, the bulk of collective protest in the colonial period was organized by strong and cohesive trade unions, which were able to discipline their rank-and-file members and use strikes effectively. In Kenya, trade unions were growing in size and organizational strength in the period immediately preceded independence, and they were also involved in political mobilization. In Zimbabwe, on the other hand, the labor movement entered the independence period in a surprisingly weak bargaining position. Not only did it lack the loyalty and support of grassroots constituencies, but organized labor was viewed with suspicion by the nationalist parties that governed the post-independence state.

LABOR DISORGANIZATION AT INDEPENDENCE

At independence, then, the Zimbabwean labor movement was divided between fairly weak affiliate unions or workplace associations and a large number of labor confederations, all of which had minimal ties to the grassroots. At the time, it seemed unlikely that the Zimbabwean state would take steps to strengthen union structures or assign workers a role in development policy. Initial statements by ZANU, the new ruling party, indicated that the beneficiaries of government policy would be rural residents. The government described urban workers as "a small and privileged urban wage income elite, and efforts must be made to avoid perpetuating this situation."[5] Even after the formation

---

[5] Government of Zimbabwe, *Growth with Equity*, quoted in Dansereau (1997: 100).

of the ZCTU, there was a perception within ZANU that urban workers and trade unionists were allied to "capitalists" and would not assist government development plans.[6] In comments to Parliament soon after independence, one junior minister argued that urban labor should not be given any special protection or privilege, since:

> If there is anyone who has deserted the government or Zanu in its struggle, it is the workers themselves. Those within the country used to hear over Radio Maputo or even from Lusaka calling upon the workers to go on strike so as to participate in the struggle [and they did nothing].[7]

The distrust of existing trade unionists was widely shared among ZANU and ZAPU MPs alike, and government officials did not view the unions as potential partners. During debates in Parliament over the 1981 Wage Act, unions were repeatedly described as being "in a shambles" and as incapable of engaging in collective bargaining on their own.

There were reasons for this skepticism surrounding the "usability" of union structures. Intermediate structures that should have linked leadership to the shopfloor had disappeared or never been functional. The most effective labor organizers had been detained during the 1970s or had left Zimbabwe to join the guerrilla struggle. The materials that exist, as well as the personal reflections of unionists who worked during this period, suggest a serious if not complete disintegration of the mobilizing capacity that unions might have possessed in the 1940s and 1950s. The report of a 1978 trade union colloquium organized by Silveira House, a Zimbabwean labor education institution linked to the Catholic Church, identified a number of problems with Zimbabwean unions, including:

1. "amorphousness" or the failure to hold regular meetings with workers either at the workplace or in the locations;

2. corruption and mismanagement of a "self-imposed leadership," composed of individuals "[who] take up trade unionism because they have no job at all";

3. lack of adequate funding, because of the small amount that unions could collect from individual workers (no more than 25 cents a month, or 0.625 percent of the wage) and the general problems of physical collection (Silveira House 1978).[8]

---

[6] Interview with Nathan Shamuyarira, August 1, 2003.

[7] Comments by the Deputy Minister of Local Government, *Zimbabwe Parliamentary Debates*, June 13, 1980.

[8] Interestingly, despite the inefficiency of physical collection versus check-off systems of dues collection, many unionists said at the colloquium that they preferred physical collection, as it created more worker access to the unions, "creating [greater] conviction" and the "construction of a sound mentality and financial democracy [amongst workers]" (Silveira House 1978: 42–3).

The Riddell Commission of Inquiry, established after independence to make recommendations on labor policy, also found a lack of grassroots union structures. It noted that "many union officials are ignorant of the broad industrial legislation or the particular regulations or agreements under which their members worked and, in addition, many appear to be ignorant of the structures of their own union" (quoted in Herbst 1990: 200).

These conditions, so different from those in Zambia, did ensure, however, a strange kind of autonomy for trade unions in the post-independence period. The ruling party neither needed nor particularly wanted to use the labor movement to bring new constituencies into the party, and politicians quickly abandoned the idea of transforming unions into party auxiliaries. The disorganization of the trade unions did not make them an attractive mobilizing structure. Further, ZANU saw itself as a rural-based party, and the nationalist movement as a whole had a tradition of politicizing cadres in residential areas rather than places of work. Though it would attempt to fill the offices of a new union confederation with pliant party loyalists, the ruling party did not seek to build a politicized labor movement. The decision to keep trade unions institutionally distinct from the ruling party had important long-term effects. Though ZANU would retain a great deal of control over industrial relations in the first decade of independence, this control was balanced by a degree of labor autonomy that allowed labor activists to creatively transform their organizations into critics of government.

THE STATE AS MIDWIFE: LABOR POLICY AFTER INDEPENDENCE

Though ZANU, the ruling party, did not view the labor movement as a potential partner, developments soon after independence forced the Zimbabwean government to turn its attention to labor policy. In 1980–1, hundreds of spontaneous strikes took place, involving at least 90,000 workers.[9] The strikes were disorganized local strikes and sit-ins, occasionally involving minor violence or threats. The labor force at the time was barely unionized, and union members amounted to no more than 12 percent of the formal sector workforce. Without usable union structures, there were no institutions that could manage the crisis of expectations among workers at independence:

---

[9] The government reported 297 strikes for 1980 (versus a mere seven for the year before), but the true number of strikes was likely much higher. See also the catalog of 178 individual strikes listed in Sachikonye (1986: 268–72).

Absent were strong mechanisms to channel the interests and demands of workers, and to mediate the conflicts between capital and labour at both industrial and
work-place levels. The colonial labour legislation had now become anachronistic
in this new context. It was therefore scarcely surprising that soon after independence, there was a massive upsurge in strikes to challenge the vestiges of the
colonial labour regime. (Sachikonye 2001: 149)

Sachikonye's language suggests that the strikes were political, exploratory, or
aimed at concrete benefits, but this was often far from the case. *The Herald*,
Zimbabwe's main newspaper, reported at the time that "some of the [striking]
workers did not seem to know why they were striking; some were acting on
incorrect information; and no doubt to others it was the expectation of large
pay packets from the word go."[10] Many of those interviewed reported that
strikes in 1980–1 often occurred for frivolous reasons, and strikers made
demands that had little to do with working conditions, such as the desire for
a personal visit from the Minister of Labour.[11] Immediate government strategy to contain these strikes was a mixture of repression and reward. Police were
deployed to worksites to forcibly disperse strikers, and the government announced significant increases in real wages, especially for miners and workers
in industry and commerce. The wage packages announced in 1980–1 were
some of the largest in Zimbabwe's history, and they were partly responsible for
reducing levels of strike activity. The number of days lost to strikes fell to
21,000 in 1982 and then to 379 in 1983, fewer than in 1978 and 1979.[12]

In the wake of the strikes, the government feared a resurgence of wage
demands and therefore moved quickly to establish a more far-reaching system
of labor control. The intention was to develop structures at both the shopfloor
and the national level that would be committed to the Government's development project and could enforce wage restraint. At the national level, the ZCTU
was established to unify the five existing union federations into a single
national labor center. The government was a key player in the formation of
the ZCTU: the Minister of Labour appointed the steering committee that
prepared for the inaugural congress, and the government oversaw all stages
of the conference (Republic of Zimbabwe 1984).[13] Appointees were chosen
from existing national centers, not the affiliates, creating a bias in favor of
older unionists. The steering committee was in charge of setting up a credentials committee to vet unions and verify membership rolls, but the Minister of
Labour intervened on the eve of the Congress and nullified the credentials

---

[10] *The Herald* (Harare), March 21, 1981; also, Republic of Zimbabwe (1984: 23).
[11] Interviews with Didymus Mutasa, August 15, 2003; Percy Mcijo, March 5, 2003.
[12] Data reported to International Labor Organization by the Registrar of Trade Unions.
Available at www.ilo.org accessed April 6, 2004.
[13] See also the comments of then Prime Minister Robert Mugabe in *The Chronicle* (Bulawayo), February 28, 1981, and *The Herald*, March 2, 1981.

committee. As a result of this nullification, unions' membership was not verified when delegates were allocated, and several unions of questionable provenance gained access to the Congress. There were allegations that ZANU formed unions just prior to the Congress in order to swing the elections of ZCTU leadership, and unions that had not affiliated to the ZCTU were given delegates and voting rights.[14] The irregularities surrounding the 1981 inaugural congress of the ZCTU had a dramatic effect, since ZANU-backed officials won the leadership positions of the ZCTU by slim margins. Large segments of the affiliate leadership and rank-and-file distrusted this new group of leaders, which included Secretary-General Albert Mugabe, variously described as a close relative or brother of the President. Many unionists argued that the close linkages between the first elected ZCTU officials and ZANU politicized the labor movement, harmed its organizational development, and prevented the ZCTU from protecting worker or union interests in the first years of independence. From 1981 to 1986, the leadership's link to the ruling party resulted in a virtual acquiescence to the economic policies announced by government.

In addition to the formation of the ZCTU, the government established "workers committees" at the shopfloor level. Government officials, including the Minister of Labour, had attributed the 1980 strike wave to a breakdown in communication between unions and workers. It was felt that workers' committees would resolve this communication gap and thereby prevent the resumption of wildcat strikes (Sachikonye 1986: 256–7). Government officials also felt that the committees would reduce the burden on the national arbitration machinery, as workplace-specific grievances could be hammered out between workers' committees and workers. Despite the important role assigned to the committees, the government did not make a serious effort to build or retain control over the structures. Workers' committees were established quickly, and there was not adequate training of employers, workers, or the newly elected workers' committee representatives. The government allocated few resources to workers' education, despite its rhetoric regarding the need to educate workers about their rights and empower them in negotiations with employers. In 1982–3, the budget allocation for workers' education programs amounted to Z$5.5 million, approximately 6 percent of the social services budget.[15] Unlike other programs, which were to be expanded in subsequent years, this allocation was essentially a one-time grant. Workers' committee representatives consequently lacked training about basic economic

---

[14] A Ministry of Labour survey of 1984 added, "On the morning after the congress only 30 unions could be verified as actually existing. The rest had disappeared into the air" (Republic of Zimbabwe 1984: 51).

[15] Republic of Zimbabwe (1982: 30–1).

principles, legislation and collective agreements governing their industries, or even the assigned role of the workers' committees.[16] Perhaps as a result of this informational vacuum, the first elections to the workers' committees were consumed by partisan politics, and candidates barely mentioned the concerns of workers or their own goals for the committees. Many of those interviewed said that the national unions were rarely divided on ethnic lines, but the workers' committees did introduce a sharply partisan dimension to *shopfloor* labor relations, which may have taken on a subtly ethnic dimension due to the rival ZAPU's base in Matabeleland. One trade unionist described these elections as consumed with sloganeering: "they would chant '*Pamberi ne Zanu*' [Forward with Zanu] and some of us were not comfortable with that because we were from Matabeleland, but that is what these workers' committees were about."[17]

The formation of both the workers' committees and the ZCTU was largely "top-down," in the sense that the demand for these institutions came from Government rather than from workers or union leadership. The weak involvement of unions in the formulation of industrial relations policy in Zimbabwe was also evident in the 1985 Labour Relations Act (LRA), which expanded central government control over industrial relations. The Act gave the Minister of Labour control over dispute settlement and he was also granted the right to intervene in the internal administration and governance of trade unions. The Ministry was responsible for registering unions, and it could also investigate union administration and records, observe intra-union elections, and dismiss union executives. The LRA had other provisions that impaired union organization and constrained the maneuverability of organized labor. The LRA prohibited strikes in so-called "essential services," a technique of strike suppression fairly common in sub-Saharan Africa. The definition of essential services was so broad as to exclude strike action in a wide range of sectors, and the Minister of Labour was able to declare any other service an essential service by publishing a notice in the government Gazette (Sachikonye 1986: 261). Public sector workers did not fall under the provisions of the Act, thereby denying them access to collective bargaining and union representation. Collectively, government actions in the first years of independence created an authoritarian and top-down system of labor relations. Crucially, however, the government also created representative structures for organized labor, at both the national and shopfloor level, which possessed formal autonomy from the ruling party and its government.

---

[16] Interviews with Eddie Cross, December 5, 2002, and Miriam Chikamba, March 7, 2003.
[17] Interview with anonymous trade unionist, Harare, November 2002.

SHOPFLOOR POLITICS AND UNION CAPACITY

As suggested above, neither the ZCTU nor the workers' committees were free from political influence during the early years of independence, even though they were not formally controlled by ZANU. The intrusion of politics into the operation of workers' committees made workplace governance problematic during the tumultuous first years of independence. Rather than stabilizing industrial relations, as had been the government's intention, the workers' committees led to conflict and confusion at the shopfloor. Norma Kriger reports that war veterans often pursued positions on the workers' committees, and the increasing influence of veterans at places of work created conflicts with white employers and black shopfloor supervisors (Kriger 2003: ch. 5, esp. 163–77). War veterans refused to take orders from supervisors they saw as "sell-outs," the veterans' term of abuse for those who had not joined the guerrilla struggle. Where war veterans and ZANU-PF cadres had power over workers' committees, they made small disputes more likely to escalate or result in deadlock:

> It could become kind of awkward. I can say the company can only afford a 14 percent wage increase. He'll say: "You have a Mercedes Benz. You don't care about the welfare of workers." I'd say: "No, it's a perk." He'd say: "No. You're an oppressor."[18]

Research conducted in 1983 roughly supports this description of the early post-independence workers' committees. Sociologist Angela Cheater reports that the workers' committees were, upon their introduction, viewed by management as a ZANU strategy to penetrate and politicize the workplace: the workers' committee was simply the party in "flimsy disguise" (Cheater 1986: 122). Trade union leadership expressed similar views on the link between workers' committees and ZANU, though some suggested a rather different motivation for the Party's encouragement of workers' committees:

> Oh yes, we had many fights after that [the introduction of workers committees], but [the Minister of Labour] used some of those workers committees to speak up for employers. They [workers committees] were taking their orders from Zanu-PF, which had taken over the Rhodesian Front offices and put themselves there, so most of the issues for workers were being decided by the offices there under political direction.[19]

Individual ZANU MPs also had close links with workers' committee members or individual workplaces, and, in the early 1980s, MPs would often be called to settle labor disputes rather than union representatives.

---

[18] Employer Saul Kangai, quoted in Kriger (2003: 165). Kriger reports one instance in which the intransigence of a war veteran-led workers' committee led to an employer lockout.
[19] Interview with Gibson Sibanda, December 4, 2002.

Despite these signs of party involvement in shopfloor labor relations, ZANU did not see the workers' committees as political resources. The party had little direct control over the workers' committees, which operated differently from workplace to workplace. Further, ZANU never seriously considered a workplace party-building strategy, and unionists do not remember party activists attempting to sell party cards at the workplace.[20] In this respect, the ruling party in Zimbabwe had a strikingly different attitude toward shopfloor-level union structures than the ruling party in Zambia, which consistently attempted to use labor structures as political instruments. ZANU party activities and popular mobilization remained concentrated in residential areas. Further, despite the initial prominence of war veterans and the politicization of early elections, partisanship did not become a deeply rooted feature of workers' committees or shopfloor labor activism. Cheater reports there already – in 1983 – existed tensions between the workers' committees and the ZANU district party committees (Cheater 1986: 128).[21] Cheater suggests that, as time passed, workers became less enthusiastic about party presence at the workplace. The party was criticized for always asking for "contributions" without delivering concrete benefits, whereas the workers' committee was seen as an organization that could "deliver" due to its direct role in workplace conflict resolution. At Cheater's research site, only five of the fourteen members of the first workers' committee were party members; new elections in 1982 and 1983 returned even smaller numbers of party members, two and four respectively (Cheater 1986: 122–3).

Politicization of the structures may not have been as great a concern as some would suggest, but the composition of workers' committees in the early days did prevent them from improving "industrial democracy" or expanding worker participation in decision-making. Representatives elected in these early rounds of elections were not chosen for their technical expertise or negotiating skill, and negotiations between employers and workers' committee representatives took place on a substantially uneven playing ground. Employers complained that committee representatives did not take into account the economic constraints facing businesses; however, representatives' lack of information and expertise also made it easy to deflect demands on grounds of economic infeasibility (Maphosa 1992: esp. 18–19). Workshops for workers' committee representatives were often held at hotels and involved food and alcohol, and one unionist said that they were essentially "bribes" intended to flatter workers' representatives and make them more sympathetic to the views of

---

[20] Interviews with Lucia Matibenga, July 30, 2003, and Percy Mcijo, March 5, 2003.
[21] Cheater's pseudonymous parastatal, Zimtex, was located in Kadoma, a city in Mashonaland West that would have been at the time a base of ZANU support.

employers.[22] The "industrial democracy" of this period was therefore management-dominated, and workers' committees had little impact on employers' policies. A Zimbabwean sociologist who undertook fieldwork at a Harare parastatal in 1988 describes the system thus:

> Workers participation remained consultative. [Workers] had no right to information, though it was given to them, mostly after the decisions had already been made. They had no veto power. The suggestion boxes presented even less opportunity for meaningful participation than the workers' committees and councils. Workers could make demands...but it was up to management to respond or not. In fact, the benefit to management was greater [because] management got to know workers' feelings and problems through this one-way communication. (Mutizwa-Mangiza 1992: 39)

Workers' committees failed to alter the balance of power between capital and labor at the shopfloor level. Nor were union structures capable of serving as a replacement and providing workers with strong representation at the workplace.

It took some time for unions to develop structures that reached the shopfloor and were able to coordinate procedures or actions across workplaces. Affiliate unions failed to substantially expand the number or improve the quality of branches in the 1980s. According to unionists active in the branches, they were meant to meet monthly, elect their own officers, usually about ten, and forward the minutes of meetings on to headquarters where demands or disputes would be followed up on by the union leadership. National unions supplied minimal support to grassroots organization. Where there existed regional union offices, branch meetings would be held there, and the national union would sometimes pay for the transport of branch officials to and from meetings. Few ZCTU affiliates had resources for more significant support, but unions and the ZCTU would occasionally arrange training workshops or other meetings for branch officials, either at the regional or at the national level. Trade unionists often reported that organization was stronger in some parts of the country than in others, and they regularly commented that branch structures often existed "on paper only" or were not functional in the early 1980s.[23] Branches perhaps had a tendency to fall into disrepair due to the small number of individuals involved in their operation. National unions did not make concerted efforts to expand participation in union elections, and elections for branch positions were organized in a somewhat ad hoc manner:

---

[22] Interview with Percy Mcijo, March 5, 2003.

[23] The most commonly reported trend was for union structures at independence to be much stronger in Bulawayo than in Harare.

In an area, we would invite all the companies that have members to come to the offices here, and maybe fifteen will come. So we say, alright, we need ten of you, and then they will elect amongst themselves. There are no shopfloor elections for union officials; that we did when we helped them to form their own workers committees.[24]

In the 1980s, only stronger, more established unions had branch structures. Unions sometimes had union organizers at the plant level but lacked intermediate structures linking these organizers to one another and facilitating communication from union leadership to the grassroots (Republic of Zimbabwe 1984: 33). In 1984, though 69 percent of unions reported that they had shop stewards, only 22 percent said that they had district branches. The lack of such structures doubtlessly contributed to unions' poor resource bases, as most unions relied on physical collection of union dues rather than check-off.

The policy of amalgamation instituted under the 1985 LRA was intended to boost the bargaining power and membership of individual unions. The LRA established the principle of "one union, one industry," making a single affiliate the sole representative of all workers within a given industry. Accordingly, the LRA established a system of mandatory check-off of workers' union dues, which immediately expanded the financial base of affiliates. The LRA did not, however, encourage improvements in union organizational structure or top–bottom communication within unions. Rather than allowing unions to build their structures on the basis of local needs and demands, the policy of amalgamation tended to yield national-level unions that lacked organic linkages between leadership and membership. The amalgamation of unions was often fairly superficial, amounting to little more than an integration of structures at the highest national level. For instance, in his examination of the Zimbabwe Farmers Union (ZFU), Michael Bratton points out that leadership control of local-level union programs was strikingly shallow (Bratton 1994b).[25] The national leadership of the new ZFU simply sat atop the organizational structures of its two component unions, and there was no real organizational integration at the grassroots level. The structure of collective bargaining institutions reinforced the disconnect between union leaders and the rank-and-file, as unions played a marginal role in wage-setting. The Employment Councils on which union representatives sat were solely advisory, and the government both made the final determination of wages and announced wage increases to workers. Trade unionists argued that this setup made unions invisible to their memberships:

---

[24] Interview with Japhet Moyo, August 14, 2004.
[25] The ZFU was formed by the merging of two smaller indigenous farmers' unions in 1991. Large-scale white commercial farmers were represented by the Commercial Farmers Union (CFU).

The problem is that government has been the trade union because all benefits to the workers have come from the government and not the unions. So people now feel that the government runs the unions . . . The Ministry of Labour is in fact the trade union because the unions don't know what they are doing. (quoted in Republic of Zimbabwe 1984: 46)

In interviews and informal discussions, trade union leadership at all levels confirmed that rank-and-file members in the 1980s saw government as responsible for setting wages, and workers did not see trade unions as having any tangible effects on standard of living or work conditions.

In the 1980s, there were developments within the labor movement that laid the groundwork for more productive and accountable union structures. These improvements in the quality of Zimbabwean unionism did not result from beneficial labor legislation or from the actions of Government; instead, the actions both of workers at the shopfloor level and of ZCTU officials gradually expanded the capacity and the zone of autonomy afforded to organized labor. Over time, unionists built a stronger and more professional labor movement that could serve as an effective watchdog and, eventually, check on government. The expansion of ZCTU education programs was particularly important. The education programs made branch structures and workers' committees more effective and boosted their efficacy in resolving workplace-level disputes. In addition, the character of higher level leadership changed. National unions became more professional, and the ZCTU boosted leadership accountability within the affiliates by intervening in cases of corruption. By the end of the 1980s, the affiliate unions were also in a better financial position. In addition to the reliable revenue from automatic dues collection, donations from international union federations increased.

In addition to the greater professionalization of the unions, a shift in the character of the workers' committees contributed to the unification of the labor movement in the late 1980s and early 1990s. The unions had vigorously opposed the introduction of the workers' committees: they argued that the committees did not have a role distinct from that of the unions, and union leaders predicted nothing but confusion and conflict on the shopfloor. In the early years, conflict did result from the introduction of workers' committees. Antagonism between trade unions and committees made it difficult to unionize workers in several workplaces, and radical workers committee leadership may have promoted splinter unions, which did proliferate during this period (Wood 1988: 298–9). Many unionists interviewed emphasized that the workers' committees chairs would "mislead" workers, turn workers "against the unions," and were often "uninformed people" who would not come to union offices or take advice from union officials about the legislation and codes of conduct governing their workplaces. As the decade progressed, there was a gradual lessening of the conflict between unions and workers' committees.

The leadership of the workers' committees underwent a gradual moderation prompted in large part by the actions of employers. Many employers sponsored educational workshops for newly elected workers' committee representatives, attempting to fill a gap that the unions themselves were neither willing nor able to address. Unionists initially distrusted the training provided to workers' committee representatives. Workshops for workers' committee representatives were often sponsored by employers, as mentioned above. There was a feeling that these workshops were biased in the direction of the employers' perspective. Later, workshops for workers' committees were held by Silveira House, a Catholic labor-training center in Harare.[26] These educational activities made workers' committees less political and more supportive of unions, said trade unionists, and trade unionists began to be elected to workers' committee posts.[27] Despite these improvements, it was not until the early 1990s and the liberalization of collective bargaining that politics entirely faded from the shopfloor.[28]

At about the same time that the workers' committees were being professionalized, changes were underway in the governance of the ZCTU that had similarly significant effects. From 1981 to 1985, a series of scandals involving maladministration and embezzlement of funds at high levels of the ZCTU resulted in leadership turnover and declining popular trust in the organization. Again demonstrating its interest and support for the ZCTU, the Government seconded senior industrial relations officials from the Ministry of Labour to the ZCTU, where they attempted to put the records in some order while preparing for the 1985 Congress (Sachikonye 1986: 265). The grip of ruling party supporters had grown attenuated during these years, partly due to the corruption scandals within the union leadership. Consequently, in 1988, an extraordinary congress of the ZCTU elected a younger and less conservative group of leaders, including Morgan Tsvangirai of the Mineworkers Union. Trade unionists unanimously described this election as a turning point in terms of the confederation's autonomy from the ruling party and its relevance to workers.[29] Isdore Zindoga, the ZCTU's first national organizing secretary, describes the significance of this leadership shift in the following manner:

> [The old guard] did not identify with anything like the class struggle; they were conservative, and they looked at trade unions like any other social group and workers as part [of the general population]. We were arguing that the labor movement should be on its own and should determine its own future without being diluted or compromised by external factors like politics. These old guys, the

---

[26] Interviews with Miriam Chikamba, March 7, 2003, and with Sylvester Rusike, July 28, 2003.
[27] Interviews with Miriam Chikamba, March 7, 2003, and with Japhet Moyo, August 14, 2004.
[28] Interview with Japhet Moyo, August 14, 2004.
[29] For more detailed analysis of this period, see Nordlund (1996) and Schiphorst (2001).

old guard, were involved in the nationalist movement, and they believed that workers needed to work as part and parcel of the overall political movement. We were saying "no."[30]

Put in these terms, the shift in leadership in 1988 to Tsvangirai and other more politically independent unionists represented a more fundamental change in the orientation of trade unions toward Government and toward their role in society. Rather than continuing to serve as partners in a government-directed program of national development intended to equalize conditions for all Zimbabweans, this new ZCTU committed itself to selfishly pursuing the interests of workers. In a move that reinforced the new autonomy of the ZCTU from the ruling party, the Congress also moved its offices out of the ZANU headquarters in 1988 (Nordlund 1996: 152).

The election of the new leadership also began a process of centralization and enforcement of discipline within the labor movement by the ZCTU. The ZCTU leadership elected in 1988 made union governance one of their primary concerns, and Tsvangirai attacked corruption in the affiliates in editorials in *The Worker* and statements at labor functions. Perhaps the last battle between the ZCTU and the older affiliate leadership, which resisted Tsvangirai's demands regarding the democratization of union governance, was fought in 1992–3 over an increase in subscription fees. The affiliates had agreed to an increased 15 cents per worker subscription rate at the 1990 and 1992 labor congresses; however, in early 1993, several of the affiliates said that this increase was unconstitutional and they would only pay 5 cents per worker.[31] Over the next year, the ZCTU took affiliates to court and threatened suspensions over non-payment; by 1995, the ZCTU had finally collected the dues owed to it.[32] There continued to be differences between ZCTU and affiliate leadership; for instance, some union leaders complained in 1996 that communication from the ZCTU often passed through union organizers rather than the formal affiliate hierarchy. But by the late 1990s, the ZCTU had consolidated its communication with and influence over its affiliates. In contrast to the situation in Zambia in the 1980s, the ZCTU provided services to its affiliates and was also capable of disciplining them. Gradually, the distancing of organized labor from the ruling party allowed the ZCTU to build up the autonomy and organizing capacity of the labor movement. In the 1990s, with the implementation of an Economic Structural Adjustment Program (ESAP), the trade unions used this autonomy and capacity to collectively protest economic adjustment and declining living conditions for unionized workers and other Zimbabweans.

---

[30] Interview with Isdore Zindoga, July 18, 2004.
[31] *The Worker*, March 1993.
[32] Interview with Godfrey Kanyenze, August 5, 2003.

CHANGING STATE–LABOR RELATIONS

By the early 1990s, workers no longer believed that the government was delivering on bargains made in the 1980s, a criticism that became stronger after the announcement of structural adjustment in 1991. At May Day celebrations in 1990, after ZANU-PF had announced plans for the introduction of a single-party state, workers carried banners calling for political pluralism. When President Mugabe came forward to speak, workers threw insults and even tomatoes at his podium.[33] Soon after the introduction of ESAP, workers blamed the ruling party for economic decline, and they accused ZANU-PF of betrayal, corruption, and favoring capital, both international and domestic, over the interests of workers. The materials used by the ZCTU for training purposes during this period changed in tone as well: criticisms of ESAP faded into sharp attacks on government, and workers were exhorted to organize and build a stronger trade union organization, which was the only way of forcing the government to abandon ESAP.[34] A banner carried during the 1993 May Day celebrations, fairly typical of the tone of these years, read: "ESAP is a plot by international capital using ZANU-PF to kill workers, peasants, and the *povo* [people]."[35]

The content of the early anti-ESAP protests was not primarily political, and the demands of workers did not include the formation of a labor-based political party. There had been discussions within the labor movement over whether and how trade unionism should be mixed with politics, reported in the union publication *The Worker*. The decision by the ZCTU to remain apolitical, to continue to negotiate with government, and to avoid overt confrontation in the early 1990s was actively debated within the ZCTU. At the 1992 Congress, a small group of younger, more radical trade unionists suggested that the ZCTU and its affiliates should back candidates for office. The feeling was that these candidates, who would run as independents, could bring to Parliament's attention the negative effects of structural adjustment on workers' living conditions and those of the population as a whole.[36] The Executive Council of the ZCTU, which was at the time split on political lines, closed debate on the topic but the Congress's President, Gibson Sibanda, explicitly did not rule out the reopening of debate on the topic in future. When asked about calls for a party, Sibanda emphasized that it was only a small, albeit vocal, minority of the rank-and-file that had supported the idea. He added that the leadership never considered the proposal seriously in the early

---

[33] Interview with Gibson Sibanda, December 4, 2002.
[34] See, for instance, ZCTU (1993*b*).
[35] *The Worker*, May 1993.
[36] Interview with Gift Chimanikire, July 13, 2004; also, interview with Japhet Moyo, August 14, 2004.

1990s: "there were some few voices, but we said no – we will weaken ourselves, we will divide ourselves."[37] The debate seemed resolved by early 1993, when the ZCTU announced that the organization would turn itself into a "political force" but would not become a political party.[38]

Walking the tightrope between political movement and party was by no means a simple task. Relations between the government and the ZCTU deteriorated in the early 1990s, and the labor movement faced additional reversals due to changes in the economic and legislative environment. In 1992, the LRA was amended to bring Zimbabwean labor law in line with IMF and World Bank demands for economic liberalization. Collective bargaining was liberalized, and the principle of "one union, one industry" was abolished, opening the door for splinter unions. The liberalization of collective bargaining did not result in immediate gains for the ZCTU, even though unionists favored decreasing government's role in setting wages. In 1990–1, the government announced that wage awards negotiated by the unions, which ranged between 19 and 30 percent, would be phased in gradually, ostensibly to control inflationary pressures (Sachikonye 2001: 155). Prices nevertheless rose more quickly than the wages were phased in, and unionized workers never saw the real value of the wage increases that had been negotiated by their affiliates. Wage increases negotiated during the 1993–4 collective bargaining exercise fell well below the 25 percent demanded by the ZCTU, amounting to no more than 10 percent in many sectors at a time when annual inflation approached 46 percent.[39] The labor movement also took more direct hits from economic reform. Mass retrenchments in the early 1990s reduced union membership: the number of workers affiliated to the ZCTU fell from 200,590 in 1990 to 152,462 in 1996.[40] Some affiliates were undermined by the formation and registration of splinter unions.[41] In some sectors, such as the railways, splinter unions were formed on a skill-level basis, causing some ZCTU affiliates to lose their most well-paid and educated members.

In part due to the reforms' immediate effects on workers, in part due to its organizational self-interest, the ZCTU announced that economic liberalization was a serious threat both to workers' livelihoods and to a strong and united labor movement. The ZCTU leadership decided to hold nationwide demonstrations in June 1992 to protest ESAP and demand the implementation of measures that would cushion its effects on workers and on organized labor. The demonstration was to consist of coordinated marches by workers in

---

[37] Interview with Gibson Sibanda, December 4, 2002.
[38] See Tsvangirai's comments and the accompanying editorial in *The Worker*, March 1993.
[39] *The Worker*, May 1994.
[40] ZCTU, "Labour Union Participation Rates (1986–2000)," Excel spreadsheet, August 22, 2002. Provided to the author by the ZCTU. See also Carmody (1998) and Mlambo (2000).
[41] Interview with Gideon Shoko, March 14, 2003.

Harare and other major cities; the demonstrators would then gather to listen to addresses by union leaders. Even after the government banned the demonstration, the ZCTU announced that the action would go ahead regardless. Riot police in Harare prevented workers from reaching the city center; in other urban centers, demonstrations were dispersed. ZCTU Secretary-General MorganTsvangirai suggested that the state response was far in excess of what was necessary to prevent the demonstration: "it was the biggest police mobilization that I have ever seen in my life. This whole town was full, 3000 police officers were mobilized, people could not understand what was going on. But it was all to demonstrate that this government was determined to suppress public expression of this kind."[42] The ZCTU leadership emerged from the failed demonstration disenchanted with confrontational mass actions. The labor movement would not organize another protest aimed at changing national policy until 1996. The ZCTU used the intervening years to build the capacity of union structures and the credibility of the ZCTU with workers and other popular constituencies. It expanded its research activities, collaborating with affiliates to survey union members and gather data that could be used in negotiations with government and employers.[43]

Trade unions' vocal objections to ESAP in 1990–2 had no impact on ZANU-PF's commitment to the reforms, and many within the labor movement questioned the utility of continued confrontation with government. Commenting on the period after the 1992 strike, Tsvangirai said:

> the government didn't want to negotiate. It was not losing anything through confrontation, and it was not going to gain anything through negotiation. So they just ignored us. So we said, ah, maybe confrontation was the wrong strategy. Maybe we should engage. So we came up with this idea of tripartitism and *Beyond ESAP*.[44]

Beyond ESAP, a 109-page report on all aspects of Zimbabwean economic policy and planning, was the result of a two-year research project that had involved the ZCTU economics department, independent economists, and business consultants (ZCTU 1996). In the early 1990s, government officials had often attacked the labor movement for criticizing structural adjustment without proposing alternative policies. The ZCTU leadership emphasized that *Beyond ESAP* was an attempt to work with government, to offer criticism *and* potential remedies.[45] The report recommended the retention of some ESAP policies, especially those that would ensure macroeconomic stability and foreign exchange availability. But it also advocated that the government

---

[42] Interview, December 12, 2002.

[43] See, for instance, the coverage of research on textile workers in *Horizon*, July 1993.

[44] Interview with Morgan Tsvangirai, December 5, 2002.

[45] Interviews with Morgan Tsvangirai, December 5, 2002; with Godfrey Kanyenze, August 5, 2003; with Timothy Kondo, November 11, 2002.

eliminate policies that hurt the informal sector, redistribute land to reinvigo-
rate rural livelihoods, and institute other policies that would correct the
underlying structural problems of the Zimbabwean economy.

Labor leadership viewed *Beyond ESAP* as a blueprint for economic reform
that would minimize the social costs of reform and also encourage sustained
employment growth. The document contained stinging criticisms of ESAP's
(and, by extension, the government's) record on unemployment, social service
cutbacks, and poverty indicators. Gradually, *Beyond ESAP* found its way onto
the desks of many civil society organizations, and it came to serve as an anti-
ESAP manifesto for both unionists and civil society activists. Importantly,
the document reflected the ZCTU's interest in constituencies outside
unionized workers and the formal sector labor force. The extensive sections
on the informal sector and on agricultural policy suggested a redefinition of
the ZCTU's imagined critical or representative role. Rather than seeing itself
solely as a representative of its members, the ZCTU defended the interests of
retrenched workers and those without access to formal employment, such as
informal traders and rural peasants. To some extent, this was not a drastic
change. As early as 1993, ZCTU publications spoke of the need to link the
organization to others representing peasants, workers in the informal sector,
and the unemployed (e.g., ZCTU 1993a: 44–6).[46] From 1996 to 1999, this
commitment was backed by concrete action aimed at integrating the civil
society sector and organizing previously marginal or ignored constituencies.

The ZCTU supplemented its research agenda with attempts to educate and
involve its members and other Zimbabweans in policy discussions. It also
urged political participation in much more direct terms than it had in the past.
By the mid-1990s, the ZCTU circulated pamphlets saying that such participation placed checks on government power and served other purposes as well.
One pamphlet explained:

> [Participation] can deepen knowledge, change attitudes, redistribute power and
> help people take control over their own development and can help people
> overcome problems of centralised planning...Failure of citizens to participate
> in democracy is like telling leaders to do as they please. Non-participation gives
> unchecked power.[47]

---

[46] In its 1993 workers' education manual, the ZCTU makes a bold statement of the rationale
for an alliance between organized labor and other popular constituencies: "workers share their
wages with their peasant relatives and spend the holidays planting or reaping together. In real life
the workers are united with the peasants in many areas. This is unity in action without unity in
organization. This should not be so. The struggle for land in Zimbabwe will never be solved
without a strong peasant organization united with workers. The workers' struggle to end
exploitation will not succeed without an organized and conscious peasant class" (ZCTU
1993b: 44).

[47] ZCTU, "Worker Participation in Civic Society," undated loose pamphlet, ZCTU archives.

ESAP had provided the ZCTU with an issue that affected the interests of both unionized workers and other urban constituencies. The ZCTU began to hold "labor forums" throughout the country, even in areas that were not viewed as traditional loci for trade unionism. These meetings were organized by local and regional ZCTU officials in order to inform workers about ZCTU activities and local collective bargaining efforts.[48] The labor forums were, in many ways, a response to the failed 1992 demonstrations: they were intended to boost the labor movement's capacity to communicate with its rank-and-file, but they also hoped to mobilize the larger popular constituencies that would be necessary for successful large-scale protest. The meetings started with attendances of 200 or 300, mostly workers; as time went on, crowds at the labor forums grew to over 1,000, and Tsvangirai and ZCTU President Isaac Matongo would address the crowds in the open space outside meeting halls.[49] Though the meetings were initially composed primarily of workers, civic activists and other interested parties began to attend the labor forums as well. In interviews, many members of civil society – especially members of the student movement – pointed to the labor forums as important places for communication and contact between the labor movement and other societal actors.[50]

Economic hardship motivated Zimbabweans to protest economic policy in more direct fashion as well, and the number of strikes and other protest actions increased in the 1990s. In 1992 and 1993, there had been spontaneous bread and maize riots to protest price increases; in January 1998, much larger scale maize riots took place in Harare and spread to other urban centers. The 1998 riots provoked both violent state repression and, unlike earlier state violence, a coordinated civil society response.[51] In contrast to Zambia, however, these riots were not accompanied by waves of wildcat strikes. Labor protest was instead controlled and channeled by national affiliate unions, not local union leaders or workers themselves. The relative discipline of organized labor in comparison to Zambia is not due to more efficient collective bargaining in Zimbabwe. After 1990, unions were free to bargain directly with employers, but dispute resolution remained lengthy and ineffective. In 1995, the Zimbabwe Labour Relations Tribunal had a backlog of 633 cases, and unions had to wait for long periods to have disputes heard, which was a

---

[48] According to Richard Saunders, these were often held at worksites or other nearby locations, either during the lunch hour or after work. Personal communication from Richard Saunders, August 1, 2005.

[49] "ZCTU Labour Forums Held Countrywide," ZCTU mimeo, file 13.06.3, dated April 2000. Also, interview with Morgan Tsvangirai, December 12, 2002.

[50] Interviews with Nelson Chamisa, September 16, 2002. Maxwell Sangweume, August 19, 2002, and Blessing Chebundo, August 2, 2003.

[51] For more on the 1998 food riots, see Amani Trust, "A Consolidated Report on the Food Riots, 19–23 January 1998" (undated), Harare.

prerequisite to striking or more confrontational bargaining with employers.[52] Unlike their counterparts in Zambia, workers did not respond to this frustration with direct action to force more timely dispute resolution or the intervention of government; instead, they waited for instructions from trade union leadership.

The affiliates and the ZCTU called their members out on strike several times in the mid-1990s, and labor unrest increased from very low levels from 1992 onward. One of the first major strikes in Zimbabwe since the strike wave of 1980–1 occurred in February 1994. Nearly 8,000 employees of the state-owned Posts and Telecommunications Corporation (PTC) went on strike after union leaders announced that management had imposed a salary scale over the union's objections (Dansereau 1997: 110). Workers remained away from work for sixteen days, shutting down the majority of the country's post offices, community savings banks (run by the PTC), and telephone offices.[53] The PTC management announced that workers would be fired, attempted to form a splinter union, and even jailed union leaders; however, the union's cause was supported by the ZCTU, public opinion, and a majority of parliamentary backbenchers.[54] The PTC was forced to give in to union demands, setting a precedent that probably precipitated more industrial action. In the months and years following the PTC strike, national unions held other strikes, and non-unionized groups – including medical staff, teachers, bankers, and civil servants – went on strike. Industrial actions were more common during the collective bargaining season, as Saunders notes (Saunders 2001: 46). Many of these strikes were successful in winning salary increases for unionized workers.

The rise in strike action demonstrated that the Zimbabwean labor movement was more willing to use confrontational tactics, including illegal strikes, to achieve its aims. It did not, however, mean that workers saw themselves as engaging in *political* protest. Lovemore Madhuku, then with the Friedrich Ebert Stiftung (FES), which provided funding and consulting support to the ZCTU, said that ZCTU criticism was not yet viewed as political:

> they were really interested more in working with government and challenging government on concrete economic issues. Like in 1996 with the civil service strike, etc, those things never translated into open political battle... If the minimum wage was low, the trade unions would say so. If the proposed laws were draconian – like in 1992 there was an amendment to the LRA that affected worker rights – the trade unions would make a lot of noise. But it was not taken

---

[52] *The Worker*, November 1995. Strikes were entirely illegal in "essential industries," a term that was applied, as in Zambia, to a wide array of industries, including nearly all civil servants.

[53] This was the first use by organized labor of the work stayaway, which would later become the chosen protest tool of the ZCTU and MDC. Interview with Gift Chimanikire, July 13, 2004.

[54] Some MPs even demanded the replacement of PTC management and the resignation of the Deputy Minister of Information (Dansereau 1997: 111).

beyond that. It was not political; it was really just traditional work of a trade union that we were doing.[55]

The vast majority of trade unionists interviewed agreed that, at that time, neither the ZCTU nor affiliates conceived of trade union actions or demands as "political." In reflecting on this period, some unionists who later became active in the Movement for Democratic Change (MDC) described unionism as having not yet developed a political consciousness, and they noted that the ZCTU leadership had not yet explicitly linked economic problems to larger issues of governance. Commented Lucia Matibenga, who was President of the Commercial Workers Union and Vice President of the ZCTU, "I really think [about] how much time we wasted just saying wages, working conditions, wages, working conditions, when we then had an opportunity to do so much more. But I think we were not identifying much as labor, as a union."[56] The ZCTU faced pressures from below as popular opposition to the government grew. At labor forums, workers began to demand the formation of a labor-based political party to challenge ZANU-PF.[57] One unionist suggested that the increasing politicization of workers at the shopfloor level was driven by the ZCTU's own human rights, workers' education, and voters' or civic education programs.[58] Workers at May Day celebrations or other rallies were free in expressing their hostility to the ruling party. At the 1996 ZCTU May Day rally, workers cheered when ZANU-PF Party Secretary Nathan Shamuyarira yelled "forward with ZCTU" but booed after he suggested "forward with ZANU-PF."[59] In the same year, a massive civil servants' strike supported by the ZCTU forced the government to allow civil servants to unionize. The ZCTU used the affiliation of the new civil servants' unions as an opportunity to affirm its autonomy from government. Tsvangirai sent a memo to all labor structures, reminding them that any alliance between trade unions and nationalist parties "cannot last forever [for] we are past that historical stage of development. The ZCTU will engage in political, social and economic struggles on a non-partisan basis."[60]

Given this prelude, it was not surprising when government–labor relations turned more explicitly adversarial in 1997. From 1995 to 1997, the ZCTU had struggled to get a meeting with President Mugabe to discuss taxation and rising prices. In July of 1997, the ZCTU was given the meeting with the president. Gift Chimanikire says that the delegation arrived with a twenty-seven-page

[55] Interview with Lovemore Madhuku, November 11, 2002.
[56] Interview, July 30, 2003.
[57] Interviews with Girai Mazenge and Tenson Muchefa, July 13, 2004; Percy Mcijo, March 5, 2003; Blessing Chebundo, August 2, 2003.
[58] Interview with Percy Mcijo, March 5, 2003.
[59] *The Worker* (Harare), June 1996.
[60] *The Worker*, November 1996.

From Protest to Parties

document drawn from the research on *Beyond ESAP*. After Tsvangirai's presentation, Mugabe commented that workers were not suffering and that people in the rural areas were "bearing the brunt" of economic adjustment.[61] After the ZCTU walked out, was lured back in, and discussed their concerns for some time, Mugabe assured them that he would consult with his cabinet and get a response to the unions the coming week. That weekend, in a newspaper interview, the Minister of Labour said that all of the issues presented by the ZCTU at the meeting had been "political." He added that, should the ZCTU wish to compete on the "rough terrain" of politics, then Tsvangirai and Sibanda must form a political party. The labor leadership saw these statements as a breach of good faith, and the ZCTU General Council subsequently approved the formation of a task force to investigate the formation of a political party. Other informants pointed to the government's massive payout to war veterans, the ZCTU's withdrawal from the Tripartite Negotiating Forum, and a ZCTU stay-away protesting new taxes – all of which occurred in 1997 – as the final breaking points in government–labor relations. Noted one trade union official, the formation of the MDC became a virtual certainty after the government and the trade unions stopped meeting in 1997: "the government lost the opportunity for dialogue, and it was inevitable that we would go outside the process."[62] The language used by the ZCTU at rallies and labor forums also took on a more confrontational tone. After the 1997 stay-away, the ZCTU rallied workers by referring to the need to resist a government that was hostile to the needs of its citizens, and it called for the government to negotiate a social contract with labor that might serve as "a ceasefire in a time of war."[63] The labor movement's change in attitude toward cooperation with government was best reflected in the ZCTU's choice of its 1998 theme: "None but Ourselves."

CONCLUSIONS

Between independence in 1980 and the late 1990s, the relationship between the ZCTU, government, and employers changed substantially. Equally importantly, the ZCTU's relationship with its own affiliates shifted, producing improvements in the capacity and unity of the labor movement. The ZCTU expanded education programs and training sessions for affiliate leaders, built ZCTU district structures to bring together the affiliate unions in particular

---

[61] Interview with Gift Chimanikire, July 13, 2004.
[62] Interview with Timothy Kondo, November 11, 2002.
[63] Morgan Tsvangirai, speech notes for "The Way Forward: towards a social accord in Zimbabwe," April 30, 1998. ZCTU Archives, folder 05.03.3.

areas, and founded regional offices of the ZCTU in Gweru, Mutare, and Masvingo.[64] In 1993, the ZCTU launched *The Worker* in order to improve communication with its membership. In addition to these services, the liberalization of collective bargaining made the assistance of the ZCTU vital to affiliates: they relied on the research department in formulating wage demands, and they also needed the ZCTU's assistance during negotiations with employers.[65] Gradually, the ZCTU became more central to the activities of the unions. Finally, perhaps most importantly for the role it would later play in a social movement and a political party, the ZCTU formed links with larger constituencies beyond unionized labor, and many Zimbabweans, particularly urban residents, began to think of the ZCTU as an association of their own.

[64] Interviews with Miriam Chikamba, March 7, 2003; Leonard Gwenzi, September 23, 2002; Percy Mcijo, March 5, 2003.
[65] Interview with Blessing Chebundo, August 2, 2003.

Four

Labor Control Regimes in Zambia and Kenya

This chapter examines labor control regimes in Zambia and Kenya, which were characterized by a greater degree of state intervention than in Zimbabwe. The goals of this intervention varied substantially in the two cases. The Zambian government crafted a strong and centralized movement in order to strengthen its penetration of society; in contrast, the Kenyan government intervened in union affairs largely to prevent the emergence of such a labor movement. States' choices regarding labor strategy were influenced by the character of labor at independence. The strong bargaining position of organized labor in Zambia made it difficult for the Zambian government to pursue labor-repressive policies, and the state instead ensured labor's cooperation with state development goals through a system of inducements and constraints. Kenyan labor, on the other hand, was not weak at independence, but it was highly fragmented, as in Zimbabwe. In contrast to Zimbabwe, the Kenyan state had little interest in building a strong, directive labor movement, and labor legislation instituted coercive control over strike activity and union governance without providing the organizational benefits that came with state policies in Zimbabwe and Zambia. Differences in labor policy had concrete effects on the form and strength of union structures in the three countries. In Zambia and Zimbabwe, labor entered the multiparty period with substantial advantages, including both organizational structures that were independent from state control and memberships that viewed unions as a source of identity. In Kenya, on the other hand, labor-repressive policies resulted in unions that were tightly controlled by the ruling party and that had very weak ties to their grassroots memberships. When rising popular discontent forced authoritarian governments to implement political reform, organized labor served as the base for protest and political mobilization in Zimbabwe and Zambia, while it remained politically captive and quiescent in Kenya.

ZAMBIA

The character of post-independence labor relations in Zimbabwe and Zambia was similar in three main respects: the degree of political autonomy allocated to labor at independence, the centrality of wage restraint to governments' development strategies, and a close initial affiliation between organized labor and ruling parties, to the extent of joint office-holding. For different reasons, organized labor in Zimbabwe and Zambia was able to resist direct incorporation into ruling party structures. This did occur in other African states. Secondly, in both Zimbabwe and Zambia, the state relied on revenue and foreign exchange earned by the mining and industrial sectors. The stability and profitability of these sectors was therefore crucial to government economic plans, meaning that wage restraint soon became a core aim of state policy toward organized labor. Consequently, mechanisms of labor control, and in particular restrictions on labor's ability to strike, were an immediate priority for post-independence governments in Zimbabwe and Zambia. Finally, organized labor in both Zimbabwe and Zambia passed through stages during which leadership was dominated by individuals with strong ties to the ruling parties. Elections of liberal, apolitical leadership – in Zimbabwe in 1987 and in Zambia in 1974 – were critical junctures in both countries, after which unions marked off their independence from ruling parties and took on more critical and activist roles on the national stage.

The Sources of Labor Autonomy

In any account of Zambian labor, one must begin with the special role played by the mineworkers union. There existed a strongly rooted tradition of worker mobilization and protest in Northern Rhodesia; in addition, the Copperbelt's miners had a sense of common identity and destiny relatively early in the colonial period.[1] Miners went on strike as early as 1935, and thousands of miners, sawmill workers, and railwaymen participated in spontaneous strikes at various points in the 1940s (Meebelo 1986: chs. 3–5). In 1935 and 1940, mineworkers held massive strikes in support of higher wages. These were fairly well-organized, and they spread from mine to mine along the Copperbelt, but the strikes also brought with them violence, looting, and property destruction. Prior to these strikes, the colonial government had relied on appointed tribal elders, a form of modified traditional rule for urban areas, as the main instrument of local government and conflict resolution in the

---

[1] The best account of pre-independence union development and, particularly, the relationship between the unions and nationalist parties is found in the very detailed Zelniker (1971).

mining areas. Labor unrest prompted a reevaluation of this strategy. For the colonial government, the 1935 and 1940 strikes, according to Michael Burawoy, demonstrated that the tribal elders were "ineffective for industrial conciliation and unreliable for social control" (Burawoy 1982: 146). Though the tribal elders were retained until 1953, when miners voted for their abolition, the system was no longer the sole prop of governance. The colonial government instead instituted a mix of union organization, investment, and infrastructural development in order to "stabilize" the newly urbanized populationof the Copperbelt towns.[2] With the encouragement of the colonial government, advisors deputized from the British Trade Unions Congress assisted in the formation of the mineworkers union and trained small groups of African miners in organization and trade unionism. The African Mineworkers Union (AMU), the first labor organization in the territory, was formed in 1948, and it soon established branches in all four of the major mining towns in the Copperbelt.

The creation of a mineworkers union in 1948 strengthened miners' bargaining power and resulted in concrete benefits for miners, despite the mines management's attempts to undermine the organization. Between 1950 and 1954, the total wage bill for African mineworkers more than doubled, even though the labor force expanded by less than 7 percent.[3] The leaders of the AMU turned their backs on the existing bases of social power in the mining towns, and they concentrated instead on developing strong links between union leaders and rank-and-file membership. Strikes garnered high participation rates among both members *and* non-members. For instance, in January 1955, the union called a strike to protest the magnitude of the wage differential between European and African workers. Of the entire African workforce, 95–96 percent observed the strike, and the government recorded that only 630 of 20,000 *non-unionized* workers reported for work (Meebelo 1986: 289). The union generated attachments of other kinds as well. The main form of recreation in the mining towns, ritualized dance competitions, moved away from expressing intertribal differences or rivalries. Instead, trade union officials were given places of honor in the dances, which came to embody a new notion of urban community (Mitchell 1956). Trade unionism did not efface traditional attachments, including workers' ethnic identities, but it did provide workers, on the Copperbelt at least, with a new form of attachment, as well as an associational space that transcended ethnic identity (Epstein 1958; Gertzel 1979: 316; Ferguson 1994).

---

[2] For more about colonial policy-making during this period, see Heisler (1971); also, Posner (2006: chs. 2 and 3).

[3] The total "emoluments" paid to Africans increased from £2,116,251 in 1950 to £4,589,840, while the number of African employees increased from 34,814 to 37,193. Northern Rhodesian Chamber of Mines figures, reported in Vander Plaetse et al. (2005): 96, footnote 7.

In contrast to Zimbabwe, where the post-independence government feared shopfloor militancy and the *absence* of trade union structures, the post-independence government in Zambia feared that powerful trade union structures could be used to organize large-scale strikes and extract concessions from the state. Despite these fears, the state found the mineworkers union to be simply too strong to dismantle or subjugate. Labor's autonomy in post-independence Zambia was assured due to the AMU's struggles *before* independence in 1964. The relationship between politics and unionism, however, remained uncertain in the early 1960s. Because of the early British influence on union organization, there was a strong commitment to economism – or apolitical unionism – on the part of many Zambian union organizers prior to independence. Lawrence Katilungu, the powerful head of the AMU, repeatedly refused to use strike action to strengthen the bargaining position of the nationalist parties that were pushing for independence. Younger trade union leaders had disagreed, and there had also been growing grassroots pressure to use the AMU structures to serve political purposes. Divisions over union strategy did not, however, yield the organizational fragmentation that plagued Zimbabwean trade unionism at independence. Leadership struggles occasionally took on partisan tones, but unions did not fragment on party lines, nor did they form rival national centers that were linked to different political parties, as in Zimbabwe. Zambian unionists were instead socialized with a commitment to trade unions as autonomous from political parties, even though these actors might be, at times, closely allied. The geographic reach of Zambian unions expanded during this period as well. By independence in 1964, Zambian unionism was not limited to the Copperbelt. The period 1960–4 was one of tremendous organizational growth for smaller unions: in 1960, only the Mineworkers Union had a membership of over 5,000; by 1964, five unions, including two truly national public sector unions, had 5,000 members or more.[4] The total unionized labor force had grown from approximately 50,000 in 1961 to 102,000 in 1964, nearly half of the total wage labor force. The Mineworkers Union was the strongest union at independence and remained the focus of government labor control policy, but it no longer dominated the labor movement as it had in the 1950s.

Labor Policy after Independence

In contrast to the fairly disorganized and weak labor landscape that existed in Zimbabwe at independence, the new Zambian government confronted a strong, autonomous labor movement with a proven history of winning wage increases for its members. Cooperation between the labor and the state was

---

[4] Labor Department figures, cited in Gertzel (1975: 319–20).

not automatic, nor did it seem particularly likely at the time. To the new ruling party, the United National Independence Party (UNIP), the loyalty of the labor movement was suspect, since many miners were supporters of the rival African National Congress (ANC), which had had stronger ties to the Copperbelt. Developments around the time of independence created further problems in the relationship between the ruling party and the country's labor movement. The pre-independence elections of 1963 were characterized by violence between UNIP and ANC supporters in many of the Copperbelt towns. There is little evidence that local violence by UNIP cadres was supported or encouraged by the party's leadership, but the party's Youth Brigades took an increasingly active and confrontational role in the mining areas in 1964 and 1965.[5] They threatened to begin checking party cards, a tactic that did much to dampen expressions of political interest in the mine townships and at the workplace. UNIP cadres also demanded that the mine management provide them with office space for meetings and coerce workers to attend party meetings.[6] The language of much of this interaction was explicitly threatening, and the UNIP Youth Brigades became known by Copperbelt residents as *mposa mabwe* or "throwers of stones" (Harries-Jones 1975: 63). The political differences between the new ruling party and the constituencies with the closest ties to organized labor complicated state-labor relations, as did other events soon after independence.

Like other African countries, Zambia was affected by a substantial strike wave in the aftermath of independence. Strikes occurred in the mining sector, the railways, local councils, and schools. The Zambian government responded to these challenges with somewhat inconsistent strategies in an attempt to strengthen control over labor. Government policy initially focused on undermining existing union structures. Thus, the government responded to the post-independence wave of strikes with an impressive lightning strategy of union leadership co-optation, and it then attempted to fragment the support bases of the existing unions by forming government-allied rival unions. These policies were largely ineffectual. The most visible failure of the second component of this policy occurred in the mining sector, where a government-backed splinter union attracted little support (Kapferer 1969). The strength and the resilience of the now-renamed Mineworkers Union of Zambia (MUZ) in the face of government interference did much to motivate a shift in UNIP policy toward labor (Harries-Jones 1975: 166–70). From this point forward, UNIP made little attempt to undermine existing union structures; instead, the party and its government would control labor by

---

[5] See, for example, "General Situation at Nchanga Chingola," January 25, 1964. File 202.2.3, Political Meetings and Correspondence, ZCCM Archives. Ndola, Zambia.

[6] "Political Meetings – Correspondence," ibid.

grafting a coercive central structure atop the already-established sectoral trade unions.

In 1964, the government put in place the first component of this labor strategy by dissolving the existing trade union center and forming a new Zambian Congress of Trade Unions (ZCTU). The ZCTU was intended to establish direct control over existing trade unions, which were organized both sectorally and geographically, and thereby exercise a dampening influence on strike activity and wage demands. The ZCTU was never intended to be an organization driven by its affiliates. For much of its early history, it served as an instrument for top–down state control, though that control was more asserted than achieved. Early actions did little to improve ZCTU–affiliate relations. The ZCTU instituted a countrywide network of information centers so it would not have to rely on affiliate reporting, and it demanded assurances from affiliates that they would not strike or engage in collective bargaining without Congress approval. These actions insinuated the Congress more directly into negotiation processes between unions, employers, and the state, and some have suggested that they were an attempt to "modernise the trade union structure by bypassing the existing unions" (Gupta 1974: 308). The ZCTU was also empowered to pursue the amalgamation of all existing unions into large single-industry or sectoral unions, a process that began even prior to the passage of comprehensive labor legislation in 1971. The formation of the ZCTU was the beginning of a large-scale centralization of union structures at the national level. Centralization was intended to expand UNIP control over politically suspicious affiliates, but there were constraints on the labor center's power. Importantly, affiliate compliance with the demands of the ZCTU remained voluntary prior to 1971 (Rakner 1994: 77–82). Thus, despite the ZCTU's rather impressive array of powers on paper, strong national unions often ignored the Congress in the early stages of its alliance with the state.

The passage of the Industrial Relations Act (IRA) of 1971 did away with this voluntarism, and it indicated a significant change from the government's prior piecemeal approach to labor governance. The Act created a set of mechanisms that constrained union behavior while strengthening union structures. The IRA required unions to affiliate with the ZCTU, and it tied union registration and participation in collective bargaining to the ZCTU structure. Rather than the toothless requirement of ZCTU approval before a strike was called, the IRA largely outlawed all strikes. The legislation failed to list which sectors fell under "necessary services," for which all strikes were illegal, leading unions to presume that all strike activity was illegal. Even outside the necessary service sectors, the means of obtaining strike permission were so cumbersome as to make legal strikes nearly impossible. Finally, the IRA established tripartite collective bargaining arrangements that gave greater power to the government's Labour Commissioner and made the decisions of the Industrial Relations Court binding and not subject to appeal.

In addition to these formal restrictions on union action, the UNIP government pursued two other policies that affected union organization and membership links at the grassroots level. The IRA introduced "works councils," which were similar to the workers' committees in Zimbabwe. As in Zimbabwe, these were meant to expand shopfloor democracy; however, according to Rakner, the councils were less participatory than coercive. They functioned for the most part as a means of supplanting the affiliate unions and "[incorporating] workers directly from the shopfloor up [into party structures] rather than trying to reach workers through the labor unions" (Rakner 1994: 83). In addition to the work councils, UNIP created "party committees" at the workplace. These changes in industrial relations transformed organized labor into an implementer of government policy and a channel for the communication of information about government policy to workers (Bates 1971). Rigid collective bargaining structures in the public sector tended to radicalize the rank-and-file, who would often choose branch leaders who were militant and willing to use strike action. The Zambian government supplemented formal constraints on labor with informal procedures for removing those union leaders who were seen as threats or as unlikely to press the government line regarding strike and wage restraint. In order to undercut the influence of branch "militants," the government would often either promote them to positions that rendered them ineligible to serve as branch officials, or it would back alternate factions in branch or union elections.[7] Government also used strategic promotion and appointments in the mining sector to remove union leaders who gained too much power or influence over the rank-and-file (Bates 1971: ch. 5). Union leaders were appointed to the Central Committee of UNIP or nominated as parliamentary candidates in order to tie these individuals more closely to the party and its policies. This last strategy occasionally backfired, since workers often resisted and voted out of office leaders perceived to be "political" or pro-government.[8]

According to the new government perspective, unions did not exist to aggregate the interests of workers or improve their bargaining strength. Instead, their primary role was to support the country's overall economic development and to act as government's "partners in development." President Kenneth Kaunda consistently urged the unions to focus on the interests of all Zambians, not just unionized workers, and argued that strong union action against strikes and wage demands would yield dividends for organized labor in subsequent periods. Bates's work on Zambian state-labor relations during this period demonstrates the way in which unions abandoned interest

---

[7] Interview with Sylvester Tembo, Lusaka, July 9, 2004; also, Liatto (1989): 44–46; *Times of Zambia*, July 18–9, 1974.
[8] Interview with Charles Muchimba, July 2004.

representation to serve as instruments of government policy. He describes the resulting labor control regime in a passage worth quoting at length:

> Instead of emphasizing the union's role as a defender of the workers' interests, however, in the field of development policy, the government emphasizes the union's role as a defender of the interests of the nation. Rather than transmitting and fighting for the demands of its members, the union is to regulate their behavior in conformity with public policy. In short, the union is to deviate from its traditional role as an input structure, and to serve as an agency for implementing public policy. (Bates 1971: 47)

This strategy of state control changed relations between UNIP and the unions, and it also affected the relationship between union leadership and rank-and-file members. As the unions were required to support government wage policy and, more specifically, enforce wage restraint, they could no longer serve as instruments for the expression of membership demands. This incompatibility between bottom-up and top-down pressures was initially resolved with an increasing disconnection between union leadership and grassroots membership. In the early period during which Bates conducted his fieldwork, he found that once militant unions with strong degrees of membership loyalty during the nationalist period suffered the loss of their members' belief in the unions' legitimacy and in the representativeness of union leadership (Bates 1971: 57–65, 106–11).

These suggestions of grassroots' discontent with union leadership hint at one of the most distinguishing features of Zambian labor relations, which was constant throughout the 1970s and 1980s. Rank-and-file membership of national unions was surprisingly militant in Zambia. Workers carried out strikes without the consent of leadership, and they punished leaders who they viewed as too moderate. By the mid-1970s, workers regularly refused to stop strikes on the request of branch and national union leaders, and they often publicly accused these officials of disloyalty to workers.[9] In the next section, I will detail how grassroots militancy gradually moved the ZCTU toward greater autonomy from the state and more critical positions on public policy.

Branch Militancy and Organizational Weakness

As suggested above, the "industrial peace" that was in turn praised by President Kaunda, ostensibly threatened by "dissidents," and occasionally used as leverage by trade union leaders was not terribly peaceful. The level of strike activity in Zambia from independence to 1990 was higher than in other countries in the region, despite harsh industrial relations legislation that

---

[9] See, for instance, *Times of Zambia*, January 30, 1975; August 6–8, 1975; October 4, 1975.

virtually illegalized strikes. In the immediate aftermath of the 1971 IRA, strike levels did decline; however, by the late 1970s, strike levels were rising once more. In the mining sector, branch officials and stewards presumed responsible for strikes could be dismissed or arrested, but this threat had little effect on labor actions. Instead, the organization of strikes was pushed underground: secret meetings became common on the Copperbelt, and strikes were coordinated through anonymous circulars and posters (Larmer 2007: 110–11). Traditionally strong unions, such as those in the mining sector, accounted for many of the job actions, but the strikes of the late 1970s and 1980s signaled the new-found reach of unions with truly national membership bases. Individual branches of the Zambian National Union of Teachers (ZNUT) and the Posts and Telecommunications Workers Union undertook a number of stay-aways and sit-in protests in the 1970s and 1980s. These local actions sometimes led to solidarity action by other union members. More often, demands were localized, as, for instance, when teachers at a single primary school in Ndola stopped work for three days demanding that the town council provide the school with water, or when primary school teachers at nine schools in Kitwe went on strike to protest "instability" in the area.[10] The earliest peak of grassroots-led worker militancy occurred in 1978 when almost 300,000 work-days were lost to strikes. As the government's alliance with the ZCTU began to fray, worker militancy escalated, leading to larger strike waves in the 1980s. Reliable strike data is not available for the immediate post-independence strike wave mentioned above, but Figure 4.1 shows that the strike-dampening effects of the formation of the ZCTU and the passage of the IRA were temporary at best.

Zambian workers more likely to go on strike than their Zimbabwean counterparts, and they also regularly used the threat of striking to extract concessions. Threats worked most effectively for state workers in essential social services, such as teaching, the railways, and the postal service. When asked why teachers held so many strikes in the late 1970s and 1980s, an organizer with the ZNUT explained, "when nobody's pushing they just sit; when we're pushing, the President goes and gets his Cabinet. The question is how to make our government dance?"[11] President of the ZCTU Newstead Zimba, commenting on doctors' demands in 1980, made a similar point about the glacial pace of the formal dispute resolution machinery: "these people have been making the same complaints to the Government as their employer, but nothing was done until it was pushed into action by the go-slow adopted by the doctors."[12] This bottom-up form of bargaining was a response to the

---

[10] *Times of Zambia*, September 16, 1980, and January 27, 1981.
[11] Interview with Leah Asaji, Joel Kamoko, Helen Mwiyakui, and Johnson Zulu, Lusaka, July 8, 2004. The comment is Mr Kamoko's.
[12] *Times of Zambia*, June 23, 1980.

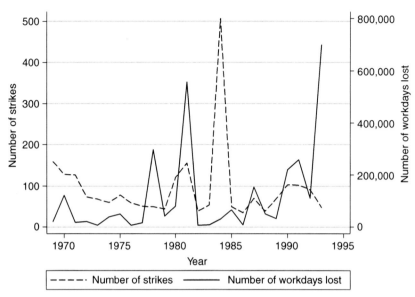

Fig. 4.1. Number of Strikes and Workdays Lost in Zambia, 1969–93

Source: Zambia Monthly Digest of Statistics; also, Liatto (1989: 83).

unwieldy character of collective bargaining institutions in Zambia, but it also reflected a lack of control over the rank-and-file on the part of the national unions. In the 1970s, the ZCTU did not have the resources to provide large-scale workers' education, one of the main ways that the ZCTU in Zimbabwe began to strengthen its control and influence over its affiliates and individual workers. In Zambia, the ZCTU developed an education module that covered the IRA, history of the labor movement, workers' rights, basic economics, and even plant management, but workers' education did not cover more than 500 participants a year.[13] The labor movement's relationship with its rank-and-file was complicated by the government Department of Industrial Participatory Democracy (DIPD), which was given direct access to workers through its own education programs. Simutanyi speculates that the Department's programs at the shopfloor level may have undercut both the union commitment to workers' education and union control over shop stewards and shopfloor members (Simutanyi 1987: 56–61).

Though the grassroots was radical, Zambian union leaders largely complied with the state's demands. Even after the introduction of structural adjustment

---

[13] Proceedings of the National Seminar on Employment, Zambian Congress of Trade Unions, and International Confederation of Free Trade Unions., held in Lusaka, February 5–9, 1979. ZCTU Archive, Kitwe, Zambia.

and grassroots-driven turnover in union leadership, union leaders attempted to stop strikes and convince workers to return to work.[14] In the late 1980s, as wildcat strikes increased, the leadership of affiliates and of the ZCTU remained strikingly apolitical. Unlike the ZCTU in Zimbabwe, there was never an attempt to harness grassroots discontent to improve the bargaining position of the labor movement. The union and ZCTU reaction to the 1987 teachers' strike is a case in point. After labor leaders met with government, they announced on March 23 that the situation was resolved and added that the continued strike was the work of "disgruntled elements." ZNUT general secretary Albert Chibale added, "The union is actually concerned at the continuation of protests because some political malcontents may take advantage of them."[15] In this and other strikes, union leaders typically bowed to government demands for an immediate cessation of strike action. This tendency to endorse a return to work, sometimes with no resolution of the grievances that had prompted strike action, created a wedge between union leaders and rank-and-file membership. Workers on strike during this period rarely abided by the decisions of national leadership, and officials of the ZCTU and its affiliates were even abused and attacked when they arrived at the locations of strikes to urge worker restraint.

The weakness of union organization at the national level was often coupled with a vibrant union politics at the local level, where elections for union posts were vigorously contested. By the mid-1970s, several candidates usually competed for union offices at the branch level, and candidates were more willing to confront their national leadership on issues of union governance and irregular election practices. For instance, in 1974, twenty-five candidates contested the six available posts in the MUZ branch elections in Chililabombwe, one of the large towns on the Copperbelt, and thirty contested the subsequent branch elections in nearby Nkana.[16] These elections were especially competitive, and candidates for branch offices sometimes ran campaigns that sharply criticized the national leadership of affiliate unions and the ZCTU. For instance, after he was re-elected in the 1974 elections, the Chililabombwe branch chairman questioned the future of the MUZ President, David Mwila, saying he had

---

[14] It is important to note that when I questioned informants about this policy, many differentiated between the public statements of leadership and "what workers really knew." Some suggested that strikes had been organized "underground" by national union leadership. This may have been true in some cases, but such statements likely also reflect a retrospective aggrandizement of the role of union leaders, especially given their later role in the MMD. I am convinced that most illegal strikes during 1975–90 were organized by the rank-and-file. For evidence supporting this interpretation, interviews with Charles Muchimba, July 3, 2004; with Leah Asaji, Joel Kamoko, Helen Mwiyakui, and Johnson Zulu, Lusaka, July 8, 2004; and with Neo Simutanyi, June 19, 2004.

[15] *Times of Zambia*, March 13, 1987.

[16] *Times of Zambia*, April 25, 1974, and May 16, 1974.

failed to prosecute union officials accused of stuffing ballot boxes.[17] These concerns over corruption were shared by other unionists: some of the Nkana candidates called on the union to use red ink to prevent miners from voting twice. Local-level union leaders presented themselves as closer to rank-and-file union members, but they did not have greater control over the grassroots than the national union leaders they criticized. Branch offices had higher levels of turnover than other levels of union leadership, and workers ignored appeals during job actions from national and branch leaders alike.

The unpredictable and often ambivalent attitude of union membership toward its leadership is perhaps best illustrated with an account of a 1980 wildcat strike undertaken by agricultural workers at one of the country's largest sugar estates. The strike at Nakambala Sugar Estates achieved national prominence because the police used excessive force in controlling the strike, opening fire on a crowd of protesting workers and seriously injuring four. The internal dynamics of the strike and, especially, the resistance of the workers to appeals from their union leadership were fairly typical of strikes during this period. The strike also highlights some of the problems in the Zambian industrial conciliation machinery that contributed to the strike waves of the 1980s, and it suggests ways in which workers used popular contestation to force circumventions of formal conciliation procedures. The background to the strike lies in the government's poor management of wage and prices policy in late 1979 and early 1980. The Nakambala strike occurred after the announcement of a collective bargaining agreement for workers at sugar-processing plants in Lusaka and Ndola, who belonged to a different union than those who harvested sugar. The collective bargaining agreement governing agricultural workers was still in force until March 31, but the Nakambala workers began to demand in early March a wage increase commensurate with that received by the sugar processors. The government had recently announced food price increases, which substantially eroded the wages of those workers who had not yet received increments. In the context of inflation, which the government itself recognized by raising food prices, once-yearly announcements of wage increases created a volatile situation. The non-harmonization of wages and prices policies and the staggering of collective bargaining announcements virtually ensured that the announcement of wage increases in one sector would be followed by the holding of strikes in others.[18]

The strike at Nakambala would have passed largely unremarked, another of the two- or three-day illegal strikes that were becoming so common in Zambia. But the Secretary-General of the ZCTU, also a Member of Parliament

---

[17] *Times of Zambia*, April 26, 1974. The branch official, Palasa Chiwaya, was later stripped of his office by the MUZ supreme council due to these comments.

[18] In contrast, in Zimbabwe, for instance, government announcements of minimum wages for all sectors were announced once a year, making strikes intended to accelerate the revision of sectoral collective bargaining agreements impossible.

(MP), raised a point of order in Parliament on March 14, calling on the Minister of Labour to justify "the serious breach of the Human Rights Charter" at Nakambala Sugar Estates. The statements delivered the next day by the Minister of Labour and Social Services and the Minister of Home Affairs provide a clear picture of the progress of the strike.[19] The Nakambala employees went on strike on March 10. Since the strike was illegal, police arrived the following day to consult with management. The police and Nakambala management called on the union's branch leadership to address the workers and let them know that their concerns would be addressed in a meeting of all parties and the Minister of Labour. After the branch leadership refused, the Vice-national chair of the agricultural union, Mr Nyirenda, arrived in Nakambala and appealed to the workers for a return to work. The police reported that "the workers interrupted Mr Nyirenda as he spoke by booing, shouting and jeering at him. As a result, Mr Nyirenda was unable to convince the workers . . . [and as the workers dispersed] there was some shouting that something would happen if their demands were not going to be met." Early the next morning, the police received a report that workers at Nakambala were attacking management and breaking the windowpanes of the office where management had barricaded itself; shortly thereafter, agricultural workers burned sixty-five hectares of cane valued at K300,000. At this point, local union leadership and the national chair of the agricultural workers union agreed to address the workers and urge a return to work. At the meeting called for this purpose, workers refused to allow any of their union officials to address them and instead shouted and jeered at the unionists and the police. The crowd then blocked a car carrying the Estate's Managing Director and began to throw stones at it; at this point, the police dispersed the crowd with tear gas and then, after the tear gas ran out, with live ammunition, resulting in the death of one striker.

The chain of events at Nakambala illustrates the tense relations between union leader and rank-and-file union members that were characteristic of this period. More and more strikes like Nakambala occurred in the late 1970s and 1980s, and unions became less and less effective at dampening wage demands and industrial actions. Union leadership partly blamed the centralization of wage determination for rising worker frustration. Because collective bargaining occurred at the national level, branch leaders were not involved in negotiations, nor were they involved in formal disputes at the factory level over non-wage issues. The centralization of the labor arbitration machinery made it more difficult for workers to see the benefits of union membership. One union leader explained:

---

[19] This account is derived from statements by the Ministers of Labour and Social Services and of Home Affairs, *Zambia Parliamentary Debates*, April 18, 1980.

[The union leadership] would communicate, but when you are not there it's different than when you're at the table. Workers weren't part of the process – that's the way it was done. So the workers were angry when leadership would come, they would call the leadership sell-outs, they would go on strike, and that was a deep problem, which led to a split [in my union] in 1991.[20]

The increase in wildcat strikes reflected a degree of indiscipline within the labor movement, but it was also a function of stark economic decline in the 1980s. From 1976 to 1986, the real wages of all workers fell by 66.8 percent.[21] Upon disaggregating this data, different patterns emerge in terms of the rate of wage erosion across sectors. Initially, miners and industrial workers were cushioned from the effects of economic decline, and their real wages actually rose in the period 1975–80 by 13 and 66 percent, respectively. In contrast, community and social services workers, including teachers and community health workers, experienced a real wage erosion of 16 percent, and workers in communications and transport faced a drop of 29 percent. The pattern is reproduced in the chronology of the "wildcat," or unauthorized, strikes during this period: strikes began with teachers and other public sector workers, spreading to other sectors somewhat later. There was rarely coordination of strikes across sectors or even across workplaces. The strikes exposed the flaws in the existing system of dispute resolution and wage determination. Inflation eroded wage increases before they were announced, and demands for wage adjustments moved slowly through the centralized arbitration machinery. In order to accelerate the adjustment upward of wages in order to keep pace with rising costs of living, workers began to organize strikes without union permission. Union leadership was seen as too moderate, which was the criticism at Nakambala, and union leadership could not prevent rolling strikes across and within sectors.

Economic conditions and grassroots militancy strained government–ZCTU relations. After the UNIP government announced new wages in 1979, the ZCTU argued that these wages were based on outdated cost-of-living figures from 1976 and failed to take into account ongoing inflation. It called on government to adopt an independently calculated poverty datum line as the basis for annual wage determinations; the government resisted. The cost-of-living calculation dispute exposed the first cracks in the partnership between organized labor and the ruling party. Union leaders' rhetoric shifted from the cooperative and supportive language that ZCTU leaders had used in the past. ZCTU Secretary-General Frederick Chiluba argued, "The Government is biased against the labor movement in that it fights against inflation by allowing prices to rise with flying colours while at the same time stamping rises in

---

[20] Interview with Joyce Noonde, July 6, 2004.
[21] All data in this section are from ZCTU (1988).

incomes mercilessly"; ZCTU President Newstead Zimba added that "it ap-
pears as if the Government is only interested in price increases and not
improving the welfare of wage earners."[22]

In the closed political environment of the one-party state, these attacks were
surprisingly harsh, and newspaper editorials began speaking of the "coming
storm" that the comments would provoke. UNIP claimed that the trade
unions were planning to form their own political party or revive the banned
United People's Party (UPP), even though there was no real political component to union demands.[23] As tensions with the labor movement continued,
UNIP became more and more estranged from the ZCTU, and the two actors
began to disagree more strongly on issues involving strike-breaking and wage
policy. Within two years, this estrangement culminated in a severe crisis when
UNIP decided to expel several union leaders from the party. The action was
intended to force organized labor back into its traditional, more cooperative
behavior toward government; instead, the expulsions prompted a massive
surge of grassroots labor protest, which undermined both the ruling party's
control over society and the legitimacy of the UNIP one-party state. The state's
repressive actions were the result of a strategic miscalculation. Union leaders
had no real control over the actions of their members and could not have
restrained strike action if they had wanted to. By sanctioning trade union
leadership for its lack of control over labor militancy, the ruling party pushed
moderate elements in the labor movement away from the state and closer to
the more radical rank-and-file. Repression both consolidated the labor movement and encouraged its turn toward oppositional unionism.

The Beginnings of Oppositional Unionism

The breakdown of relations between the Party and the labor movement
reached a crisis point during a dispute over a new system of local government
introduced by UNIP in 1980. The Party's reaction to the crisis vividly conveyed the limits of the freedom that UNIP was willing to grant to the labor
movement. The conflict also laid the groundwork for the political project that
the ZCTU would pursue in the late 1980s, both in terms of strengthening
ZCTU control over the labor movement and of launching the ZCTU leadership to positions of national visibility and popularity. The 1980 Local Administration Act was introduced ostensibly to decentralize power and fund-raising

---

[22] *Times of Zambia*, September 13, 1979.

[23] The UPP was a largely Copperbelt-based political party formed in the late 1960s after Vice
President Simon Kapwepwe resigned from government in protest at the ejection of three Bemba-
speaking ministers. The UPP was banned in 1972. Throughout the 1970s, union branch officials
that were considered "too radical" by UNIP would be arrested or stripped of their union posts for
allegedly supporting the UPP. For more, see Larmer (2006).

authority to local governments, which had had persistent financial problems in the 1970s.[24] In reality, the Act grossly centralized UNIP party control over local government by integrating party and other institutions of local government into a single body, the District Council. The leadership of the labor movement came out strongly against the Act. Affiliate unions announced that members would not be eligible to hold any posts, regardless of level, in the union structures if they ran as candidates for local government office. And they followed up on this threat. Immediately after the first local government elections under the new system, while backbenchers in Congress were still debating whether the legislation was constitutional, the Mineworkers Union suspended sixteen shop stewards for pursuing offices. This provoked a larger political crisis. The ZCTU made clear that it would support the MUZ's action, citing the labor movement's collective decision to not participate in local administration. UNIP then suspended seventeen members of ZCTU and MUZ leadership from the party and confiscated their passports.[25]

Though union leaders were themselves fairly conciliatory toward the ruling party, rank-and-file union members were outraged by the government's actions. The suspended leadership immediately wrote letters revoking the suspension of the shop stewards and apologized for interference in the implementation of the Local Administration Act. The UNIP Central Committee nevertheless moved to expel the seventeen ZCTU and MUZ officials, adding that "all organizations in the country must realize that they are inferior to the Party and must obey its instructions."[26] The workers' response was immediate. Four days later, 5,000 workers in Chililabombwe, historically one of the more militant and strike-prone mining areas, did not report for work. The following morning, the strike spread to at least five other mines on the Copperbelt. Administrative staff walked out in the afternoon. Newspaper accounts of the strike underline the exuberance of the miners and the lack of union involvement in the planning or control of the strike:

> Shouts of 'solidarity forever' were a common feature in bus loads of miners traveling from Chambeshi division to Mufulira. The miners were waving tree branches reminiscent of the pre-Independence days. According to some miners, the strike started when some morning shift workers went from one department to another ordering their colleagues to go home ... The Branch Chairman of MUZ [at Luanshya] said: 'The trouble is we were taken unaware. We just noticed that people were leaving their working places and going home.'[27]

---

[24] For more on the changes proposed in the Local Government Act, see Rakodi (1988) and Mukwena (1992).
[25] See *Times of Zambia*, January 10–12, 1981.
[26] Comment by UNIP Secretary-General Mainza Chona, *Times of Zambia*, January 20, 1981.
[27] *Times of Zambia*, January 21, 1981.

Over the subsequent days, the crisis deepened, as Copperbelt towns degenerated into riots and other national unions joined the call for reinstatement of
the expelled union leaders. The explicitly political tone to the strike intensified.
Striking workers dubbed their action "six feet versus four feet," referring to the
respective heights of President Kaunda and ZCTU leader Chiluba. Attacked
party officials, refused to sing the national anthem at union meetings, and, in
one extreme instance, set UNIP offices in Kitwe ablaze.[28] A strike flyer
produced in Parliament read, "All workers out; in defense of trade union
rights; against Party dictatorship; human rights violated; leave trade union
leaders alone; respect the Industrial Relations Act Cap. 517; expulsion of union
leaders from Party means expulsion of all workers belonging to trade unions.
Workers are one."

Within a week of the strikes and riots, the Party was forced to backtrack,
first announcing that the administration of mining townships would be
exempted from the Act, then reinstating the union leadership, and finally
removing high government officials perceived to be anti-labor. Humphrey
Mulemba, who was considered a party moderate and friend of organized
labor,[29] was appointed the Party's new Secretary-General. The former
Secretary-General, Mainza Chona, who had long advocated tighter control
over labor, learned about his replacement and his appointment as ambassa-
dor to an "unnamed socialist country" via the radio.[30] The government's
conciliatory stance toward the trade unions would not last for long, but the
government response indicates the degree to which the balance of power
between the actors had shifted. The ZCTU, which had previously been an
instrument of state control of labor, a role reinforced by institutional design,
suddenly had the power to force policy concessions and reappointment
of high party officials. The change that this outcome represented was not
due to a fundamental change in the organizational capacity or reach of the
labor movement, though affiliates' branch structures had somewhat expanded in the 1970s. Instead, the increased power of organized labor stemmed
from its ability to piggyback on rising popular discontent over economic
conditions and its ability to serve as a symbol for a still larger constituency,
the urban poor. It was this social group that was likely responsible for the
riots that followed the strikes.

Even within the ranks of the formal sector workforce, the ZCTU's greatest
resource was affective rather than organizational. The labor movement in
Zambia derived its power not just from its formal organizational structures
but also from its ability to trigger loyalty and willingness to act *even where*

---

[28] *Times of Zambia*, January 21–28, 1981.
[29] In 1991, Mulemba resigned from UNIP, joined the MMD in strikingly public fashion, and
became a member of the party's executive committee.
[30] *Times of Zambia*, February 21, 1981.

these structures were generally weak. Workers had ignored the directives of union leaders in the past, but they still viewed these leaders as their representatives, as their willingness to protest in 1980-1 suggests. The ZCTU possessed mobilizing structures and some concrete political resources, but it benefited from more amorphous forms of linkage to workers across the country.

This dynamic is well expressed by the role that ZCTU district committees played over the course of the 1980s. As we will see in later chapters, the ZCTU district committees became important mobilizing structures for the Movement for Multiparty Democracy (MMD) after its formation. They also functioned as the seedbeds for an oppositional labor identity built on identification with the ZCTU. The ZCTU formed the district committees after UNIP introduced plans in the late 1970s to incorporate the labor movement into the Party as a mass wing. The committees were seen by many in the labor movement as a means of protection and self-preservation. By 1980, thirty-one district committees (DCs) were in operation, though by the ZCTU's own admission, these operated "largely on paper," and members were often unclear about the role of the DCs and how they were to function.[31] Correspondence between the ZCTU and its DCs shows that some workers in fairly peripheral areas of the country felt a strong connection to workers in urban areas and strongly identified with the ZCTU by the mid-1980s.[32] In addition to the minutes of local meetings that DCs sent to the union headquarters, committee officials sent letters requesting more communication from the main office, offering assistance in planning May Day celebrations or "any other mobilization" the ZCTU might need, and pledging support for the activities of workers in other parts of the country.

The correspondence from Serenje, one of the districts, demonstrates how DCs composed a far-flung network of dormant mobilizing structures, which could be called into service when needed. This was despite limited resources and little in the way of regular correspondence from higher levels of ZCTU leadership. Serenje is a small, somewhat isolated, town of less than 8,000 in Central Province. It is located on the Tazara (Zambia–Tanzania) rail link, but it is not near the main line of rail that serves as the axis of labor organization and economic development in Zambia. Around the time of the 1981 strikes, despite indications that it had received no communication from union structures and had learned of the expulsions through newspapers, the Serenje committee sent a letter stating that it was "dismayed" by the expulsions and "hoped that the matter will come to a good end soon, and that the action taken by our friends in urban areas is a good one and the

---

[31] Report of the Secretary-General to the 7th Quadrennial Congress of the ZCTU, Livingstone, October 15–18, 1986. QC/D No. 1, ZCTU Archives, Kitwe, Zambia.
[32] District Committee Correspondence, DC/2–63. ZCTU Archives, Kitwe, Zambia.

Committee supports our friends and may God be with them."[33] Over time, despite the headquarters' non-response, about which the Committee often complained, and despite the exhaustion of its union-provided stamps, the Serenje DC continued to regularly send letters requesting tasks and reporting that it had "sold the name of ZCTU in the District in that the Authorities have come to know it, that ZCTU is operating in Serenje (*sic*)."[34] The Serenje DC, on its own volition, undertook organizational activities, attempting to form local branches of "absent" national unions without informing the affiliates' national leadership.[35] Though all DCs were not the equal of Serenje in terms of their enthusiasm, DCs provided a means for the ZCTU to expand its geographical reach in the wake of the Local Administration Act dispute.

Following the protests in 1981, the relationship between the ruling party and the trade unions initially improved, only to turn adversarial again fairly quickly. The government's attempts to implement ESAP from 1985 to 1990 were hindered by numerous wildcat strikes and urban food riots, which necessitated the moderation of announced austerity measures at several points. The UNIP government responded to strikes and other forms of popular resistance with increasingly authoritarian tactics. At one point, it discontinued the dues check-off system for all unions whose workers went out on wildcat strikes, a policy that had little impact on strike levels. The government also expanded the number of workers who were designated as working in emergency services, thereby outlawing strikes for an ever-larger portion of the workforce. Finally, in 1987, UNIP announced that union leaders would no longer be allowed to address May Day celebrations, since union leaders had been using the event to "abuse" the government.[36] This event can be viewed as the formal announcement of the end of the corporatist partnership between organized labor and UNIP. From this point forward, organized labor moved steadily in the direction of political opposition and the formation of the MMD. This will be discussed further in Chapter 6. The pages above show, however, that organized labor's relationship with the state and with popular constituencies shifted significantly before the political liberalization of 1990–1. The emergence of a consolidated labor movement in the 1970s and 1980s laid the groundwork for the mobilization of Zambian workers into a political movement.

---

[33] District Committees Correspondence, DC/54, letter dated January 1981. ZCTU Archives.
[34] Ibid.
[35] For instance, after some minor disputes at a local station of the national grain marketing board, the DC recruited members on behalf of NUCIW and then petitioned the national union leadership to recognize the branch.
[36] *Times of Zambia*, May 1, 1987.

KENYA

In the late 1980s, as in Zambia, the ruling party in Kenya faced a rising tide of discontent. In contrast to Zimbabwe and Zambia, organized labor in Kenya was silent. In the midst of economic protests, union leaders surfaced only to issue statements in support of the ruling party, and trade unions were never involved in the formation of new parties. The following section argues that organized labor's role during this period was a direct consequence of the labor-repressive policies undertaken by the Kenyan state in the decade after independence. These policies weakened the structures of union affiliates, resulted in a small and fragmented membership base, and created a labor center with little autonomy from the state. The structure of the Kenyan economy does differ from the other two cases, notably in its lack of a mining sector, but structural factors and "starting conditions" were not determinative of labor outcomes in Kenya. In the pages below, I first address two alternative arguments that might be used to explain labor weakness in Kenya: (*a*) the formal sector was not large enough to support a powerful labor movement; and (*b*) because of the primacy of ethnic identity, mobilization by organized labor was bound to be weak. The chapter then examines the events that led up to the formation of the state-imposed Congress of Trade Union (COTU) in 1965. The remainder of the discussion is devoted to various aspects of the labor control regime in Kenya, focusing especially on the ways in which it differed from labor policies in Zimbabwe and Zambia.

Potential Obstacles to Organized Labor in Kenya

In the early years of independence, an independent observer would have had solid grounds for predicting a strong and active labor movement in Kenya. In 1972, unions represented 290,500 workers, which was 43 percent of the formal sector labor force (Muir and Brown 1975: 700). Had union membership been made mandatory for formal sector workers, as it was in Zimbabwe and Zambia, trade unions would have represented over 900,000 workers by the end of the 1970s, since the formal sector workforce expanded substantially over the decade (Collier and Lal 1986: 87–92). Again, this does not suggest a working class that was too small to play a political role in Kenya. Further, as suggested in the introduction, size is less important than leverage. The political and economic strength of labor is increased where unions have the capacity to threaten disruptive strike action. The Kenyan state was acutely aware of the dockworkers' ability to shut down the Mombasa port, which is East Africa's largest port and the major entry point for cargo bound for Uganda, Rwanda, Burundi, and other parts of central Africa. The manufacturing sector, concentrated in Nairobi, was also large enough to make strikes costly to the government. Prior to independence, large and successful strikes had been organized by fishermen at Kisumu, dockworkers at Mombasa, and employees of the railways (Singh 1969; Cooper 1987). Put simply, one can easily imagine a Kenya in which a relatively small labor movement played a strong opposi-tional role.

Unions had emerged late, but they built up membership bases quickly from a level of relative weakness in the 1940s. In 1951, Singh estimated that there were 15,000 dues-paying members of registered trade unions, the bulk of whom were from Kenya's Asian community, as well as another 50,000 work-ers who belonged to unregistered workers' associations, which were primarily African (Singh 1969: 306). By 1956, the majority of these African workers had been gathered under the umbrella of the newly formed Kenya Federation of Labour (KFL). Tom Mboya, the Nairobi-based unionist who had organized the KFL, estimated that the organization had a paid membership of 55,000 in 1956, out of an estimated African workforce of 450,000 (Mboya 1956: 3). This compares favorably to levels of unionism in Zimbabwe before independence. The state of emergency imposed by the colonial state during the Mau Mau rebellion impacted organized labor, but it had a less disruptive effect on Kenyan unionism than the liberation war had in Zimbabwe. During the Emergency, trade unions were closely monitored, and unions that maintained ties with the banned nationalist movements – or those that seemed to practice "political unionism" – were threatened with deregistration. Despite some constraint, the emergency did not prevent the growth of unions in Nairobi and Mombasa, and the KFL amassed a significant membership during this period (Clayton and Savage 1974: 387–401). By independence in 1964, it seems likely that the unions had doubled their membership from the 1956 figure above. Four of the largest unions, those that represented civil servants, postal workers, teachers, and railway workers, together had 90,000 members in 1965.[37] Precise membership numbers do not exist for the powerful Dock-workers Union at this point, but well over 15,000 dockworkers participated in the 1947 and 1956 strikes. These workers were represented by either the Dockworkers Union or the Kenyan Distributive and Commercial Workers Union.[38] Unions had reached a diverse collection of workers by the early 1960s, but large portions of the workforce still lacked effective union repre-sentation. In 1965, for instance, a strike of over 2,000 sisal plantation workers was settled without union involvement.[39] The plantation workforce, which

[37] *Daily Nation*, April 9, 1965.

[38] In 1965, 7,500 workers were eligible to vote in internal elections for the Dockworkers Union (i.e., were dues-paying); given that check-off was not yet implemented, the Union claimed to represent, and negotiated on behalf of, a larger membership. *Daily Nation*, September 18, 1965.

[39] *Daily Nation*, May 15, 1965.

numbered 250,000 workers, was eventually unified after several competing unions were amalgamated after independence, but ties between workers and the resulting union remained weak.[40]

Organized labor served as a mobilizing structure independent from ethnicity in the pre-independence period. During the colonial period, prominent trade unionist Tom Mboya – later General Secretary of Kenya African National Union (KANU) and holder of several ministerial portfolios – had used his base in the trade unions to build a cross-ethnic political base in Nairobi. Mboya chose to run for the colonial Legislative Council in the late 1950s from Nairobi rather than his home area of South Nyanza, a decision that was motivated by his desire to retain this cross-ethnic base (Goldsworthy 1982: 115). At this point, ethnicity, which later became the sole relevant political identity in Kenya, was a more contingent determinant of political behavior. Both before and immediately after independence, cross-ethnic mobilization remained a viable route to power. Goldsworthy, for instance, notes that Mboya's popular base was built on the delivery of patronage to workers regardless of their ethnic origin:

> Mboya won because he was, above all, the most effective patron figure in Kenyan African politics. In this period, his was very much a 'politics of utility.' As K.F.L. leader and an M.P., he was a man of established and proven power who got results – whether in negotiating wage rises for workers, securing educational opportunities abroad in the intensely political 'airlifts,' or pressuring the British and Kenyan Governments for political freedom. But more specifically, he was a major patron of the Nairobi Kikuyu...Once again, it may be said that an ethnically neutral approach in Nairobi was also a rational strategy. (Goldsworthy 1982: 118).

One should not underplay the importance of ethnicity during this period. Ethnic divisions heightened conflict within the unions in 1963–5, and ethnicity had ever-greater effects on labor organization and labor politics in subsequent decades. My point is simpler. At independence, Kenyan workers had the choice of multiple political identities, only one of which was ethnic. State policies in the post-independence were responsible for narrowing the range of political identity choices from which Kenyans could choose. What is striking about modern-day Kenya is the absence of what Melson terms "cross-pressured worker" (Melson 1971). When multipartyism was reintroduced in 1991, Kenyan workers were not forced to choose between loyalties to labor and loyalties to ethnic group; instead, the actions of the Kenyan state in the post-independence period removed labor mobilization as a possibility. By pursuing repressive rather than corporatist labor policies, the KANU state ensured that union structures could not be used as a political base. These labor

---

[40] For a detailed account of the struggle to unionize agricultural labor, see Hyde (2000).

policies also made the state less effective in dampening strike activity and wage demands. COTU may initially have been meant to serve this purpose to a limited degree, but political anxieties always trumped economic utility when it came to the formulation of labor policy in Kenya. A weak labor movement was the result.

The Formation of COTU

Kenya became independent in December 1963, and the new government announced the formation of a centralized trade union congress, the COTU, less than two years later. The common wisdom about the imposition of COTU in 1965 is that Kenyatta and his Kikuyu allies wished to bring the trade unions' structures under their own political control and thereby deprive potential rival Tom Mboya of his organizational base (e.g., Anyang' Nyong'o 1989). The implication is that COTU served as a check on Luo power within the new state, as both Mboya and the Luo nationalist leader Jaramogi Oginga Odinga were viewed as threats by the increasingly Kikuyu-dominated KANU. This interpretation of COTU's formation relies on viewing all Kenyan politics through the heavily tinted lens of ethnic maneuvering. This is generally a sound strategy, but, in this particular case, the reality is more complex. The period from 1963 to 1965 was characterized by extreme polarization within the labor movement, polarization that was initially organized around the affiliation of the KFL to the International Confederation of Free Trade Unions (ICFTU), which some unionists saw as associated with imperialism and with a Cold War alignment with the West. Ethnicity played a marginal role in these battles. During this period, factional conflict was primarily played out through the disaffiliation of affiliates from KFL, the suspension of union officials on both sides, and poaching and counter-poaching of branch-level structures by rival affiliates. In a few instances, however, conflict escalated. In 1964, the anti-ICFTU faction forcibly occupied the KFL headquarters in Nairobi. Factional conflicts also led to a wave of strike actions in Mombasa and violent confrontations between workers associated with the two factions. Union conflicts fueled increased strike activity in 1964 and 1965, but the state seemed uninterested in mediating these conflicts or encouraging the formation of well-ordered union structures. In April of 1964, the government announced that it would not recognize more than one labor center, nor would it allow further splintering of affiliates.[41] But then it continued to register splinter unions, and it registered the KFL's rival, the Kenya Africa Workers' Congress

---

[41] *Daily Nation*, April 22, 1964.

(KAWC), first as a society in May of 1965 and subsequently as a union in August of 1965.[42]

In September, the government abruptly reversed its own decisions by deregistering both the KFL and the KAWC. It subsequently announced the formation of a new labor center, which would take over the assets and liabilities of its two predecessor congresses. It seems unlikely that this decision was motivated by the desire to use trade union structures to dampen strike activity, nor was it a considered strategy to undercut the base of support for Kenyatta's Luo rivals. Instead, it seems to have been a response to events on the ground: three days earlier, armed clashes at a union affiliate meeting in Mombasa had led to three deaths.[43] Factional battles within the unions were affecting the larger political environment in Mombasa, Kenya's second largest city, and KANU's own structures had begun to be implicated in union politics. Faced with this challenge to political order, the government established COTU by fiat, on the order of the President. The government had fairly limited aims with regard to its new trade union center. A handful of union officials, including the sitting General Secretary of the KFL, vied for KANU nomination to parliamentary seats. For the most part, however, the ruling party was suspicious of the kind of party–union alliances that characterized Zimbabwean and Zambian labor relations. This tradition of economism stretched back to the early days of union organizing: Mboya had been trained in labor relations at Ruskin College, Oxford, and the British TUC and Labour Party had been active in organizing the KFL and several of its affiliates. The unions' commitment to the separation of unions from politics had allowed them to remain operational during the Emergency, and economism had also underlain interactions between the nationalist parties and unions in the pre-independence period. Unionists occasionally held offices in both parties and unions, but there was recognition of sharply delimited roles for each of the organizations:

> Although Mboya was General Secretary of both organizations, and there was significant cooperation between KANU and the KFL, neither the party nor the union sought to dominate the other, and the KFL relinquished to KANU those political activities that it had undertaken in the absence of a national African political party. (Goodman 1969: 341)

After COTU was formed, the separation of unionism from party mobilization continued. Government announcements of economic policies and wages were not accompanied by public pronouncements of support from COTU, nor did labor leaders appear at the *harambee* rallies that became important components of party-building after Daniel arap Moi assumed the presidency in 1978.

---

[42] *Daily Nation*, June 2 and August 12, 1965.
[43] See *Daily Nation*, August 31–September 9, 1965.

In comparison to Zimbabwe and Zambia, government rhetoric urged unions to represent their own memberships, not to sacrifice interest representation for the good of the nation.

There were, however, several aspects of labor relations that resembled industrial arrangements in the more corporatist labor control regimes of Zimbabwe and Zambia. Like their Zimbabwean and Zambian counterparts, Kenyan trade unions were accorded a dues check-off system under labor relations law, and the central trade union confederation automatically received 15 percent of these dues (Henley 1978: 229). However, union membership was not mandatory in Kenya, and the onus of organizing and instituting check-off arrangements at individual workplaces lay with the unions. The financial base of Kenyan unions was, therefore, weaker than in the other two countries. As in Zimbabwe and Zambia, tripartite agreements committed the unions to non-militancy. In 1970 and 1978, for instance, employers agreed to increase the formal workforce by another 10 percent, yielding more union members, if unions would refrain from industrial action and wage demands (Chege 1987: 255).[44] These agreements did little to strengthen organized labor or improve living standards for workers. Wage freezes that accompanied some agreements resulted in an erosion of real wages, which the government exacerbated by periodically removing price freezes without concomitant adjustment of wages (Mukui 1983). In contrast to Zimbabwe and Zambia, the state initially played little role in collective bargaining, though it did occasionally mediate labor-employer negotiations. From 1973 onward, the state grew more involved in wage policy, and the Minister of Labour started to play a fairly active role in the approval and amendment of collective bargaining arrangements. But tripartite agreements and labor policies did not amount to any form of alliance between organized labor and the ruling party: trade unions and the COTU were given little access to government, and the ruling party never viewed unions as a key channel for communication or implementation of policies.

Union Disorganization and Labor Decline

Kenya differed most substantially from the other two cases in terms of the amount of autonomy accorded to organized labor. This was most significant for staffing and policy formulation at COTU. The COTU leadership was appointed by the President, who was not obliged to follow the "recommendation" of the

---

[44] Mukui points out that these wage freezes were undertaken partly in the interests of political stability: the first was signed in the midst of the instability over the Kenyan People's Union (KPU), a rising opposition party, and the second major tripartite agreement was signed soon after Kenyatta's death (Mukui 1983).

officials of COTU's affiliate unions (Henley 1978: 230). After COTU's first elections, Kenyatta disregarded the choices made by union delegates and instead appointed representatives from all the existing factions to the executive leadership of COTU, in the hopes that the move would yield buy-in from the fragmented affiliates.[45] The government's initial involvement in the establishment of COTU and the President's role in selecting the first union executive did not differ substantially from state actions in Zimbabwe and Zambia when trade unions congresses were first formed. Nor were the formal powers of the Kenyan Registrar of Trade Unions more expansive than those of his counterparts in the other two countries: in all three countries, Registrars had the power to examine union books, initiate audits, and remove leadership. In contrast to the other countries, however, the COTU constitution was drafted by the Attorney General's office. This constitution granted the state formal representation on COTU's governing council and other decision-making bodies of the union center. In the late 1970s, COTU's constitution was once again redrafted by the Attorney General's office, and it was adopted without a general debate within the labor movement (Henley 1978). The state also demonstrated a consistent pattern of interference in affiliate union elections.[46]

In this environment, election-driven change in the composition and character of union leadership – which were so important in transforming the labor movements in Zimbabwe and Zambia – was not possible. Both COTU and affiliate elections demonstrated the disorganization of labor structures and the suffusion of union politics with state influence. For instance, in 1980, the election of new office-holders by the COTU Governing Council had to be postponed for several months after seventeen of the organization's thirty affiliates missed the deadline for the holding of their internal elections.[47] Even when elections were held, they were characterized by disorder, occasional violence, the selective expulsion of voting members by union leaders, and allegations of vote-rigging and violations of union constitutions.[48] In 1986, for example, local elections in the teachers' union were disrupted by scuffles and police intervention, eventually leading President Daniel arap Moi to order district commissioners to step in and administer the union elections.[49] In the teachers' union election, as in other affiliate elections, there were allegations of powerful KANU ministers and officials bankrolling the campaigns of individual union leaders. Because there was little scope for organizational responsiveness through internal union

---

[45] *Daily Nation*, November 18 and December 2, 1965.
[46] See, for instance, *Daily Nation*, April 15, 1966; *Daily Nation*, August 4, 1971; *Daily Nation*, September 1 and 5, 1980; *Financial Review*, November 3 and 10, 1986; *Financial Gazette*, May 11, 1987.
[47] *The Weekly Review* (Nairobi), September 26, 1980.
[48] See, for instance, *The Weekly Review*, November 7, 1980, and October 17, 1986.
[49] *The Weekly Review*, July 4, 1986.

elections, links between union leadership and rank-and-file members remained weak. The vibrant union congresses in Zimbabwe and Zambia, which brought together delegates from several different levels of the union hierarchy and which were responsible for the elections of radical leaderships, never occurred in Kenya.

The actions of the Kenyan state undercut union autonomy, but state policies also contributed to the organizational weakness of affiliate unions. In contrast to Zimbabwe and Zambia, most formal sector workers were not represented by unions. In the 1970s and 1980s, unionized workers composed no more than one-third of the formal sector workforce (Chege 1987: 253). Though the implementation of the check-off system made unnecessary the physical collection of dues, Kenyan unions still struggled to organize work-places and recruit members. Both COTU and the affiliates had trouble cover-ing their basic running costs, and the trade union confederation provided affiliates with limited assistance in collective bargaining. Because of these financial problems, unions' ties with rank-and-file membership became even more attenuated. In 1971, for instance, most of COTU's affiliate unions lacked the funds to hold internal union elections.[50] Of COTU's thirty affiliates, the bulk could afford only one full-time advisor or official. COTU was not able to diversify its membership base geographically, nor was it successful in amalga-mating the fragmented affiliates it inherited. In 1980, Nairobi and Mombasa still accounted for half the country's trade membership (Ochieng' and Maxon 1992: 359). Splinter unions continued to form and were occasionally recog-nized by the state throughout the 1970s and 1980s. In the 1980s, the state registered two breakaway unions, even though COTU refused to recognize or affiliate these unions (Ochieng' and Maxon 1992: 360–6).

Strike patterns in Kenya differ substantially from those in Zimbabwe and Zambia, once again suggesting the limitations of KANU's repressive labor regime. In theory, COTU was given expansive powers to police affiliates (Sandbrook 1972); in practice, however, COTU's authority was weak. The post-independence strike wave, which had been fueled by wildcat strikes, peaked in 1965. There was an overall decline in the number of strikes post-1964; however, union affiliates continued to threaten and to hold strikes after 1965. Even as late as 1981, well after most commentators say labor was co-opted and tamed, the Minister of Labour warned of increases in illegal strike activity.[51] In many of these cases, newspaper coverage of the strikes makes no mention of COTU involvement or COTU statements urging workers to practice restraint.[52] Figure 4.2 shows the overall pattern of strike activity in Kenya, though readers should note that strike data for the post-1974 period is

---

[50] *Daily Nation*, August 21 and 24, 1971.
[51] *Daily Nation*, June 9, 1981.
[52] See, for instance, *Daily Nation*, January 28, 1969.

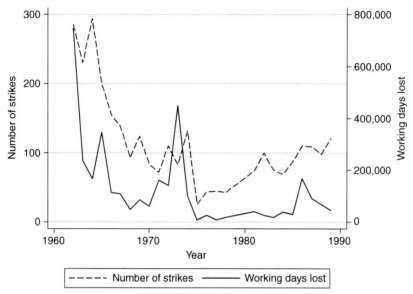

Fig. 4.2. Number of Strikes and Workdays Lost in Kenya, 1962–74

Source: Collier and Lal (1986: 47); ILO, available at laborsta.ilo.org

highly unreliable, as it is based on official Kenyan government data that do not seem to tally well with the fragmentary strike information provided in newspapers and by COTU.

Strikes remained a consistent feature of the landscape in Kenya. Strikes from 1965 to 1974 tended to be longer and involve fewer workers, which is suggestive of a larger affiliate role in their organization. For instance, in 1964, 167,767 workdays were lost to strike activity, but this represented the participation of 67,155 workers; in 1971, a roughly similar number of workdays (162,108) were lost in strikes that involved only 17,300 workers (Collier and Lal 1986: 47). The Kenyan state's attempts to control labor through co-optation and interference did not prevent workers from striking. These policies did, however, prevent organized labor from building a cohesive grassroots structure that could be later used to challenge the state. Unlike labor movements in Zimbabwe and Zambia, organized labor in Kenya played no role in organizing large-scale strikes, even as workers' fortunes fell throughout the 1980s. In the late 1980s, the unions seemed to be focused on their own internal leadership squabbles, which seemed to reach a new high in 1989.[53] Nor did unions emerge as critical voices during the protests that preceded multiparty elections in 1992. In terms of the political

---

[53] See *Financial Review*, January 16 and February 20, 1989.

loyalties of labor, they lay with the ruling party, not with the pro-democracy coalition that was emerging in the late 1980s and early 1990s.

CONCLUSIONS

There are several factors that explain why organized labor is politically influential in some countries while it remains irrelevant in others. I have emphasized here the importance of labor autonomy from direct state control. Where organized labor was not granted formal associational autonomy from the ruling party, it was rarely able to disentangle itself from the ruling party and build an independent organizational structure capable of coordinating workers across sectors. In Tanzania, for instance, the ruling party responded to post-independence strike waves by dissolving the trade union federation that had been its ally during the nationalist period. The new trade union center had little if any autonomy from the ruling party, and its incorporation into the ruling party in 1977 was little more than a formality. In Kenya, the trade union confederation was similarly captive to the state, though it never became a wing of the ruling party. Zambian and Zimbabwean ruling parties, though they occasionally interfered with the operations of individual unions and the labor center, never seriously considered abolishing these organizations' autonomy from the state or from the party. Workers retained control over union governance, and they used this freedom to elect oppositional leadership and gradually transform their organizations from within. As we will see in the next two chapters, these zones of autonomy allowed unions to play a role in organizing resistance to states' implementation of economic structural adjustment and, eventually, to the authoritarian system itself.

Part Three

The Organization of Protest

★

———————

POLITICAL OPPORTUNITY IN PARTY-STATES

"We don't eat politics here."
— Morgan Tsvangirai, Secretary-General of the ZCTU (Zimbabwe)[1]

"We are tired of the same faces. We want a change now. We cannot eat
peace and unity which our leaders always talk about just because they and
their families are comfortable."
— A "handicapped tailor from Luanshya [Zambia]"[2]

In January 1998, thousands of Zimbabweans rioted in Harare and other
urban centers. The riots were prompted by a government announcement that
it would raise the price of mealie-meal by 24 percent. The price of the foodstuff,
the staple food in Zimbabwe, had already increased 36 percent in October and
another 21 percent in December 1997.[3] Protests against the price increases
began in Harare's high-density townships and the neighboring city of Chitungwiza; on the second day, they spread to four other urban areas.[4] Over the
course of four days, the riots resulted in over 2,500 arrests, eight deaths, tens of
thousands of dollars in property damage, and widespread looting. Though the
government claimed that the Zimbabwe Congress of Trade Unions (ZCTU)
and whites organized the riots to undermine the government, no organizations
had issued calls for protests against the price increases. The riots seem to have
been, instead, entirely uncoordinated. One account of the first day of rioting in
a single Harare township underlines its spontaneous nature:

———

[1] Address to the Bulawayo provincial rally of the ZCTU, March 29, 1998. Videotape in
possession of the ZCTU, translation by Memory.
[2] Letter to the editor, *The National Mirror* (Lusaka), June 23, 1990.
[3] *Zimbabwe Standard*, January 25, 1998. Price increases for other basic commodities were
similarly devastating: cooking oil had increased 45 percent since December, and rice by 59 percent.
[4] There were riot-related incidents in fourteen urban centers, though these incidents differed
widely in terms of severity. Amani Trust (1998: 15).

People gathered early in the morning at the main shopping centre in the Mabvuku/Tafara area. A small group of women, around 6 am, began demonstrating against the recent price hikes by turning away a bread truck. Most people were just watching in amusement and the situation was calm, then for some reason things suddenly got out of hand and tensions rose. The demonstration turned violent and riots and looting began. People went into supermarkets, pharmacies, and butcheries taking things from the shelves and refrigerators. (Amani Trust 1998: 17)

Food riots had occurred in Zimbabwe before. They had never been connected to political claims in the past, nor were they on this occasion.

It is not the content of the riot that I mean to emphasize but its lack of connection to larger organizational structures. The Zimbabwean food riots of 1998 were not a coordinated protest, nor did they advance the goals or interests of the labor-led social movement that was already active at that time. To give the reader another example of what uncoordinated protest looks like, consider the food riots that occurred in Zambia in June of 1990. These riots were also triggered by price increases, and they were similarly uncoordinated. Unlike the riots in Zimbabwe and unlike earlier food riots in Zambia, there was a political component to the riots. As in Zimbabwe, the riots were sparked by increases in food prices. The government announced that it would end price controls on refined mealie-meal, one of the two varieties of Zambia's staple cornmeal, and millers doubled the price of breakfast maize meal overnight. The capital city of Lusaka and other urban centers erupted in riots. The subsequent military and police crackdown left twenty-seven dead and hundreds injured or arrested. The protests began outside government stores, but these were not the only government symbols targeted. The *Times of Zambia* painted a vivid picture of the progress of the riots in Lusaka:

Mtendere marketers joined in the rampage by burning the UNIP flag there while at nearby Chainama college of health, the Zambian police post was set ablaze. Some vehicles along Great East Road were burnt and others stoned as the rampaging mob marched to the city center, demanding that Government revoke the prices . . . Most roads in the affected townships were barricaded by residents who trapped police. Defence forces had to clear their passage under a barrage of stones. Later defence forces in nine Land Cruisers headed for Mandevu and Marrapodi townships and were trapped near NIEC [government] stores . . . Thousands of residents closed in on the police for close to two hours in Mandevu, blocking all four roads. The Times [of Zambia] vehicle was [also] pelted with stones. Residents destroyed council offices barely 100 metres away and scattered documents. Defence forces had to fire their way out of the area with live bullets and teargas canisters as mobs grew in size by the minute . . . Realising the forces were not shooting to kill, residents teased them shouting 'wabepa fye' (you are lying) and 'come we fight'.[5]

---

[5] *Times of Zambia*, June 26, 1990.

Other sources comment further on the political overtones to these strikes. The rioters shouted the names of former coup leaders, notably Christon Tembo, and destroyed government offices and vehicles; in one township, rioters looted Kaunda's old house, which had converted into a museum, and burned the historic Land Rover parked outside (Chisala 1991: 43). In the aftermath of the riots, the trade union leadership denounced rioters and called on workers to refrain from strike activity, despite worsening economic conditions.

These kinds of uncoordinated, unruly protests became common across sub-Saharan Africa in the 1980s and 1990s, as economic liberalization imposed shocks on urban livelihoods. But not all protest was uncoordinated. Protest took a very different form in Zimbabwe in December of 1997, just a few months before the food riots discussed above. The ZCTU called a one-day national strike to protest tax increases. It planned peaceful marches in towns and cities nationwide, for which the Congress obtained police permits in advance. The ZCTU announced an itinerary for the morning hours of the strike, and it announced the times at which workers would be addressed by trade union leaders. Following the ZCTU's timetable, Zimbabwe's urban centers were shut down on December 9, 1997, as workers, including those employed by the government, observed the strike in overwhelming numbers. In Bulawayo, Zimbabwe's second largest city, a crowd of approximately 50,000 converged on the City Hall to hear addresses from ZCTU leaders, after which the crowd dispersed.[6] Police reported no incidents of violence or looting. In the capital of Harare, the police reacted to the mobilization of workers brutally. Riot police shut down roads into the city center, violently dispersed those workers who had already assembled for the march, and continued to pursue and teargas individuals who were trying to leave the city center. The disruption of the demonstration turned into "running battles" between demonstrators and security forces, and some looting oc-curred following the breakup of the protest. Importantly, however, protesters complied when ZCTU Secretary-General Morgan Tsvangirai announced that the demonstration was canceled and workers should return to their homes. In the aftermath of the melee in Harare, the Police Commissioner confirmed the level of compliance with the ZCTU's strike and went on to wonder at the meaning of this new tactic:

> This has never happened before [and] it's a surprise to us ... Today throughout the country no industry, no shops, no business was open or was running. What was the idea? Were all these people members of the ZCTU, what did the employers themselves contemplate? What did they want to achieve by doing that?[7]

---

[6] *Chronicle* (Bulawayo), December 10, 1997. In Bulawayo, the timing of the protest strictly followed the timetable previously announced by the ZCTU. *Chronicle*, December 9, 1997.

[7] Augustine Chihuri, interview in the *Financial Gazette*, December 11, 1997.

In subsequent years, the ZCTU and the opposition Movement for Democratic Change (MDC) regularly resorted to stayaways to protest both economic policies and political events. The ZCTU held two further national strikes in 1998, and participation rates regularly topped 80 percent.[8] During this same period, its social partners held similarly disciplined marches and other demonstrations. Participants in these demonstrations rarely defined their aims in terms of concrete aims and goals; instead, when asked the reasons for protests, participants would regularly mention the need to "send a message" and "to show our strength."

These different incidents of mobilization – some spontaneous, others planned and disciplined – might be lumped into the same category by some observers of political transitions in Africa. All could be seen as examples of a rising tide of discontent, driven by economic decline and structural adjustment, which forced weakened neopatrimonial states to implement political reform (Bienen and Gersovitz 1986; Bratton and Van de Walle 1992). Indeed, this is the common narrative of the protest-led origins of democratic transitions across the continent. There are similarities across these protests, especially in terms of tactics (marches into city centers, occupation of urban spaces, the building of barricades) and state response (the shutting down of roads into the city center, the mobilization of riot police and the military). But protest events are also defined by their differences. Coordinated protests have clear-cut demands and participate in ongoing processes of framing and claims-making. They serve as a form of communication between government and opposition. Uncoordinated protests may have clear demands (the revocation of price increases, for instance), but they exist apart from larger campaigns and processes of mobilization. Moreover, as the editorials and comments of observers following the Zambian riots suggest, uncoordinated protests do not generally redound to the benefit of particular movements or opposition parties. Protests and riots may mark off regimes as vulnerable, but they do not serve as signals of the organizational strength or mobilizing capacity of opposition movements and parties.

The differences between uncoordinated and coordinated protest elicit the questions that animate this set of chapters: How do movement leaders connect concrete grievances to larger, more abstract claims? What accounts for the differential capacity of organizations to channel and control protest behavior and claims-making? The three cases examined in these two chapters differ widely in the ability of elite-led movements to connect with and discipline grassroots demands. On one end of the spectrum, the labor movement in Zimbabwe built strong alliances between labor and other civil society groups

---

[8] Regarding the March 1998 stayaway, the government's own national news service, Ziana, reported participation rates of 80–90 percent in cities nationwide. *Zimbabwe Independent*, March 6, 1998; also, November 13, 1998.

even prior to the emergence of protest. These alliances expanded the mobilizational reach of the labor-led movement, and the process of alliance-building transformed the relationships between movement leaders and grassroots constituencies. Social movement organizations used protest to mobilize constituencies and signal strength, but they also formed links with popular constituencies through non-protest events, such as public meetings and congresses. By the time an opposition party was launched by labor and its movement partners, activists and supporters shared a common set of values, a common vocabulary, and a common identity. In contrast, opposition movements in Zambia and Kenya made little attempt to coordinate large-scale protests, and their interactions with popular constituencies were much less regular than in Zimbabwe. Organized labor in Zambia served as a focal point for protest, but it did not build the structures and relational ties that would have allowed it to sustain mobilization or discipline claims-making over time. Similarly, protest in Kenya was largely uncoordinated, and civil society was fractured and ethnically divided when opposition parties were launched. Absent the organization that labor provided in the other two cases, grassroots-driven protest in Kenya coalesced in a brief moment of unity at the time of the "Saba Saba" protests and the formation of the Forum for the Restoration of Democracy (FORD). As founding elections approached, mobilization quickly spun off into particularistic and more sharply delimited patterns of popular mobilization. Part Two of the book centered on the construction of mobilizing structures that spanned ethnic and geographic boundaries. This set of chapters focuses on the degree to which these mobilizing structures were repurposed for the expression of general grievances and, eventually, larger political demands.

Five

Opposition and Collective Identity in Zimbabwe

In Zimbabwe, the implementation of structural adjustment undid the coalitions that had stabilized authoritarian rule in the 1980s, and it pushed both organized labor and other popular constituencies toward overt confrontation with the state. In order to understand the character and the durability of the movement that emerged, we must examine how the social movement led by organized labor forged new links between the unionized labor force, civil society organizations, and the urban poor. This coalition started as a string of only tenuously connected networks but was transformed into a cohesive political base for the opposition Movement for Democratic Change (MDC). The economically motivated protests of the mid to late 1990s forged links across a diverse set of actors, and they exposed activists to a new language, which would slowly become shared by protesters and ordinary Zimbabweans alike. In the 1990s, Zimbabweans launched new organizations, ranging from national lobbies to local residents' associations, while older organizations, like the trade unions, expanded their reach. In contrast to Zambia and Kenya, civil society organizations in Zimbabwe often collaborated and even borrowed one another's institutional capacity during particular campaigns. By the time that the MDC was launched, separate sectors of civil society were no longer strangers. Activists had met and spoken together at public meetings and demonstrations, and they had urged their constituents to support one another's causes.

Though its roots lay in protests against economic structural adjustment policies, the loose movement that launched the MDC in September 1999 had also collaborated on more political campaigns. Before the MDC, the Zimbabwe Congress of Trade Unions (ZCTU) and other civil society organizations had created the National Constitutional Assembly (NCA) together. The NCA forced the government to address the issue of constitutional reform in Zimbabwe, and NCA partners successfully mobilized a "no" vote in the popular referendum on the government's own constitutional draft. In this chapter, I examine the breakdown of the state-labor alliance discussed in Chapter 3. I then turn to the process by which the ZCTU expanded its organizational reach and its constituency base, a process that began long before the launch of a labor-backed opposition party.

THE FRACTURING OF STATE–SOCIETY BARGAINS

Like many other African countries, Zimbabwe was driven to adopt an Economic Structural Adjustment Program (ESAP) in 1991 by poor export performance, high levels of foreign debt, and overstrained state budgets. Zimbabwe had never approached the levels of state intervention that characterized Zambia's economy, but the state had subsidized unprofitable parastatals, rationed foreign exchange, and set prices and minimum wages. Pressures from both the domestic business community and the international donor community pushed the government toward reform (Skalnes 1993; Dashwood 2000), and, in 1991, ESAP began to be implemented. The reforms represented a sharp break with past government policy. Prior to ESAP, the Zimbabwean state had concentrated its efforts on social services provision, and ordinary Zimbabweans had come to expect a certain degree of state paternalism. In the 1980s, the government dedicated large sums of money to social services and development projects. The budget allocated to education grew in constant Zimbabwe dollar terms from ZW$119.1 million in 1979/80 to ZW$315.0 million in 1981/2 to ZW$651.6 million in 1985/6 (Dashwood 2000: 42). Government spending on health care more than trebled in the same period. The Zimbabwean government drastically expanded basic social services coverage over the course of the 1980s, providing health care and primary education to nearly all Zimbabweans. In order to lessen the previously sharp urban-rural gap in social welfare indicators, the Zimbabwe state directed the bulk of development funds to rural areas.[1] As Bratton (1987) points out, the delivery of social services and agricultural extension to rural areas fueled a dramatic expansion in the size of the Zimbabwean state, thereby laying the groundwork for ESAP.

Despite government claims that the program was "homegrown," Zimbabwe's ESAP was a standard, fairly orthodox version of the neoliberal reforms that the IMF and World Bank had helped implement elsewhere. Civil society, including the labor movement, had little influence over the content or timing of reforms (Moyo 1991). As in Zambia, structural adjustment imposed significant costs on grassroots constituencies due to the extent of the state's past commitments to subsidies, universal health care and education, and other

---

[1] For the strongest government statement of rural prioritization, see Republic of Zimbabwe (1982: 22–8); also, Republic of Zimbabwe (1986: 12–13). For results, see Dashwood (2000: 43–5).

Table 5.1. Real Wages in Zimbabwe in 1990 and 1993 as a Percentage of Real Wages in 1980, Selected Sectors

Sector	1990/80 real wages	1993/80 real wages
Agriculture	130	51.5
Construction	77	44.3
Education	83.2	50.5
Electricity and water	95	68.4
Health	91.2	54.2
Manufacturing	105	69.2
Mining	117	81.5
Public administration	61.5	34.4
Total	103	61.9

Source: Zimbabwe Congress of Trade Unions (ZCTU 1996: 68).

benefits, such as agricultural extension. The state introduced cost recovery measures in health care and education, which meant that all households above a certain (very minimal) income level were required to pay for basic health care and education. School enrollment began to decline, especially for girls.[2] According to Renfrew, the fee for most services at rural hospitals and health care facilities more than doubled in the period from 1990 to January 1992, and the rate for in-patient care increased from ZW$1.75 to ZW$10 per day during the same period (Renfrew 1992: 20).[3] The consequences for Zimbabwe's prior goal of equal access to health care were immediate: the figures for admissions for various treatments in rural Murehwa fell by between 11 and 52 percent; maternity admissions dropped by 33 percent. Urban dwellers were also hurt by the introduction of cost recovery. In the course of one year, admissions at Harare Central Hospital dropped by 25 percent due to increased patient fees (Dashwood 2000: 173). The effects of this restricted access to health care are perhaps best demonstrated by rising maternal mortality, which may have doubled over the course of the 1990s. Official statistics from UN agencies report an increase from 570 deaths per 100,000 live births in 1990 to 1,100 in 2000.[4] These kinds of

---

[2] In 2000, the Ministry of Education, Sport, and Culture reported that an average of 300,000 children dropped out of school each year from 1993 to 1999. *Zimbabwe Standard*, February 6, 2000.

[3] For more on social costs of reduced government education and health expenditure, see Nyambuya (1994).

[4] The UN data is compiled by the WHO, UNICEF, and the UNFPA and is available in the UN Millennium Indicators Database, http://unstats.un.org/unsd/mi/mi_goals.asp accessed February 14, 2005. The WHO/UNICEF data corrects for missing data and derives several data points from its own model: Zimbabwe's 1990 figure for maternal mortality is one of these model-derived estimates. Research conducted in Masvingo and Harare provinces during the 1989–90 period suggests an *even lower* figure prior to ESAP, of 85–169 deaths per 100,000 births (Fawcus and Mbizvo 1996: 319–27).

welfare shocks triggered bread riots in Zambia. In Zimbabwe, popular reaction was initially more muted, even though economic reforms led to sharp declines in quality of life for urban and rural dwellers alike. Bread riots in Zimbabwe did not occur until 1998, and economic grievances did not spur spontaneous protests over the course of the 1990s, even as economic conditions worsened.

In addition to the government's retreat from services provision, ESAP had immediate effects on levels of employment, wages, and living conditions for unionized formal sector workers. By the end of 1992, 15,000 private sector and over 10,000 public sectors workers had been fired; in 1994, another 23,000 workers in the private sector were retrenched (Saunders 1996; also, Carmody 1998). Between 1990 and 1993, real wages in the formal sector dropped precipitously due to inflation and increases in the prices of basic commodities. In 1993, real wages in the manufacturing sector were 69.2 percent of 1980 levels; real wages in public administration, the sector most heavily hit, were 34.4 percent of 1980 levels. Even the most insulated sector, mining, experienced a sharp erosion of real wages, as Table 5.1 shows.

Between May 1991 and June 1992, urban families experienced a 43.6 percent rise in their overall cost of living. The price of food rose even more rapidly, increasing by 64.5 percent (Sachikonye 1993). Since the poor spend a greater proportion of their incomes on food, the removal of price controls and subsidies on basic goods hit the poorest households hardest. Poverty figures perhaps best convey the heavy social and economic costs of structural adjustment in Zimbabwe: the percentage of households living below the poverty datum line (PDL) grew from 40.4 percent in 1990/1 to 63.3 percent in 1995/6, while the percentage of households that could be classified as "extremely poor" (living below the lower food poverty line) increased from 16.7 to 35.7 percent over the same period (Republic of Zimbabwe 1998: 36).

In order to deal with the social dislocations of reform, the World Bank and the Zimbabwean Government inaugurated a Social Dimensions of Adjustment program, one of the first of these programs to be implemented in Africa. The centerpiece of the program was the Social Dimension Fund (SDF), which was intended to provide targeted food subsidies, exemptions from cost recovery measures, support for small-scale enterprises, and an employment and retraining program. The Zimbabwean SDF was poorly administered and reached few of those it was meant to target (Moyo et al. 2000: 15). By 1994, the ZCTU estimated that the SDF was benefiting only 10 percent of *retrenched* workers, who were meant to be the primary beneficiaries of the employment and retraining program.[5] In a survey of clothing and textiles workers, the ZCTU found that only 22 percent of workers had heard of the Fund.[6] Even for those who were able to access the SDF, the facility's chronic underfunding

[5] *The Worker*, August 1993.
[6] *The Worker*, June 1993.

Table 5.2. Voter Turnout in National Elections in Zimbabwe, 1980–2008

Year	Type of election	Total votes cast (in millions)	Turnout, voting age population	Turnout, registered voters	Percentage vote for ZANU-PF
1980	Parliamentary	2.65	84.1	N/A	63
1985	Parliamentary	2.89	75.5	N/A	77.2
1990	Presidential	2.59	56.4	53.9	83.1
1990	Parliamentary	2.24	31.8	46.6	80.5
1995	Parliamentary	1.49	26	30.8	81.4
1996	Presidential	1.56	26.7	32.3	92.8
2000	Constitutional referendum	1.31	23.4	—	45.3
2000	Parliamentary	2.56	45.5	48.3	48.2
2002	Presidential	3.05	54.3	54.3	56.2
2005	Parliamentary	2.7	48.7	47.7	59.6
2008	Harmonized	2.42	45.5	43.2	45.9

Sources: Institute for Democracy and Electoral Assistance (IDEA), available at idea.int/vt; author's own data.

meant that payouts were not large enough to deal with rising costs (Gibbon 1995: 16–17). The food subsidy was so minimal that urban dwellers stopped applying for it. By 1995, financial constraints forced the SDF to cancel training programs and scale back the payment of health and education bills (Dashwood 2000: 172–4).[7] There were rumors that the funds had been plundered by well-connected political elites. In 1999, this was confirmed, when an investigation into the SDF fund found that over ZW$10 million (US $1.1 million in 1996 dollars) had been lost due to fraud.[8] By the end of the 1990s, the SDF's financial problems were acute. The department of social welfare instructed its provincial officers to stop processing applications for reimbursement of school fees in 1999.[9]

Though policies meant to cushion Zimbabweans from the costs of reform failed, worsening economic conditions – and evidence of increasing state corruption and misuse of funds – significantly changed state-society relations. Incumbent elites lost their access to patronage resources due to ESAP, weakening the ruling party's control over constituents and party structures. The ruling party also faced a rising tide of popular discontent. Popular songs, which remained triumphalist celebrations of Zimbabwe African National Union – Patriotic Front (ZANU-PF) and independence throughout the 1980s, began to express anger at the ruling party, corruption, broken promises,

[7] For more analysis of the shortcomings of the program, see *The Insider* (Harare), November 29, 1999.
[8] *Zimbabwe Independent*, February 26, 1999.
[9] *Zimbabwe Standard*, February 6, 2000.

and economic decline in the early 1990s (Vambe 2000). In the early 1990s, the student movement organized scattered protests against economic reform and government corruption, but students received little support from other quarters. Even as support for the ruling party fell, opposition parties could not capitalize on discontent. The major opposition parties in 1995 captured far less than the 20 percent of the popular vote that the largest opposition party, the Zimbabwe Unity Movement (ZUM), had won in 1990. Rather than voicing dissatisfaction or dissent through the ballot box, most Zimbabweans preferred to disengage from the political realm, as falling voter turnout in elections in the 1990s suggests (Table 5.2). After the 1995 parliamentary elections, the government announced a voter turnout of 57 percent, lower than in any preceding election; many suspected that the real figure was well below 50 percent (Makumbe and Compagnon 2000: 235–43). Turnout was particularly low in the urban constituencies that would later become the MDC's strongholds. Elections were not held in 55 of Zimbabwe's 120 parliamentary constituencies, since opposition candidates did not field candidates in those constituencies.

This choice of exit rather than voice was also notable in the presidential elections of 1996. President Robert Mugabe was re-elected with 92.5 percent of the popular vote and an embarrassingly low turnout of 29.5 percent of registered voters (Makumbe and Compagnon 2000: 288–94). One should note that the 1980 and 1985 elections, which were vigorously contested, had much higher turnout rates. These occurred prior to the forced merger in 1987 of the country's main opposition party, the Zimbabwe African Patriotic Front (ZAPU), into the ruling party.[10]

The weakness of popular political response to ESAP was due to the weak connections between opposition parties, which were largely urban and elite-focused, and popular constituencies. Prior to the MDC, Zimbabwean opposition parties shared a common organizational form, one that tended to limit party impact, prevent cooperation between parties, and inhibit material grievances from being transformed into political action. Some parties, such as the Zimbabwe Union of Democrats (ZUD) and ZUM, were the personal vehicles of single individuals. New parties, including Forum, the Liberty Party, and ZAPU 2000, were launched by small groups of elites without any prior constituency-building or broader consultation. These parties shared some common features: little interest in mobilizing rural constituencies, over-

---

[10] As it did in the post-2000 period, ZANU used violence and intimidation during this earlier period of party competition (Alexander 1998; Kriger 2005). Most notably, from 1981 to 1987, the government deployed a military force to western Zimbabwe, ZAPU's base of support, in order to contain supposed "armed dissidents." The military operation resulted in over 10,000 civilian deaths; the use of torture and terror tactics against civilian populations was widespread (CCJP 1999). The ZAPU–ZANU merger was viewed as the best means of ending the "disturbances" in Matabeleland.

reliance on ethnic or regional power bases, centralization of power, and a lack of internal democracy (Sylvester 1995; Nkiwane 1998). The centralization of party decision-making made it difficult for these parties to attract and retain promising candidates for office. More fundamentally, opposition parties did not connect their campaigns to the concrete grievances of the working class and the urban poor.[11] In response to this poor track record, scholars of Zimbabwean politics consistently underestimated the possibility of political change. Reflecting on the fragmentation of the party landscape, Sithole argued that, even if an electoral alliance were forged by the parties, "it is unlikely that the united opposition could make a serious dent in ZANU's electoral hegemony" (Sithole 1997: 139). In the final chapter of their book on the 1995 elections, Makumbe and Compagnon (2000) concluded that opposition parties "face an almost impossible task." The general consensus was that extra-ZANU-PF opposition was likely to remain irrelevant to political outcomes, and scholars argued that political opposition had shifted to intra-party struggles by the late 1990s (Sylvester 1995; Sithole and Makumbe 1997; Du Toit 1999).

What these observers seem to have neglected is that a vibrant opposition politics was emerging in the 1990s *outside and apart* from formal party politics. Protest actions, including street demonstrations, boycotts, and strikes, became more frequent and well organized from 1995 onward. Trade unions played a significant role in the organization of protest, and the labor leadership also became increasingly involved in larger civil society struggles. Protest actions were coordinated by the ZCTU, and they initially advanced purely economic claims. But these actions allowed the ZCTU to build its mobilizing reach and credibility with a mass constituency of urban dwellers (and, to a lesser extent, some rural dwellers). This new base of ZCTU supporters reached far beyond the unions' formal membership. The ZCTU and its affiliates were the most vocal and most consistent critics of ESAP, and the labor movement slowly formed alliances with other civil society actors in the hopes of rolling back structural adjustment. This cooperation between trade unions and other non-governmental organizations (NGOs) would lead to the formation of the NCA and, eventually, the MDC. In order for this to occur, however, civil society had to become stronger and more politicized than it had been in the 1980s. In the next section, I trace the increasingly critical role played in the 1990s by the civil society sector, which had been sympathetic and supportive of government policy in the 1980s.

---

[11] See, especially, the discussion of the Forum Party in Makumbe and Compagnon (2000): 11–15 and 140–9.

STRUCTURAL ADJUSTMENT AND
CHANGES IN CIVIL SOCIETY

In 1990, Zimbabwean civil society was larger and more developed than civil society in many other African countries. There were hundreds of NGOs and community-based organizations (CBOs), in both urban and rural areas nationwide. One of the country's first rural development organizations, the Organization of Rural Associations for Progress (ORAP), was large enough by the early 1990s to serve as a major distributor of food assistance during the drought of 1991–2.[12] A handful of smaller organizations relied on small government grants for their operations, but NGOs generally remained financially and organizationally autonomous from the government. NGOs were not, for instance, incorporated into government development plans (Moyo et al. 2000: esp. 75–7). Nor did the government show a keen interest in regulating civil society in the early 1990s. Legislation governing the registration and operation of NGOs was rarely enforced.[13] This would change later, as structural adjustment made government more dependent on NGOs and more interested in their control (Raftopoulos 2000). There were scattered episodes of government intervention in the 1980s and 1990s, some of which will be discussed below, but the government did not use civil society to implement government policy. The sector therefore possessed some degree of autonomy from government in the 1980s.

Despite their autonomy from the state, most civil society organizations maintained a cautious distance from advocacy or any other activities that could be construed as political (Kuperus 1999; Rich Dorman 2002). In a study of the NGO sector completed in 1991, Sam Moyo found that only twenty NGOs – less than 1 percent of the total – were actively engaged in advocacy programs (Moyo 1991: 5–6). To some extent, civil society organizations saw themselves as government partners during this period, and there was a degree of loyalty toward the ruling party. The social policies of the 1980s, which rapidly expanded health care and access to education, were enthusiastically supported by all segments of civil society. Some civic activists felt a strong loyalty and gratitude toward the ruling party due to its role in the liberation war. This undoubtedly dissuaded criticism:

> There was that euphoria and I think we allowed the leadership to do as they pleased, we gave them the benefit of the doubt and we thought, "if they made

---

[12] Interview with Themba Ndiweni, March 6, 2003.
[13] In terms of the lack of enforcement, it is likely that the government had nowhere near the administrative capacity to force NGO compliance with the Welfare Associations Act – or even to inspect the audited accounts of the 800 NGOs that did register, as the law required. Interview with John Makumbe, October 5, 2002.

mistakes they were minor mistakes, after all, we had peace, stability and independence." (Reginald Matchaba Hove, quoted in Saunders 2000: 10)

Many NGOs and church organizations often worked closely with ZANU-PF structures, and they viewed their mission as one of contributing to state development policy (Maxwell 1995). Nor did this attitude immediately change when economic conditions worsened. Even as party elites scaled back social spending and reformed the economy on neoliberal lines, civil society actors remained willing to give the government "the benefit of the doubt" on economic policy. For instance, Silveira House, a Catholic NGO that provided training and education to trade unionists, put together in 1993 a small booklet on economic policy in Zimbabwe since independence. The language used to describe outcomes included "successful," "well-managed," "not a bad record," and "quite a good performance when compared with most African countries" (MacGarry 1993).

Secondly, state actions influenced the character of civil society and probably dissuaded some organizations from critical action. In 1983, the government closed the Matabeleland training center of the ORAP, due to fears that it would be used by "dissidents". Three years later, two officials of the Catholic Commission for Justice and Peace (CCJP) were arrested for allegedly providing information to Amnesty International (Bratton 1989a; Auret 1992: 215–16).[14] ZANU-PF repeatedly intervened in the internal governance of the Zimbabwe Council of Churches (ZCC) and replaced the Council's head, who was considered a political opponent, with more cooperative leadership (Maxwell 1995: 112–13). Leadership struggles were also politicized in the Zimbabwe Farmers Union (Bratton 1994b) and the Indigenous Business Development Centre (Taylor 1999). ZANU-PF used patronage and other means in order to "insinuate itself deeply into civil society" (Sylvester 1995: 406–8). Several scholars go so far as to suggest that civil society was essentially captive in this period, in the sense that it was tied to the ruling party and permeated by state influence (e.g., Rich Dorman 2003: 847). The civil society sector was also disorganized and fragmented, which prevented collaboration or effective lobbying. NGOs in the rural development sector, in particular, were isolated from one another and tended to coordinate programs with government ministries rather than other NGOs. Moyo, Raftopoulos and Makumbe note that "even during the drought effort [of 1991–2] few NGOs knew exactly what others were doing" (Moyo et al. 2000: 89). Rather than lobbying for changes at the national level that would make NGO activities more effective, NGOs tended to negotiate with local officials on a case-to-case basis (Bratton 1989a: 580–4). As a result, NGO

---

[14] The government also refused to allow the publication of the CCJP's report on the 1980–8 massacres in Matabeleland. It was finally published in Zimbabwe in 1999.

activities were often limited to local, ad hoc solutions. Policy-focused lobbying at the national level was rare.

After the introduction of ESAP, civil society organizations became more willing to criticize government and demand a role in policy-making. New grassroots organizations were formed to fill gaps left by the retreat of the state, but most civil society organizations and local associations formed in response to ESAP were often initially "welfarist" in orientation (Chitiga 1996: 13–14). During this period, the vast majority of grassroots organizations did not coordinate actions, exchange information, or analyze the sources of the challenges they confronted. Instead, they simply served as "rudimentary bulwarks against the deepening incursion of poverty" and had limited agendas "defined by the basic survival needs of the group" (Saunders 1995: 28). Though civil society was better developed in Zimbabwe than in Zambia and Kenya, it was not naturally oppositional. This trajectory of development would not have yielded strong opposition parties without a ZCTU-led process of politicization. Civil society organizations were not an opposition-in-waiting: they had to be taught to serve as critics.

Church organizations and the trade unions were the first to openly criticize government actions. Their public statements initially focused on concrete state violations of human rights, such as the massacres of civilians in Matabeleland and the police mistreatment of student demonstrators. After the introduction of ESAP, the churches expanded their focus to deal with economic and social rights and broader national issues. The CCJP and Silveira House, a labor and rural development organization supported by the Catholic Church, subsidized the publication costs for a large number of small, affordable books that called attention to poverty and inequality in Zimbabwe.[15] *Moto*, a Catholic monthly, published numerous articles critical of ESAP. When the CCJP spoke out against the government eviction of homeless "squatters" at Churu Farm, it phrased its opposition in the language of economic and social rights (Auret 1994). The CCJP is commonly seen as the frontrunner of religious human rights activism in Zimbabwe, but church institutions that were more conservative and closely linked to the ruling party were also vocal in their criticism of the state's human rights record. The two main church institutions – the ZCC and the Catholic Bishops Conference – issued public statements in the early 1990s criticizing plans for single-party rule, the treatment of student protesters, and other human rights issues. In the early 1990s, the ZCC established a Justice, Peace, and Reconciliation desk in order to coordinate advocacy programs and campaigns on economic and social rights. The JPR desk would later

---

[15] The topics of these books ranged from single-issue tracts, such as forced evictions of squatters, to broader examinations of economic justice, such as *ESAP and Theology: Reflections on ESAP in Light of the Bible and the Social Teaching of the Catholic Church* (Harare: CCJP, 1992).

play a key role in the organization of the National Constitutional Assembly (NCA). The ZCC General Secretary argued in 1995 that churches should rethink their ecumenical missions in order to include popular mobilization around economic issues and involvement in economic decision-making.[16] Criticism was not limited to the traditional churches: in 1992, the Evangelical Fellowship of Zimbabwe (EFZ), which represents many of Zimbabwe's smaller evangelical churches, denounced the single-party state and called for an inquiry into the torture and killing of civilians by state security forces in western Zimbabwe in the 1980s (Maxwell 1995: 119). This string of actions is suggestive of an increasing autonomy and outspokenness on the part of Zimbabwean churches. There were limits to church activism, however. Churches in Zimbabwe were willing to criticize economic policy after ESAP was implemented, but they were reluctant to engage more overtly political issues.

In addition to the new-found autonomy demonstrated by established NGOs, structural adjustment prompted the formation of new advocacy and welfare associations. The blossoming of associational life was particularly marked in urban areas. Residents' and ratepayers' associations, which had been concentrated in middle- and upper-income suburbs in the 1980s, were formed in the poor, high-density neighborhoods of Harare and other cities. By the late 1990s, thirty municipalities had active resident associations, and the larger cities had citywide residents associations with many local affiliates.[17] One of the strongest associations, the Bulawayo United Residents Associations, was an umbrella body for more than forty-five local residents' associations, each of which had 1,000–2,000 dues-paying members.[18] There was often strong political component to individuals' involvement in the residents' associations. Residents' associations in Glenview, Budiriro, Highfields, and Mufakose, all of which affiliated to the Combined Harare Residents Association (CHRA), became particularly strong in the late 1990s. Monthly meetings of each association were attracting approximately 500 people in the late 1990s, and these public meetings took on a more and more anti-government, anti-ZANU-PF tone.[19] Muncipal councillors ceased attending the meetings at some point in 1997, and the associations began to publicly lobby for the dismissal of the Harare City Council. Nor was this activism limited to

---

[16] Comments of M.C. Kuchera, General Secretary of the ZCC, reported in "Economic Justice NORDIC-FOCCESA Workshop Report," conference sponsored by ZCC, April 10–14, 1996: 41–50, Mimeo in possession of the author.

[17] See the extended discussion of urban civics in Saunders (2000: ch. 2).

[18] Membership was open to any resident upon payment of a small membership fee, and each local association elected a representative to sit on the BURA board. The board scrutinizes city council budgets and activities, and it also coordinates community participation in local development and other projects (Saunders 2000: 40).

[19] Interview with Last Maengehama, July 28, 2003.

Zimbabwe's large cities. For instance, in 1998, a residents' association in the provincial town of Chinhoyi threatened to hold a rates boycott if the town's mayor did not step down.[20] In addition to ratepayers' and residents' associations, other urban-based associations were established that provided concrete benefits and thereby attracted large memberships quickly. In 1997, a group of community activists set up savings schemes in Harare for the most marginalized of urban dwellers, those resident in "temporary" squatter settlements or townships (Chitekwe and Mitlin 2001). The savings schemes quickly spread to other urban areas, and residents soon began to request more contact and information-sharing between communities. In late 1998, these savings schemes launched a national organization, the Zimbabwean Homeless People's Federation (ZHPF). By 2000, the organization had 20,000 members (Chitekwe and Mitlin 2001: 86).

This expansion of associational activity was accompanied by greater education and "conscientization" of grassroots constituencies, as evidenced by the institution or expansion of civic education programs in the 1990s. Later to become active in the constitutional reform movement, the Legal Resources Foundation (LRF) was one of the first Zimbabwean organizations to mix advocacy programs with outreach and education of grassroots constituencies. After a rural pilot study in Seke from 1986 to 1988, the LRF leadership shifted the organization's mission from casework toward broad-based education on legal rights (Manase 1992). The Seke evaluation team argued that equitable access to the legal system presupposed basic knowledge of human rights on the part of the citizenry: "for people to be able to identify a wrong, they must be educated first that a right exists from which, if they are wronged, they can seek a remedy" (Manase 1992: 12). As early as 1990 and 1991, the numbers of individuals reached by the LRF education program were impressive. The LRF's National Director reported that "advice volunteers" held 333 meetings in 1990–1 with a total attendance of 19,593 persons in Harare province alone.[21] Tens of thousands of pamphlets on aspects of Zimbabwean law were handed out nationwide.

The LRF programs were an early example of collaboration across civic groups, and they built contacts between activists from different organizations and different parts of the country. The individuals trained to run the LRF education programs were not recruited by the LRF directly but were officers or grassroots members of the Association of Women's Clubs (AWC), the Zimbabwe Women's Bureau, and other developmental organizations (Manase 1992: 13). In addition to the LRF programs, many of these organizations implemented their own civic education programs, including voter education,

---

[20] *Zimbabwe Standard*, March 22, 1998.
[21] Interview with Albert Musaruwa, March 24, 2003.

at different points in the 1990s.[22] For instance, Silveira House had long held training seminars for ZCTU staff and union members; in the 1990s, human rights, including economic and social rights, were mainstreamed into these training sessions.[23] Another example of the growth of a rights-based civil society was the formation of ZimRights. The membership-based human rights organization was launched in 1992 and had 14,000 members and forty full-time staff by the mid-1990s (Rich Dorman 2001: 145–9). ZimRights was itself an example of the coalitional nature of Zimbabwean civil society: Morgan Tsvangirai, the ZCTU Secretary-General, sat on the first executive of the organization, and the organization worked through existing small-scale community associations to build a membership base that spanned urban and rural areas.

Alliance-building across these civil society groups initially operated at the level of elites. The LRF sought out the ZCTU and other organizations in order to put together "test cases" to challenge aspects of existing law or government actions that it saw as unconstitutional.[24] The ZCC initiated its Economic Justice Network Project in 1994, which focused on research and analysis of the social effects of ESAP. It sponsored a series of workshops beginning in 1995 that brought together organizations and civil society activists from several organizations to discuss economic policy. Groups of related NGOs formed small, issue-oriented coalitions to draft policy recommendations and lobby Parliament. Civil society organizations also cooperated in order to defend the autonomy and political space they had won for themselves. For instance, in 1996, the government dismissed the executive of the AWC for alleged mismanagement, which it had the power to do under its new Private Voluntary Organisations (PVO) Act. Many civil society organizations declared their support for the AWC, and a Campaign for the Repeal of the PVO Act was formed. Even after the AWC's dismissed executive was restored, the campaign continued to meet weekly, held several public meetings, and collected 5,000 petition signatures (Rich Dorman 2003). With the assistance of its civil society partners, the AWC legally challenged the clause in the PVO Act that allowed the government to dismiss the leadership of NGOs, and the High Court declared the law unconstitutional in 1996.

In addition to the increased communication between organizational leaderships, the mid-1990s were characterized by a flourishing of public discussions and greater contact between civil society elites and grassroots activists. The student movement, which had been fairly alienated from the rest of civil society in the late 1980s, is a good example of this change. Previously, there had been few opportunities for students to meet with trade unionists and civil

[22] Interview with Sekai Holland, April 8, 2003.
[23] Interview with Sylvester Rusike, July 28, 2003.
[24] Interview with David Coltart, March 11, 2003.

society activists. In the 1990s, however, research organizations like SAPES Trust and the African Association of Political Science sponsored regular seminars to discuss issues of governance and economic reform. The audiences that attended these seminars included students, academics, members of NGOs, and even members of government.[25] Students also gathered in large numbers at "labor forums," discussed in Chapter 3, which were organized by the ZCTU to discuss structural adjustment and its effects.[26] Trade unionists, students, and other social groups interacted at public meetings sponsored by the neighborhood associations that were founded in many Harare townships through the 1990s. Finally, as ESAP sharply reduced the number of jobs available in the public sector, bright University of Zimbabwe graduates turned to civil society organizations for employment. The junior and senior staff of many Zimbabwean NGOs is now composed largely of UZ graduates of the 1990s, most of whom were active in student politics.[27] Isolated rural NGOs were similarly incorporated into the civil society community, through conferences sponsored by donor agencies, through increased contact with grassroots human rights organizations like ZimRights, and through training workshops given by Silveira House, which also trained trade unionists.

In the late 1990s, after these changes in civil society were fairly well consolidated, there was a turn from more routine or "contained" civil society campaigns to transgressive, large-scale mass actions. As discussed in Chapter 3, the labor movement initially tried to work with government to reform ESAP. It was only after the failure of this cooperative approach that the ZCTU began to emerge as a more vocal and oppositional critic. In addition to publishing the *Beyond ESAP* proposals, the ZCTU started a new advocacy program in 1996 as part of the same program. It assigned the advocacy program three major tasks: (*a*) to build the capacity of the labor movement, especially at the grassroots level; (*b*) to lobby government and otherwise "create an environment conducive for meaningful national policy dialogue"; and (*c*) to engage civil society organizations "*so as to create common understanding of the positive and negative effects* [of ESAP] . . . *and develop common positions, common perceptions, and common strategies.*"[28] Unlike organized labor in Zambia, the ZCTU in Zimbabwe placed a priority on forging strong links with other civil society organizations. Labor leadership viewed the creation of "common positions, common perceptions, and common understandings"

---

[25] Field notes, June 1999.

[26] Interviews with Percy Mcijo, March 5, 2003; Leonard Gwenzi, September 23, 2002; and Timothy Kondo, November 11, 2002. MDC MPs from many different backgrounds also mentioned these labor forums as important early meeting spaces for discussion.

[27] Field Notes, December 2002.

[28] Isdore Zindoga, Acting SG of ZCTU, "Foreward," ZCTU (2000: i–ii), emphasis added. For a more detailed review of the advocacy program's founding terms, see T. Kondo, "ZCTU General Policy Guidelines, November 1996," in ZCTU (2000: 20–9).

between labor and civil society as an integral step to achieving the policy reform laid out in *Beyond ESAP*. As we will see, the ZCTU advocacy department played an important role in the process within the ZCTU that led to the formation of the MDC. In terms of the ZCTU's success at leading the NCA and then the MDC, the organization's prioritization of collaboration with civil society partners was as important as its ability to mobilize its own members.

The ZCTU's expansive definition of its own mandate led it to involve itself in the creation of several civil society organizations, none of which catered to workers exclusively. The trade unions were involved in the formation of the previously mentioned ZimRights in 1992.[29] The ZCTU played an even more active role in the creation of NGOs that catered to the urban poor. The Zimbabwe Unemployed and Retrenchees Organisation (ZURO) was largely a creation of the ZCTU. ZURO, with planning and material assistance from the ZCTU, started in Harare and later spread to other urban centers.[30] The ZCTU also held two-day training workshops in the late 1990s for the Informal Traders Association of Zimbabwe (ITAZ); these workshops were held in six different provinces, targeting peri-urban areas and growth points.[31] These outreach activities allowed the ZCTU to remain in touch with former union members who had lost their jobs, in the case of ZURO, or come into contact with individuals who lived in areas with little to no union presence, as in the case of ITAZ. As civil society grew, it developed more ambitious aims.

THE NCA AS OPPOSITION CLEARINGHOUSE

The campaign for constitutional reform represented a final stage of the growing interconnectedness of civil society. The NCA, a coalition of over forty civil society organizations, was formally launched in January 1998. The organization demanded a new constitution, to be drafted with the input of all Zimbabweans. This would then replace the existing, heavily amended Lancaster House constitution that had been signed as part of Zimbabwe's

---

[29] Interview with Gift Chimanikire, July 13, 2004. Chimanikire says that ZimRights was "formed" by Morgan Tsvangirai, Chimanikire, and other unionists, and they then found Reginal Matchaba-Hove, a medical doctor, to chair the organization "because we did not want someone who could be construed to be forming a political party." Nick Ndebele, seen by others as the founder of ZimRights, agreed that trade unions were approached very early in the process, long before the organization began to have a strong membership. Personal communication, Sara Rich Dorman, January 18, 2005.

[30] ZCTU, "Advocacy Programme Summary Report (July 1996 to February 2000)," included in ZCTU (2000). Also, interview with Dennis Murira, October 22, 2002.

[31] Ibid.

independence negotiations. Neither legal activism nor demands for constitutional reform were new. In 1997, the Zimbabwe Lawyers for Human Rights, which defended clients who had suffered arbitrary detention, had begun advocating for a new Bill of Rights. Women's groups and other organizations were using the courts to challenge aspects of customary law and other rights-related issues in the courts. Members of Parliament (MPs) were engaged in a donor-supported Parliamentary Reform Project, which involved gathering opinions from Zimbabweans about the proper role of Parliament. As a result of this process, conversation among many parliamentary backbenchers turned to constitutional reform as a means of empowering Parliament.[32]

From the beginning, the NCA spoke a public language of apolitical, non-partisan, narrow-minded interest in constitutional reform, but the leadership and many of the organizational members had a much more far-reaching campaign in mind. The ZCTU was already committed to confronting government, and other civil society activists felt that negotiation with the ruling party was fruitless, if not actually dangerous. In contrast, many of the more moderate civil society organizations that joined the NCA were uncomfortable with demands that seemed overtly political or anti-ZANU-PF, and they felt that dialogue and cooperation with the government was the proper channel for pursuing issues of governance and institutional reform. In the words of one of the NCA's founders, they were working with some organizations that had not realized that "when ZANU PF says civil society should not be political, it is very much akin to the old family ruse of the greedy man who claims to his family that if they eat eggs they will go blind, and that therefore this delicacy must be reserved for him alone" (Mutasah 2001: 2). The more radical (and influential) elements in the NCA saw the constitutional reform process as a means of convincing civil society, and the population more generally, of the "true nature" of the ruling party.[33]

In May 1997, in what is commonly seen as the first meeting of the NCA, about twenty civil society leaders met in Harare. The meeting had been arranged and funded by Friedrich Ebert Stiftung (FES), which had earlier approached the ZCC to ask it to coordinate a "civic alliance" to advance constitutional reform.[34] The job of reaching out to NGOs and approaching "experts" was tasked to the JPR desk of the ZCC, which was staffed by activists Tawanda Mutasah and Deprose Muchena. The FES and the ZCC director, Reverend Kuchera, wanted the early meetings of the NCA to simply provide a forum for discussion, but the JPR desk approached its close contacts with a

---

[32] Interview with Victor Matinde, November 26, 2002.

[33] The student movement and the trade unions saw themselves and were seen to be natural leaders for the more oppositional NCA. Interviews with Brian Kagoro, November 5, 2002; Tendai Biti, December 9, 2002.

[34] Interview with Lovemore Madhuku, November 11, 2002.

different task in mind. Put simply, the challenge for this "core group" was to find a way of selling the NCA to the segment of civil society that was still committed to dialogue with government. It is unclear whether their aims were fully shared by Morgan Tsvangirai and the ZCTU leadership at this point, but Tsvangirai was "primed beforehand." The core group feared that some civil society leaders would be hesitant to join the NCA if it was seen as confrontational or anti-government; it was therefore decided that the aims of the organization would initially be presented in an apolitical, "legalistic" tone at the first meeting. Brian Kagoro recalls that potential disagreements over the long-term strategy were hidden or downplayed:

> The churches didn't want any suggestion that we would come up with our own constitution: they wanted it written that we would consult, and we would give the product of our consultation to government and encourage government to come up with a new constitution. We all realized at the time that it was foolish to argue [with this perspective], because we wanted to build [a coalition].[35]

"Radical" activists like Kagoro, Tendai Biti, Muchena, and Mutasah – all of whom had come from the student movement of the late 1980s – saw the NCA as an intermediate step toward a more overt confrontation with the ruling party. Other civil society partners viewed the process very differently. For instance, Bishop Peter Nemapare of the ZCC, a member of the organization's first task force, wrote in a 1997 NCA report: "in this process, nobody is wrong and nobody is right . . . [instead] the emphasis is the coming together of all Zimbabweans – across the race line, across the tribal line, across the gender line, in government and outside it."[36] Given that the NCA was initially housed by the ZCC's JPR desk, these differing views of the goal of the constitutional reform movement were initially downplayed. Within the ZCC, those working on constitutional reform issues were more radical than the executive board of the ZCC, but activists did not make these differences clear. As the NCA became more confrontational, the JPR desk started "running by itself without the support of the leadership."[37]

The division between these two groups centered mainly on the boundaries of the constitutional reform issue – in other words, on what constituted "success" for the NCA. Those most closely associated with the formation of the NCA saw the value of constitutional reform as reaching far beyond the issue itself. Kagoro added that the NCA was seen, by himself and others, as the

---

[35] Interview with Brian Kagoro, October 21, 2002. Tawanda Mutasah, another founder, phrases this division differently, saying that the NCA was supported by groups that saw its mission as solely educative and by others who wanted the NCA "to spearhead the movement for constitutional change" and directly place pressure on government (Mutasah 2001: 5–6).

[36] Quoted in *The Insider*, November 23, 1998.

[37] Interview with Perpetua Bwanya, November 28, 2002; also interview with Deprose Muchena, October 1, 2002.

beginning of a process that would culminate in electoral turnover rather than just political opening: "*We wanted to end the politics of reform, but the only entrance was the constitutional argument.* And it was going on elsewhere – South Africa, Malawi, Kenya, Uganda – so it made sense to talk in the terms of constitutionalism."[38] From the beginning, the leadership of the NCA connected constitutionalism to broader questions of power distribution, which perhaps makes it easier to see how the organization was a logical outgrowth of earlier struggles over corruption, ESAP, and bread-and-butter grievances.[39] Constitutionalism was seen as a neutral issue that could serve larger purposes, namely the unification of a fragmented civil society sector: "Given the growing despondency in civil society, there was a need for a major initiative that would be a rallying point for civil society in Zimbabwe.... The Constitution could bring all of us together, we thought" (Mutasah 2001: 22). Many within the churches, on the other hand, saw the process as firmly limited to civic education: the NCA would raise awareness, perhaps strengthen government respect for human rights, but the organization had no politically transformative mission. According to this perspective, the drafting and adoption of a new constitution could easily be a collaborative process between government and civil society, which did not need to yield changes in the country's leadership. These disagreements would later play out in how different actors reacted to the separate government-initiated process of constitutional review.

The early activities of the NCA papered over the potential divisions between different civil society groups, including disagreement about the project's long-run aims. In June, the small circle present at the first meeting was expanded to include all the major organizations active in the human rights arena. In the early meetings, it was decided that the NCA would operate as an umbrella group of loosely connected organizations, each of which would retain its independence and would pursue its own programs. The ZCC agreed to host the NCA within its JPR unit, and the ZCC also covered some of the organization's operating costs for 1997–8. The organization established its own offices several months after the formal public launch of the organization on January 31, 1998. In marked contrast to Garden House in Zambia, or the closed-door organizational meetings of Forum for the Restoration of Democracy (FORD) in Kenya, 560 "delegates," including some government officials, MPs, and High Court judges, attended the launch of the NCA (NCA 1998: 8). Throughout 1998, the NCA organized meetings targeting core civil society constituencies: the business community, commercial farmers and other agrarian interests, women, and youth. These seem to have been moderately well attended, but the NCA struggled to organize regional and community

---

[38] Interview with Brian Kagoro, October 21, 2002.
[39] Interview with Deprose Muchena, October 1, 2002.

workshops. For much of 1998, as Rich Dorman observes, grassroots education and organizing often took a backseat to "a more typical NGO agenda of urban-based meetings" (Rich Dorman 2003: 849). Only two community meetings, both in Harare townships, were planned in 1998, and one of these was cancelled due to poor attendance (NCA 1998: 17). The NCA held three fairly well-attended regional workshops in Marondera, Mutare, and Masvingo; however, as the NCA's annual report observed, the success of these meetings was dependent on communication from the NCA's constituent organizations to their own members. Both during this early stage and even later, the NCA seems to have relied on "borrowing" the capacity of its NGO partners. Despite plans to expand NCA structures quickly, the organization did not establish provincial field offices and constituency committees until 2000 (NCA 2000: 26–7). Thus, the NCA's campaign in the run-up to the government's February 2000 referendum was largely coordinated through the offices and structures of other civic organizations. The NCA was, both in spirit and in organizational structure, an alliance rather than an autonomous actor.

Like the labor movement, the NCA moved from cooperation to confrontation in its attitude toward government. Initially, the government seemed willing to cooperate with the NCA process: it accepted proposals on the constitutional reform process from the NCA in July 1998; in October, Eddison Zvobgo, the ZANU-PF Legal Affairs Secretary, met with the NCA leadership to discuss the proposals.[40] Very quickly, this initial space for collaboration closed. NCA affiliate organizations found themselves forced to decide whether to cooperate with government plans for constitutional reform. In early November, the NCA organized a march to press for constitutional reform and also protest the government's military involvement in the Democratic Republic of Congo (DRC).[41] The ZCC, one of the NCA affiliates, felt that the criticism of the DRC involvement was not constructive, and it did not take part. After the NCA march was broken up by riot police and tear gas, NCA affiliates felt increasingly uncomfortable with pursuing dialogue with government. Soon after the NCA demonstration, President Mugabe amended the Labor Relations Act (LRA) to ban all industrial actions that were intended to press for political or policy reforms.[42] Since national strikes and stayaways had become an important part of civil society's repertoire in the late 1990s, civil society associations issued public statements protesting the new restrictions. Many NCA affiliates were further politicized by events in early 1999. In

---

[40] *Zimbabwe Independent*, October 9, 1998; also, the discussion of Zvobgo in Mutasah (2001: 8).

[41] *Zimbabwe Independent*, November 6, 1998; also, *The Insider*, November 23, 1998.

[42] "Zimbabwe: Government Bans Workers' Strikes," press release of the Media Institute of Southern Africa, December 3, 1998. Available at www.allafrica.com, accessed January 17, 2009.

January, an editor of the independent *Standard* newspaper was arrested, to be
shortly followed by the detention of a journalist who had written about a
rumored coup attempt. Shortly thereafter, over 4,000 attended an NCA march
in Harare to protest the detentions and push for constitutional reform; they
were tear-gassed and dispersed by riot police.[43] Two weeks later, 300 lawyers
congregated outside the High Court; they were also tear-gassed and dispersed.[44] Despite this government response, public protests against the detentions continued in Harare, and both the churches and civil society
organizations grew even more outspoken about the government's human
rights record after evidence emerged that the journalists had been severely
tortured.

In the first nine months of 1999, therefore, NCA affiliates increasingly
found themselves forced to choose sides. The ruling party established its
own Constitutional Commission, which was intended to gather opinions
from the public and draft a new constitution, and it attempted to appoint
several prominent civil society leaders to the Commission. In March, the NCA
and the ZCTU both announced that they would not cooperate with the
Commission's work. The NCA's criticisms centered on the selection process
for the 395 commissioners, who were to be individually appointed by the
President, and the regulations that governed its operation. In a joint statement,
Zimbabwe's main women groups said that the appointment of commissioners
by government "negates the very principle of inclusion and participatory
democracy which we understand is lacking in our current discredited constitution."[45] Others argued that the Commission was disproportionately composed of ZANU-PF office-holders.[46] In addition, the Commission had been
formed under the Commissions of Inquiry Act, which gave the Executive the
power to accept, reject, or modify the recommendations of the Commission as
it saw fit.[47] Overall, NCA activists felt that the constitutional reform process
had been "hijacked" by ZANU-PF, which hoped to manipulate the process
and prevent substantive political change. This is reflected clearly in the NCA's
official justification of its non-participation in the government Commission:

> [The government's initial positive reaction to the NCA] was indeed welcome, but
> the NCA cautioned (*sic*) against being absorbed into a party process that would
> hoodwink the people into believing that it is a popularly-based process... The
> current moves by Government (i.e., the Constitutional Commission) are indica-
> tive of the Government's desire to control the process in order to influence the

[43] *Zimbabwe Standard*, January 17, 1999.
[44] *Zimbabwe Mail and Guardian* (Johannesburg), January 29, 1999.
[45] *Zimbabwe Independent*, March 26, 1999.
[46] *Zimbabwe Independent*, April 16, 1999; *Zimbabwe Independent*, April 30, 1999.
[47] For an exhaustive discussion of the NCA's objections to the Constitutional Commission,
see the guest columns by Welshman Ncube in *The Financial Gazette*, April 15, 1999, and in
Zimbabwe Independent, May 14, 1999.

results in favour of ZANU-PF's political survival beyond the year 2000. (NCA 1998: 4)

Conflict quickly escalated between the two constitutional reform bodies. In March, the NCA Executive formally ejected a member who had taken a position with the government Commission.[48] In May, the government replaced Zvobgo, who had been considered a moderate who was interested in incorporating NCA views, with Emmerson Mnangagwa, a ZANU-PF hardliner who said he would not take a "conciliatory" stand toward the NCA.[49]

As the broader constitutional debate grew polarized, there were voices within the NCA who were uncomfortable with the organization's "political drift." The JPR desk of the ZCC, which continued to run the NCA through the ZCC, was increasingly monitored by nervous members of the church leadership. ZCC staff felt that President Mugabe and other ZANU-PF leaders were pressuring Bishop Nemapare, the ZCC Vice President responsible for the NCA, to distance the ZCC from the NCA.[50] After the NCA announced that it would not cooperate with the government, Nemapare eventually pulled the ZCC out of the NCA entirely, saying that the organization was becoming a political party. The increasingly confrontational approach of the NCA created divisions in other organizations as well: Zimbabwe Lawyers for Human Rights found it necessary to poll its members on whether to stay within the NCA, and divisions between the CCJP and the more ambivalent Catholic Bishops Conference were repeatedly reported in the press.[51] The ZCC, however, was the only major defection from the NCA. Its demands for moderation were not taken up by any other member organizations. Constituent organizations talked through the decision to remain within the NCA or cooperate with the government commission: for the most part, Zimbabwean civil society chose continued confrontation over engagement. Through the first months of 1999, the more radical wing of the NCA – that associated with the ZCTU – gradually pulled the rest of the organization in their own direction. The NCA that emerged by late 1999 was a far more cohesive organization, which had a greater commitment to confrontation with government.

In August 1999, the government's Constitutional Commission began a whirlwind tour of the country, gathering input from Zimbabweans on what they wanted and did not want in a new constitution. The NCA started a "parallel campaign," using both inclusionary and exclusionary strategies to draw distinctions between itself and the Constitutional Commission. The NCA not only held local meetings and workshops on constitutional issues

[48] *Zimbabwe Independent*, April 16, 1999.
[49] Zimbabwe *Independent*, May 14, 1999.
[50] Interview with former employee of ZCC, November 2002.
[51] *Zimbabwe Standard*, August 8, 1999; on the Catholic Church, see *Financial Gazette*, August 5, 1999; *Zimbabwe Standard*, August 8, 1999.

but also distributed printed materials, patterned cloth emblazoned with the NCA symbol, and T-shirts to rural populations. In Zimbabwe's political culture, material goods are not just means of raising public awareness or advertising an organization's cause; they are also powerful markers of belonging. For instance, the first membership-based civil society organization in Zimbabwe, ZimRights, had several thousand registered members during its peak in the mid-1990s. By the end of the decade, it had largely lapsed into insignificance and had ceased its rural outreach programs. Despite this, several rural residents continued to carry their ZimRights membership cards, one of their few personal possessions, along with their national identity cards a decade later. NCA paraphernalia seems to have had a similar power. At the NCA's 2002 Annual General Meeting, attended by hundreds of NCA members from all over the country, the one agenda item that seemed to have some grassroots resonance was the issue of individual membership cards.[52]

The NCA campaign did not just teach popular constituencies who they were; it also, perhaps even more effectively, created an image of who they were not. The NCA used exclusionary strategies to portray the sitting government as isolated from the people, uncaring about their concerns, and unwilling to allow them to participate in the process of constitutional revision. The advertising campaigns of the two bodies underlined their different conceptions of the link between the people and the state. The NCA advertisements showed different groups of Zimbabweans engaged in discussion, some sitting outside and others in modern houses. The Constitutional Commission advertisements featured pictures of national monuments and swirling graphics. The NCA advertisements spoke of "the people," the Commission of "the nation." In addition to these less direct means of creating a divide between the ruling party and popular constituencies, NCA activists disrupted meetings and even assaulted members of the Constitutional Commission on scattered occasions. One student and NCA activist recalled that they often traveled long distances in order to attend Constitutional Commission meetings, only to disrupt the Commission proceedings by asking questions "that showed how they were against democracy and the NCA was the true voice of the people."[53] On other occasions, Commission meetings were prevented from taking place, commissioners were barred from entering particular areas, or potential attendees were accosted and convinced not to attend. Another student activist active in the NCA, now an MDC MP and minister in the coalition government, remembered one occasion when members of the Constitutional Commission, including prominent former minister and ZANU-PF MP Edson Zvobgo, were unable to hold a meeting at the

[52] The NCA allows only organizational, not individual, membership, and it seems that the bulk of the grassroots NCA membership neither understands this distinction nor supports its continuation. Field notes and anonymous interviews, August 2002.

[53] Interview with Maxwell Sangweume, August 19, 2002.

Harare Polytechnic.[54] Students physically barred them from entering the campus, and commissioners, frightened that the students were violent, called riot police. Toward the end of the process, commissioners and others began to complain of "tokoloshis" (small supernatural creatures) who would announce changes of venue or otherwise impede local people from attending Commission hearings.[55]

The government's Constitutional Commission responded with similarly polarizing statements, attacking the NCA as a "group of stupid protesters [who are] being paid and used by overseas donors who do not want to see anything good coming out of the country."[56] In July 1999, the Constitutional Commission announced that it would no longer be advertising in independent media, which it viewed as biased in favor of the NCA.[57] By the middle of 1999, polarization had intensified between the two constitutional reform camps. The media was full of reports of groups "defecting" to one side or the other, and attempts to foster debate across the debate often degenerated into attacks on the credibility of one side or the other.[58] In August, the Anglican Cathedral in Harare informed the NCA that it would no longer allow the organization to use the Cathedral hall, since the Bishop of Harare was serving as vice-chairman of the Constitutional Commission.[59]

By this point, the MDC had already been launched, and the NCA and MDC were cooperating in organizing the "no" vote for the referendum on the Constitutional Commission draft. Indeed, in many places, it was difficult to distinguish between NCA, MDC, and trade union efforts: the structures of these three organizations were usually overlapping, often composed of the same individuals, and used the same appeals and tactics. The campaign was unexpectedly helped by disarray within the government's Constitutional Commission. The Commission only allocated one week to the review of its findings and the drafting of a new constitution. Constitutional experts invited to observe the Commission's deliberations suspected that a draft constitution already existed; in addition, they noted that debate was often turned away

[54] Interview with Nelson Chamisa, September 16, 2002; *Zimbabwe Standard*, February 6, 2000.

[55] Field notes, August–November 2002; interview with anonymous civil society member, November 2002; interview with ZANU-PF MP, May 2003.

[56] Jonathan Moyo, spokesperson for the Constitutional Commission, quoted in *Zimbabwe Independent*, June 25, 1999. For further criticism of the NCA by Moyo, see his guest column in *Zimbabwe Independent*, April 30, 1999.

[57] *Zimbabwe Independent*, July 30, 1999.

[58] Field Notes, June–July 1999. The round tables on constitutional reform at SAPES Trust in Harare continued to be held during this period, but it was increasingly difficult to get individuals from different sides to sit together or soberly discuss issues. Also, personal communication, Sam Moyo, June 10, 2004. For an illustrative example of the repositioning of groups on either side of the constitutional divide, see the discussion of traditional chiefs who had decided to back the NCA in *The Financial Gazette*, June 23, 1999.

[59] *Financial Gazette*, August 19, 1999.

from the views expressed by the majority of respondents.[60] In December, a high-ranking Lutheran bishop resigned from the Constitutional Commission, saying that the draft constitution had not been debated by commissioners and did not reflect the public submissions to the Commission (Rich Dorman 2002: 90). Other defections followed. Surprisingly, conflicts between commissioners and the drafting team were extensively covered in the government-controlled media, and the protests of some commissioners at the plenary session were even broadcast on state television. Particular clauses in the draft constitution released at the end of the conference – especially those regarding the powers of the Presidency – disagreed with the majority of both public respondents and commissioners. As the draft was passed on to the President, twenty-four members of the Commission resigned and announced that they would start speaking to the NCA.[61]

These last-minute changes in the draft constitution made it much easier for the NCA's "no" campaign, according to individuals involved in grassroots campaigning. Previously, it seems that there had been some confusion about the difference between the two organizations. One commercial farmer reported, "we were actually not aware that there were two separate processes taking place in the country [and] we invited these people (the NCA) believing they were all the same with the government commission. It is hard to know whom to follow."[62] Other Zimbabweans expressed concern about what the NCA could offer since the "ZANU-PF Commission" had access to government.[63] In contrast, after the government's adoption of the draft constitution, there was a widespread feeling, expressed in the media, that Zimbabweans had been ignored. The "no" vote campaign quickly incorporated this criticism of the draft constitution into their typical appeals:

> [When we went to the countryside] the rural people would really understand, because the constitution issue was simple. We said this is the constitution left over from the Smith regime, all the government has done is amend it, and we want a fresh thing for us. And then the other thing, the point on which we hit [ZANU-PF] hard, was then we said: 'you were consulted by the commission from Mugabe – but, for instance, on abortion, what did you say?' And the people would tell you, and then you open the government draft, and you say, they didn't take what you said, so go and vote no.[64]

---

[60] *Zimbabwe Standard*, November 21, 1999.
[61] *Zimbabwe Independent*, December 3, 1999.
[62] *Financial Gazette*, September 9, 1999. The comment is especially ironic since the government claimed that commercial farmers were working hand-in-glove with the NCA.
[63] Field notes, June 1999 and May–July 2002.
[64] Interview with Lucia Matibenga, July 30, 2003.

The NCA also ran advertisements in the independent press comparing what appeared in the draft constitution to submissions to the Constitutional Commission (NCA 2000: 23).

On February 9–11, 2000, Zimbabweans voted on the proposed government draft constitution. To the surprise of many ZANU-PF leaders, the NCA won a resounding victory–54.7 percent of Zimbabweans voted "no" to the government's constitution; more surprising, the results were not clearly split on urban–rural lines. In some rural districts, up to 60 percent of voters rejected the government draft. Turnout was, however, quite low, at only 20 percent. The government's loss in the 2000 referendum had deep implications for the ruling party itself, as will be discussed in Chapter 6. Because of the low turnout, it should not be read as too significant an indicator of popular mobilization. But the referendum did signal to Zimbabweans, across the lines of ethnicity and different areas of the country, that the opposition coalition that had coalesced behind the NCA was a viable threat to ruling party rule. More importantly, the organizational ties developed during the NCA campaign subsequently benefited its political party successor, the MDC. The mass constituency mobilized by the NCA during the constitutional campaign formed the base of the MDC's support.

ROOTED COALITIONS AND THE
BEGINNINGS OF THE MDC

In order to reinforce the importance of the strong ties forged prior to the MDC's launch, let me comment briefly on another process – spearheaded by the ZCTU and independent from the NCA – that occurred at the same time as the NCA's referendum mobilization. The ZCTU laid the groundwork for the MDC's mobilizational reach some months, even years, before the formal launch of the party. At roughly the same time that it was involved in the NCA's formation, the ZCTU initiated a parallel process of grassroots outreach. In 1997, after the breakdown of tripartism, the ZCTU Secretariat formed a working group to organize and plan a National Working People's Convention in late 1999. The Convention was intended to bring together all stakeholders, including trade unionists and representatives of other constituencies, to discuss the linked political and economic crises in the country. The working group designated to plan the Convention reflected this inclusiveness. It was composed of all heads of ZCTU departments as well as representatives from ORAP (Nomalanga Zulu), the ZCC (Deprose Muchena, also active in the NCA), ZURO (Dennis Murira), "technical expert" Renee Loewenson (Training and Research Support Centre, a health NGO) and another "expert" from the Ministry of Health.[65] The working group tasked Timothy Kondo, head of the ZCTU advocacy program, and Dennis Murira of ZURO to hold a series of preconvention consultation meetings throughout the country. The meetings were held in October and November of 1998 in most of the significant urban centers in Zimbabwe.[66]

The meetings were explicit attempts to build still stronger links with NGOs, not just at the national or Harare leadership level but at the local activist level as well. Invitations were sent to all NGOs, and they were instructed to send their local representatives to the meetings in different areas.[67] The twenty meetings were all fairly small, never exceeding an attendance of forty individuals. They were dwarfed in size by ZCTU labor forums and by NCA meetings and marches that were occurring during this same time period. In addition to the meetings with open attendance of all NGO activists, the ZCTU separately held six meetings in Matabeleland North and Midlands with branches of ORAP, the rural development NGO mentioned earlier and in Chapter 3. ORAP was chosen as a partner because it was seen as the only rural grassroots organization with a structure that could be used to communicate with grassroots constituencies and mobilize rural activists. These meetings were also small, with between twenty and forty participants.[68] In addition to these meetings, the ZCTU continued to work through its affiliate structures, and, as Alexander and McGregor point out, the unionized workers in Rural District Councils were important means of reaching into rural constituencies as well (Alexander and McGregor 2001: 524–5; McGregor 2002: 15–16).

At the time that the meetings began, there were disagreements within the ZCTU over where the process would go. According to Morgan Tsvangirai, the ZCTU leadership had decided on the formation of an opposition party already,[69] but this plan was not brought to the General Council for debate. Nor were the individuals involved in the process leading up to the Working People's Convention informed of the presumed end point. The main coordinator of the meetings, for instance, saw his pre-convention meetings as a process of consultation, and he believed that the results would be used as the basis for negotiations with government:

---

[65] "Summarised Report: Preconvention Consultative Meetings, November 1998 – 'The Raw Data'," reprinted in ZCTU (2000), 47–8.

[66] The locations of meetings were, in chronological order: Mutare, Nyanga, Chipinge, Chiredzi, Beitbridge, Masvingo, Zvishavane, Beitbridge (for the second time), Hwange, Bulawayo, Gweru, Kwekwe, Chinhoyi, Chegutu, Kadoma, Bindura, Norton, Marondera, Harare, and Chitungwiza.

[67] Interview with Timothy Kondo, November 11, 2002.

[68] See Nomalanga Zulu, "Consultative Report (ZCTU-ORAP)," reprinted in ZCTU (2000), 78–95.

[69] Interview with Morgan Tsvangirai, December 12, 2002.

No, there was no discussion of a party before the [Working People's] Convention. What we hoped would be the outcome of the Convention was the adoption of policy positions to bring to government . . . [and at the preparatory meetings] the action these people would talk about would be an action of dialogue with the government.[70]

Rather than instruments of mobilization, the meetings served the ZCTU's strategy of alliance-building. By incorporating grassroots activists into the pre-convention process, the ZCTU was building links with civic organizations at the local as well as national level. They were also expanding the geographic base of the soon-to-be-formed political party, though this secondary aim was not communicated to all ZCTU officials or to participants.

The series of meetings coordinated by Kondo culminated in the ZCTU-sponsored National Working People's Convention, which was held in Harare on February 26–28, 1999. The Convention brought together over 400 delegates drawn from more than forty civic associations, and it was intended to be a serious forum for discussion of economic and social policy in Zimbabwe.[71] In marked contrast to the Garden House conference in Zambia, the meetings were structured in order to stimulate discussion on concrete problems and solutions, and all delegates contributed to the drafting of the Convention's resolutions. The form of the meetings, therefore, departed from the highly orchestrated opposition party launches that are characteristic of Anglophone Africa. After opening plenary sessions, participants at the Zimbabwean National Working People's Convention were split into eight issue-based groups.[72] The groups were in charge of drafting reports on their sectors' problems and "the way forward," which were then presented for discussion to the whole Convention. The reports of these groups were used to draft the final resolution of the Convention. Informants noted that the discussion at the Convention, which was conducted mainly in Shona and Ndebele, was lively and inclusive.[73]

Economic concerns were at the heart of the demands emanating from the Working People's Convention. The declaration passed by delegates demanded the adoption of a development strategy that would prioritize "basic needs for food security, shelter, clean water, health and education, the equitable distribution of resources, [etc.]" and a constitutional guarantee of "a minimum

---

[70] Interview with Timothy Kondo, November 11, 2002.

[71] See "Report of the National Working People's Convention: Agenda for Action," March 1999. Reprinted in ZCTU (2000), 96–127.

[72] The issue areas were: economy and labor market; education and human resource development; gender; health/social security and housing; industry and commerce; land and gender; constitution and national integration; and governance.

[73] Interviews with Gibson Sibanda, December 4, 2002; Timothy Kondo, November 11, 2002.

standard of health inputs (food, water, shelter)."[74] The emphasis on basic economic and social rights has led some commentators to present the Working People's Convention as a radical, socialist project driven by the grassroots, which was later betrayed by the moderate, neoliberal MDC (Alexander 2000: 390–1; Bond 2001: 33–4, 40–6).[75] A careful reader would instead note the presence of well-established ZCTU and NCA demands: the Declaration requested a constitutional commission "not based on Presidential appointment"; and it also revived the ZCTU's treasured ZEDLAC ("a mechanism for national consensus that involves all stakeholders" that is "mandated to negotiate a social contract"). Nor did the Declaration demand deviations from long-standing ZCTU economic policy. Its economic vision is instead profoundly similar to the fairly neoliberal one advanced in *Beyond ESAP*. The Declaration stated that the state's role in the economy should be "redefined toward facilitation rather than interference" and "targeted, end user-directed and time-bound" subsidies should be used only to correct for market failures.

The Declaration of the Working People's Convention was a statement of economic grievances and a set of specific policy demands; however, it was also a call to action. In this sense, the process inaugurated by the ZCTU in 1997 might be considered the hinge by which the economic grievance-driven protests of the ZCTU (i.e., the national stayaways of 1997 and 1998) were fused with the wider political campaigns (i.e., the NCA) in which the ZCTU leadership had been engaged. The Declaration closed by calling on the "various organizations of working people" (which the delegates specified as including the labor movement, informal traders' organizations, and peasant farmers' associations) to:

> take these issues to the people across the country, to mobilise them toward the working peoples agenda, and to implement a vigorous and democratic political movement for change.[76]

Immediately after the close of the Convention, the ZCTU announced at a workers' rally in Bulawayo that it would facilitate the launch of a labor-based political party, which would be guided by the discussions and resolutions of the Working People's Convention.[77] Civic organizations were told that they

---

[74] "Declaration of the National Working People's Convention," February 26–28, 1999. Reprinted in *The Insider*, March 22, 1999.

[75] Some labor leaders, like Collen Gwiyo, made public statements to this effect and also spoke at length on this "betrayal" in an interview with me. Interview with Collen Gwiyo, November 6, 2002. Munyaradzi Gwisai, a radical MDC MP and leader of Zimbabwe's International Socialist Organization, was perhaps the harshest critic of MDC economic policy, arguing that businessmen like Eddie Cross had "hijacked" and "bought" the party. Gwisai was subsequently ejected from the party. For an extended discussion of his criticisms of the MDC, see Gwisai (2002).

[76] "Declaration of the National Working People's Convention," *op. cit.*, 3.

[77] The ZCTU also announced that it would pull out of tripartite discussions (i.e., the National Economic Consultative Forum, discussed in Chapter 5) with government. It should be noted

should report back to their constituencies and obtain their approval to participate in the process of building the party. Report-back meetings and rallies, organized by the ZCTU and by the civic organizations that attended the Working People's Convention, began shortly afterward.[78] In order to obtain its membership's official approval to launch a political party, the ZCTU held a special extraordinary congress in August 1999, where the motion to launch a political party was adopted unanimously. In Chapter 8, I will turn to the party that emerged out of these different processes of civil society collaboration and mobilization. Briefly, though, it is important to point out that the participatory processes that produced the MDC continued to mark the party and, perhaps, the broader political culture in Zimbabwe. In stark contrast to their Zambian and Kenyan counterparts, MDC activists and partisans developed stronger ties to the party, as we will see in Chapter 8, as well as a greater belief in their own personal efficacy. This is unsurprising, as the party was built around consultative and participatory processes, generating an internal party culture that remained somewhat resilient, at least until 2005–6, despite intense state campaigns of repression and violence.

CONCLUSIONS

As in Zambia, political opposition in Zimbabwe benefited from mobilizing structures that it had inherited from earlier periods. Much of the organizational capacity of the labor movement had been built prior to the emergence of opposition to the regime. Thus, in order to explain the ability of the movement to mobilize and to discipline unionized workers, one must look to the initiatives the ZCTU took in the 1980s and early 1990s to strengthen its own affiliates and build stronger linkages between the labor center and rank-and-file union membership. In this chapter, I have examined how the ZCTU moved beyond its own natural constituency and built alliances with other civil society organizations and grassroots constituencies. In this effort it differed markedly from organized labor in Zambia or from the individuals associated with the pro-democracy movement in Kenya. What was unusual in Zimbabwe – and what differentiated Zimbabwean opposition from the protest

that, in statements to the media and workers' rallies, Tsvangirai and Sibanda declined to use the term "party," preferring "movement for change" as in the declaration of the Working People's Convention. Several months later, Tsvangirai again clarified: "The movement is not the party. It is a broad-based instiuttional membership organization . . . but before we launch a party, we have to have a base which is what this movement intends to do." *Inter-Press Service*, May 19, 1999.

[78] "Post-Convention Report-back Meetings with ORAP Groups," June 1999, reprinted in ZCTU (2000), 135–50.

politics that emerged in Zambia and Kenya – is that the opposition found ways of channeling societal discontent into large, sustained campaigns of mobilization. It displayed a talent for disciplining the constituencies it brought together, allowing it to guard against both fragmentation and mobilizational decline. By 1997, the trade unions and their allies almost entirely monopolized protest activity. Mass constituencies – the ordinary people who participated in protest actions, built movement structures, or supported the movement in other ways – demonstrated a remarkable flexibility in terms of the demands they were willing to back. Initially, protest was coordinated by the trade unions and centered on high taxation and declining social services; later, the same social movement campaign moved fluidly from economic demands to the need for constitutional reform to a straightforward party campaign. The movement formed new organizations to coordinate these different phases of the same campaign.

As we will see in Chapter 6, the movement forged in Zimbabwe through this sustained period of social mobilization differed substantially from the more limited, more opportunistic links made between social actors in Kenya and Zambia. Instead of strong alliances and shared values, popular protest in the other two cases was characterized by a lack of strong organization and by fairly fragile links between elites and mass constituencies. Rather than being marked by durable relationships, as in Zimbabwe, opposition coalitions in Zambia and Kenya were characterized by weak ties. These differences emerged during the first waves of overt protests against incumbent regimes, but they had long-run effects on the structures, internal governance, and durability of opposition party organizations when they were formed.

Six

Weak Ties in Zambia and Kenya

In both Zambia and Kenya, periods of protest differed markedly from the Zimbabwean experience. Popular protests in these countries were less organized, and economic decline and protest did not spark collaboration between previously unconnected actors. In Zambia, organized labor served as a natural focal point for elites and ordinary Zambians alike, but trade unions did not pursue alliances with other civil society organizations. In the years preceding the formation of the Movement for Multiparty Democracy (MMD), economic protests occurred, but organized labor did not undertake campaigns or outreach programs that capitalized on economic discontent. Therefore, despite the subsequent electoral success of a labor-backed opposition party, Zambia lacked the strong and focused mobilization that was characteristic of protest campaigns organized by the ZCTU and MDC in Zimbabwe. This would have effects on party organization later on. In Kenya, popular protests were political, but they were, once again, driven by grassroots constituencies rather than well-structured social movements. Popular mobilization by the pro-democracy movement and by parties in Kenya mirrored the underlying structure of Kenyan civil society, which was occasionally strong at the local level but was strongly demarcated by regional, ethnic, and sub-ethnic boundaries. Unlike Zambia, there was no focal point or cross-ethnic network that allowed for the coordination of opposition to the ruling party. Opposition parties in Kenya fragmented quickly prior to founding multiparty elections, and the ruling party was able to retain power with less than 40 percent of the parliamentary and presidential votes.

It is perhaps useful to think of the differences between Zambia and Kenya in network terms. Granovetter suggests that social networks are structured by a combination of strong and weak interpersonal ties (Granovetter 1973). Strong interpersonal ties predominate in densely connected networks: individuals in these networks interact frequently with one another, and individuals' personal networks overlap substantially with those of their friends. Within these enclaves, individuals are likely to be strongly influenced by one another, and ties of trust and reciprocity facilitate collective action (Gould 1993; Fearon and Laitin 1996). Granovetter's distinct contribution lies in pointing out that weak ties that serve as "bridges" linking otherwise distant and disconnected social sites. These ties do not require the same social or time investment as strong ties, nor are they likely to carry with them the notions of trust, reciprocity, or common identity that characterize networks of strong ties. Weak ties are, however, vital for the spread of information, ideas, and behavior across diverse societies. Where they are absent, new information is likely to remain stuck in the eddies of internally dense, yet outwardly isolated, communities of strong ties. The presence of these ties, also referred to as brokers or bridges, has been used to explain a wide variety of "contagious" societal and political phenomena, from the coordination of collective action to the efficiency of labor markets to fads in music and footwear (Watts 1999; Hedstrom et al. 2000; McAdam et al. 2001; Diani 2003; Centola and Macy 2007). In terms of how this applies to the two cases of Kenya and Zambia, this chapter argues that Kenya's political system relied on systems of ethnic brokerage that created hierarchical patronage networks that were limited to districts. This encouraged politicians to invest in strong, exclusive ties with small constituencies, and it prevented the coordination of political action across space or ethnic boundaries. In Zambia, state power was not premised on ethnic brokerage, yielding a different landscape for mobilization. Though the labor movement was not large, it provided a network of weak ties that linked individuals from different regions and ethnic groups, which facilitated the spread of information and action once the Zambian Congress of Trade Unions (ZCTU) moved into political opposition.

In order to understand the organization of protest and the subsequent pattern of party organization in Kenya, therefore, it is necessary to look at the structure of associational and clientelistic links that were in place in the late 1980s. One might argue, probably correctly, that associationalism was overall much weaker in Zambia than in Kenya, particularly given the size and vitality of the local self-help associations known as *harambee* in Kenya. What differs between the two cases, and what I argue accounts for different patterns of protest and party mobilization, is the presence or absence of ties that span districts and ethnic boundaries. In Zambia, organized labor provided a network of weak ties, often composed of little more than a dozen individuals in a single location, which allowed mobilization by the ZCTU to move quickly across districts and regions. Protest could therefore be coordinated behind the labor-backed MMD once it was launched. Kenyan civil society, on the other hand, was characterized by an occasionally vibrant civic life at the local level, but it was lacking in links that connected constituencies or activists across district lines. Local communities, characterized by dense internal networks, swung their support behind elites with personal ties to those communities. The absence of weak ties connecting these communities to the outside made it quite difficult for mobilization to proceed by any route other than through personal networks. Larger social movements or party coalitions had little to offer politicians, since a politician's individual electoral chances depended on the strength of his or her own ties to voters. Party fragmentation and constant cycles of defection and counter-defection are less surprising given this context.

There has been a tendency to assume that the MMD's electoral turnover in 1991 was due to the role of the mineworkers or the size of the formal sector workforce. This tends to mark the Zambian transition as unique or less generalizable to other contexts on the continent. I argue, however, that the contribution of organized labor to the MMD was less numbers than network. The MMD captured large majorities throughout the country, not just on the Copperbelt, and their success at doing this was due to the presence of ZCTU DCs throughout the country. The number of individuals who were linked to these trade unions structures was very small, perhaps comprising no more than ten or fifteen individuals in a particular constituency. As discussed in Chapter 4, these isolated branches devoted energy to mobilizing small groups of workers, three or four electricity workers in one place, five or six civil service employees in another. These small groups developed strong bonds of loyalty to the ZCTU, and they served as the "weak ties" that allowed MMD mobilization to jump from one local network to the next and thereby politicize large numbers of Zambians, the vast majority of whom were not union members. The difference between Kenya and Zambia lies in the absence of these weak ties in Kenya, which left opposition parties with few means of tapping into local communities except through direct personal ties. As we will see, party leaders relied on their ethnic and clientelistic links with small, geographically bounded constituencies, leading to a speedy fragmentation of the opposition landscape. This chapter will look at how protest was organized (or not organized) in Zambia and Kenya, and I also devote time to establishing how associational networks differed in the two countries. Party organization and electoral outcomes will be discussed in Chapter 8.

ZAMBIA

Economic Decline and Grassroots Protest

The early 1980s marked a turning point for the Zambian state. The continued low price of copper, upon which Zambia depended for more than 90 percent of its export earnings, created chronic balance of payments problems, as did the high price of oil. From 1976 to 1982, the country's balance of payments had been consistently negative (Shaw 1982). Many hoped that Zimbabwean independence in 1980 would spark economic recovery, but it instead shifted investment and trade away from Zambia. In 1983, the Zambian government signed a first economic structural adjustment agreement with the IMF; in

October 1985, a second agreement committed the country to additional re-forms.[1] The government devalued the currency, the kwacha, and it also implemented a foreign currency auction system. Due to continued high government spending, the two measures sparked spiraling inflation in 1985–6. The effects on Zambian workers' living standards were immediate. Liatto reports that the consumer price index for low income Zambians increased dramatically in the months following the introduction of the auction system, from 513.3 in 1985 to 794.9 in July 1986 (1975 = 100) (Liatto 1989: 52). By the end of 1985, the real purchasing power of wages had fallen below 1967 levels (Meijer 1990: 677). Real GDP per capita fell 19 percent from 1981 to 1986 (Loxley 1990: 22), and the erosion of living standards escalated from 1986 onward. In 1987, 25 percent of urban households were below the poverty line; by 1988, it had increased to 31 percent and, by 1990, to 40 percent (Geisler 1992: 123).

In December 1986, the government began the process of dismantling state subsidies. The government announced that it would no longer support the price of refined breakfast cornmeal, though it would continue to support the lower cost staple "roller" mealie-meal. Overnight, private millers doubled the price of breakfast meal, leading to runs on roller meal, which many believe would be the government's next target. One day after the price announcement, large crowds began to assemble at milling plants, complaining of shortages in the stores.[2] The following day, looting began in the Copperbelt towns of Ndola and Kitwe, spreading quickly to the rest of the Copperbelt and then to Lusaka and Kabwe. Workers did not seem to play a prominent role in the riots; instead, observers suggested that children, students, and unemployed youths composed the bulk of the rioters.[3] The press reported that rioters targeted government shops, attacking twenty of its National Import and Export Cor-poration stores and looting K80 million worth of property.[4] The government first reacted with repression: a dusk to dawn curfew was imposed on the Copperbelt, and thirteen were killed in the subsequent police crackdown.[5] Under pressure and facing opposition to the price increases within his own party, President Kaunda announced the reimposition of price controls. Private millers were subsequently nationalized (Good 1989: 311–12).

---

[1] For a detailed account of these plans, see Meijer (1990: esp. 669–77).

[2] *Times of Zambia*, December 9, 1986.

[3] One report from Kitwe judged that 50 percent of rioters were between the ages of 12 and 16 and only 5 percent were over the age of 22. *National Mirror*, January 24, 1987. In one Copperbelt town, the government press reported that "hundreds of youths *between eight and 20 years* went on an orgy of destruction." *Times of Zambia*, December 10, 1986, emphasis added. A later report concluded that the bulk of those leading the riots had been under the age of 15. *National Mirror*, November 28, 1987.

[4] *National Mirror*, December 28, 1986. Two NIEC employees were killed by rioters.

[5] *Times of Zambia*, December 10–12, 1986.

The government reversal of price increases in the wake of the 1986 riots may have raised individuals' assessment of the likelihood of strike success and thereby encouraged further mass actions. In the first six months of 1987, wildcat strikes exploded across sectors. In March, teachers went on strike, followed by nurses and clinical staff, doctors, and postal workers. Wildcat strikes were not coordinated by the union leadership, but they spread from their origin points and involved workers nationwide.[6] Economic reforms also motivated collective action from groups other than workers, especially in urban areas. In October 1989, hundreds of miners' wives twice marched to the Zambian Consolidated Copper Mines headquarters, smashing ZCCM signs along the way, to protest the introduction of fees at the mines' hospitals.[7] Like participants in many of the wildcat strikes, the wives were successful, and the introduction of fees was revoked.

In the short run, popular protests were successful in reversing the state's commitment to price liberalization and to the broader package of IMF-sponsored reforms. In the wake of the 1986 riots, the Zambian government suspended relations with the IMF in May 1987. It inaugurated a new adjustment plan, the National Economic Recovery Program (NERP) – with a slogan of "Growth from Own Resources" – shortly thereafter. This decision gained the ruling party some temporary popular support, and it mended divisions within the party between radicals, who had long opposed the IMF reforms, and the more technocratic cabinet (Simutanyi 1996b). NERP's track record was mixed. As in Zimbabwe, government attempts to allay the social costs of liberalization failed. The Zambian government introduced a coupon system under NERP, which was intended to give poor households access to lower priced food. However, due to poor policy design, the coupons never reached those most in need of assistance. Bates and Collier found that the majority of urban households, including the poorest quartile, had no means of accessing the coupons since they had no link to formal-sector wage-earners (Bates and Collier 1993: 427).[8] Many suggested that the system simply shifted black market activity from commodities to the coupons.[9] Government attempts to cushion consumers from market liberalization backfired in other ways as well. Producers evaded price controls by packaging commodities in quantities for

---

[6] Interviews with Leah Asaji, Joel Kamoko, Helen Mwiyakui, and Johnson Zulu, July 8, 2005.

[7] See *Times of Zambia*, October 10–12, 1989 and October 17–18, 1989.

[8] Initially, the coupons were available to whoever applied; later, the program was targeted on formal-sector wage-earners, and coupons were distributed through the workplace. In 1988, formal-sector wage-earners represented only 19 percent of the labor force. Bates and Collier estimated that 62 percent of urban households were "almost entirely unrepresented in the formal sector."

[9] *National Mirror*, January 7, 1989; *National Mirror*, August 4, 1990. Also, see Geisler (1992: 124).

which no prices were set. Retailers carried large cash balances that allowed them to stockpile commodities, which led to shortages.

NERP initially relieved pressure on the regime, but the retreat from the IMF was no more than temporary. Under NERP, the government considerably lowered its debt servicing: repayments had accounted for 95 percent of export earnings in 1987 versus a cap at 10 percent under NERP (Loxley 1990: 12; Meijer 1990: 682). Even with these savings, the budget was simply unsustainable. Since independence, the Zambian government had used the National Agricultural Marketing Board (Namboard) to maintain artificially low food prices.[10] But it had done so at great cost. The collapse of copper prices in the late 1970s meant that the state could not cover the cost of price subsidies or the vast state infrastructure that purchased, transported, milled, and marketed grain. Food subsidies consumed 15 percent of government expenditure by the mid-1980s (Loxley 1990: 15; also, Kydd 1988). Nor did the cost of the marketing infrastructure ensure efficiency. Namboard failed to collect 20 percent of the 1985 bumper maize crop; it managed to collect only two-thirds of the much smaller 1987 harvest; and, in November 1990, "rotting remains of the 1989 harvest were littered all over Northern Province" (Geisler 1992: 116). After cutting relations with the IMF, the bulk of these budget burdens remained, but the government had to cope with the loss of almost all access to external finance. Even Scandanavian donors, who had consistently given significant amounts of development aid over several decades, were unwilling to extend further assistance without the restoration of relations with the IMF (Simutanyi 1996b: 827). Wildcat strikes, riots, and protests at universities and secondary schools continued.[11] In September 1989, the government resumed negotiations with the IMF, and it adopted a new adjustment program in early 1990.

Even at the beginning of the volatile dance between government, donors, and popular constituencies, the ruling party in Zambia had a thin base of support. In Zimbabwe and Kenya, ruling parties made larger investments in maintaining grassroots links and local presence. In Zambia, the ruling United National Independence Party (UNIP) faced the fairly rapid collapse of its branch structures after the imposition of single-party rule in 1972. Party presence at the local level was already uneven by the early 1970s, and Zambians retreated from the party to a greater extent than their counterparts in Kenya and Zimbabwe. Surveys conducted in 1970 and 1971 found that 72 percent of the University of Zambia students polled opposed the formation

---

[10] Grain marketing boards across the continent served roughly the same purpose. Partly, the intent was to secure the quiescence of potentially disruptive urban dwellers and formal sector workers, with the costs of the system accruing, of course, to rural farmers. See Lofchie (1975) and Bates (1981).

[11] For reports of the student rioting, see *Zambia Daily Mail*, January 9, 1989; January 21, 1989; February 7, 1989; and April 11, 1989.

of a UNIP branch on campus and only 11 percent agreed with the statement "the time is now ripe for the declaration of a single-party state" (Burawoy 1976: 89).[12] Robert Bates found similar processes of disillusionment and dissent in the rural areas of Zambia. By the early 1970s, 78 percent of households in a village in remote Luanshya province agreed with the statement "public officials don't care what people like [me] think," and 71 percent believed that government served only the interests of a few (Bates 1976: 206). Perhaps the best evidence of the decline of the party is the sharp decline in party membership after the introduction of one-party rule. On the Copperbelt, UNIP membership dropped from 25 percent of the population in 1968 to 8 percent in 1974 (Scott 1978: 331). By 1980, party membership had fallen to less than 8 percent nationwide.[13] Local party structures disintegrated in the 1970s (Scott 1978; Bratton 1980: ch. 7). Voting turnout in Zambia's one-party elections was substantially lower than in Zambia's two multiparty elections in 1964 and 1968 (Baylies and Szeftel 1992: 77). There were occasionally expressions of discontent. But the retreat from the party was not counterbalanced by the development of new associations and lobbies, as it was to some extent in Zimbabwe. Zambians exited. They did not seek out other means of expressing voice.[14]

Despite the party's shrinking connection with its popular base, it maintained a firm grip over associational life and the expression of demands. The centralization of the trade union structures was discussed in detail in Chapter 4, and the labor movement was effective, to some extent, in dampening strike activity and wage demands. Other state interventions in the associational realm had less clear-cut aims. Two of Zambia's most prominent professional organizations, the Law Association of Zambia and the Zambia Institute of Mass Communications, were established by Acts of Parliament in the early 1970s and early 1980s, respectively.[15] These organizations possessed some autonomy from government – autonomy that they would begin to use in the early 1990s – but they did not function as vibrant, independent civic associations. Local women's clubs were more closely tied to UNIP, as affiliation to the

---

[12] In earlier periods, there had been a strong party presence at the University of Zambia. Interview with Njekwa Anamala, July 21, 2003. For more on the oppositional student movement of the early 1970s, see Rothchild (1971).

[13] Statement by MP Francis Nkhoma, citing UNIP figures. *Zambia Parliamentary Debates*, November 26, 1980.

[14] State repression may have played some role in dampening enthusiasm for independent associationalism in Zambia. The UNIP state had, for instance, violently repressed non-mainstream religious organizations in the 1960s and 1970s (Van Binsbergen 1976; Hudson 1999; Smith 1999). Even after the opposition United Progressive Party (UPP) was banned in 1972, UNIP continued to target individuals suspected of UPP sympathies. As mentioned in Chapter 4, trade unionists were a particular target.

[15] See the discussion in USAID Zambia, *Project Proposal: Democratic Governance Project* (Project # 6110226), 1992–5: 84–7.

UNIP Women's League was a prerequisite for receiving government funds
(Touwen 1990: 25–6). Women's organizations outside the UNIP Women's
League had no more than 100 active members, according to one estimate, and
their membership was primarily composed of upper-class urban women
(Geisler 1987: 56, ftnt 3).

Where grassroots associations did exist, they rarely served as channels for
the communication of demands and were, instead, oriented toward state
patronage (Bratton 1980; Pletcher 1986: 614–17). For instance, the Zambian
state urged farmers to form cooperative societies, which it suggested would be
used to distribute inputs and technical expertise. Cooperative societies mush-
roomed in the first years of independence: by 1970, 1,280 societies had been
registered, claiming 53,000 members (Lombard 1972: 294). These societies did
not yield strong ties or individual commitment. As Lombard points out, few
members felt that they "belonged" to their societies, and most were planning
to leave as soon as they found better work (296–7). Though the cooperatives
were not strong grassroots organizations, they also fell prey to UNIP's drive
toward centralization. In 1973, the state founded the Zambian Cooperative
Federation (ZCF), which was to act as an apex organization in the same way
that the ZCTU did. The government increasingly intervened in the internal
running of the cooperatives, leading members to view the cooperatives even
more instrumentally than they had in the past. Poor policies created "an
environment in which efficient, self-reliant and economically productive
behavior was discouraged [and in which] members came to expect endless
handouts from the Government" (Quick 1977: 385; also, Ludwig 2001: 74–6).
Corruption and internal squabbling within the cooperatives increased, and
they lost membership and administrative capacity.

In comparison to Zimbabwe, Zambian civil society was underdeveloped. In
the 1970s and 1980s, few associations or non-governmental organizations
(NGOs) were operational outside urban areas. Further, as the example of the
cooperatives suggests, the associations that did exist were not given space to
build structures or ties with membership independent of state and ruling party
control. Organized labor had an established membership and geographic
reach, and the churches were similarly well rooted. Beyond these two actors,
however, other grassroots organizations and civic associations were simply not
present by the 1980s. In 1990, on the very eve of the MMD's campaign, the
National Mirror reported that there were only twenty-six NGOs in Zambia – a
stark contrast to the hundreds of NGOs in Zimbabwe in the same year.[16]
According to the *Mirror*, the majority of Zambian NGOs were welfare organizations that targeted women or children exclusively. Neither the trade
unions nor the churches had partners with whom to collaborate on popular

---

[16] *National Mirror*, June 9, 1990.

movements to resist economic reform. Equally importantly, both organized labor and the churches were ambivalent about their aims in the 1980s. Though the state–labor alliance was disintegrating in the 1980s, it was only at the end of the decade that the ZCTU was willing to consider political mobilization against the state. In the next section, I will show that the protests of the 1980s were important in placing pressure on the UNIP regime, but they were not the work of a well-organized social movement.

Protest and the Absence of Organization

Grassroots demands became politicized in the last half of the 1980s. Protests and strikes in the late 1980s were initially motivated by concrete and short-run concerns over the prices of commodities or other economic grievances, as the 1985 rioters had been. Protesters were often placated by concessions from the government. For instance, when the government announced that it would reverse the removal of maize subsidies that had led to the 1986 riots, it was reported that children and other former rioters sang praise songs to Kaunda in the streets.[17] As time went by, however, protesters proved to have an omnivorous appetite, slowly incorporating new grievances about quality of governance, elite corruption, the actions of ruling party "vigilantes," and the corruption of local officials. To give an example of this shift, consider the political framing of 1990 maize riots versus that of the 1986 riots discussed in the introduction to this set of chapters. The government announced in 1990 that it would, once again, remove price supports on mealie-meal. As in 1986, large-scale riots convulsed the Copperbelt and other urban centers in response to the announcement and the corresponding price increases. The catalyst for both the 1986 and the 1990 riots was the same, but contentious politics had shifted in the four intervening years. The 1990 riots were more violent, the crowds more confrontational, and the discontent expressed by the rioters both economic *and* political. Commenting on this transformation, Bates and Collier remark: "while the food riots of December 1986 had focused on the price of maize, those in June 1990 focused on the political system itself" (Bates and Collier 1993: 429). The riots did not force the reinstatement of price controls, as riots had in 1986, but they further increased the ruling party's sense of threat. The riots may also have emboldened dissident politicians and the labor movement to move in a more explicitly political and confrontational direction, as the MMD was officially launched at a conference held roughly four weeks later.

---

[17] *National Mirror*, January 24, 1987.

Was this politicization of protest directed by the ZCTU, as it had been by the labor movement in Zimbabwe? For the most part, despite the seemingly coordinated timing of protest and MMD activity, grassroots protest in Zambia was undirected. The ZCTU played no role in organizing early economic protests, nor did it seem desirous to speak on behalf of protesters. In 1986, the maize meal price increases had been announced a full month before the riots, but the trade unions did not issue any public statement denouncing the price increases, nor did they organize or threaten demonstrations or strikes.[18] The ZCTU explicitly disassociated itself from popular protests, but grassroots militancy and the inability of labor leadership to control strikes led to increasing antagonism between the ruling party and the ZCTU. The government's public attacks on unionists, as well as the economic hardships of the 1980s, began to forge the perception of a community of interest between workers and other segments of the Zambian population. In interviews long after these events, Zambian unionists remember the 1980s as a period of greater solidarity between labor and other constituencies for reform:

> [Workers] were radical. [Leaders] were also radical. Because of the things that were happening. The workers saw what was happening in the country. They would queue for everything ... This is where the Congress received not only support from workers but also from ordinary people, including members of [the UNIP] Central Committee who were coming to us privately and saying "we have problems with the system, but it is not easy to resign from the system – but we support you."[19]

The alliance between the labor movement, the urban unemployed, and informal sector workers was more affective or emotional than institutionalized. Again unlike the labor movement in Zimbabwe, the ZCTU did not build links with these constituencies, and it seemed to remain firmly focused on the interests of union members, even as structural adjustment steadily shrank the size of that membership.

In addition to their reluctance to build links with popular constituencies, the labor leadership did not build structures or communication channels that would bring them closer to their own grassroots. The correspondence files of the ZCTU district committees do not show increased communication or assistance from the ZCTU to district committees (DCs) from 1986 to 1989, nor does it seem that there was a marked increase in the formation of committees.[20] There was no explicit program of politicization. Instead,

---

[18] See *Times of Zambia*, November 3–13, 1986.
[19] Interview with Alfred Mudenda, July 2, 2004.
[20] District Committee Correspondence, DC/2-63. ZCTU Archives, Kitwe, Zambia. It is important to note that these correspondence files are not available for all the district committees that were listed as operative during this period. Nor did all district committees provide the center with minutes or updates, which may or may not be an indication of the vibrancy of that DC. Taken as

workers and the urban poor were politicized by unplanned contentious actions throughout the 1980s. National or affiliate union leadership remained relatively apolitical during this period. The ZCTU did not declare its political opposition to the state until fairly late in the protest cycle. In 1986, after government criticized labor for not contributing to policy formulation, ZCTU Secretary-General Newstead Zimba stated that the trade unions should remain autonomous from politics.[21] In the same statement, shortly after advocating political non-involvement, he then stated that the trade unions "love" the government and wish all political leaders to remain in their current posts.[22] After three years of economic decline and government repression, this "love" seems to have dissipated. In 1989, in response to a more pointed attack on labor, Zimba responded: "he [Minister of State for Labour] thinks that by attacking unions he will get his promotion. What he should know is that the confidence of Zambians in this government is long lost because of the manner that the government handles financial affairs of the state."[23] Even at this point, it is not clear that labor leadership was strongly in favor of political mobilization against the UNIP regime. Akashambatwa Mbikusita-Lewanika, one of the organizers of the Garden House conference where the MMD was formed, remembers trade union leaders as being reluctant to commit to attending the conference, which he attributed to their uncertain position on opposition to UNIP.[24]

In many ways, the breakdown of relations between the Zambian government and the Christian churches proceeded by a very similar route. Like the trade unions, the effects of structural adjustment alienated the mainstream Christian churches in Zambia from the government that they had previously supported. Conflicts between the church and the UNIP government often played out in the Christian press, which was the only non-state-controlled media in Zambia. It is in the interactions between the government and the Christian press that we can best chart changes in church–state relations over the course of the 1980s. The formal autonomy of the papers

---

a whole, the files do not suggest any substantive changes in ZCTU policy toward the DCs during the 1980s. Some DCs were formed from 1987 to 1989, but others seem to have folded.

[21] *Times of Zambia*, October 12, 1986. This was actually a departure from earlier policy. In the 1970s, labor leaders had repeatedly requested *more* involvement in policy-making, and the ZCTU had consistently sought trade union representation on government bodies.

[22] *Times of Zambia*, October 12, 1986.

[23] *National Mirror*, June 10, 1989.

[24] Interview, July 23, 2003. Both the ZCTU Chairman Frederick Chiluba and the Secretary-General Newstead Zimba, for instance, refused to sign the invitation letter to the conference; in addition, Lewanika said that Chiluba and other unionists did not arrive until 4 hours after the meeting had started, when they saw that it would not be disrupted by the police. It seems that there was anxiety within the unions that Garden House would lead to massive arrests. Also, interview with Ben Mwila, July 17, 2003.

from Church leadership allowed them to take stands that were far more critical than those advanced in bishops' pastoral letters. For instance, the *National Mirror* was owned and operated by the protestant Christian churches, but the paper was autonomous and church leaders had no control over its editorial content. *Impact*, the official publication of the Catholic Secretariat, may have steered clear of controversy, but the other Catholic publications, such as *Workers Challenge* and the Bemba-language *Icengelo*, were more insulated from political pressures and were free to take positions that were sharply critical of the UNIP government. As early as 1981, President Kenneth Kaunda criticized the churches for their "attacks" on the government and the party in the *National Mirror*.[25] By the mid-1980s, the Christian press had become even sharper in their criticism, regularly running stories critical of economic liberalization and supportive of trade union leaders. *Icengelo* was widely read on the Copperbelt; after the introduction of ESAP, "it became so popular that parish priests and catechists discouraged its sale before the Sunday service [in order] to avoid seeing the congregation reading it during their sermons" (Hinfelaar 2004: 346). The paper's advocacy of social justice and pro-poor policies earned it a following among churchgoers and trade unionists alike, but it also attracted the attention of the state. In November 1989, *Icengelo*'s editor, Father Umberto Davoli, was detained and interrogated by government ministers and by state security, who accused him of being a foreign spy. In a justification of Davoli's arrest, which was released only later, the government alleged that the magazine "spread tension and fear by forecasting the collapse of the economy and suffering for the poor [and] encouraged disorder and unrest to change the situation."[26] In the same statement, the government objected to *Icengelo*'s coverage of the Pope's visit to Zambia. The newspaper ran stories on popular upheavals that had occurred in other countries that the Pope had visited, which the government viewed as "suggesting that something of the kind should also happen in Zambia." Thus, though the press was increasingly willing to challenge government policy, political criticism remained, even in *Icengelo*, fairly oblique.

In addition to the role played by economic liberalization in politicizing the churches, other factors also pushed churches in a more political direction. In the 1970s and 1980s, after Vatican II, the Catholic Church in Zambia became more committed to the school of Catholic social teaching that emphasized the importance of a "preferential option for the poor."[27] Clergy were urged to

[25] *Times of Zambia*, January 12, 1981.

[26] *National Mirror*, May 12, 1990.

[27] The "preferential option for the poor" has often been lumped together with Latin American liberation theology, but the two are distinct. The first was mainstream Church theology from Vatican II until the late 1980s, when Pope John Paul II started to urge churches to remain out of politics. The second was a very different body of thought about the sources of poverty and the role of the church. See the discussion in Levine (1988).

incorporate social and economic justice into their ministries, and Small Christian Communities (SCCs) were established at the diocesan level all over Zambia. The Catholic Secretariat established a new Social Education and Research department in 1982. After a study trip to Zimbabwe, this department became the Catholic Commission for Justice and Peace (CCJP) in 1986, and it modeled itself in part on the confrontational CCJP in Zimbabwe. Diocesan peace and justice committees followed. There is a lack of in-depth research on the Catholic Church's role in the democratic transition in Zambia, so my comments on the consequences of these organizational and ideological changes are speculative. The SCCs and diocesan peace and justice committees in Zambia were similar in form to Christian Base Communities established in Latin America and elsewhere (Mainwaring 1987; Burdick 1993). They were intended to involve the laity, especially the poor, in church governance, and they also provided a forum for church members to study and reflect on economic and social justice, as well as immediate problems in their own lives. The strengthening of SCCs in Zambia was a priority area for Catholic church leaders, and the CCJP used the SCC structures to carry out its social justice education (Hinfelaar 2004: 357–60, 395–6). By the late 1980s and early 1990s, social justice had become part of the core of Catholic Church activity in Zambia, reaching down to the grassroots level.[28]

In other countries, Christian Base Communities have served to politicize the poor, and they played an integral role in several regime transitions (Alves 1984; Levine and Mainwaring 1989; Canin 1997). In Zambia, they played a more limited role. The SCCs, along with the CCJP and other mass-based Church organizations, educated grassroots constituencies about human rights, economics, and social policy. They also provided many Zambians with their first experiences of organization and discussion outside the state realm.[29] This grassroots network was weaker than what the ZCTU in Zimbabwe built, and it did not bring activists from different part of the country together at events or training sessions. The role of Christian communities might have played in protest and political opposition was also limited by the opposition of the church hierarchy to political involvement. The question of politics was controversial beyond the leadership as well. Hinfelaar notes that "in the years that followed [the creation of civic education programs] the SCCs became gradually politicized while the increasingly independent movements of the lay apostolate remained traditional and uninvolved" (Hinfelaar 2004: 359). Finally, it is important not to overstate the size or reach of changes in churches' attitudes toward political involvement. It was only the Catholic Church, which represents only about 25 percent of Zambians, that established SCCs. After the launch of the MMD, no church hierarchies formally endorsed the movement,

---

[28] Interview with Fr. Peter Henriot, October 11, 2002.
[29] Interview with Fr. Joseph Komakoma, July 22, 2003.

but individual pastors gave "political sermons" that advocated multipartyism and, later, urged Zambians to vote (Phiri 1999: 341). Bartlett suggests that many MMD activists were pulled from the church youth movements, and the churches may have played some role in mobilizing the women's vote (Bartlett 2000: 435).[30] Overall, however, church institutions provided support for the MMD only on the margins. The activism of the CCJP and some of the SCCs may have politicized Zambians in directions that made them more receptive to the MMD's appeals. But MMD activists and office-holders did not mention churches as mobilizing structures for the movement, and there is no evidence of MPs emerging from diocesan structures. In Zimbabwe, on the other hand, the director of the CCJP was elected as a MDC MP, and the ZCC played a central role in the formation of the NCA.

Mobilization by the MMD

There is limited information available on early MMD planning and organization at the local level. Informants, the majority of whom were either unionists or Lusaka-based businessmen and academics, consistently referred to the MMD structures as "self-organizing." The MMD itself has kept no archives of any kind,[31] and it is unclear how often the National Interim Council corresponded with local committees, whether committees received formal instructions, or whether the party circulated campaign materials through the local committees. Informants active in the MMD at the time remember only the circulation of MMD manifestos. In terms of assistance from civil society organizations, several associations assisted MMD politicians and helped secure the political space that allowed the MMD to campaign and reach voters. The Law Association of Zambia provided free legal services to advocates of multiparty rule, and it defended Chiluba and other MMD figures when they were arrested in October 1990.[32] The Press Association of Zambia expanded

---

[30] Much of Bartlett's support for this argument is inferred. He argues that the churches must have had political influence because of religion's centrality in Zambian life. He notes that 83.3 percent of Zambians belong to a church, the Catholic Secretariat and the CCZ are both among the eight largest NGOs, and even agricultural training centers are church-linked (Bartlett 2000: 435–6). Obviously, concrete evidence of church participation in MMD campaign committees would be more convincing.

[31] The lack of any documents or official party record is a disappointment. Not only does the MMD lack any record of early organizing, but it has not retained copies of public statements, circulars, or correspondence from the period *following* the party's election. It is possible that MMD leaders, notably Frederick Chiluba, or Arthur Wina, kept party documents in their own personal possession, but it seems likely that the historical record of the party has been lost. Field notes (Lusaka), June 2004.

[32] The association passed a resolution supporting all the major demands of the MMD in September 1990. Law Association of Zambia, "Resolution of the Special General Meeting," September 2, 1990. Mimeo provided by LAZ.

the MMD's access to media by obtaining a court injunction that removed the managing editors of the major newspapers and the director of Zambia's one broadcasting company for their bias against the MMD (Momba 2003: 46). Churches provided meeting places for the MMD when it could not obtain permits for party meetings.[33] The reach of the independent Christian press has been mentioned above. The Catholic Church publication *Icengelo* was an important resource, especially on the Copperbelt: by 1990, the magazine had an estimated circulation of 60,000 and an estimated readership of 300,000.[34] The mobilizing structures provided by labor, however, are most responsible for the MMD's reach and its ability to field candidates in 149 of Zambia's 150 constituencies in the 1991 elections.

In contrast to informants in Zimbabwe, who emphasized that several coalition partners played a role in mobilization, there was an overwhelming consensus in Zambia that the trade unions "brought the organization." In August 1990, soon after the formation of the MMD, the ZCTU General Council decided that "multiparty campaign committees" should be formed at the district level, and it recommended that funds be dispersed from the ZCTU to these committees (Rakner 1994: 59–60).[35] In the minds of the MMD leadership, the MMD committees would simply be built atop existing ZCTU DCs, perhaps even sharing personnel. There were a number of ZCTU DCs that were operational in 1990, but these were rickety structures on which to build a movement. As discussed in Chapter 4, the ZCTU had formed the DCs in the late 1970s after UNIP introduced plans to incorporate the labor movement into the Party as a mass wing. At the time, the committees were seen as a means of protection and self-preservation. They helped the ZCTU establish an organizational presence in areas beyond the towns and industrial areas that clustered on Zambia's north–south line of rail. To some extent, the DCs built community and an incipient collective identity for workers across Zambia. These were, however, "weak ties," to use Granovetter's terminology. By 1980, thirty-one DCs were in operation, though by the ZCTU's own admission, several of these operated "largely on paper." Members were often unclear about the role of the DCs and how they were to function.[36] In the 1980s, the organization department did little to either support or build capacity and interconnections across DCs, partly due to a lack of funds and the death of the department's director.[37]

Even as state–labor relations grew more conflictual, the ZCTU did not significantly invest in an organization-building campaign, as the ZCTU in

---

[33] Interview with Father Joseph Komakoma, July 22, 2003.
[34] *National Mirror*, April 28, 1990.
[35] Interview with Austin Liato, June 22, 2004.
[36] Report of the Secretary-General to the 7th Quadrennial Congress of the ZCTU, Livingstone, October 15–18, 1986. QC/D No. 1, ZCTU Archives, Kitwe, Zambia.
[37] ZCTU, "Secretarial Report for 1989, National Centre," undated mimeo, ZCTU Archives, Kitwe.

Zimbabwe had. The new director of organization undertook three organizational tours of Copperbelt, Luapula, Lusaka, and Western provinces in order to evaluate the state of the DCs between March and November 1989.[38] He found that DCs were in particularly good shape in the Lusaka and Copperbelt provinces, though three important Copperbelt DCs were in need of "reorganization." Few concrete plans seemed to result from this tour. It is important to underline that, at this point, the DCs were not a priority for the ZCTU leadership, and the ZCTU did not rely upon DCs for communication. Occasionally, they were asked to assist in membership drives or were given funds to hold Labour Day celebrations, but several of the DCs went long periods without direct contact with the ZCTU. From their formation to the present, DCs would periodically fall inactive and then be revived when needed by ZCTU leadership.[39]

After the formation of the MMD, the DCs were seen as the best means of quickly extending the MMD's national reach. In 1991, the ZCTU again organized a tour of the DCs. In contrast to the 1989 tour, however, the 1991 tour included all districts in five provinces, including four of the five that had not been visited in 1989.[40] The change in DCs' priority within the ZCTU was also reflected in the list of those participating in the district tour, which included the ZCTU Chairman and deputy Chair, two Assistant Secretary-Generals, ZCTU trustees, and affiliate heads. The prioritization of the DCs explains how the MMD was able to organize large rallies nationwide within two months of its formation. T.Z. Tembo's personal account of the MMD district committee in Livingstone indicates that ZCTU leadership was in touch with the DC there the day after the MMD was launched at Garden House (Tembo 1996). The formation of an MMD "referendum committee" was first discussed at the home of the Provincial Secretary of the local administration workers union (ZULAWU), a resident of Livingstone. Five of the seven initial planners of the MMD committee were trade unionists, and the initial meetings of the MMD branch were held in ZULAWU headquarters (Tembo 1996: 1–2). Austin Liato, who was President of the electricity workers union at the time, said that overlapping leadership of the ZCTU DCs and MMD branches was common nationwide:

> So what was happening was the DCs, the leaders there became the pioneers of the MMD. So that, for example, if you had a MMD person come or travel there, they

[38] Affiliates were invited along on the tours of Luapula and Western provinces, which have traditionally been areas of low trade union presence. Those that did come, noticeably the Guards Union of Zambia and ZNUT, gained new members. Few affiliates, however, expressed interest in the DC tour.

[39] See District Committee Correspondence, DC/2-63. ZCTU Archives, Kitwe, Zambia.

[40] ZCTU, "Report of the SG to the 9th Quadrennial Congress, October 25 to 27th 1994, Livingstone," mimeo, ZCTU Kitwe. The provinces visited were Southern, Eastern, Western, Northern, and Central provinces. Northwestern Province was not included in either visit.

would say this is union politics, we [ZCTU] are doing this now, can you help? And you would find that the chairman of the DC – because that is who they would talk to – is suddenly the chairman of the newly formed MMD branch.[41]

Trade unionists formed the heart of most MMD local branches or committees, but the DCs also performed another crucial task that national union leadership could not have achieved on its own. DC officials identified local businessmen and local government officials that could be incorporated into the new MMD structures. These small-scale local businessmen, who were shopkeepers or commercial farmers, provided funds and transport for the first MMD rallies. Mbikusita-Lewanika suggests that their support was far more crucial to the success of the MMD than the support of elite members of the national business community, such as former UNIP members like Vernon Mwaanga.[42]

The ZCTU leadership assisted the organization of the MMD and mobilization of mass constituencies in other ways as well. One ZCTU official said that, in the early days of the MMD, the ZCTU provided funds and facilities for the printing of MMD flyers and other materials.[43] Rakner, who was conducting fieldwork immediately prior to the 1991 elections, notes that ZCTU vehicles were repainted with MMD letters and colors and used in the election campaign (Rakner 1994: 60, footnote 9). Direct assistance of this kind was risky, however, and union leaders always feared that their involvement in the multiparty campaign might result in a backlash against organized labor. Unionists emphasized that the formal boundaries between trade union work and MMD work had to be respected, especially after UNIP passed legislation limiting how trade union funds could be used.[44] Alfred Mudenda, who was then General Secretary of ZULAWU, said that MMD business was regularly mixed into normal union activities:

> So you are strengthening the district officials, but you would not say 'how do we strengthen the district committees and help the MMD.' You couldn't say that. [But it was understood? Strengthening the DCs meant strengthening the local MMD?] Oh yes, yes, at the time. But you would not say you want to strengthen the MMD. You would say you want to change the political understanding. You would say I think this movement is progressive, and you should consider supporting it. And Zimba and Chiluba would come, but you could not invite these solely political figures [other MMD leaders].[45]

When directly asked if DCs were given money in order to organize MMD rallies, Mudenda again emphasized the importance of maintaining the

---

[41] Interview with Austin Liato, June 22, 2004.
[42] Interview with Akashambatwa Mbikusita-Lewanika, July 23, 2003.
[43] Interview with Maria Kamuchele Kabwe, July 2, 2004.
[44] Interviews with Alfred Mudenda, July 2, 2004; Sylvester Tembo, July 9, 2004; and Charles Muchimba, July 3, 2004.
[45] Interview with Alfred Mudenda, July 2, 2004.

appearance of autonomy between the ZCTU and the MMD. He said that DCs were given funds in order to visit local chiefs, councillors, and ordinary people – ostensibly on union business – and they also might be provided with MMD manifestos "to study" in order to determine if it was a progressive party that workers might want to individually support.

Organized labor was every bit as important in explaining the mobilizing reach of the MMD as other scholars of Zambia have suggested (Akwetey 1994; Rakner 1994; Nordlund 1996; Larmer 2007). But my account differs substantially from other accounts. At the elite level, the MMD was an alliance of business, labor, "academics," and civil society, as the literature emphasizes. At the grassroots level, however, Zambia was marked by a dearth of strong mobilizing structures. Apart from the ZCTU, only the churches had the ability to reach large numbers of Zambians in different corners of the country. Other MMD allies had essentially no ties to mass constituencies. This fact is sometimes lost in overviews of the party's formation, which devote much of their attention to "high politics" and intra-elite bargaining. Nor are scholars alone in their failure to interrogate the picture of the MMD as a coalition. MMD informants often emphasized the importance of the coalitional nature of the party, only to admit – sometimes after further questioning, sometimes only in informal conversations – that the structures and mobilizing capacity of the movement were derived almost entirely from just one of the movement's partners. In the remainder of this chapter, we will investigate the shape of political opposition where this kind of focal actor – and the weak ties that it is able to provide – is absent.

KENYA

Protests against Single-Party Rule

In most African countries, economic structural adjustment was the background condition that made political liberalization possible (Decalo 1992; Bratton and Van de Walle 1997; Joseph 1997; Diouf 1998). Prolonged fiscal crises weakened states, and austerity measures, particularly the removal of price controls, further undermined the legitimacy of unpopular authoritarian regimes. Kenya was a partial exception to this rule. The government of President Daniel arap Moi was particularly adept at maintaining funding flows from the IMF and donors while making very little progress in the implementation of market reforms. The country's economic troubles led to engagement with the international financial institutions and the commitment, at least in theory, to economic liberalization and market reforms. Standby arrangements were negotiated with the IMF beginning in 1979, and the

Kenyan shilling was devalued several times during the 1980s as part of these arrangements. The deregulation of maize marketing, as in Zimbabwe and Zambia, was a central requirement for most of the loans Kenya received through the international financial institutions.[46] Unlike the other two countries, though, the Kenyan government never braved popular discontent by implementing unpopular reforms like maize price deregulation. Similarly, though the IMF demanded that the Kenyan state significantly scale back the size of the state bureaucracy and civil service, the state resisted. Public employment actually grew 4.3 percent from 1985 to 1989. Unlike most other African states during this period, the government continued to hire university graduates, such that 75 percent of new graduates still received government jobs in the early 1980s (Cohen 1993: 455). The economic reforms that were implemented may have created some losers, but they also created winners. In 1988, for instance, when Zambia was experiencing shortages and mass retrenchments, the annual GDP growth rate in Kenya peaked at 5.2 percent. It was not until *after* the first round of multiparty elections in 1992 that the economy began to slip into free fall, driven in large part by KANU's inflationary electoral tactics (Holmquist and Ford 1992: 104).[47]

For these reasons, protests in Kenya were less economically motivated than those in Zimbabwe and Zambia. Mobilization against the KANU government was motivated to a greater extent by political grievances that had accumulated in the years since Moi's assumption of the presidency in 1978. As Widner discusses in great detail, Moi aimed to build KANU into a centralized, coercive party organization that would be able to reach directly to the grassroots level (Widner 1992). Moi had limited success in achieving this aim, but his attempts to transform the ruling party and local administration upset the delicate structure that had secured political order in the Kenyatta period. Many KANU politicians saw Moi's party-state project as an assault on the structure of power that they had helped erect (Barkan and Chege 1989; Southall and Wood 1996). Under Kenyatta, regional- and district-level leaders structured their own clientelistic networks: they were relied upon to deliver support and votes to KANU, but they had significant autonomy within their own areas. From independence to 1978, state control was built atop a strong yet flexible network of ethnic brokers. In Barkan's words, Kenyatta ensured that the system remained effective by "encouraging secondary and tertiary echelons of regional elites to emerge through the [intra-KANU] electoral process," which were then incorporated via patronage and the allocation of

---

[46] The precise details of these early agreements – and the Kenyan government's relative non-implementation of them – can be found in Mosley (1986).

[47] Barkan notes that the money supply was estimated to have increased 40 percent in the last quarter of 1992 due to spending on KANU party campaigns (Barkan 1993: 94).

cabinet positions (Barkan 1993: 87). Even without opposition parties, one-party electoral competition was vibrant, and MPs who did not comply with their home constituencies' "role expectations" – which largely centered on the delivery of patronage – were not re-elected (Barkan 1976: esp. 453–4; also, Barkan 1979). Authoritarian state institutions, notably the provincial administration, remained important (Branch and Cheeseman 2006), but single-party elections in the Kenyatta period were surprisingly participatory and contentious (Barkan 1979; Cheeseman 2006: 9–11). Moi did not allow the continuation of this election-led fluidity, nor did he wish to rely so directly on the direct distribution of patronage. Moi's regime was built on a different ethnic calculus than Kenyatta's – it depended on the support of small tribes, particularly the pastoralist tribes of the Rift Valley – but it also envisioned a different relationship between state and society. Rather than depending on ethnic brokers to deliver grassroots constituencies, Moi's strategy of rule depended on a direct insertion of the party into local communities, as well as the expansion of authoritarian or coercive controls over popular constituencies. Thus, during the 1980s, there was an increasing centralization of power around party institutions. Local authorities were more aggressively policed and sanctioned by the center. The party established disciplinary committees that vetted candidates, expelled party critics from party membership, and reduced local constituencies' freedom to elect and sanction their own MPs. In 1986, KANU implemented a system of "queue voting," which further undermined the freedom and competitiveness of elections. In lieu of the secret ballot, voters were required to line up behind their candidate of choice physically. In the subsequent 1988 elections, there were charges that, even when local communities braved state sanctions to line up behind their own choices, candidates preferred by the party leadership still prevailed.

According to VonDoepp, it was this "disruption of the legacy of accountability and civil autonomy left by [Moi's] predecessor Jomo Kenyatta" that laid the groundwork for the emergence of political protest in the late 1980s (VonDoepp 1996: 35). Two other state choices must, however, also be mentioned. First of all, the Moi regime substantially shifted the flow of patronage within the state, generating hostility among many segments of society, especially the Kikuyu community that had most benefited from Kenyatta's rule. The underlying philosophy of the regime was a leveling of economic wealth and opportunity across Kenya's regions: the beneficiaries of this redistribution were to be the poorer regions, which were inhabited primarily by the smaller ethnic groups that had been excluded from Kenyatta's ruling coalition (Barkan and Chege 1989: 436). If one looks at the list of politicians involved in the formation of Forum for the Restoration of Democracy (FORD) and other opposition parties before the 1992 elections, a large number of these individuals were former government ministers and state officials who lost office due to the shift in power and resources toward Moi's own Kalenjin group and other small tribes. Secondly, the Kenyan state grew increasingly authoritarian over the course of the 1980s. The hurried imposition of one-party rule was followed by the enthusiastic application of colonial-era public order laws to an ever-widening set of targets, especially after a failed coup attempt in 1982.[48] Political detentions increased, public meetings were routinely canceled on the grounds of national security, and the regime began to chip away at the autonomy of the judiciary. After the arrests of a handful of prominent lawyers and the introduction of an annual licensing system for lawyers, the previously state-allied Law Society of Kenya (LSK) became increasingly critical of the government (Ross 1992; Mutua 2001; Press 2004: esp. 120–34). Other social actors also began to express discontent. These events set the stage for the series of political protests that would result in the formation of FORD in 1991. Opposition to KANU was significant in the period preceding the founding multi-party elections of 1992, but opposition lacked the mobilizing structures that labor movements had provided in Zimbabwe and Zambia. As I suggest above, Kenyan civil society did not have other networks of weak ties that would have allowed the coordination of protest and voting.

Civil Society in Kenya

The first proponents of multiparty democracy did not have a strong associational base in civil society on which to draw. As discussed in Chapter 4, the Kenyan state was not supportive of organized labor in the early independence period, and it subsequently manipulated union elections and governance to splinter or disorganize affiliates that were seen as threats. Increasing control over the remnants of unionism in the 1980s was part of a broader strategy to ban and harass civil society. Several unions were deregistered in the early 1980s. In 1984, the Kenya Farmers Association was dissolved and then reformulated into the Kenya Grain Growers Cooperative Union, a move intended to reduce the organization's autonomy from the state. Over the next few years, in a dizzying series of moves, the government disbanded the organization once again in 1987, then reconstituted it, and finally took direct control over its finances and purged its primarily Kikuyu leadership (Burgess 1997: 142). In 1986, Maendeleo ya Wanawake, the country's largest women's development organization, was also forcibly affiliated to the party, and it changed its name to KANU-MyW shortly thereafter (Adar and Munyae 2001).[49] Though the Congress of Trade Unions (COTU) narrowly avoided a

---

[48] For an overview of the legal environment of the late 1980s, see Ndegwa (1998).

[49] Holmquist and Ford suggest a less formal affiliation between KANU and Maendeleo (Holmquist and Ford 1994: 14).

similar fate,[50] it remained under the firm control of the ruling party, which was actively involved in internal union elections throughout this period. These state-co-opted organizations were politically marginal, and their close ties with the state meant that they were not viewed by opposition leaders as potential mobilizing structures. From 1990 onward, even as protest escalated, the country's leading trade union officials made no public pronouncements on the multiparty issue. Perhaps the best evidence of KANU's co-optation of the labor center is the outcome of an attempt by COTU to place pressure on government after the 1992 elections. In 1993, the Secretary-General of COTU called for a general strike to press for a 100 percent increase in wages, and he also called for the dismissal of a top government official suspected of corruption (Holmquist and Ford 1994: 11). KANU responded swiftly, maneuvering the Secretary-General out of power within the organization; plans for the general strike were dropped.

As with professional associations and national lobbies like Maendeleo ya Wanawake, the Moi regime attempted to control or dismantle other networks that might have been used to mobilize opposition to the state. During the Kenyatta period, informal networks of ethnic brokerage had been supplemented by larger ethnic associations, which had some ability to coordinate action across districts within ethnic zones. First and foremost among these was the powerful Gikuyu Embu Meru Association (GEMA), which represented agricultural and business interests of the Kikuyu, Embu, and Meru communities. It had powerful ties to state and party bureaucracies during the Kenyatta period. These related tribes, concentrated in Central Province, had been beneficiaries of state policies and patronage during the Kenyatta period, especially in relation to land. In 1980, Moi banned all ethnic welfare associations, which he feared might serve as rival bases of political power (Widner 1992: 138–44). This did not affect GEMA alone: the Luo Union and Abaluhya Union, among others, also discontinued their operations. Perhaps because the move was perceived as a fairly transparent ploy to undercut Kikuyu influence, this restriction on associationalism did not arouse protest from the churches or civil society. Anyang' Nyang'o argues that it was the particularistic organization of the ethnic associations that allowed Moi to restrict civil liberties without overt challenge: "in identifying their primary constituency so narrowly, [GEMA's leaders] isolated themselves from the rest of the nation and could not expect much support from either the bourgeoisie as a whole or popular

---

[50] Relations between the party and the unions were schizophrenic in the late 1980s. Prior to the March 1988 polls, Moi announced that unionists would not be eligible to stand as party candidates; six months later, KANU ordered COTU to merge with the party as a mass wing. Though the plan was resisted, potential affiliation with the party shaped internal union wrangles from 1988 onward. See, for instance, the coverage in *Financial Review*, October 3, 1988, and January 16, 1989.

classes from other ethnic groups" when they were targeted by the state (Any-ang' Nyong'o 1989: 249).

With ethnic associations gone, there were few remaining associations that linked Kenyans across district lines. For instance, even though a large propor-tion of informal sector traders in smaller Kenyan towns belonged to associa-tions, sectoral or industry-wide organization of these interests was absent. Widner argues that patronage and patrimonial linkages undermined incen-tives for traders or other groups to organize: traders' clientelistic ties to local patrons made them "able to secure what they need[ed] without achieving policy change that might benefit other members of the sector" (Widner 1991: 45). Community associations existed, but demands were funneled through local elites, who controlled access to the state and to patronage. Farmers and smallholders lacked regional and national lobbies. Instead, these consti-tuencies were given influence and voice only through local *harambee*, the fund-raising rallies that served in Kenya as a means by which local commu-nities could hold their representatives accountable (Holmquist 1984; Burgess 1997: 135). With changes implemented during the Moi period, the democratic qualities of the *harambee* system diminished, the powers of the district councils over *harambee* funds increased, and there was increasing evidence of misuse of funds (Widner 1992).[51] Of course, the balkanization of associ-ational life into district or even sub-district realms was not a result of the Kenyatta and Moi periods alone. As a number of scholars have noted, the current ethnicization of Kenyan politics has its origins in the structuring of political space in the colonial period (Anderson 2005; Branch 2006; Cheese-man 2006; Orvis 2006). Indeed, the strength and centrality of ethnic associa-tions prior to their banning suggest that the weakness of cross-regional and cross-ethnic political mobilization has deep roots.

As for the urban-based movements from which FORD drew many of its members and activists, these organizations had few if any linkages to grass-roots constituencies. Civic education efforts and paralegal programs in rural areas were not in place until the late 1990s (Orvis 2003). Even then, NGOs did not serve as truly national entities; instead, like political parties, individual NGOs' activities catered to the ethnic constituencies of the organization's leadership. Though the churches played an important role as a critical voice on the national stage, it seems that they were also not well placed to serve as grassroots mobilizing structures. Orvis' work, for instance, gives us a window

---

[51] Indeed, it may be in this context of the degeneration of *harambee* that we should interpret Miguel's finding that multi-ethnic communities in Kenya are less successful in supplying public goods than either their multi-ethnic counterparts in Tanzania or their monoethnic counterparts in Kenya (Miguel 2004). Although this is speculative, it seems logical that weak or politicized *harambee* would function better in monoethnic communities, as these communities might be better able to leverage their position as ethnic vote blocks to constrain state officials' predatory use of *harambee*.

into the activities of the Kenyan Catholic Justice and Peace Commission (CJPC), which is the direct corollary of the CCJPs in Zimbabwe and Zambia. The Catholic Church was active in pushing for political reforms, especially after the implementation of queue voting in 1986. There were disagreements across the church hierarchy over political involvement (see Gitari 1991), and these disagreements affected the implementation of CJPC programs at the diocesan level. For each pastor that advocated democracy and urged support for FORD, there were others that believed the churches should remain apolitical. The CJPC in Kenya was not able to form parish-level justice and peace commissions until the late 1990s (Orvis 2003: 253).[52] The lack of a strong, well-connected civil society sector had implications for the shape of protest in Kenya during the days leading up to political liberalization. Though there were popular protests, these were uncoordinated. And though politicians attempted to form inclusive opposition partnerships, they did not have the common interests or the mobilizing structures to hold these coalitions together.

Mobilization for Multiparty Elections

The first voices for democracy emerged from within the Kenyan churches. In the mid-1980s, individual pastors delivered sermons that attacked the Moi regime's human rights record. The mainstream church establishment began to openly criticize the state following the ruling party's implementation of queue voting in 1986. Both the Anglican and Catholic churches' leaderships spoke out against the elimination of the secret ballot, and they released a petition, signed by 1,200 pastors, that threatened a boycott of the 1988 elections (Sabar-Friedman 1997: 33). After the 1988 elections, the churches attacked the overt rigging that had occurred during the polls, and individual pastors became more confrontational vis-à-vis the Moi regime. From the pulpit, one prominent pastor reflected on events in Eastern Europe and asked when similar political change would come to Kenya (Throup and Hornsby 1998: 57). Another publicly attacked KANU plans to introduce party membership as a prerequisite for voter registration, saying it amounted to the disenfranchisement of Kenyans who could not afford the membership fee (Sabar-Friedman 1997: 34). As in Zambia and Zimbabwe, the state attacked the churches for meddling in politics, and "patriotic churches" were urged to leave the National Council of the Churches of Kenya (NCCK), the cross-denominational umbrella association

---

[52] It may be that those areas that were under the control of clergy critical of the state organized these committees earlier. Sabar-Friedman, for instance, mentions that the Nakuru Diocese Justice & Peace Commission was active in 1990 (Sabar-Friedman 1997: 39). Overall, however, there does not seem to have been a nationwide structure that linked the CJPC to the grassroots.

of the churches. Though increased pressure from the churches did not have an immediate effect, it encouraged a public dialogue over the acceptable limits of state power. In July 1990, KANU accepted the recommendations of its own internal party commission and instituted several reforms that the churches had consistently demanded, including the repeal of the queue voting system.

The Kenyan churches started making political demands earlier, but many view the February 1990 murder of Foreign Minister Robert Ouko as the beginning of the pro-democracy movement in Kenya. After a Judicial Commission of Inquiry was appointed to look into the death, investigations began to point toward Moi's close associates, and the president disbanded the commission (Throup and Hornsby 1998: 58–60; also, Mutua 2001: 113). Calls for political reform increased. In May, former KANU ministers Kenneth Matiba and Charles Rubia held a press conference at which they denounced government corruption, blamed single-party rule for economic decline, and called for political opening. Over the following four months, Matiba and Rubia enlisted the support of urban-based associations, notably the LSK, and began to lay out plans for a series of public rallies. Scholarly accounts of this period often attribute a great deal of organizational capacity to this small cluster of individuals (e.g., Throup and Hornsby 1998: chs. 4 and 5). Large-scale protests and riots occurred during this period, but their connection to elite-level politics is either assumed or riots are dismissed as the actions of an "inchoate urban crowd [that] reemerged as a political factor in July 1990" (Holmquist and Ford 1992: 99). Assuming a connection between elite-level politics and grassroots protest is problematic. Where coordination and disciplining of protest exists, we can assume that there are formal or informal structures that link elites to constituencies, which could potentially be repurposed to serve as party structures. This was not the case in Kenya.

From 1990 onward, political protests in Kenya were spontaneous and undirected, as the economic protests in Zambia had been from 1986 to 1989. Movement leaders had little control over the constituencies they mobilized, and political protests regularly degenerated into riots. For instance, Matiba, Rubia, and their LSK allies called for an unauthorized public rally in support of multiparty democracy in Nairobi on July 7, 1990. After the police violently dispersed those who had gathered for the rally, riots broke out in Nairobi's high-density townships, quickly spreading to urban centers across Central Province, the home area of Matiba and Rubia. After FORD was formed in 1991, popular protests followed a fairly similar repression-to-rioting script. FORD made a second attempt at a large-scale rally in Nairobi in November 1991. Police repression once again triggered violent resistance from protesters, and several FORD leaders were arrested under public order laws. Fearful that arraigning FORD leaders in Nairobi would spark further unrest, individuals were deported back to their home areas to stand trial. Rather than neutralizing the popular component of the movement, these trials seem to have exported popular mobilization to the rural areas. As FORD leaders arrived at rural courts, they were greeted by large crowds, who waved branches and sang pro-FORD songs.[53] Crowds protested in favor of FORD, but they also arranged their own demonstrations without prior contact with leaders or organizers. Throughout the latter half of 1991 and in 1992, the papers report what seem unorganized demonstrations by a diverse set of groups. If anything, it seems that FORD created a political opening that allowed for autonomous mobilization by a diverse set of constituencies.

During subsequent protests, alliances were struck between groups of protesters, so we can discern links between separate protest events during the 1991–2 period. For instance, in March 1992, a small group of mothers of political prisoners occupied a corner of Uhuru Park in Nairobi and embarked on a hunger strike.[54] After the police violently evicted the "Mamas" from the park, an eviction that left Green Belt leader and Nobel laureate Wangari Maathai in the hospital, street hawkers and bus touts in central Nairobi launched a boycott in support of the protesting mothers that, unfortunately, degenerated into a riot. Subsequent protests by the mothers were supported by FORD and by the student movement. For several weeks, the mothers held public meetings outside the Cathedral of All Saints, where they had relocated, at which the public gathered to discuss corruption and the lack of respect for human rights. In early April, the police stormed the Cathedral in order to arrest student activists who had taken shelter there, and the Mamas' moment seems to have slipped away. Thus, though there is evidence of these kinds of informal linkages, the demands of different constituencies were not incorporated or institutionalized into opposition party-building; indeed, Tibbetts notes that, as elections neared, "the issue of political prisoners was marginalized and the coverage of the mothers' protest diminished over time" (Tibbetts 1994: 35). In sum, there were fairly weak ties between leaders of the pro-democracy movement and the grassroots constituencies involved in protest. The weakness of these ties partly explains why FORD so quickly lost segments of its original constituency to defections and party splinters, as we will see in Chapter 8.

CONCLUSIONS

Differences in the organization of protest and in the character of civil society during this period had important effects on party-building. In Zambia, as in

---

[53] See, for instance, the coverage in *The Daily Nation*, November 16–18, 1991.
[54] I depend on Tibbetts's fascinating account of the "Mamas" protest (Tibbetts 1994).

Zimbabwe, state corporatism created a labor movement that had political visibility and an organizational structure that stretched, however tenuously, across much of Zambia. In contrast to Zimbabwe, however, the Zambian trade unions did not actively involve themselves in the planning and organization of protest, nor did they pursue coordinated campaigns with other social actors during the period preceding party formation. When the MMD was launched in 1990, its leaders and activists had little experience of working together, nor were they knit together by shared priorities or a strong collective identity.

In Kenya, the organization of opposition faced even greater obstacles. Governance in Kenya had long been structured around decentralized systems of ethnic brokerage. This arrangement tended to mold civic life in the same direction. When disgruntled politicians and their allies in urban-based civic associations began to make demands for greater democracy and state account-ability, they found themselves without formal or informal networks upon which a broad-based, cross-ethnic democracy movement could be based.

In the two countries, the outcomes were different. The presence of a strong and autonomous labor movement provided Zambians with a means of co-ordinating protest behind a single actor, while the long-standing ethnicization of politics and civic life in Kenya made a unified opposition impossible. But there was one basic similarity between Zambia and Kenya. In both countries, new opposition parties did not possess the long history of collaboration or the social rootedness that Zimbabwean opposition had built. Protests in Zambia and Kenya did not yield disciplined social movements capable of sustaining mobilization over time. New opposition parties, therefore, lacked established means of resolving internal conflict, and their links with grassroots constitu-encies were based on personal networks. These factors would shape party development in founding multiparty elections and the period that followed.

Part Four

The Formation of Parties

★

_____

PARTY ORGANIZATION AFTER PROTEST

"We are saddened that there are others who want us [Zimbabweans] divided. But people must not listen to small, petty little ants which we can crush."

— President Robert Mugabe at a 2000 election rally[1]

"And then it is the party that is changing their office and repainting. This party is no longer the LDP, it is now the ODM. Another flag goes down, another flag goes up. The officials remain the same, but even then, you can't ever find them."

— Kibera resident[2]

In 2005, just after a second round of violent parliamentary elections in Zimbabwe, the leadership of the Movement for Democratic Change (MDC) announced that it would hold a series of rallies in several sites around the country.[3] The party said there was a need to consult the party's grassroots about the party's course of action following the loss of several seats in the parliamentary elections and the subsequent forced eviction of over 700,000 urban dwellers, many of them MDC supporters.[4] Mobilization and consultation of popular constituencies were established routines within the MDC by this point, even in periods between elections. But the turn to meetings and rallies as a means of determining strategy also reflected a broader commitment and orientation within the MDC. The party's internal culture and governance had been shaped by the ethos of consultation and grassroots participation, and the national executive, even when in disagreement, regularly took into account how decisions might affect mobilization and grassroots support. Despite intense campaigns of state-sponsored violence, especially from 2000 to 2005 and again in 2008, the MDC maintained grassroots structures and some

_____

[1] Reported in ZHRNF (2001: Annexes, Section J).
[2] Focus group, Kibera (Nairobi, Kenya), June 6, 2008.
[3] _Financial Gazette_, August 25, 2005.
[4] These evictions occurred under the government's Operation Murambatsvina. For more, see UN-HABITAT (2005) and HRW (2005).

degree of participatory decision-making. At first glance, this seems a puzzle. When we look at opposition parties in Zambia and Kenya, or indeed elsewhere in Africa, investment in party-building or in maintaining ties with constituencies during inter-electoral periods is exceedingly rare. So why did the MDC prioritize mobilization and grassroots participation, particularly given the high costs that state violence and repression imposed on these activities? Secondly, participatory decision-making opens up more opportunities for disagreement and conflict within organizations, and it also makes organizational planning and control more difficult. How did the MDC maintain participatory party structures without triggering organizational fragmentation?

In this set of chapters, I argue that opposition parties approach both mobilization and the perennial threat of fragmentation in different ways. In all three of the cases I consider, opposition parties were formed as diverse coalitions, but they demonstrated different levels of success in holding these coalitions together. Success was partially due to the strength of the identity and mobilizing structure upon which a party could draw. The MDC in Zimbabwe, for instance, did have a stronger and more cohesive social movement base upon which to build, and both elites and grassroots organizers had collaborated on protest campaigns in the past. But party governance and elite–mass linkages are also shaped by the choices made during and after party formation. More specifically, I argue that parties that use polarizing or confrontational appeals can manage high levels of internal disagreement without organizational collapse. The MDC could manage both intense demands from below and differences at the elite-level precisely because long periods of confrontation with the ruling party had built walls around the party that were difficult to cross. Barriers to defection were reinforced through state violence, which targeted MDC members and also those who merely shared the attributes of MDC supporters (e.g., were teachers, lived or spent time in urban areas, were active in trade unions or other civic associations). MDC party structures could be given voice because, even when their input was overturned at the national level, they abided by party decisions and continued to mobilize mass constituencies on behalf of the party. Even after a factional split in the MDC's leadership resulted in the formation of a splinter party, grassroots party structures remained intact.

Opposition parties in Kenya and Zambia displayed very different patterns of decision-making and popular mobilization. In opposition parties in these countries, the loyalties of popular constituencies often lay with local leaders or visible ethnic elites rather than with the party per se. Parties might be tied to grassroots constituencies via informal linkages, but the weakness of clientelistic and personalized bonds meant that popular support remained volatile and often fleeting. Decision-making in party organizations was highly centralized, which reflected party leaders' fear of factionalism. This was also a cause of further factional splintering. Finally, in the absence of party-based polarization, there was little to hold diverse coalitions together. In Kenya, campaigns of state-sponsored violence institutionalized violence into party competition in the early years of democratization. But violence was not organized around a single cleavage, nor did it constrain the fluidity of the politics of alliance and defection that continue to shape the Kenyan party system. Polarization forged the parties that face each other in Zimbabwe, while fluidity and organizational weakness have produced the less stable party systems that characterize the other two cases.

Because its impact on organizational development and behavior has been seldom discussed by comparative party scholars, party-based polarization requires more explanation here. Some degree of polarization is a common, perhaps a universal, feature of party campaigns. Parties must mobilize their base constituencies and attract new voters. The deployment of "us–them" distinctions – and the conscious attempt to heighten the salience of those distinctions – is perhaps the most effective means of accomplishing these tasks (Horowitz 1985; Zaller 1992; Mendelberg 2001). In majoritarian first-past-the-post systems, parties may alter the appeals or the attributes they stress to different voters, but identity features and policy preferences are presumed to sort into two party blocks with varying degrees of internal consistency. In times of high party polarization, it is more difficult for politicians to activate new issues or to reorient voters along new cleavages, but this increased inflexibility rarely endangers political stability in established democracies.

In hybrid or democratizing regimes, however, polarization can quickly approach dangerous levels. This is partly due to the character of mobilization in closed political environments. Because participation is inherently high-risk, "radicals" – those who are least amenable to compromise and negotiation – often dominate, at least initially, the grassroots structures of opposition movements. Mobilization also takes place in environments that lack the strong institutions that moderate discourse and channel conflict into institutionalized, non-violent modes of interaction (Huntington 1968; Snyder and Ballentine 1996). Natural tendencies toward differentiation can also be magnified by the conscious choices or "craft" of political elites. In particular, polarizing strategies – those that divide the electorate into two opposing camps and heighten the perceived incompatibility of interest between parties – are chosen by opposition party elites because they are likely to politicize constituencies, increase mobilization, and prevent organizational fragmentation. Power-holders often respond by mirroring the confrontational stands of the challengers they confront. This is particularly true where the stakes of party competition are high and the consequences of electoral loss are uncertain, as they are in hybrid regimes. The loss of political office could lead to prosecution for crimes committed during authoritarian rule, and the transfer of power could threaten other incumbent interests, such as the security of property rights. Where incumbents still possess resources and popular support, polarization and deadlock can continue for some time. Mutual distancing, organizational radicalization, and violence often result.

Polarization can build new social boundaries, or it can increase the salience of those that already exist. This can yield substantial changes in the political landscape, as groups' attempts at self-policing change dynamics *within* the groups on either side of a boundary. Social boundaries are not merely a division or distinction between groups: they are fixed pieces of the social and political landscape, which mediate interactions within and across groups (Tilly 2004*b*). Thus when polarization occurs, processes of inclusion (internal solidarity) and exclusion (mediation of relations across the boundary, justification of the boundary) are intensified. Other social boundaries recede in importance, and the cleavage around which polarization is built comes to organize social interaction in multiple arenas. Other realms of economic and social life are politicized, and identification with one of the two camps is imposed if it is not chosen. Groups define themselves in opposition to one another, they limit interaction to conflict or violence, and they silence moderates by accusing them of disloyalty. Polarization thereby collapses previously complicated identities and interactions between multiple political actors into a simple battle between two. As we will see in Chapter 7, polarization produces stronger and more cohesive party organizations, but it has less positive effects on the development of a democratic political culture. Where polarization is absent, party leaders find it more difficult to prevent the defection of candidates and other allies. The involvement of activists is harder to sustain, and relations with grassroots constituencies remain sporadic and, often, conflictual.

Most broadly, this set of chapters examines how parties make decisions and how they structure interactions between party elites, local candidates, and grassroots constituencies. Competition in elections is obviously part of this story, so I spend some time disentangling patterns of party support and party system development over election cycles. To a larger extent, though, the chapters are intended to shed light on internal party organization and the key questions of organizational strength and societal linkage that were posed in Chapter 2. The effect of party strength on electoral success is contingent on a number of factors. The weakness of opposition party structures in Kenya and Zambia is a reason that party systems in the two countries have been characterized by fragmentation and volatility. But even strong opposition parties sometimes face strong and skilled incumbents. Strong parties do not always win elections, but they do shape the character of representation in new democracies. Where parties are strongly centralized and limit their activities to electoral periods, accountability will remain weak. Where parties instead devote energy to grassroots communication and mobilization, voters and grassroots activists have a greater ability to influence and sanction the behavior of their representatives.

Seven

Polarization and Party-Building in Zimbabwe

On the eve of the 2000 elections in Zimbabwe, both the ruling Zimbabwe African National Union – Patriotic Front (ZANU-PF) and the opposition Movement for Democratic Change (MDC) faced potential fragmentation. ZANU-PF's grassroots organization had eroded substantially over the course of the 1990s, the party's leadership was sharply divided on regional lines, and there existed what might be termed reformist and loyalist wings of the party. From 2000 to 2002, however, ZANU-PF found new means of mobilizing mass constituencies through land redistribution, and it created new party structures to enforce intra-party discipline and to police the opposition. Despite precipitous economic decline, the ruling party did not suffer notable defections until 2008, and its popular support also remained relatively stable during this period. Its opponent, the MDC, was a coalition of diverse interests, which many predicted could not hold together. From 2000 onwards, the party faced targeted repression, legal harassment, and larger, less precisely targeted campaigns of state-sponsored violence. Despite this intense pressure, the MDC resisted fragmentation and retained its popular base. How did these two parties build internal solidarity in the midst of incentives for fragmentation?

This chapter argues that the puzzle of party solidarity – for both the ruling party and the opposition – can be explained with reference to a single process: party-based polarization. By making defection and the formation of third parties less attractive, polarization prevents the escalation of intra-party disputes into party fragmentation. And by tying candidates' electoral success to membership in one of two parties, polarized party systems are more likely to lead politicians to make investments in party-building. The causes of polarization may be different across countries. In Zimbabwe, party-based polarization was intensified by state-sponsored violence, the repression of civil society organizations that were perceived to be supportive of the MDC, and the expansion of targets to include "disloyal" elements in the judiciary and the churches. Rather than splintering the MDC, these developments forced the party to pay still greater attention to maintaining grassroots ties and activist commitment. Party structures adapted, and party activists and officials began to speak of the party's struggle in explicitly moral terms. Following the failure of inter-party talks in 2002, grassroots pressures and shifts in the party's internal balance of power pushed the MDC toward a still more confrontational stand vis-à-vis the ruling party. This process of defensive radicalization sustained the MDC's reach and the loyalty of its grassroots activists, but it also laid the groundwork for a split in the party's leadership in 2005.

Overall, this chapter demonstrates how party strategy affects individual politicians' and voters' calculations about the potential utility of defection. Where vote choice coincides with strong and salient social cleavages, we would expect parties to be more stable. Voters are more likely to vote in accordance with party labels, so party affiliation provides substantial benefits to candidates. This is true even if parties do not provide more tangible assistance for campaigns or constituency services. The comments on party polarization here contribute to a larger discussion about how the number and overlapping or non-overlapping nature of identity cleavages affect party behavior. As Chandra points out, the multiplicity of ethnic and communal cleavages in India has generally pushed parties toward more centrist positions that lessen the salience of any one boundary (Chandra 2005). Varshney has similarly stressed the way that the presence in India of multiple, cross-cutting cleavages can drive parties toward accommodation and inclusive appeals (Varshney 2003). According to these kinds of models, where ruling parties are pushed toward the center of the political spectrum, opposition parties will face particular challenges in coordinating the disparate group of voters that lie outside the central zone that the ruling party targets (Sartori 1976; Cox 1996). In African settings, theories of party positioning and coordination have less traction, as parties are rarely positioned on a programmatic left–right spectrum. But opposition parties still face the challenge of diversity. In many cases where opposition parties cannot unite disparate anti-incumbent constituencies behind a single identity claim, they cannot coordinate protest voters.

The unique qualities of Africa's ruling parties tend to intensify this difficulty. In Africa, the presence of multiple ethnic or ethno-regional cleavages has tended to produce ruling parties with a non-ethnic or "catch-all" form at the national level. In these contexts, there are few visibly and uniformly excluded identity groups from which opposition parties could build constituencies large enough to force an election turnover. As I argued in Chapter 5, social movement and party campaigns can provide a way around this dilemma. Protest and confrontational tactics can generate new social boundaries and new communities of interest. As we will see, polarization can contribute to the process of identity creation, and it can give parties a powerful tool with which to discipline the responses of grassroots constituencies. The structuring of conflict and identity around a single party-based cleavage can provide a solution to the problem of opposition coordination, as it tends to yield more cohesive organizations on either side of the partisan divide. But we should exercise caution in viewing confrontation and party polarization as a short-cut to more competitive party systems. Viewing the consequences of polarization through the lens of party positioning and vote coordination obscures the deeper consequences of polarization and conflict for mobilization and internal organizational culture. Though ZANU-PF is not the focus of the analysis here, party-based polarization did much to "trap" moderates within the ruling party. This increased the control of the center over provincial and local party structures, and it made it more difficult to place brakes on the path of violence and economic destruction that ZANU-PF undertook. It is also difficult to argue that violence and repression produced any benefits for the MDC and its supporters. Political violence in Zimbabwe has left a trail of destruction in its wake. But the MDC's ability to hold together a fractious coalition and maintain high levels of activist commitment – *despite* the very significant risks that party membership and participation entailed – suggests that polarization may have paid party-building dividends. This chapter will also show that violence and polarization significantly shifted the internal organization of the party over time.

BUILDING THE INCLUSIONARY PARTY

By the time the MDC was formally launched in September 1999, the Zimbabwe Congress of Trade Unions (ZCTU) and National Constitutional Assembly (NCA) had together created political space and built a base of support for the new opposition party. Earlier ZCTU campaigns and protests created ties to popular constituencies that reached beyond unionized workers. The NCA's constitutional campaign had knit together activists from different parts of Zimbabwean civil society. In addition to these coordinated and overlapping campaigns, the ZCTU leadership had done a great deal of preparatory work before the party's launch. The ZCTU's 1998 outreach meetings and labor forums, discussed in Chapter 5, built links with a number of grassroots constituencies. These ties were further strengthened through the stayaways and demonstrations of the late 1990s. This process of inclusion operated at the elite level as well. As early as 1997, ZCTU Secretary-General Morgan Tsvangirai began to target key members of civil society and request their input on planning.[1] Prior to

---

[1] For instance, Sekai Holland of the Association of Women's Clubs, Trudy Stevenson of the Combined Harare Residents Association, and human rights lawyer Tendai Biti were all invited onto the ZCTU's task force that was formed by the General Council to consider the formation of a labor-backed party. Interview with Gift Chimanikire, July 13, 2004; interview with Sekai Holland, April 8, 2004.

the formal launch of the party, he approached the same individuals to see if they would be interested in serving as parliamentary candidates. Civil society activists were strategically incorporated into the MDC structures, but the ZCTU and its affiliates remained the dominant forces in party organization and decision-making. At the launch in September of 1999, the composition of the MDC's interim leadership clearly reflected the centrality of the labor movement: twelve of the thirty-four interim National Executive Council (NEC) posts were allocated to trade unionists, and labor leaders held three of the MDC's top four positions (President, Secretary-General, and Deputy President).

There were strategic motivations for including the leaders of other civil society organizations in party planning, since these individuals had skills, expertise, and, occasionally, ties to some popular constituencies that labor lacked. But it was also natural for trade union leaders to turn to civil society activists with whom they had worked in the past. Many of the individuals who later served as MDC parliamentary candidates and as members of the National Executive had personal relationships with the ZCTU stretching back to the mid- or early 1990s. Lawyer David Coltart had brought the ZCTU onto Legal Resources Foundations (LRF) human rights test cases; Paul Themba Nyathi, another lawyer, had allowed ZimRights to use his offices for their early meetings; while Tendai Biti had represented union leaders in court when they were arrested for organizing strikes and stay-aways. By bringing these individuals into the MDC, the ZCTU was simply relying on a pre-existing network that linked the labor confederation to other sectors of civil society. The resulting coalition effectively incorporated all associational networks outside the state realm. In addition, the early inclusion and consultation between the ZCTU and its partners fostered a sense of popular ownership of the party. This was one of the most consistent impressions I gleaned from interviews and discussions with activists and officials at all levels of the party bureaucracy. Even though the party emerged from the union structures and remained dependent on labor for organization and leadership, each coalition partner was able to view itself as the determinative factor in the party's success. Student leaders believed that the student structures in polytechnics and colleges *were* the MDC structures. Unionists believed the party simply piggybacked on the labor organizations. Intellectuals and civil society activists believed that the NCA and the earlier struggles of civil society produced the political opening that made the MDC possible. This inclusive process of identity mobilization yielded an organization that was capable of resisting tendencies toward fragmentation. It also built a party that was capable of staying on message, the message being, in the words of one activist, "all about making every-thing a two-horse race."

The MDC's manifesto reflected the diversity of interests that underlay the various linked civil society campaigns of the 1990s. The ZCTU's mid-1990s set of suggestions for national economic policy, laid out in *Beyond ESAP*, resurfaced in various parts of the manifesto, especially in its demand for a "labour intensive development strategy that integrates the formal and non-formal sectors of the economy" and in its thinking on land reform. The familiar demands of the ZCTU's social partners were also reflected in the document: the MDC demanded constitutional reform using the NCA's language, its gender policy reflected the demands of women's organizations, and its "social agenda" incorporated the demands that had emanated from residents' associations and other issue-based non-governmental organizations (NGOs). Nor did the MDC merely reflect the interests of its target constituencies and organizational allies. From the beginning, the concrete tactics and appeals used by the party were interlinked with those of civic groups, most notably that of the NCA, as discussed in Chapter 5. The NCA and the MDC worked together in mobilizing Zimbabweans to vote "no" to the government Commission's constitutional draft in a popular referendum in February 2000. After the draft was rejected by 55 percent of the relatively small number who voted, the MDC quickly shifted gears from campaigning for the "no" vote to campaigning for parliamentary elections. The interim provincial structures were charged with coming up with lists of parliamentary candidates. Even at this stage, there was an effort to integrate grassroots structures into party decision-making and candidate selection. In contrast to the MMD in Zambia, there were few accusations of NEC "imposition" or central control during the 2000 parliamentary campaigns. In contrast to opposition parties in Kenya, there was a formal process for the selection of candidates, and the party sought to run candidates in all areas of the country, even in constituencies where the leadership had few ties or contacts.

From the beginning, priority was placed on policing the party against "infiltration" by the ruling party. MDC activists and leaders, from 1999 to 2006, consistently expressed fears that the party would be "swallowed" by ZANU-PF. In order to protect against this, the interim NEC restricted eligibility for party candidacy to those who had become official members of the MDC prior to the date of the referendum. Had the MDC's commitment to maintaining sharp boundaries between itself and the ruling party been somewhat weaker, there were members of ZANU-PF who would have been likely candidates for recruitment. More than twenty former ZANU-PF Members of Parliament (MPs) and city councilors boycotted their party's primaries in 2000, claiming various irregularities, and they subsequently contested the general elections as independent candidates.[2] This group included several MPs known to be more progressive than the ZANU-PF leadership. Prominent MPs like Moses Mvenge, Richard Shambambeva-Nyandoro, and Lazarus Nzarayebani

[2] *Mirror*, May 26, 2000.

had led efforts in Parliament to force the government to undertake constitutional reform and to block the 1997 war veterans' levy, the cost of which sparked
the ZCTU anti-tax protests of 1997 and 1998.[3] These MPs, as well as other
moderates, contested their seats as independent candidates in 2000, but they
were outpolled by MDC and ZANU-PF candidates alike. This was true of
candidates running on third-party tickets as well. Had ZANU-PF moderates
been free to join the MDC – or had voters been less hostile to independent
candidates in the 2000 elections – subsequent party and party system development may have taken a different path. The defeat of the non-aligned in the 2000
parliamentary elections suggests that the party polarization was entrenched, to
some extent, by the time of the elections.

The MDC's parliamentary candidates were not recent defectors from ZANU-
PF, but many were veterans of earlier political campaigns. Of the fifty-five
members of the first MDC parliamentary delegation for whom I have biographi-
cal information, seventeen identified themselves as former members of
Zimbabwe African National Union (ZANU), Zimbabwe African Patriotic
Front (ZAPU), or their armed wings.[4] Fidelis Mhashu, who became the MDC
MP for Chitungwiza, served as a ZANU-PF city councilor in the mid-1990s and
had run as an independent candidate for mayor of Chitungwiza in 1996 and
1998. David Coltart, who became the MDC MP for Bulawayo South, had been
active in the Forum Party in 1995, as had Trudy Stevenson (MDC MP, Harare
North) and Elias Mudzuri (MDC Mayor of Harare). The Forum Party was the
only one of Zimbabwe's existing opposition parties that formally disbanded and
joined the MDC.[5] Other opposition parties were not targeted by MDC
leadership, as they had both weak personal ties to the interim executive of the
MDC and, more importantly, lacked popular constituencies that would make
them attractive targets for co-optation. In the months before the elections,
these small opposition parties suggested that they would agree to a "voting
pact" only if the MDC agreed to not contest particular constituencies in favor
of the other parties' candidates.[6] Even had these parties been seen by the MDC
leadership as attractive partners, these demands were incompatible with the
MDC's process of locally-based party nominations. The MDC NEC never

---

[3] Nzarayebani had also been one of eleven MPs who responded to ZCTU attempts to
engage Parliament in discussions about economic structural adjustment plans in 1997.
Interview with Timothy Kondo, November 11, 2002. The important point is that if the
MDC had been interested in engaging with the ruling party, these are the individuals who
would have been approached.

[4] Movement for Democratic Change, "MPs CVs Summary: Confidential," undated mimeo.

[5] *Financial Gazette*, December 9, 1999.

[6] *Mirror*, April 14, 2000. The voting pact was proposed by Margaret Dongo's Zimbabwe
Union of Democrats, regional party Zanu-Ndonga, the United Parties, and the small pro-
federalism Liberty Party, which seemed to be largely South-African-based when I met party
leaders in August 1999.

pursued negotiations with other opposition parties, and these parties remained politically irrelevant in 2000 and subsequent elections.

According to many MDC candidates, candidate selection in 2000 proceeded with little friction. Local structures were given the responsibility of identifying and recruiting candidates. Where there were multiple candidates, district or provincial party structures supposedly put candidates together in a room and let them decide by consensus on the party's nominee. Some MDC activists attributed this early unity to the exceptional character of the 2000 campaign, which party aspirants and activists saw as historic. For instance, trade unionist Lucia Matibenga, who held a position on the NEC and stood in a rural constituency in Midlands, noted in 2003:

> The interim structures would work things out without it reaching the point of a fight. But now things have changed, and there are always protests and people saying they will fight and get appointed to the position no matter what. I think at the time there was real excitement, there was a feeling that it was a revolution, so the structures solved problems easily.[7]

Other evidence suggests that nominations may have been more contentious than Matibenga and other party leaders suggested. In the Harare urban constituencies, for instance, there was an average of eight candidates per constituency.[8] But disagreements rarely became public. Where defections from the party occurred or were threatened, they were quickly suppressed. There were, for instance, three MDC members in 2000 who lost their candidacy bids and announced that they would contest the seats as independent candidates. After a meeting with MDC National Chairman Isaac Matongo, the three announced that they were withdrawing their bids and again backing the MDC.[9] There were clear losses during the primary stage: both Learnmore Jongwe, a student leader who became the party spokesperson and MDC MP for Kuwadzana, and trade unionist Pauline Gwanyanya were initially interested in contesting the Harare Central seat.[10] After the local structures decided on advancing Catholic Commission for Justice and Peace (CCJP) leader Michael Auret for the seat, both Jongwe and Gwanyanya contested and won Harare seats that were considered less certain victories for the party. For prominent party officials like Jongwe and Gwanyanya, a loss in one constituency at the primary stage would typically result in placement elsewhere. In several instances, however, prominent members chose to contest seats in rural areas, in a risky attempt to give the party a foothold in rural areas. For instance, AWC (Association of Women's Clubs) leader Sekai Holland lost

---

[7] Interview, July 30, 2003; also, interviews with Morgan Tsvangirai, December 12, 2002, and Ian Makone, August 13, 2003.

[8] *Mirror*, March 24, 2000; interviews with MDC MPs and activists, 2002–3.

[9] *Mirror*, June 24, 2000.

[10] *Standard*, April 17, 2000.

her contest in the rural constituency of Mberengwa East; MDC Deputy Secretary-General Gift Chimanikire lost the rural Guruve South seat; Lucia Matibenga, who headed the powerful Commercial Workers Union, similarly lost her Shurugwi seat. Most notably, MDC President and former ZCTU Secretary-General Morgan Tsvangirai lost a hard and violent campaign in Buhera North. Members of the national leadership put aside their own personal interest – and the salaries they would have gained if they had contested urban constituencies – in order to further party-building. There are striking contrasts between this kind of electoral strategy and those that characterize the more personalized opposition parties we find in most African countries.

In terms of the structures of the MDC, the party relied overwhelmingly on the organizational resources of the ZCTU. Trade union district committees were used to recruit branch members and plan meetings and rallies nation-wide, and trade unionists reported that they often sold MDC membership cards from their desks or did other party-organizing activities while in the workplace.[11] The MDC also borrowed the organizational capacity of other members of the NCA, such as the nationwide network of the AWC. In urban areas, the local branches of the Combined Harare Residents Association and other residents' associations provided the MDC with many of its party orga-nizers and activists, who then traveled to rural areas during the 2000 election campaign or served as campaign workers for various MDC MPs.[12] Because of high rates of unemployment in Zimbabwe, urban youths, many of whom were well educated, were often willing to work for civil society organizations and the MDC without pay, in hopes that this would translate into some formal position. In high-density suburbs, young men between the ages of 18 and 22 – many of whom were school-leavers or university graduates – became involved with the residents' associations or with other civil society organizations in the late 1990s. Some of these youths had been politicized through student politics; others became supporters of the ZCTU after the national stayaways of 1997 and 1998. In later periods, taking advantage of urban–rural linkages, many of these youths shuttled back and forth between rural areas and Harare on behalf of the MDC. At meetings during the violent 2002 rural district council elections, for instance, urban youths were a very visible presence at report-backs and meetings in Harare, and they carried back information from the rural areas on violent confrontations at nominations courts.[13]

---

[11] Interviews with Miriam Chikamba, March 7, 2003; Gideon Shoko, March 15, 2003.

[12] Interviews with Last Maengehama, July 28, 2003; Dennis Murira, October 22 and 30, 2002; Maxwell Sangweume, August 19, 2002; Taona Mwanyisa, October 4, 2002. Field notes, 2002–3.

[13] Field notes and anonymous interviews, September–December 2002. For more on the rural district council elections, see ZESN (2002).

In western Zimbabwe, the Organisation of Rural Associations for Progress (ORAP) likely played a significant role in mobilizing MDC voters, though it is not mentioned by scholars who were conducting fieldwork in Matabeleland during the 2000 campaign (Alexander and McGregor 2001). In 2002 and 2003, ORAP members were consistently mentioned as MDC activists and supporters by grassroots organizers, civil society figures, and MDC party officials in interviews in Harare, Gweru, and Bulawayo. ORAP would have had formidable reach. In early 1991, ORAP already had more than 300,000 members (Sibanda 2002: 321), roughly double the size of the ZCTU. By 2000, it had 100 full-time staff.[14] ORAP's structure was hierarchical, like the ZCTU's, but it also allowed for participatory decision-making at the grassroots level, which encouraged strong identification with the organization among members (ORAP 1987; Hughes 1989: 64–73; also, Nyoni 1987). The MDC's relationship with ORAP, however, was never as clear-cut as it was with NCA partners. The national leadership of ORAP itself never directly supported the ZCTU, the MDC, or their demands; instead, the use of the organization's grassroots structures proceeded through pathways that largely circumvented the national leadership of the organization.[15] As mentioned in Chapter 6, the ZCTU conducted meetings at ORAP district branches prior to the Working People's Convention, and several ORAP organizers attended the Convention as delegates. After the Convention, report-back meetings were held in Matabeleland North and South. The report-backs were attended by between twenty-five and forty village organizers each, and the meetings' recommendations consistently stressed support for the new party and the desire for closer contact with the ZCTU. The recommendations of the Esigodidi Mzingwane District (Matabeleland South) are somewhat typical:

> People must be brave to vote for the person they want, also that this is the time to change the leaders at top levels. Also that people are now waiting for a go ahead from the new party they want, which is ZCTU, to tell them to start organising the whole district ... We have to work with the ZCTU closer to people such as one [ZCTU member] at Esigodini. If MDC comes to Nswazi, they must be escorted by ZCTU so that we know who they are also the message is to be given to Mr J. Ndlovu the Organiser.[16]

The mentions here of the loyalties of ORAP and urban youths are meant to underline a larger point. The labor structures of the ZCTU did not merely

---

[14] Interview with Themba Ndiweni, March 6, 2003.

[15] The national leadership of the organization repeatedly stressed its non-partisan nature, and Sithembiso Nyoni, one of ORAP's founders, was a ZANU-PF minister. Interview with Themba Ndiweni, March 6, 2003.

[16] See reports of ORAP Post-Convention Report Back Meetings, reprinted in ZCTU (2000: 135–50).

provide a focal point for voters. Instead, there was widespread identification with the ZCTU by diverse constituencies prior to the MDC's launch.

In the previous pages, I have stressed the organizational aspects of MDC party-building. The alliances with civil society organizations, the process of grassroots candidate selection, and the exclusion of ZANU-PF moderates all played an important role in building a rooted and well-disciplined party. These factors were also important in holding together the party's vote base. In the next section, I will briefly consider how the MDC performed in the parliamentary elections from 2000 to 2008. The section provides more evidence that the MDC's organizational cohesion in the midst of repression constitutes a "puzzle." The rest of the chapter will then reflect on how the MDC managed this feat. It is in this latter section that I will discuss state-sponsored violence in greater detail.

PATTERNS OF ELECTORAL SUPPORT

In the June 2000 parliamentary elections, the MDC ran candidates in all 120 constituencies. It won fifty-seven of these seats, and it captured 47 percent of the national vote. Support was concentrated in the urban provinces of Harare and Bulawayo and the two Matabeleland provinces of western Zimbabwe, but the party also won more than 30 percent of the provincial vote in four of Zimbabwe's remaining six provinces. Because its support was greatest in urban areas and in the Western provinces where most ethnic Ndebele live, the MDC has sometimes been popularly described as an urban and ethnic party with minimal appeal to rural Shona, the country's other main ethnic group. The 2000 election results, and the results in subsequent local and rural district council elections, belie this claim. The party's vote was concentrated in what were considered its regional strongholds, but the MDC also won a significant number of rural votes outside of Matabeland. It captured several rural seats in Manicaland, and it won more than 30 percent of the vote in a large number of rural constituencies, including those in ZANU-PF "no-go" zones in the Mashonaland provinces. In subsequent election rounds, the MDC maintained this vote base and geographic reach, and it also won a number of rural district council seats in 2002 elections. Most notably, the opposition vote did not significantly fragment until the 2008 elections. Even in those elections, levels of vote fragmentation remained well below those in other African first-past-the-post systems, including Zambia and Kenya (Figure 7.1).

The MDC's electoral fortunes suffered in the 2005 parliamentary elections: it lost sixteen of its parliamentary seats, and it received about 130,000 fewer votes than it had in 2000. These results should not, however, be interpreted as a significant erosion of MDC support or a strengthening of ZANU-PF, as the

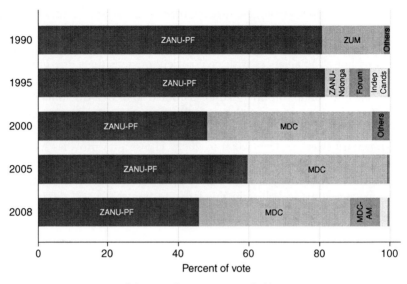

Fig. 7.1. Fragmentation of the Popular Vote in Zimbabwe, 1990–2008

released official results are unlikely to be a fair representation of voting. In addition to the array of informal tools used by the ruling party to manipulate the vote, most notably the politicization of emergency food aid, vote-rigging was prevalent in 2005.[17] Large numbers of MDC voters were either turned away at the polls or were forced to stand in long lines due to the under-provision of polling stations in areas of opposition support. If one looks closely at the 2005 constituency-level returns, however, the MDC significantly improved its performance in a number of rural constituencies where it had previously been uncompetitive. In some of these – for instance, Gutu South in Masvingo and Chipinge South in Manicaland – the party doubled or more the number of votes it received, even though it was still not within striking distance of winning these seats. The majority of the party's lost votes occurred in constituencies where it had previously had strong levels of support, which suggests that apathy or election rigging may have kept many MDC supporters away from the polls.

---

[17] See MDC (2005), ZESN (2005: 45–7), Crisis (2005), and, especially, the Sokwanele blog post, "What happened on Thursday night: an account of how ZANU-PF rigged the parliamentary elections," April 5, 2005 (available at www.sokwanele.com). Observer reports compiled by the African Union and the Southern African Development Community are considered biased in favor of the ruling party; other observers were barred. The political use of food began long before the 2005 elections. For an analysis of how partisanship was used to limit the access of Zimbabweans to food, see HRW (2003a).

In the harmonized parliamentary and presidential elections of 2008, the main MDC faction's inroads into rural areas outside Matabeleland were significantly widened.[18] In areas where ZANU-PF candidates had won by 65 or 70 percent of the vote in 2000 and 2005, the MDC either won seats or came within small margins of victory. The elections signaled a significant erosion of ZANU-PF's popular support, but they were not an unmitigated success for the MDC. Due to a split within the party, briefly addressed below, two factions of the MDC ran candidates against one another. Even though the larger faction, under Tsvangirai's leadership, retained the bulk of the party's structures and its electoral base, the splitting of the vote across two factions cost the party at least eight of 210 seats. More importantly, it cost the party the presidency.[19] Tsvangirai once again stood as the presidential candidate of the MDC's main faction, but he split the opposition vote with an independent candidate who had been endorsed by the MDC's splinter faction. The result triggered a run-off, as the state claimed that neither Mugabe nor Tsvangirai won 50 percent of the votes cast. In the run-up to the run-off, state security forces, including the military, launched a campaign of violence nationwide. In the assessment of many observers, MDC local party structures were largely destroyed during the three months between the first round of elections and the presidential run-off (HRW 2008; Solidarity Peace Trust 2008).

The MDC's most significant accomplishment from 2000 to 2008 – and an indication of the party's organizational strength – was its ability to discipline the opposition vote. In all three elections, ZANU-PF and the MDC together monopolized the parliamentary vote. In 2000, other opposition parties and independent candidates accounted for a mere 5 percent of total votes; in 2005, these candidates won less than 1 percent. In order to give the reader a sense of how fragmentation of the vote changed over election rounds, Figure 7.2 plots the constituency-level fragmentation of the vote against the share of the vote won by ZANU-PF in each of these constituencies. The measure of fragmentation used is the effective number of parties at the constituency level.[20] Unlike the total number of parties running candidates, or the

---

[18] See, for instance, "Rural areas turn their backs on Mugabe," *IRIN News*, March 31, 2008 (www.irinnews.org).

[19] Civil society organizations spearheaded, though the use of cell phones, a parallel vote tabulation effort in the 2008 elections that made the count fairly reliable. The MDC's candidate, Morgan Tsvangirai, won 47.9 percent of the popular vote against President Robert Mugabe's 43.2 percent. Former government minister Simba Makoni won the remaining 8.3 percent of the vote. Even though Makoni endorsed Tsvangirai in the subsequent presidential run-off, it was too late. Severe state repression, orchestrated by the military, destroyed the MDC's party structures and its ability to campaign. Tsvangirai announced the party's withdrawal from the run-off one week before it was scheduled to occur. For more on the elections and on the brutal campaign of state violence between the two election rounds, see Alexander and Tendi (2008).

[20] This is calculated as the inverse of the sum of squares of each party's proportion of votes received. The effective number of electoral parties is typically calculated at the national level.

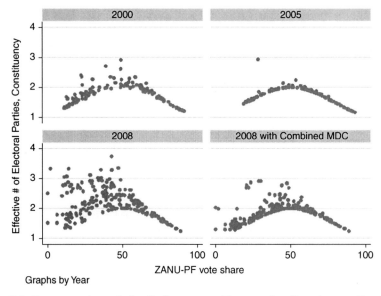

Fig. 7.2. Fragmentation of the Parliamentary Vote at the Constituency Level in Zimbabwe, 2000–8

proportion of the vote received by the ruling party, the effective number of parties gives us a sense of how coordinated voting was around the main parties' candidates. In a disciplined two-party system, we would expect to see a curve fairly similar to that in Figure 7.2 for the 2000 election. As the ruling party's percentage of the vote rises, the effective number of parties falls to one, indicating that the ruling party captures nearly all votes. In competitive constituencies, measures of fragmentation near two indicate that two parties split the vote somewhat evenly; in constituencies where the ruling party did poorly, the effective number of parties again approaches one, as a single opposition party captures the bulk of the vote.

After 2000, the MDC actually increased the level of cohesion in its vote base, save for the single exception of Tsholotsho, where a former ZANU-PF minister ran and won the seat as an independent candidate. In 2008, however, we do see a significant disordering of the opposition landscape, signaled by

Calculating the measure at the constituency level gives us a more precise picture of the degree of vote coordination in different areas of the country, especially in countries where party support may clump on regional or ethnic lines.

the number of constituencies in which both opposition support and the effective number of parties were high. This higher level of constituency-level fragmentation was due almost entirely to competition between the two MDC factions. When compared to Zambia or Kenya, countries in which opposition parties are volatile and highly fragmented, the Zimbabwean party system still displays very low levels of fragmentation. The split within the MDC did not result in the launching of multiple third parties, nor did voters lose their confidence in MDC candidates, though they disagreed over which faction represented the "true" MDC. In 2008, only two former MDC candidates chose to run as independents: both won only a few hundred votes and performed no better than other independents.[21] The rest stood as MDC-Mutambara or MDC-Tsvangirai candidates, or they abided by primary losses and did not stand. In the end, independent and opposition candidates won less than 3 percent of the votes cast. In Figure 7.2, the fourth graph presents the 2008 constituency-level fragmentation had the two MDC factions contested as a single party. This demonstrates the degree to which the Tsvangirai and Arthur Mutambara factions of the MDC continued to dominate the opposition landscape.

Before examining how vote cohesion was connected to organizational party-building and party polarization, let me briefly address the common claim that the MDC's patters of electoral support suggest an ethnic base to the party. MDC campaigns have differed in areas that are dominated by either the Ndebele or the Shona, the two major ethnic groups in Zimbabwe. In their excellent analysis of the 2000 election campaign in Ndebele-dominated western Zimbabwe, for instance, Alexander and McGregor point out that the MDC consciously evoked memories of the region's earlier opposition party, Joshua Nkomo's ZAPU, which merged with ZANU-PF in 1987 (Alexander and McGregor 2001: 524–6). MDC campaigns in Bulawayo, Zimbabwe's second city, have also played on the marginalization of the Ndebele in terms of national development plans and social spending. Differences in party appeals, however, do not indicate an underlying ethnic base to the party. It is worth noting again that the MDC ran candidates in all areas of the country from 2000 to 2005, for both national and local elections. Since the split, the Tsvangirai-led main faction has continued to wage similarly national campaigns, and the smaller faction has only been marginally less national in its campaigns.[22] This is a sharp contrast to opposition parties in Kenya, for instance, where parties run far fewer candidates outside the ethnic zones of their leaders.

---

[21] One of the two, sitting MP Timothy Mubawu, had been implicated in the intra-party violence mentioned below, and he had been suspended from the party for comments made in Parliament that expressed opposition to legislation that the MDC endorsed.

[22] In the 2008 elections, the MDC faction led by Arthur Mutambara (the smaller faction) ran only 152 candidates for the 210 constituencies that make up the recently expanded House of Assembly, while the larger MDC ran candidates in 200 constituencies.

More persuasively, following the factional division, voter support did not break in ways that would support an "ethnic party" interpretation. In 2005, most of the Ndebele or western Zimbabwean members of the MDC NEC crossed to the newly founded faction, which was subsequently headed by expatriate academic Arthur Mutambara (MDC-AM). Rather than following these leaders, large proportions of MDC voters in Matabeleland continued to vote for the Shona-led main MDC faction (MDC-Tsvangirai). Several Ndebele MPs who defected from the main faction were punished by their home constituencies and lost their seats to newcomers who ran on the main faction's ticket. These included former MDC Secretary-General Welshman Ncube and the party's founding Vice President Gibson Sibanda, who held top leadership positions within the new party faction. Secondly, as mentioned above, the MDC has consistently won more than 25 percent of the vote in the majority of constituencies nationwide, despite very real constraints on its ability to campaign. Most rural Shona voters have little access to independent newspapers or other sources of political information, and the state-owned media – to which they do have access – regularly depicts the MDC as a Ndebele party or as "British-led." Despite this, rural Shona voters have voted for the MDC in increasingly large numbers. The MDC's ability to coordinate a large cross-ethnic constituency is directly related to the organizational structures and identity appeals that the party's social movement partners made even before the party's launch. The construction and reinforcement of party-based polarization also played a role in holding both ZANU-PF and the MDC together. State-sponsored violence played an important role in the reinforcement of this party divide. It is to the effects of violence on party organization that we will now turn.

VIOLENCE AND POLARIZATION

Immediately after the February 2000 referendum, invasions of white-owned commercial farms began. In the last weekend of February 2000, groups of peasants and war veterans, some numbering up to 400, invaded commercial farms all over Zimbabwe, most of which were owned by white farmers. In the weeks after the referendum, "war veterans were involved in an extensive outreach programme in their local areas, recruiting people to go and occupy farms" (Marongwe 2003: 178). So-called "mobilization committees" called meetings on farms and in communal areas, told crowds that invasions had government backing, and then arranged the date and gathering point for the occupation of a given farm before moving on (Marongwe 2003: 179). The ruling party denied any involvement in the land invasions, saying that they were spontaneous grassroots responses to land hunger. As the invasions continued, however, these statements became less credible. Analyses of the political violence in 2000 underline the intimate links between farm invasions, ZANU-PF MPs, and local party structures (HRW 2002; Amani Trust 2002). In 2000 interviews, some war veterans indicated that they had received direction from the national leadership of the Zimbabwe Liberation War Veterans Association (ZLWVA) about which farms to occupy (Alexander and McGregor 2001: 511, ftnt 2). The ruling party provided ZW$20 million (US$500,000) to the ZLWVA to campaign for the party in the upcoming election, which allowed the association to pay ruling party youths and war veterans to participate in the farm invasions (Laakso 2002: 448). War veterans received food and other support from the Association, including weekly allowances, when they were resident on occupied farms (Marongwe 2003: 169).

By the end of March 2000, the Commercial Farmers Union (CFU) reported that there had been 731 invasions so far, a large proportion of which occurred in the ZANU-PF heartlands of Mashonaland Central (172) and Mashonaland East (179).[23] There was a partisan cast to the farm invasions. After the MDC's launch, state television had broadcast footage of white commercial farmers handing donations to MDC officials. During the referendum campaign, the NCA had often held meetings on commercial farms, and commercial farmworkers were seen as a potential vote bank for the MDC (Rutherford 2008: 89–90). Internal ZNLWVA documents suggest that commercial farmers' political affiliations were sometimes involved in the selection of farm targets: one occupied farmer allegedly "used his farm for military training of MDC supporters under the guise of training farm guards"; another "urged his workers to attend MDC rallies"; yet another also "contributed to the military training of MDC supporters" (Marongwe 2003: 176). The majority of farm invaders likely did not view the occupations primarily through the lens of party affiliation. Popular invasions of commercial farms had occurred in Zimbabwe throughout the 1990s (Moyo 2001), and farms were typically targeted because of their proximity to communal areas, a history of poor relations between farmers and nearby residents, or underutilization of farmland.

Violence began on the commercial farms, but it did not remain isolated on the farms. In terms of interactions between ZANU-PF and MDC activists, the 2000 parliamentary election campaign was characterized by lower levels of organization and coordination of violence than in subsequent elections. During the 2000 campaign, groups of MDC and ZANU-PF party supporters routinely clashed in violent scuffles, often as they traveled to or from rallies or other party meetings. Participants were usually armed only with sticks or iron bars and were often evenly matched. There were also more serious attacks on MDC activists, party headquarters, and those presumed to be MDC supporters,

---

[23] *The Farmer*, March 30, 2000.

notably teachers. Overall, approximately 12,000 MDC supporters fled from the rural areas into the towns during the election period, bringing with them stories of property destruction, arson, beatings, and torture.[24] In later periods, when ZANU-PF militia were trained and strategically deployed by party leaders, the degree of coordination increased. By 2002, violence little resembled the disorganized and opportunistic patterns of conflict that Tilly terms "violent brawls"; instead, patterns of violence reflected the high levels of coordination and salience that he associates with "coordinated destruction" (Tilly 2003b). It was no longer the accidental encounter with MDC activists that provoked violence; instead, there was a systematic seeking-out of political activists, teachers, and any other individual who was perceived to be an MDC member. The actual perpetrators of violence were also more tightly organized by the presidential elections of 2002. The government established permanent training bases for what became known as "Green Bombers," a paid and trained ruling party youth militia known for its green uniforms. At these bases, recruits received instruction in torture techniques, interrogated and beat suspected opposition supporters, and were deployed to outlying areas depending on by-election schedules (Reeler 2003).

In addition to violence, the ruling party used other means to increase the salience of partisan affiliation. The state media reframed the debate between the ruling party and the MDC in the language of nationalism and betrayal, with continual references to Zimbabwe's liberation war. Ruling party rhetoric presented ZANU-PF as the sole legitimate representative of the nationalist legacy, and it painted the opposition as unpatriotic at best and an operative of the British government at worst (see Chikwanha et al. 2004; Ranger 2004). Early attacks began with articles in the government newspapers about "unholy alliances" between white employers and black trade unionists. In the run-up to the referendum, these attacks escalated, as demonstrated by a Constitutional Commission advertisement that ran in *The Herald* shortly before the referendum. Over a photo of two whites wearing "Vote No" T-shirts, the caption read:

> What are they up to? Vote Yes and show them the way! Don't follow them back to the dark past when they were queens and kings while you suffered. Send a clear message to them by voting 'yes' and take control of your destiny today and forever.[25]

Attacks on urban dwellers ("totemless individuals," "little better than cats and dogs") remained muted until after the referendum. By the time of the 2002 presidential elections, government-controlled radio continuously broadcast patriotic songs glorifying the violent seizures of commercial farms. In 2002

---

[24] The estimate for the number displaced is from an interview with an Amani Trust official, March 2003.

[25] *The Farmer* (Harare), February 17, 2000.

and 2003, the country's one independent television station was shut down, and the remaining Zimbabwe Broadcasting Corporation (ZBC) channel devoted ever-larger portions of its airtime to talk shows on the liberation war and to history programs on European colonialism in Zimbabwe and elsewhere. Nightly news programs often included reports on MDC "terrorist" actions and sabotage, which journalists presented as part of a neo-imperialist plot orchestrated by Great Britain.

What were the aims of this campaign of violent polarization? Did the ruling party in Zimbabwe use violence to hold onto tenuous "battleground" constituencies, as its counterpart in Kenya did? Was violence intended to dissuade MDC voters from voting, or was it directed at an altogether different constituency? In order to look at how violence was used to achieve particular political aims, it is necessary to look at patterns in its geographic dispersion and timing. Unfortunately, there are several problems with the aggregate data on political violence in Zimbabwe for this early period of party interaction (2000–3) that make analysis difficult. First of all, violent episodes were only sporadically reported with sufficient detail to establish where violence occurred, the degree to which it was organized, and the number of victims. Secondly, the data that exists was drawn largely from testimonies collected from victims by Amani Trust, an organization that provided medical treatment, and the Zimbabwe Community Development Trust (ZCDT). The Zimbabwe Human Rights NGO Forum collected these testimonies and also included incidents of violence reported in the press, a practice that is deeply flawed, in its monthly tabulations. Victim testimonies were only taken at offices in Harare and the six other urban centers in which either Amani or ZCDT had offices; consequently, incidents were reported only if the victim was willing and able to travel to these offices.[26] Most victims found their own way to the offices, but a significant number were ferried by their former (white farmer) employers or by the MDC.[27] In this data, there were occasionally clusters of well-documented cases of political violence in one or two constituencies.[28] Because civil society and donor agencies had only sporadic access to large portions of the country

---

[26] NGOs provided food and other assistance to victims of political violence and displacement; however, in many cases, such a trip was necessarily one-way. Victims, including those who have no ties to the opposition party, were typically not welcomed back once they left their home areas.

[27] Interviews with victims of political torture on behalf of Human Rights Watch, March 2003.

[28] A very good case of this is found in a February 2002 report by the Zimbabwe Human Rights NGO Forum, which contains an annex listing reports of militia bases in operation nationwide. These reports rarely list any details about how many individuals were based at particular sites, how long they had been there, etc. Suddenly, in one report and solely for the province of Bulawayo (the second largest city), there is a list of bases with details on how many individuals are at each base, whether they are youths or war vets, etc. It is easy to imagine this list the work of a single, enthusiastic activist. The point is that there is no information given on how many reports are used to establish presence of a base, how information is compiled, or the number of substantiating reports used.

in 2000–3, it is difficult to tell whether these clusters are an artifact of data collection or reflections of a more consistent, sustained pattern of high political violence in particular constituencies. Finally, as with activists' estimates of meeting attendance or their assessments of their own role in decision-making, self-reporting is prone to exaggeration and misrepresentation. The essential point here is that there do not exist clear and reliable data on patterns of violence in Zimbabwe during this period.

Some generalizations can still be made about the geographic distribution and severity of violence from place to place. If we assume a consistent bias in the data due to collection problems, we would expect the number of violent incidents in ZANU-PF strongholds to be grossly underestimated and the scale and intensity of violence in urban, predominantly MDC areas to be over-stated.[29] Instead, all available data suggests that *violence was more serious and more systematically organized in ZANU-PF strongholds.* Mashonaland Central and Mashonaland East, the two provinces that polled the greatest "yes" (pro-government) votes during the 2000 referendum, accounted for the bulk of the collected reports of political violence in the run-up to the 2000 parliamentary elections. This level of violence was sustained in subsequent years. Within provinces, the most violent constituencies were usually those that voted strongly in favor of the government's proposed constitution; these constituencies also polled unusually low levels of support for the MDC in 2000. Since the referendum preceded political violence, the low MDC vote cannot be attributed to the out-migration or successful intimidation of likely MDC voters. In one of the most violent constituencies in the country, Mount Darwin, 80.5 percent of the population voted in favor of the government constitution, and only 9 percent voted for the MDC in the 2000 parliamentary elections. Mudzi and Mutoko, among the most violent constituencies in Mashonaland East, polled the lowest levels of opposition support in the province (22 and 18 percent voting "no" in the referendum, only 7.8 and 5.6 percent voting for the MDC in the parliamentary elections). The association was equally strong in Mashonaland Central, where the most violent constituency similarly polled the lowest level of opposition support, and valid to a lesser extent in provinces that experienced lower levels of violence overall.[30]

---

[29] That is, victims in ZANU-PF areas would be more likely to be intimidated from reporting the violence, either to civil society organizations or the police, and they would be less likely to travel to urban areas to file testimonials.

[30] The assertions about concentrations of violence across constituencies are based largely on the reports of violence contained in the monthly reports of the Zimbabwe Human Rights NGO Forum and on the lists of alleged perpetrators sometimes contained in the organization's special reports (which list the constituencies in which perpetrators are active). This data roughly concurs with data provided to me by the MDC and with ruling party leaders' own assessments of "hot spots" provided during interviews.

Why would violence be more intense in the areas where the MDC was least competitive? To this point, political scientists have often assumed that incumbents use violence to intimidate those who might potentially vote for the opposition, or that violence is aimed at changing electoral geography by forcing out-migration of opposition supporters. In some countries at some times, this seems accurate. In Kenya, for instance, political violence was intended to evict suspect ethnic groups in order to deliver electorally close constituencies to the ruling party. In Zimbabwe, political violence served other purposes. As I argue in greater detail elsewhere, ZANU-PF concentrated violent campaigns in its strongholds not to swing voting in those areas but to rebuild the teetering cohesion of its own party organization (LeBas 2006). Prior to state-sponsored violence, moderate ZANU-PF MPs and members of the Central Committee had sometimes advocated negotiation with the NCA, compromise on constitutional reform, or even agreement on electoral provisions demanded by the MDC. Others called for the decentralization of party power. As violence increased, these signs of internal disagreement disappeared. Hardliners seized control over local party structures, silenced moderates at the national level, and gradually built tighter command-and-control over ZANU-PF MPs, governors, and local party activists.

The referendum results were important in explaining this change in party governance. In some constituencies, the number of registered party members exceeded the number who had voted "yes" in the constitutional referendum, and there was a suspicion that local party leaders and traditional chiefs had not campaigned for the proposed constitution.[31] ZANU-PF therefore initiated an internal party audit, which was intended to purge moderates and supporters of regional leadership and replace them with party activists who had tighter links to the national party leadership. Some ruling party MPs felt that those in control of violence specialists were using the implicit threat of violence to enforce discipline and expand their personal control over the party; others simply noted the slow consolidation of power within the party by those either concretely linked to violence or based in violent constituencies.[32] One MP described in 2003 how he routinely encountered roadblocks manned by youth militia on one of the major roads in his constituency. When he instructed the police to dismantle the roadblocks and arrest the youth militia, he received a telephone call from a member of the Politburo asking him to release "his boys" from police custody and "just generally reminding me who was in charge of my constituency."[33] Rather

---

[31] Interview with Chen Chimutengwende, November 14, 2002; field notes October and November 2002.

[32] Interviews and informal conversations with ZANU-PF MPs and former party officials, August 2002, October–November 2002, April–May 2003.

[33] Interview with anonymous ZANU-PF MP, May 2003.

than being solely focused on the MDC and its supporters, violence was often used by particular ZANU-PF politicians to expand their control over party decision-making, threaten those they suspected of opposing the centralization of party, and pursue specialized, somewhat reactionary ideological agendas.

THE CLOSURE OF POLITICAL SPACE

Violence was used to build a stronger, more cohesive ZANU-PF, but violence and repression had equally significant effects on MDC party structures and supporters nationwide. As mentioned earlier, diverse constituencies that were considered MDC supporters were driven from rural areas from 2000 onward. Teachers were the most visibly affected group. The labor movement was also a target of ZANU-PF militants, as ZANU-PF activists and youths under the leadership of war veteran Joseph Chinotimba invaded factories and demanded workers disaffiliate from the ZCTU. During this period of factory invasions, Chinotimba and his supporters resuscitated the defunct Zimbabwe Federation of Trade Unions (ZFTU), announcing that it would serve as a "patriotic" labor alternative to the ZCTU.[34] Though the ZFTU remained marginal, seeming to exist only in the pages of the state-run *Herald* newspaper,[35] its formation is representative of the reconstitution of civic space into partisan blocks over the course of 2001–3. A similar process of partisan-fueled splitting occurred within the Zimbabwe Teachers Association (ZIMTA), as teachers disgruntled with the association's allegedly pro-government orientation formed a rival teachers' union, the Progressive Teachers Union of Zimbabwe (PTUZ), which affiliated to the ZCTU.[36] Rural district councils and their workers were also targeted for their presumed disloyalty to the ruling party, an assault that peaked in 2001 and 2002. As McGregor notes, at the same time as the farm invasions, ZANU-PF launched a "parallel and largely unnoticed assault on the institutions of the local state, their procedures, their personnel and their day-to-day running, which the police did nothing to stop" (McGregor 2002: 17; also, Hammar 2003). These attacks on civil servants were the beginning of a slow hollowing-out of state capacity, which had previously been much higher

[34] Unionists and other Zimbabweans regularly mentioned that the ZFTU received a government budget, something that the ZCTU – even during its early days – never had access to. There was no means of confirming whether the ZFTU actually received funding from ZANU-PF or the state.
[35] Some unionists did report disruption and the formation of splinter unions, but these were relatively small and did not substantially affect the membership base of the ZCTU. Interviews with Leonard Gwenzi, September 23, 2002; James Gumbi, July 14, 2005.
[36] Interview with Raymond Majongwe, July 14, 2005, also see *Zimbabwe Independent*, September 15, 2000.

in Zimbabwe than in other African states. Attacks on local government workers, ZCTU members and teachers were often linked to the election calendar, as they escalated in areas prior to parliamentary elections or other local government elections. But repression and violence were not deployed simply to serve electoral aims: teachers and public sector workers were also targeted in advance of strike actions.[37] Overall, ZANU-PF's actions reflected a sorting of groups into loyal and disloyal categories, a process that would merely intensify over the following years.

The attacks on the rural district councils were part of a larger dismantling of the political space that had allowed the MDC's vibrant civil society base to emerge. For instance, the Zimbabwean judiciary had been an important neutral ground in the 1990s, and its decisions had guarded the rights of civil society organizations and trade unions throughout the decade. Even in 2000 and 2001, the judiciary served as the last best check on the ruling party's drift toward authoritarianism. In 2000, the High Court ruled that the government's plan to seize commercial farms without compensation was unconstitutional; in 2000 and 2001, the judiciary ruled against state searches, detentions, and bans on demonstrations, and the High Court refused to postpone the hearing of MDC election challenges. Frustrated with these "pro-opposition" verdicts, the government intensified a campaign of intimidation against the judiciary and forced several justices, including the Chief Justice of the country's Supreme Court, to resign.[38] Among the most blatant of these episodes was the thronging of the High Court by war veterans in January 2001, after which the Justice Minister informed High Court judges that the government could not ensure their personal security, given popular sentiment about Court rulings.

In addition to these informal assaults, the state passed new legislation that seriously restricted civil and political rights. A new Public Order and Security Act (POSA) went into effect at the end of January 2002, over the objections of MDC MPs.[39] POSA made statements intended to "undermine confidence" in the institutions of government punishable by imprisonment of up to five years. The law also granted the police extensive powers to restrict public meetings and demonstrations. The police could prohibit any meeting that they felt might lead to public disorder, a decision that was not subject to appeal. Police

---

[37] *Zimbabwe Independent*, March 2, 2001; *Financial Gazette*, January 25, 2001.

[38] *Financial Gazette*, January 17, 2001; *Zimbabwe Independent*, February 17, 2001; *The Herald*, February 13, 2001; *MMPZ Media Update*, January 22–29, 2001; and January 29 – February 4, 2001. The government repeatedly attacked individual judges and the judiciary as a whole in the state-owned press and in public statements. In January 2001, ZANU-PF MPs threatened to introduce legislation that would allow cabinet ministers to impeach judges. Over the course of 2001 and 2002, judges and magistrates resigned, and the courts increasingly began to rule in favor of the government.

[39] For more on the content of these acts and their application, see Legal Resources Foundation, "Justice in Zimbabwe," WO 41/84, September 30, 2002; also, Feltoe (2002).

were also entitled to ban all demonstrations in a particular area for up to a month, if it was felt that these events would lead to public disorder of violence. From 2002 onward, POSA was repeatedly invoked to justify bans on MDC meetings and rallies, mass detentions without charge, and the arrest of sitting MDC MPs.[40] Another piece of legislation, the Access to Information and Protection of Privacy Act (AIPPA), required journalists to be approved and registered by the government-appointed Media and Information Commission, and it made publication of "falsehoods" punishable by jail-time. Together, these two pieces of legislation restricted civil and political liberties and the ability of civil society organizations, independent newspapers, and the MDC to operate freely.

ZANU-PF also directly targeted organizations and sectors of civil society that were considered support bases for the MDC. Polarization therefore came to reshape civil society as well, and the period 2000–3 resulted in a progressive politicization of all realms of associational and civic life in Zimbabwe. Where party affiliation was not chosen by civil society organizations, it was imposed. NGOs that documented human rights violations – or those that provided assistance and medical care to victims – were particularly targeted. The government described human rights NGOs as "hatcheries of opposition" in the state press, and it increasingly restricted their operations in the run-up and aftermath of the March 2002 presidential elections. The Amani Trust, one of Zimbabwe's oldest and most respected human rights organizations, is a case in point. Amani's primary activity was providing medical assistance to MDC activists and other victims of political violence: it established a system of safe houses for those displaced by political violence, and it also collected affidavits from victims for use in legal cases.[41] In 2002, after the organization released reports that provided medical evidence of torture and rape by ZANU-PF militia, Amani's director was arrested, only to be released later without charge. In November 2002, the government announced that Amani was operating illegally and said that staff could be arrested at any time; later that month, Amani was forced to close its Harare offices.[42] Throughout 2003, as

---

[40] The best analysis of arrests remains the excellent IJR and SPZ (2006). Of the nearly 2,000 arrests on which the report is based, the state obtained convictions in only 1.5 percent of cases, though nearly a third of those arrested were tortured during detention. As the Zimbabwe Human Rights NGO Forum points out in a 2002 report, both POSA and AIPPA were applied in a partisan fashion, and POSA was often applied retrospectively in order to charge MDC MPs for statements critical of ZANU-PF Ministers (ZHRNF 2002). Also, interviews with Albert Musaruwa, March 24, 2003; Geoff Feltoe, April 1, 2003.

[41] Interview with Amani Trust official, March 2003; field notes, March and April 2003. In the state-owned press, the safe houses were described as "killer houses" that sheltered MDC "terrorists" who were responsible for the torture of ZANU-PF supporters. For a statement on these press attacks, see "Statement by Mashonaland Trustees of Amani," press release, January 28, 2002 (available at www.kubatana.net).

[42] *The Herald*, November 14, 2002; see also, "Amani Trust a Legal Entity," Amani Trust press release, November 15, 2002.

government repression intensified, the organization operated largely under-ground.[43] As it did with Amani, the government regularly detained civil rights activists under POSA, only to subsequently release them without charge. Arbitrary detention was used to harass and bankrupt civil society organiza-tions, lawyers, and journalists, especially from 2002 to 2005. By 2003, the problem had reached such proportions that the Zimbabwe Lawyers for Human Rights established an emergency fund that would allow the "rapid reaction" provision of legal services to human rights activists.[44] Outside the human rights sector, the government clamped down on organizations involved in food distribution using similar rhetoric and tactics. In 2002, when ORAP was serving as one of the World Food Program's (WFP) im-plementing partners, ZANU-PF and government officials accused ORAP of working with the British High Commission and withholding food aid from ZANU-PF supporters in the heated run-up to a by-election in rural Matabele-land South.[45] State-owned television and radio reported that food aid was being distributed by "active members of the opposition MDC and not by ORAP as initially believed," and editorials in the state newspapers accused ORAP of openly campaigning for the MDC in the by-election.[46] ORAP and the WFP subsequently terminated all distribution of food assistance in the constituency. The CCJP's feeding programs for children were also shut down in 2002, after the Minister for Local Government said that the CCJP and other NGOs were setting up "structures parallel to those of the government."[47]

DEFENSIVE RADICALIZATION IN THE MDC

Changes in the political environment forced the MDC to adapt. In the wake of the March 2002 presidential elections, another 18,000 MDC members were forced to flee violent retribution in their home areas.[48] After the September 2002 rural district elections, there was another wave of violent evictions, as the ruling party targeted winning MDC candidates and drove them from their homes. This new wave of repression had significant effects on party structures. In a report after the post-presidential election violence, the MDC's organizing

---

[43] I became acquainted with the organization when I served as a consultant for Human Rights Watch for portions of 2003. For more on government repression during this period, see HRW (2003b).

[44] ZLHR, "The Human Rights Defenders Emergency Fund," press release, April 24, 2003, available at www.kubatana.net.

[45] See MMPZ, Weekly Media Update no. 38, October 14–20, 2002.

[46] Ibid.; field notes, October 2002.

[47] *Daily News*, June 5, 2002.

[48] *Zimbabwe Independent*, March 28, 2002.

department noted that party structures had "disintegrated"; further, there was "very little or no activities" by provincial structures, due in some cases to misappropriation of funds.[49] Nor could the national executive remain well informed about conditions outside Harare: an audit in late 2002 found that most provincial leaders were passing along false information about structures and membership.[50] Even in urban areas, there were indications that party structures were weakening. The structures in Harare had been accustomed to meeting almost every week; after the passage of POSA, MDC activists found it more difficult to hold meetings or talk to members of the public.[51]

The most immediate response to violence and the disruption of visible party structures was a turn to more amorphous, socially embedded networks. The party went partly underground, and it used personal and social networks to communicate with both electoral constituencies and party activists. Candidates for mayoral elections in 2003, for instance, used commuter omnibus operators and market women as their primary campaign structures, especially in wards that had strong ZANU-PF structures or militia bases in operation.[52] The organization and oversight of formal party structures became similarly indirect. Because it was difficult for MDC activists and officials to travel to large portions of the country, the MDC approached teachers or pastors from inaccessible areas on "neutral" ground. Thus, provincial and national organizing secretaries would seek out a potential party organizer either through personal contacts or when the individual attended a training workshop or ecumenical gathering in an urban area. This individual would be provided with party flyers, instructed in how to organize a branch structure, and sent off to the constituency. Report-backs from these branches were sporadic, depending almost entirely on when a member of the structure would be in an urban area. Even in ruling party-controlled no-go areas, ZANU-PF MPs and party officials themselves admitted that MDC party structures remained "somehow" organized throughout 2003.[53] Though these informal strategies assured a minimal party presence in areas nationwide, they were not amenable to top-down control or even the simple coordination and communication of party plans.

Toward the end of 2002, there were extensive discussions within the MDC about the best means of reorganizing the party in light of this new political

---

[49] MDC, "Organising Report June 2002," mimeo.

[50] MDC, Memorandum from Secretary for Organising to National Executive, October 17, 2002.

[51] Interview with MDC official, April 2003; interview with Last Maengehama, July 28, 2003; field notes, February–May 2003.

[52] Field notes, MDC mayoral candidate training session, July 30–31, 2003.

[53] Interview with Didymus Mutasa, August 15, 2003. The comment relates to party activities in the constituency of Makoni North and in the province of Manicaland more generally. This was not true of all areas, particularly the more violent constituencies of Mashonaland Central and Mashonaland West. Field notes, Hurungwe West, September 28–30, 2002.

climate. The need for reassessment was underlined by the party's incoherent and conflicting reaction to the presidential elections of March 2002. Partly acknowledging the grassroots demand for popular protests, MDC leaders and officials told supporters to prepare for mass action if ZANU-PF would not agree to an election rerun.[54] Inter-party talks, mediated by South Africa, were held in April and May of 2002,[55] but there was widespread disagreement within the party structures about whether the MDC should pursue any kind of dialogue with ZANU-PF. Many party activists, especially those in the party's youth structures, felt that party talks were a betrayal of MDC victims of political violence. There was significant grassroots pressure for a return to the strikes and mass actions of the late 1990s. After inter-party talks collapsed, the MDC initiated consultations with its grassroots structures over the form of mass action, and party leaders announced that the national executive would hear report-backs from the provinces and make final decisions on the mass action in early June 2002.[56] Over the next two months, the status of the mass action remained unclear: some party officials announced that the executive had been forced to reconsider mass action, and others announced that mass action was imminent.[57] The MDC's National Executive Committee (NEC) did decide on a short parliamentary boycott, but the party did not take any larger scale actions for the rest of 2002. After violent rural district council elections in September 2002, grassroots frustration with the party's reliance on legal challenges grew. Publicly, the party leadership said that there were no popular demonstrations or protest actions because "we knew what the people felt, and we knew that any kind of protest would turn into a bloodbath on both sides."[58] Privately – and only after the MDC's success in organizing mass stayaways in March and June of 2003 – party officials admitted that the party had tried but been incapable of organizing a mass action.

Members of the national executive pointed to the disruption of local party structures to explain the failure of the planned post-election mass action, saying that plans were simply "lost" in the party structures. The national leadership had placed a call out to the provincial and local structures, requesting that they prepare for a coordinated protest campaign.[59] According to the general narrative offered by several MDC officials at the national level, the

[54] *Daily News*, April 29, 2002; *Zimbabwe Standard*, May 19, 2002.

[55] For an analysis of why the talks collapsed, see *Financial Gazette*, May 16, 2002; also, ICG (2002).

[56] *Financial Gazette*, May 30, 2002; UN Integrated Regional Information Networks (IRIN), May 30, 2002.

[57] IRIN, June 27, 2002; *Financial Gazette*, July 18, 2002. In August, the MDC national youth chairman was arrested for allegedly announcing at a party meeting that a mass action would occur on August 14. *Daily News*, August 16, 2002.

[58] Interview with Morgan Tsvangirai, December 5, 2002.

[59] *Financial Gazette*, July 18, 2002.

structures reacted by questioning the directions and expressing some degree of anger that the grassroots structures had not been previously consulted. This would seem to tally with complaints at the grassroots level of the party. By late 2002, local MDC activists were frustrated with their inability to communicate and get information from the party leadership. Activists complained that party leaders could not hear "the people's" calls for action; still others complained that "programmes always come from the top."[60] Similar frustrations were regularly expressed outside formal party channels by activists and ordinary party supporters alike. It was during this time that grassroots party activists began to attack MDC Secretary-General Welshman Ncube and other "academics," who they felt were forcing the MDC to "sell out" and negotiate with ZANU-PF. This sentiment was particularly strong within the party youth.

The failure to organize a response to the presidential elections prompted significant changes in party governance. The NEC decided at the end of 2002 that formal party structures would be bypassed when political events required an immediate MDC response, popular mobilization, or mass action. The solution was the creation of a "parallel structure," a shadow party structure, which would be designed to facilitate top-down organizing and speedy response to orders from national leadership. The "action committees" that composed this parallel structure were still organized on the geographic, district-branch-cell model; however, they were seen to be superior to official party structures precisely because they were less democratic, required less explanation of party motivations or strategy, and were composed of more militant party followers.[61] This new form of party organization was not created from scratch. The party had been using so-called parallel structures since 2000 for special tasks, sometimes including violence and property destruction.[62] For instance, the destruction in 2000 of a Harare surgery belonging to Chenjerai Hunzvi, the leader of the war veterans' association, is widely credited to be the early work of the parallel structures. The consequences of this decision were not foreseen at the time, but the establishment of the parallel structures would substantially shift power within the party, and it would intensify disagreements over the proper role of mass action and confrontation in pushing forward political change. These changes are essential to understanding the factional split within the MDC that occurred in December 2005.

---

[60] Field notes, March–June 2003; MDC, Minutes of Manicaland Province Organisers Meeting, November 20, 2002.

[61] Interviews with MDC local activists and national party officials, June–August 2003.

[62] Both MDC local party activists and those involved in national planning emphasized that violent actions were entirely defensive. The vast majority of violent actions during this period have been perpetrated by ruling party activists and sympathizers against those perceived to be opposition supporters.

Because they were developed as informal networks to deal with violence, the parallel structures were less "civic" in their orientation, and structures were sometimes used to coerce popular participation in mass actions or to undertake other actions that ran counter to the MDC's liberal democratic principles. This willingness to use "whatever means necessary" is, of course, part of the reason the structures were effective. One MDC official directly involved with the parallel structures commented: "what kind of people are in these parallel structures? They're the militant ones, people who can get things done, who follow orders without question – youths, obviously, urban unemployed, commercial sex workers, thieves. [You mean they're *jambanja* types?] Yes, exactly. They're *jambanja* [break-up] types."[63] The agreement with the term "*jambanja*" is an important sign of how these parallel structures are viewed by those in charge of them. *Jambanja* is the term commonly used to refer to war veterans and other "rabble" who invaded commercial farms beginning in April 2000: it is associated with a willingness to destroy and break things, a potentially uncontrollable violence. The closest English approximation would probably be a "heavy." The structures may have been initially intended to serve as underground and impermanent groupings, which would remain delimited in their role, but they quickly began to compete with the elected party structures.[64] This tension partly resulted from the degree of autonomy granted to the structures: there was a dual reporting system, so district action committees did not report to the district party structures they existed alongside. Because younger, more militant party members were specifically recruited or transferred to the action committees, many of those involved in planning and executing mass actions had previously been very junior members of the party within their districts and provinces. District structures were not involved in the staffing of the action committees, which was instead undertaken by nonelected staff members at the national headquarters.[65] The creation of parallel structures therefore exacerbated an existing division within the MDC, with some saying that they reflected a further shift in power away from the party's "politicians" in favor of unelected party "technocrats."[66] Many party members, including those who had initially approved of the parallel structures, felt that "the democratic process within the party ended when the executive made the decision to establish action committees."[67]

After the formation of the parallel structures, broader party strategy and rhetoric turned more confrontational. In large part, the change of strategy was a response to increasing grassroots and civil society pressure on the MDC's

---

[63] Interview with MDC official involved in the planning and organization of mass action, March 2003.

[64] Interview with Nelson Chamisa, July 13, 2006; interview with Itai Zimunya, July 10, 2006.

[65] Interview with Gift Chimanikire, July 14, 2006.

[66] Interviews with Ian Makone, August 13, 2003; and with Last Maengehama, July 28, 2003.

[67] Interview with Ian Makone, August 13, 2003.

national leadership.[68] The disjuncture in sentiment between grassroots and leadership was explicitly acknowledged by the party when it finally did announce plans for mass action in March 2003.[69] After several years in which the ZCTU and the NCA were the only organizations that pursued marches and demonstrations, the MDC held a two-day stay-away in March. Heavy police mobilization prevented protesters from assembling for marches, but the stay-away shut down urban centers as effectively as ZCTU national strikes had in 1997 and 1998. Party officials and activists believed that the mass action would signal the revitalization of party structures to the ruling party, and this initial protest was supposedly timed to dissuade ZANU-PF from using fraud in two crucial Harare by-elections. In the aftermath of the March stayaway, state paramilitaries launched brutal sweep operations in the Harare high-density suburbs, in an attempt to decapitate party structures (HRW 2003b). Though officials associated with the elected structures suffered substantially, as did ordinary residents and civil society activists, the parallel structures seem to have largely escaped this assault.

In June of 2003, the party once again called for mass action, which they expanded to a week-long stayaway. This action – labeled the "final push" – was intended to paralyze the economy and prove that ZANU-PF rule was unsustainable. During this action, the MDC called for members of the security forces to defect, and rumors circulated in Harare about MDC infiltration of police forces and the military. Officials within the party believed that parallel structures were integral in assuring the mass actions' success. In some areas, MDC party youths coerced participation in the stay-aways, largely by taking over transport routes. Workers and transport operators reported that MDC youths would not allow buses to leave the Harare high-density suburbs for industrial areas or the central business district during the June stay-away.[70] Despite a frightening intensification of state repression, levels of mobilization and expressions of commitment to the party were much higher in the wake of the first mass action. MDC activists and party supporters believed that change was imminent. This was a marked contrast from the increasing apathy and frustration felt within the grassroots structures after the presidential elections. Members of the MDC's National Executive were arraigned on charges of treason, other MPs went into hiding or fled the country, and hundreds of MDC activists were detained and tortured. Despite this, the organization

---

[68] Field notes, February 2003; also, *Daily News*, January 23, 2003; *Standard*, January 27, 2003.

[69] *Daily News*, March 8, 2003; *Financial Gazette*, March 13, 2003.

[70] Field notes, June 2003. At the few open businesses in the Harare central business district and northern suburbs, workers reported walking to work. State media reported several instances of "terrorism" during the stay-aways, including the burning of two Zupco (state-owned) buses. See, for instance, *The Herald*, March 19, 2003. Within Harare and other urban centers, these overt acts of violence were widely perceived to be the work of ZANU-PF youth militia.

of and levels of participation in the June stay-away were very high. Activists excitedly talked of the need for confrontation and even violent resistance in order to achieve "regime change." The creation of the parallel structures gave the party greater capacity to organize the mass actions that the party grassroots demanded, but the structures also opened up conflicts within the party's NEC.

Different attitudes toward mass action would shape party development over the next two years, eventually yielding the party split at the end of 2005. Differences within the party were reflected in the sharply different rhetoric used by leaders to describe the aims of the mass action. Where Tsvangirai encouraged Zimbabweans to "rise up" and embraced the grassroots description of the June stay-away as the "final push," party Secretary-General Welshman Ncube repeatedly stressed that the mass action was only intended to force ZANU-PF to restart inter-party negotiations.[71] Changes in party organization became one element of this larger disagreement over party stategy. The structures created to establish direct control over grassroots activists soon came to be seen as means of sidelining particular elements of the leadership, especially the moderate Ncube. The parallel structures were not the first "security" organs created within the MDC, but they expanded the number of party youths active in party operations and also gave the most militant members of the party's rank-and-file significant power within the organization. In 2004 and 2005, these youths were directly implicated in episodes of intra-party violence, including violent Harare party primaries and the near-fatal assault on the MDC's Director of Security at the party's own headquarters in September 2004. In his comments to an internal party inquiry, the Director of Security suggested that the parallel structures began to be used as a weapon in programmatic and strategic disagreements between different elements of the party's leadership.[72] By 2005, the parallel structures were also affecting democratic processes at the grassroots level. In the run-up to the 2005 parliamentary elections, several MDC party primaries became hotly contested affairs, occasionally involving violence, and they were marked by competition between those allegedly linked to parallel structures and those more strongly linked to elected party structures. Informants suggested that some MPs and party officials formed their own groups of youths and had been responsible for

[71] An analysis of this is found in IRIN, "Focus on the MDC's Final Push," June 5, 2003 (available at irinnews.org). The party's own newspaper, *The Changing Times*, also abounds with examples of polarizing language; for example, a banner headline following a by-election defeat reads "Temporary Victory of Thuggery and Evil over Good." *The Changing Times*, November 1–7, 2002.

[72] MDC, Commission of Inquiry into Disturbances at Party Headquarters, December 2004, cited in Raftopoulos (2006: 8).

violence in some constituencies in the run-up to party nominations prior to the 2005 parliamentary elections.[73]

Grassroots demands for more visible and direct action by the party leadership emerged following the 2005 parliamentary elections, as they had after the presidential elections in 2002.[74] The state's forced eviction of 700,000 urban dwellers in May of 2005, which was termed Operation Murambatsvina ("drive out trash"), likely reinforced this preference for confrontation (Bratton and Masunungure 2007). The grassroots demand for mass action once again suggested the need for mass action and, perhaps, violent resistance: the MDC Manicaland provincial chair was quoted as saying, "this is the work of a sophisticated dictator. We will never beat ZANU-PF [in elections] while it is in power. We need *other means*."[75] In the same article, an unnamed activist used language almost identical to that used in conversations I had with grassroots activists in 2002–3: "We discovered that the leadership has no plan B. We are going away empty-handed. All this sitting around at tables achieves nothing. We should be talking regime change." The party leadership's response also bore a striking resemblance to the actions taken in mid-2002. An emergency meeting of the National Executive was called. The meeting did not produce any resolution, other than a statement that legal challenges were unlikely to be pursued, as challenges arising from the 2002 elections were still in the courts. The debate over whether to pursue mass action led to divisions with the National Executive, and competition for executive party offices may have been affected by the debate as well. There are suggestions, for instance, that party branches were opposed to re-election of supposed moderates such as Welshman Ncube and Paul Themba Nyathi.[76] MDC youths had allegedly been instructed to impound party vehicles from party officials linked to NEC members who were opposed to mass action, which included most party officials from Matabeleland.

In May 2005, these differences over whether the party should pursue mass action prompted outbreaks of intra-party violence involving party youths at the Harare headquarters and provincial offices in Bulawayo and Gwanda. Over the following months, disagreements over larger party strategy – over negotiation versus confrontation – began to focus on participation in elections to a new Senate, which the ZANU-PF government had just formed. Tsvangirai argued that grassroots party structures were against participation in Senate elections, which many party activists saw as legitimating ZANU-PF rule and

[73] Interview with Sekai Holland, July 13, 2006; interview with Last Maengehama, July 12, 2006.

[74] The media coverage of the election aftermath emphasized this angle strongly, quoting MDC activists and ordinary residents of high-density urban areas. See, for instance, "Mugabe threatens to eradicate opposition," *Sunday Telegraph* (London), April 3, 2005.

[75] Prosper Muchamyi, quoted in *Sunday Times* (London), April 3, 2005. Emphasis added.

[76] *Zimbabwe Independent*, May 20, 2005.

betraying victims of political violence. A disputed NEC vote on participation in the elections eventually split the party. Five of the party's top six officials attempted to initiate disciplinary procedures against MDC President Morgan Tsvangirai, alleging that Tsvangirai had violated the party's constitution by overruling the National Executive recommendation to participate in November 2005 Senate elections.[77] These officials alleged that MDC President Morgan Tsvangirai was working too closely with his own "kitchen cabinet" and not properly consulting with the National Executive and the "top six" party officials.[78] In interviews in 2006, MDC officials confirmed that the term "kitchen cabinet" referred to those involved with the parallel structures.

After the party split, the bulk of the grassroots seems to have remained with the Tsvangirai faction, the leaders of which had argued against participation in Senate elections in 2005 and had been consistently associated with a more confrontational, mass action-based party strategy. But there was also evidence that a deeper culture of violence had taken root within the MDC by late 2004.[79] The reliance on youths and "security" was not limited to the Tsvangirai faction. In the wake of the party split, each faction accused the other of fostering intra-party violence and using youths to violently disrupt party activities. Youths belonging to either wing of the party were linked to violent assaults on the opposing faction, including invasions of each other's party offices.[80] The language used by faction leaders to attack their former colleagues – which abounded with accusations of dictatorship, collaboration with ZANU-PF, and corrupt dealings with international donors – was strikingly reminiscent of the MDC's former attacks on the ruling party. In my interviews with party activists and some members of the leadership in June and July 2006, I was struck by the extent to which the violence of party youths was considered legitimate or at least justified as a natural or even necessary response to the violent political system (for a similar point, see also Raftopoulos 2006). Even within the main faction's Women's Assembly, there seemed to be ambivalence about the acceptability of the use of violence. Following a violent assault on

---

[77] Arguments over the disputed vote center on the issue of proxies: members of the Tsvangirai faction allege that the President held two proxies of absent NEC members, who voted against participation in the elections, while the Ncube–Sibanda faction (subsequently the Mutambara faction) argued that the vote was 33–31 in favor of participation. See "Full text of MDC disciplinary committee letter expelling Tsvangirai," available at www.kubatana.net accessed April 19, 2006.

[78] For example, *Zimbabwe Independent*, October 28, 2005; *Business Day* (Johannesburg), November 1, 2005; Raftopoulos (2006: 12–15).

[79] For the best statement on this, see the blog post by former MDC shadow minister David Coltart, "The reasons why I cannot join the Tsvangirai faction," May 26, 2006 (at davidcoltart. com).

[80] For one account of the continuing intra-MDC violence, see the editorial by MDC MP David Coltart, former shadow minister for justice, "MDC must deal with violence in its own ranks," *Zimbabwe Independent*, May 26, 2006.

former MDC MP Trudy Stevenson, who had defected to the other faction, the
Harare women's structures reluctantly agreed with Assembly Chair Lucia
Matibenga's suggestion that a delegation be sent to visit Stevenson's hospital
bed, but some also suggested that "Trudy should have known better than to
come to our place."[81] Though it is hard to assess party sentiment after 2006,
many of those who remained with the Tsvangirai faction interpreted grassroots calls for mass action to mean potentially violent resistance to ZANU-PF.

CONCLUSIONS

The question that looms over this chapter – and, indeed, over any analysis of
the evolution of the MDC – is how the party has been affected by developments
since the 2008 harmonized elections.[82] In the wake of a flawed and violent 2008
presidential run-off, both MDC factions signed a power-sharing agreement
with the ruling party. The agreement, brokered by South Africa, resulted in the
division of ministries and the appointment of MDC leader Morgan Tsvangirai
to the newly created post of Prime Minister. Though there have been improvements in social service delivery and in economic stability since the agreement
was implemented, the post-agreement period has also been characterized by
repeated violations of the power-sharing accord by the ruling party. Farm
invasions have continued; MDC activists continue to be harassed, tortured,
and arrested; and the willingness of the military to cooperate with MDC office-
holders is unclear. In terms of the MDC itself, the effect of the power-sharing
agreement on the party's structures and internal discipline remains uncertain.

The MDC's decision to participate in the power-sharing agreement marks
a significant shift in the strategies and tactics that have been used by the
party and by its social movement predecessors in the past. In the pages
above, I discussed how state-sponsored violence and repression intensified
party-based polarization, but it is important to underline that the campaigns
of the ZCTU, the NCA, and the MDC were largely premised on the idea of
unbridgeable positions and identities. MDC leaders did not see dialogue
or cooperation with government as a possibility from fairly early on:

> We knew, for instance, when we took on the election challenges, that that would
> polarize and reduce the area of compromise. [So there was an explicit party
> decision to make compromise difficult?] Yes, but I think that decision was
> reached long before that. I think it was reached in the late 1990s, I know in my
> own mind it was.[83]

---

[81] Notes, meeting of the MDC Women's Assembly, Harare chapter, July 11, 2006.
[82] For a more detailed analysis of the 2008 elections, see Alexander and Tendi (2008).
[83] Interview with David Coltart, March 11, 2003.

So what changed? And what does the abandonment of the MDC's commitment to confrontation mean for the durability of the party and its base of support? The power-sharing agreement has eased the economic and humanitarian crisis in the country, but some MDC leaders felt that the coalition government would allow the party to assemble a track record in government that would appeal to voters. Though funding shortfalls and strikes continue to plague the public sector, the slow rebuilding of the shattered educational and health care systems may win the MDC even greater levels of support in future elections. At the time of writing, donors remain unwilling to extend significant funds to the coalition government so long as violence and other ZANU-PF violations of the accord continue to occur. The MDC is therefore engaged in a risky strategy. On the one hand, if it can deliver social services and improvements in governance, it may be able to attract former ZANU-PF supporters, whose loyalties to the ruling party have already proven tenuous. On the other hand, power-sharing deprives the party of many of the appeals and tools that held its organization together in earlier periods, despite repression and the lack of access to patronage. For instance, cooperation with ZANU-PF may have eroded the commitment of party activists and local structures, which have often been more confrontational than the party leadership. Finally, it is worth noting that polarization and conflict are still being used by ZANU-PF to enforce internal solidarity, as the continuation of land invasions, MDC harassment, and war-based rhetoric suggest. Even if the coalition government hangs together until elections are held in 2011 or 2012, this does not preclude a return to the politics of polarization and violence during the campaign period. Indeed, this seems the most likely scenario.

Putting aside these speculations about the future, this chapter sheds light on the ties between party-based polarization and the forging of party organizations. Though state-sponsored violence obviously harmed local party structures that were in place in 2000, it also consistently focused the attention of the MDC national leadership on the task of maintaining contact with grassroots constituencies. In the later stages of this early period of party-building, the party adapted to an increasingly violent political environment by forming party structures that could mobilize the grassroots without exposing themselves to government repression. This innovation had both positive and negative effects. On the one hand, parallel structures allowed the party to maintain levels of mobilization and popular commitment; on the other, it triggered processes that slowly unraveled solidarity at the level of party elites. The party split in 2005, but the larger of the two resulting fragments retained the bulk of the party's structure and support. Viewed through a comparative lens, the MDC split looks quite different from the pattern of opposition fragmentation characteristic of other African hybrid regimes. In Zimbabwe, the opposition vote remained relatively disciplined. The MDC label remains an important determinant of vote choice. The factional split was driven by very different factors than those that promoted party system fragmentation in Zambia and Kenya. The elite disagreements that led to the MDC split centered on issues of party governance, decision-making procedures, and the role of grassroots structures in decision-making. Unlike defections in Zambia and Kenya, which were driven by personal conflicts or candidates' own interests, issues of party strategy and organizational change were at the root of the party conflict in Zimbabwe. As we will see in Chapter 8, where party organizations are weak, candidates and voters face very different sets of incentives, and party decisions have much weaker effects on political outcomes.

Eight

Fragmented Parties in Zambia and Kenya

In Zambia and Kenya, opposition parties have had varying levels of electoral success, but they have been similarly weak in terms of organization and institutionalization. Since founding multiparty elections in 1991 and 1992, the two countries demonstrate high levels of party system fragmentation and fluidity, as well as routine party-switching by political aspirants. Party organizations were characterized by weak party structures and little involvement of grassroots constituencies and activists in party decision-making. Rather than privileging consensus and grassroots consultation, as the MDC leadership has at different points, opposition party leaders in Zambia and Kenya centralized decision-making. Parties were governed by their national executives alone or, even more commonly, by still smaller groups that were tightly connected to party presidents. In both countries, wars for control of top party positions were hard-fought, and losers were often excluded from party planning, decision-making, and patronage. In addition to gross centralization, Kenyan and Zambian opposition parties made few investments in local party structures. In Zambia, the party leadership broke its ties with organized labor after the Movement for Multiparty Democracy's (MMD's) election in 1991, leading to the erosion of the loyalties and networks that had brought the party to power. In Kenya, party leaders relied on their personal connections with ethnic constituencies in order to mobilize votes. They did not build party branches at the local level. In both countries, there was a sharp decline in the value of party labels from 1991, as demonstrated by increases in party system fragmentation and in the frequency with which candidates switched their partisan affiliations.

As a result of these early choices, party organizations in both countries have demonstrated strong tendencies toward volatility and fragmentation. Office-holders and elected representatives have occasionally left parties due to substantive differences over policy or strategy, but defections more often reflect tensions arising from highly centralized – and personalized – party structures. The creation of a new party organization, or defection to rivals, places defectors closer to positions of authority, or it generates new opportunities for patronage or co-optation by the sitting regime. Defections have also been fueled by the relatively low costs and risks that accrue to defectors.[1] There are high rates of incumbent turnover in the two countries, especially in Kenya, but floor-crossing does not typically lead voters to sanction their representatives. In by-elections triggered by defection or expulsion from a party, incumbents have generally been able to retain their seats. In contrast, disgruntled elites in Zimbabwe remained within their parties (either the MDC or ZANU-PF) because they recognized that their electoral fortunes are tied to their party affiliation. Losers of MDC primary contests, for instance, abide by the party's decision and wait to contest again the following election cycle. In Zambia and Kenya, this logic is not operational.

Where party organizations are weak, as they are in Zambia and Kenya, they provide few "side benefits" to political aspirants, either in the way of concrete campaign resources or clear electoral dividends. Candidates' electoral chances hinge on their own qualities and resources. High levels of floor-crossing and party splintering are symptoms of party weakness, but they also perpetuate and intensify party system volatility and fragmentation. As we will see in both cases, weak party organizations are not capable of building strong and enduring ties with mass constituencies. In this chapter, I first provide an overview of the founding elections in Zambia and Kenya and the opposition party organizations that contested them. I then turn to changes in patterns of party system fragmentation, paying particular attention to whether ethnic diversity or ethnic mobilization might explain these outcomes.

ZAMBIA

The Founding Elections

In Chapter 6, I showed how a lively protest culture, driven forward by grassroots labor militancy and large-scale protests against structural adjustment, emerged in Zambia prior to 1991. Opposition elites could channel this undisciplined mobilization on the margins, and the MMD was the beneficiary of organized labor's ability to act as a focal point for opposition. In this chapter, I will show that the opposition MMD's early momentum and electoral success cannot be seen as evidence of organizational strength. MMD politicians did not lay the groundwork for a cohesive, institutionalized, or

---

[1] The electoral penalties incurred by candidates who cross to other parties are variable across countries. In some places, especially those with well-institutionalized party systems, defections are rare and are likely to be penalized by voters. In other countries, defection may increase incumbents' chances for re-election. On this particular point, see Kato (1998), Desposato (2006), Samuels (2000), Shabad and Slomczynski (2004).

well-governed party. The early choices of MMD leaders regarding strategy and party structure did much to shape the fluid and fragmented party landscape that continues to characterize Zambia. Corporatism provided a strong national labor movement that could serve as a focal point for protest voters. This explains the MMD's landslide 1991 victory. Economic protests and wildcat strikes occurred throughout the 1980s, but the transformation of this ungoverned economic discontent into a political movement occurred over a remarkably compressed period of time. There was no investment, however, in party-building, and the MMD's early organizational advantage was squandered.

The MMD was launched as a movement at the Garden House Conference in July 1990. The first MMD rallies, which were focused only on calls for multiparty elections, were held in August and September. In August, President Kenneth Kaunda announced that a popular referendum would be held on multiparty rule; in September, he canceled the referendum and announced that multiparty elections would be held the following year. Less than a year after the MMD's registration as a party, it won parliamentary and presidential elections by overwhelming margins. The MMD captured 81 percent of the presidential vote and 125 of the 150 National Assembly seats.[2] The former ruling party's support was largely limited to constituencies in the Eastern Province that were considered the heart of President Kaunda's political – and ethnic – base. Outside Eastern Province, the MMD captured over 65 percent of the presidential vote in all other provinces, and the MMD vote topped 80 percent in Copperbelt, Luapula, Northern, Southern, and Western provinces. Most parliamentary contests were similarly uncompetitive.[3] Of Zambia's 150 constituencies, MMD candidates won more than 65 percent of the vote in 106, and they won more than 75 percent of the vote in ninety-one constituencies. Though MMD candidates performed well in the Bemba-speaking provinces of the Copperbelt, Northern, and Luapula, where MMD President Frederic Chiluba's support was presumed to be concentrated, they also won more than 75 percent of the vote in the majority of constituencies in all provinces apart from Eastern Provinces. As I suggested in Chapter 6, much of the credit for this early success can be attributed to the mobilizing structures and organizational reach of the Zambian Congress of Trade Unions (ZCTU).

Despite its strong base in the labor movement, MMD party-building relied heavily on defections from the ruling party. Defectors from the ruling United National Independence Party (UNIP) quickly filled leadership positions

---

[2] For a more detailed analysis of the 1991 elections, see Baylies and Szeftel (1999). Evaluations of the election results should take into account that turnout was rather low at only 45 percent of eligible voters, which was lower than in some of Zambia's past one-party elections (Baylies and Szeftel 1992: 77). The low turnout may be partly explained by a flawed and badly organized registration process (Andreassen et al. 1992: 31).

[3] All election results were provided to me by the Electoral Commission of Zambia. Some election results are available at www.elections.org.zm

within the MMD and provided means of resolving party nominations. UNIP was ineffective in stemming the flow of defections; indeed, party policies actively encouraged or even forced such defections. Along with the visible defections of highly ranked party officials, punitive ruling party policies toward multi-party advocates triggered a disintegration of UNIP party structures, which had long been weak, throughout the course of 1991. At the grassroots level, the party experienced a mass exodus of officials during the months preceding the elections.[4] In addition, nine sitting MPs ran and were re-elected to Parliament on MMD tickets, and a larger number of former UNIP MPs and officials crossed to the MMD to contest on the new party's ticket.

Apart from a handful of ZCTU officials and trade unionists, the national leadership structures of the MMD were soon dominated by former ruling party politicians, including both recent defectors and those who had been purged from the party in earlier periods. The Zambian opposition's welcoming attitude toward defectors differed markedly from the Zimbabwean opposition's attempt to erect and police walls between itself and the ruling party. In Zimbabwe, the MDC instituted party rules that prevented ZANU-PF defectors from standing on MDC tickets, and it did not seek the support of prominent ZANU-PF politicians, including those who were seen as moderate or pro-reform. At the grassroots level, the MDC concentrated on building new structures rather than co-opting the weakened grassroots party structures of the ruling party. In contrast, the MMD in Zambia erected no such barriers to party entry. A ZCTU official active on the first steering committee of the MMD commented, "if one crossed over to the new political party, one was welcome, because what we wanted was to be strong."[5] To a great extent, the new party was less about the building of a new political coalition than about the disintegration of the old. Baylies notes:

> a consideration of the MMD candidates in the 1991 elections makes it tempting to conclude that, in 28 years in office, Kaunda managed to sack, detain, humiliate or otherwise frustrate enough individuals to form an opposition. (Baylies and Szeftel 1992: 83)

Given the prominence of defectors, MMD rallies in the latter half of 1990 focused to a large extent on the symbolic exit from UNIP and the breaking of prior links with the party. Attendees were encouraged to turn in their UNIP membership cards, which were collected in large piles.[6] The appearance of former UNIP elites or famous UNIP opponents was a frequent occurrence. At

---

[4] UNIP, "Preliminary Report: 1991 Presidential and General Elections Post-Mortem," mimeo, UNZA special collections (no date).

[5] Interview with Maria Kamuchele Kabwe, July 2, 2005.

[6] Interviews with Vernon Mwaanga, July 21, 2003; Benjamin Mwila, July 17, 2003.

the Kabwe rally, MP and former Minister Joshua Lumina apologized to the crowd for supporting UNIP; at an August MMD rally in Lusaka, MPs Bennie Mwiinga, Humphrey Mulemba, and Sikota Wina publicly resigned from the party, as did UNIP Member of the Central Committee Ludwig Sondashi.[7] One former UNIP member commented on the resemblance between the MMD rallies and the "slogan shouting" of earlier UNIP rallies (Zukas 2002: 179).

The "cascade" of elites and mass constituencies to the MMD did not seem inevitable at the time. Several MMD activists mentioned that repression and violence seemed very real possibilities up until the elections.[8] UNIP adopted hardline rhetoric, which differed only slightly from the polarizing language used a decade later in Zimbabwe. Immediately after Kaunda's announcement that multiparty elections would take place, UNIP announced that all Members of Parliament (MPs) who had advocated multiparty politics were suspended from attending the party's National Council and also risked expulsion from the party and from the National Assembly. MPs who had appeared at MMD rallies were barred from provincial and council meetings, and at least one member of the Central Committee instructed district governors to fire ward chairmen suspected of MMD sympathies.[9] At a UNIP party rally in November, the Secretary of State for Defence and Security told the crowd that they should identify multiparty advocates in their own neighborhoods:

> We have to demarcate our sections, branches and wards and know how many of the houses are not UNIP. Mark the enemies by their language and notify the government which will find means of converting them to UNIP. If that fails, the government will find other means of making it practically impossible for them to live in Lusaka.[10]

UNIP had control of the police and military forces, and the party had also established in the 1980s a decentralized system of "vigilantes," informal UNIP youth militia, who policed marketplaces and enforced government policies. Vigilantes were ostensibly meant to enforce price controls, remove illegal traders from marketplaces, and "maintain order" in urban areas. In practice, they were outside the control of party elites, and they used their power to extort money or goods.[11] After the formation of the MMD, vigilantes occasionally harassed vendors who did not have UNIP cards. Overall, despite real potential for party-based conflict, party-linked violence was rare (ZIMT 1992: 60–2).

In contrast to its counterparts in Zimbabwe and Kenya, the Zambian ruling party did not take advantage of its incumbency to subvert election results

---

[7] *National Mirror*, September 29, 1990.
[8] Interview with Austin Liato, June 22, 2003; Japhet Moonde, June 24, 2003.
[9] See, for instance, *Times of Zambia*, October 9, 1990, and November 23, 1990.
[10] Quoted in *National Mirror*, November 24, 1990.
[11] See, for instance, *Times of Zambia*, October 5, 1986; June 2, 1987; February 5, 1991.

(Andreassen et al. 1992; NDI and the Carter Center 1992). As Bratton points out, the head of the civil service issued regulations that limited civil servants' involvement in UNIP party campaigns, and other formal attempts to delink the party from government institutions were also made (Bratton 1992: 90; also, Andreassen et al. 1992: 20–1). Given the short time before the election, however, delinkage was more a stated principle than a fact on the ground (NDI and the Carter Center 1992: 43–4; ZIMT 1992: 57).[12] Ultimately, the ruling party in Zambia chose to act differently than its counterparts in Kenya and Zimbabwe. Hard-liners within the party, notably those who attacked international observers, were restrained.[13] Vote rigging and violent displacement were not used to remake electoral geography. The party occasionally threatened that disorder and violence would result from multiparty rule, but it did little to make this a reality. At the time, it seemed that UNIP's restraint augered well for democratization in Zambia (e.g., Bratton 1992; Joseph 1992). The lack of polarization and threat, however, meant that the opposition MMD did not face the same obstacles that the MDC did in Zimbabwe. Not only was there less need to build a strong, rooted party organization in Zambia, but the MMD lacked the solidarity and sense of common identity that struggle and state repression helped build in the Zimbabwean opposition.

The Internal Organization of the MMD

Disagreements over economic policy and party organization would later loom large in intra-party conflicts, but these were not discussed during MMD's early days. In contrast to the National Working People's Convention in Zimbabwe, which had laid out a skeletal agenda for "the Zimbabwe we want," the Garden House Conference ignored specific policy positions and focused largely on the flaws of one-party rule. At the time, there was little thought devoted to how the groups allied at Garden House would govern or how they would make collective decisions. Said one participant: "All energies went toward removing KK [Kaunda]. We forgot about institutional reform, we forgot about quality of leadership."[14] Rather than formulating procedures for resolving disagreement

---

[12] The core problem was the virtual fusion of state and party institutions during single-party rule. The overlap was formalized in 1980 with the passage of the Local Administration Act, discussed in Chapter 4, which prompted large-scale protests from the ZCTU and organized labor.

[13] In late October, just weeks before the election, UNIP party officials placed an ad accusing the observers of being "a big imperialist plot" intended to install "a puppet [MMD] government" in Zambia (Bjornlund et al. 1992: 425). There were also other verbal attacks preceding the advertisement (Andreassen et al. 1992: 60–2). Kaunda moved quickly to restrain these voices, and he publicly called on Zambians to support the observation mission.

[14] Interview with Chileshe Mulenga, October 11, 2002.

or setting up the norms that would govern decision-making, MMD leaders focused their attention on the allocation of party offices. Competition for the party's executive was fierce, and the jockeying at the convention foreshadowed the kinds of disputes that would soon split the MMD. In addition to Chiluba, three other candidates announced that they would contest the party presidency at the MMD's first party convention; multiple candidates were also to contest the chairs of the party's different committees.[15] Upon losing their contests at the party convention, several MMD notables, including the first interim chairman of the party, threatened to form another party; eventually, the group was lured back into the MMD.[16] Some attacked provincial imbalances in the awarding of party positions, which led a small number of local and provincial MMD officials to resign from the party after the convention.[17] Others alleged that ZCTU Chairman Frederic Chiluba won the party presidency via rigging, vote-buying, and strong-arm tactics.[18] There were conflicts within the party between those from organized labor and those who had come to the party via other paths. Still other tensions stemmed from ethno-regional cleavages.[19] These disagreements did not sharpen into coherent factional divisions, but there was no moment in the MMD's history when the leadership was truly united. This had effects on party institutions and decision-making.

In terms of the grassroots party structure, lines between local branches and national leadership were not well developed.[20] MMD activists at the local level were not involved in party decision-making or policy formulation, nor did the national leadership place a high premium on intra-party solidarity or on local activists staying "on message." Ihonvbere, for instance, provides several examples of provincial MMD officials ignoring or reversing the decisions of the central party leadership during this period (Ihonvbere 1995a: esp. 9–13). Indeed, promises made by MMD local activists were often diametrically opposed to the statements of the NEC. Local MMD campaigns revolved around promises of cheap maize or provision of social services and employment; the MMD leadership, meanwhile, announced that the new party supported economic liberalization and less state intervention in the economy. Other signs of party indiscipline emerged. At the first party convention, it was reported that party organizers in several districts had lost or stolen funds.

[15] *Times of Zambia*, February 26–27, 1991.
[16] *Africa Confidential*, November 8, 1991. See also, "Statement by Arthur Wina affirming his loyalty to the MMD, released in Livingstone, February 1991," reprinted in Tembo (1996: 27).
[17] *Times of Zambia*, March 20, 1991.
[18] Some, for instance, allege that university students and other delegates were used to "pack" the Convention with Chiluba supporters. Interview with Choolwe Beyani, October 3, 2002; *Times of Zambia*, March 14, 1991; also, Larmer and Fraser (2007: 624).
[19] Interview with Simon Zukas, July 18, 2003; also Rakner (1994: 63).
[20] Informants, for instance, could not recall – after the election of the NEC – any training sessions or other occasions on which activists or candidates from different parts of the country were brought together.

After the 1991 elections, there were reports of similar incidents in the run-up to by-elections and local government elections. The national party leadership did not address these problems, nor were there attempts to establish directive control over the provincial and branch structures that had been recently established.

Even though the national leadership had weak authority over party structures and local officials, decision-making in the MMD was strongly centralized. Most notably, the MMD national leadership retained control over the selection of parliamentary candidates. Provincial chairs, largely appointed from within the circle of Lusaka-based MMD politicians, were given the task of identifying and recruiting potential MPs, with final decisions resting with the NEC. Shortly before the 1991 elections, perhaps beginning in September, Chiluba and other NEC officials toured the provinces and interviewed prospective candidates. In areas like Livingstone, where there were multiple candidates, the NEC decided on the basis of interviews alone, without consulting the MMD district structures (Tembo 1996: 30–3).[21] The lack of consultation in Livingstone was characteristic. Bratton notes that the MMD "often pushed local preferences aside, creating an unfortunate precedent of arbitrary, patrimonial decision-making" (Bratton 1994a: 118). Parliamentary seats were offered to businessmen or UNIP politicians without consultation with MMD structures in the constituency itself.[22] Articles in the press suggested that the NEC was using its vetting powers to exclude popular candidates.[23] Local MMD activists, including the trade unionists who had played such an integral role in the organization of the movement, were displaced by individuals with connections to the NEC or money to fund their own election campaigns (Larmer 2007: 280).

The accelerated nature of the MMD's 1990–1 campaign, as well as the limited resources available to the party, perhaps partly explains the centralization of decision-making and indiscipline discussed above. After the MMD won office, however, the leadership took few steps to institutionalize the party. The Elections Committee, which was responsible for internal party elections and some elements of organization, was not given a budgetary provision in the first MMD budgets.[24] In its report to the party's 1993 convention, the Organisation Committee reported that party structures were eroding due to poor flow of information, inadequate resources, and non-payment of salaries to

---

[21] Tembo notes that the MMD district committee in Livingstone supported this means of choosing candidates; indeed, in June 1991, Tembo and another member had written to Chiluba suggesting that primaries would sow tribal divisions and splinter the party.

[22] See, for instance, the account of nominations in Northern Province in Mwanakatwe (2003: 433–5).

[23] *Weekly Post*, September 13, 1991.

[24] Sikota Wina, "Election Committee Report to the National Executive Committee [of the MMD]," August 1994. Mimeo, MMD Headquarters, Lusaka.

provincial coordinators and district organizers.[25] Within a year of the MMD's election, commentators remarked on the scale of intra-party divisions and noted that local party structures were hurt by the fact that "many of the best organizers have been 'kicked upstairs' to Lusaka" (Kibble 1992: 105). The MMD leadership recognized that party elections were needed by the end of 1992 to fill posts left vacant by provincial and district officials who had taken positions with the state. These elections, however, were not held until 1994, and they were then "characterized by a lot of bickering and mudslinging."[26] Escalating intra-party tension was also driven by the provincial and national leadership's practice of "[building] political networks by imposing, or rigging the elections of, favoured candidates" (Bartlett 2000: 441; also, Burnell 1995: 679). In advance of the 1992 local government elections, Chiluba refused the grassroots call for primary elections and defended candidate vetting by the NEC. In subsequent election rounds, the MMD's Lusaka-based NEC continued to impose MP candidates on local constituencies after little to no consultation with local structures (FODEP 1996: 29; Gould 2002: 317).

The overall picture that emerges is of a top–down party structure with few regularized links with grassroots constituencies. After its election in 1991, the MMD leadership also grew increasingly authoritarian in its tactics toward internal dissent, opposition parties, and ordinary voters. Many individuals, including those who had crossed to the MMD from UNIP, blamed these developments on the replication within the MMD of the political culture that had been prevalent in UNIP.[27] In 1992, a first MMD minister resigned, citing corruption in the new government; in August 1993, Chiluba fired another four of the MMD's founding members from their ministerial posts, triggering a further ten MP resignations.[28] The MMD reacted to this spate of defections by further closing the political space available for intra-party dissent: another four MPs were subsequently expelled from the party for their links to the defectors. Even though "few opponents of the MMD leadership remained in the party" by the 1993 party convention, Bartlett notes that some delegates' credentials were still challenged and other delegates were expelled in favor of the clients of provincial or district leaders (Bartlett 2000: 444). Nor were these authoritarian tactics limited to party officials. Focus groups convened in 1993 reported that the MMD was intimidating voters

---

[25] "Recommendations of the Party Organisation Committee to the 2nd Convention of the MMD," Mulungushi, November 27–28, 1993. Mimeo, MMD Headquarters, Lusaka.

[26] Ibid.

[27] Interviews with Akashambatwa Mbikusita-Lewanika, July 23, 2003; Simon Zukas, July 18, 2003. Also, "Statement by Arthur Wina," op. cit. Ihonvbere (1995a); Bartlett (2000).

[28] Corruption, barely mentioned here, escalated throughout the Chiluba administration. There is a general feeling, among both scholars and ordinary Zambians, that corruption has lessened since President Levy Mwanawasa was elected in 2001. For a comprehensive overview, see Szeftel (2000) and Van Donge (2009).

and curbing criticism of the party, just as UNIP had in the past (Bratton and Liatto-Katundu 1994). By 1996, most members of the MMD's first interim executive had left the party and had been re-elected to their seats on opposition party tickets.

MMD Ties to Grassroots Constituencies

As the MMD centralized internal decision-making, there was an erosion of the party's ties to organized labor and the other social actors that had brought the party to power. Organized labor initially remained loyal to the party it helped create, even as the new government implemented structural adjustment policies that harmed workers' interests.[29] The personal loyalty of trade unionists toward President and former ZCTU Chair Frederick Chiluba, in particular, restrained protest against government policy. During the 1990s, affiliates called strikes to protest economic policy, only to have their branches refuse out of loyalty to Chiluba.[30] When explaining the MMD's support for neoliberal policies, which few within organized labor had supported, unionists typically deflected blame from Chiluba, suggesting instead that business elements and UNIP politicians had "hijacked" the party.[31] During the first years of the Chiluba administration, the ZCTU and affiliate unions lost their access to government and were given little input into policy-making. On some occasions, organized labor was not given advance notice of decisions that most directly affected workers. An official with the mineworkers union noted that labor, when it began to complain about the effects of economic reform, was told:

> Wait, we're not elected by you workers alone. This landslide is a landslide of all Zambians. When we implement policies, this is a multiparty democracy where groups are not going to just answer to workers, to farmers, to business.[32]

Over the course of 1993 and 1994, the MMD's coalition unraveled quickly, as every one of the party's societal allies expressed opposition to the way in which economic reforms had been implemented. It was not merely labor that was excluded: the influence of the business community, the agrarian lobby, and

---

[29] A comprehensive account of labor–state relations in this period is found in Larmer (2005).

[30] Interview with Neo Simutanyi, June 19, 2004. It should be noted that this loyalty was personalized. Some informants spoke of the MMD as the "baby" of the unions, as trade unionists described the MDC in Zimbabwe, but many more mentioned Chiluba and spoke of him as being "our" president or "our man."

[31] Interview with Charles Muchimba, July 3, 2004. See also issues of the labor-oriented *Workers' Challenge* (Ndola) during this period, especially the cartoon and pieces in the March 1993 issue.

[32] Interview with Charles Muchimba, July 3, 2004. Similar sentiments were expressed in interviews with Japhet Moonde, June 24, 2004, and Joyce Nonde, July 6, 2004.

other interests also declined during this period (Rakner 2001, 2003). Rakner argues, quite rightly, that organized social interests had fewer "channels into the political system" under multiparty rule than in the UNIP period (Rakner 2001: 540). In terms of popular and organizational responses to this exclusion, many informants suggested that loyalty to the MMD government dissipated rapidly, especially as organized labor was ever more visibly marginalized within the MMD and in government decision-making. Officials of the national teachers union said that by 1993, workers no longer supported Chiluba uncritically; however, there were few strike actions because "it was now multiparty so there was no common enemy."[33] Despite these claims, however, it is striking that the ZCTU failed to condemn the ruling party's imposition of a state of emergency in 1993.[34] Over time, trade unions and the MMD's other organizational partners became less willing to give the government the benefit of the doubt. Strike action resumed: large numbers of railways workers, teachers, and public sector workers went on strike in 1993 and 1994. In 1993 and 1994, the churches began to openly criticize government policy; other interest groups followed suit.[35] Rather than modifying its adjustment plans or incorporating interest groups into the decision-making process, the MMD government responded by further insulating itself from popular pressures. From 1994 onward, business, organized labor, the churches, and other associations found themselves largely cut off from dialogue with government.

Even as labor's discontent with the MMD government grew, changes within the ZCTU eroded the capacity of the labor movement to exert pressure on the government and to coordinate protest. At the Quadrennial Congress of the ZCTU in 1994, a leadership battle led to a larger split and the disaffiliation of five unions from the ZCTU. These included the mineworkers and teachers unions, which accounted for 80 percent of the federation's revenue. Together, these disaffiliated unions accounted for more than 50 percent of the ZCTU's total membership (Banda 1997a: ch. 4). Unionists on both sides of the split suggested that relations between the MMD and labor leaders lay at the heart of the battle.[36] The MMD's actions against unions that remained affiliated to the ZCTU bear out this interpretation. In 1997, the government amended the

[33] Interview with Leah Asaji, Joel Kamoko, Helen Mwiyakui, and Johnson Zulu, July 8, 2004. Despite this claim, however, it is striking that the ZCTU failed to condemn the ruling party's imposition of a state of emergency in 1993. *Times of Zambia*, March 27, 1993.

[34] *Times of Zambia*, March 27, 1993. For a detailed analysis of the state of emergency and its political effects, see Ihonvbere (1995b).

[35] See the statements of the Catholic Bishops of Zambia (July 1993) and the Zambia Episcopal Conference (August 1994), reprinted in Komakoma (2003: 292–303, 313–23). For the response of business and agricultural interests, see Rakner (2003).

[36] Interviews with Joyce Nonde, July 6, 2004; Japhet Moonde, June 24, 2004; Austin Liato, June 22, 2004. Also, Rakner (2003: 97–9).

Industrial Relations Act to remove the "one industry, one union" clause
that had governed labor relations since 1971. The new Act allowed for the
registration of splinter unions, which the ZCTU and its affiliates saw as an
attempt to break the negotiating power of the trade union center. In 1998,
the government deregistered the electricity workers union, allegedly for financial mismanagement.[37] The ZCTU and several of its other affiliates were also
threatened with deregistration. The late 1990s were characterized by increasing confrontation between the MMD and the ZCTU. Structural adjustment
and economic decline had, however, reduced the size of the unionized labor
force. In addition, the liberalization of labor laws led to greater disorganization
within union structures and also weakened the links between the ZCTU and
its rank-and-file members. Had the ZCTU decided to back an opposition
party, it would have provided a much weaker organizational base in 2000 than
it did in 1991.

The measures taken to undermine organized labor were part of a larger
closure of political space during the first years of MMD government (Banda
1997b; Lungu 1997; Polhemus 1997; Gould 2002). These authoritarian tactics
seem to have undermined rather than reinforced the party's control over local
constituencies. The results of a series of by-elections suggest that MMD
support was tenuous even before the 1996 elections: of the forty-two by-
elections held from 1991 to 1995, the MMD won only twenty-four (Chikulo
1996). Of those who defected from the party in 1993 and 1994 and subsequently contested their seats on the National Party's (NP) ticket, the majority
retained their seats. But the more marked change was the increasing popularity of the former ruling party, UNIP. In the nineteen by-elections held in 1995,
UNIP won back five seats that had previously been held by the MMD, retained
four of its own seats, and lost a handful of other contests by narrow margins
(Chikulo 1996: 449). During the 1996 elections, Human Rights Watch documented substantial abuses during the registration process (HRW 1996; also,
Kees van Donge 1998: 79–83); other observers documented instances of vote-
buying, violence, intimidation, and misuse of state resources by the MMD
during the election campaign (FODEP 1996). As Bratton and Posner note,
Zambia's performance in this respect was indicative of a broader trend of
declining quality of second elections across Africa (Bratton and Posner 1999;
also, Lindberg 2006). In 1996, even though the MMD won the presidency and
over 85 percent of seats in Parliament in the 1996 elections, there were
expressions of local discontent with the centralization of MMD candidate

---

[37] The union's president, Austin Liato, viewed the move as an attempt to subvert his
campaign for the presidency of the ZCTU, a contest that he subsequently lost. Interview with
Austin Liato, June 22, 2004. See also *Times of Zambia*, October 15, 1998; *The Post*, October 9,
1998.

selection. In Kabwe, the party's imposition of the MMD National Secretary Paul Tembo as the party's MP candidate led to violence, when a rally attended by Tembo and Chiluba was disrupted by party activists loyal to local favorite Austin Chewe, a trade unionist. After the MMD refused to overturn the NEC's decision, the constituency elected Chewe, who ran as an independent, by a significant margin (FODEP 1996: 31).

As the MMD's party structure became more centralized and less responsive to grassroots pressures, it lost ever-larger sections of its vote base that had accounted for its landslide 1991 election success. Though the 1996 election results do not mark a significant change from 1991, the erosion of MMD support was more significant outside the Bemba-speaking provinces of Northern, Luapula, and the Copperbelt. In these provinces, the MMD retained over 60 percent of the vote; elsewhere, opposition parties were able to make greater headway. Support for opposition parties, many of which were led by politicians who had previously held offices with the MMD, was fragmented on regional lines. The NP won the bulk of its votes in Northwestern Province, the home of its party leader and presidential candidate; the Zambian Democratic Congress (ZDC) only managed to capture two parliamentary seats in Western Province, though it won some support in other provinces. These parties, as well as smaller ones that contested in 1996 and in subsequent elections, were the personal vehicles for individuals or a small group of political elites. They lacked organizational structures that linked them to mass constituencies, and parties were launched and disbanded depending on their leaders' assessment of their fortunes vis-à-vis the MMD. Burnell describes the resultant landscape as "a continual circulation of politicians, contributing to the emergence and in some cases later disappearance of small parties, proto-parties, and political groups" (Burnell 2001: 244). These tendencies toward organizational volatility and reorganization led to a significant decomposition of the party landscape in the 2001 elections. The 2001 elections pitted an MMD weakened by the Chiluba succession struggle against a large field of opposition parties, many of which were headed by politicians who had defected over Chiluba's campaign for a third term or over his selection of Levy Mwanawasa as his successor. Overall, the 2001 elections were notable for the fragmentation of both the presidential and the parliamentary vote: the winning presidential candidate, the MMD's Mwanawasa, won only 28.7 percent of the presidential vote, just over 2 percent more than the UPND's Mazoka. The remainder of the vote was split across nine other candidates. The parliamentary vote was fragmented on similar lines, as Figure 8.1 suggests.

The MMD's dip in electoral support in 2001 corresponded with the period of greatest disorganization and erosion of party structures. Prior to the elections, Chiluba had attempted to amend the constitution to allow him to stand for a third presidential term, which triggered a series of conflicts within the party.

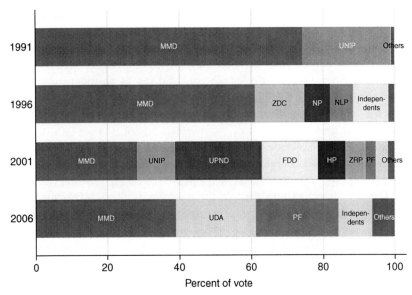

Fig. 8.1. Fragmentation of the Parliamentary Vote in Zambia, 1991–2006

Over fifty sitting MMD MPs resigned or were expelled from the party.[38] The MMD also purged branch- and provincial-level structures of party officials who were seen as opposing the third-term bid.[39]

But there are other potential explanations for fragmentation. For instance, Zambian voting patterns have often been explained with reference to ethno-regional cleavages and, to a lesser extent, economic conditions.[40] Thus, Posner argues that party labels in the multiparty Zambia serve as ethnic cues for Zambian voters, who coordinate their votes behind the candidate of the party that is most likely to represent their group's interest (Posner 2006; also, Posner 2004b). In line with other constructivist research on identity, Posner argues that individuals choose from a variety of potential identities when formulating their political choices.[41] He reduces the complexity of these individual identity choices, however, to the size and political relevance of an individual's group. Ethnic groups in Zambia are too small to achieve power singly, so Zambians

[38] The best account of the third-term debate and the reasons for MMD fragmentation is found in VonDoepp (2005), which usefully places Zambia alongside the similar third-term debates in Malawi and Namibia.

[39] *The Post*, November 11, 2000; *Times of Zambia*, December 9, 1999.

[40] Both Posner and Simon and Simon find that increased district-level poverty rates depressed turnout and voting for Chiluba in 1996, but they argue that ethno-regional identity and urban residence had larger effects on individual voting (Posner and Simon 2002; Simon 2002).

[41] See the discussion in Posner (2006: 2–15); also, Laitin (1986, 1998), Chandra (2001), and Posner (2003).

mobilize on the basis of language group. Posner used the 1996 elections as the empirical base for his conclusions about how multiparty politics affects individual vote choice and ethno-regional mobilization, and other scholars come to similar conclusions about this round of elections and the subsequent 2001 elections. Scarritt, for instance, suggests that parties in Zambia rely on ethnic appeals to win the votes of their ethnic bases, from which they receive the bulk of their votes (Scarritt 2006). Reflecting on the 1996 elections, Gould also notes that the party competition was highly ethnicized, though he attributes that to the "unanchored, transitory nature of existing political structures" (Gould 2002: 321).

These accounts overstate the uniformity of individuals' responses to parties, and they neglect how weak party organization undermines a party's ability to coordinate votes even within its own ethnic block. The 2001 and 2006 elections, in particular, suggest that Zambian parties have often failed to serve as strong ethnic cues or informational shortcuts for ethnic voters. The fragmentation of the vote in the 2001 election is associated, to some extent, with patterns of ethno-regional mobilization that had been practiced in the past. But increases in the number of candidates and significant party competitors cannot be explained with reference to ethnic mobilization alone. It was not that new parties drew away the votes of smaller ethnic groups, or split the vote bases of existing parties on sub-regional or sub-ethnic lines. Instead, changes in the party system indicate the inability of the larger parties to construct durable political coalitions and, equally importantly, discipline and prevent the defection of candidates and voters. When we look at patterns of vote fragmentation at the constituency level, the "solid ethnic coalitions" that Posner posits prove illusory. To give readers a sense of changes at the constituency level, the average effective number of electoral parties (ENEP) at the constituency level rose from 1.93 in 1991 to 3.36 in 1996 and then jumped to 6.46 in 2001. ENEP, as discussed above, is simply a measure of vote fragmentation. In 1996, only five constituencies had ENEP scores of more than 3.5 and none of these had scores over 5.0. In 2001, eighty-one constituencies – or just over half – had ENEP scores of greater than 3.5, and twenty-four constituencies had scores over 5.0. In 2006, there was a slight decline in fragmentation at the constituency level, but nineteen constituencies still had scores over 3.5 and four had scores over 5.0. I have plotted this measure of constituency-level fragmentation against the MMD's vote share, which gives us a graphical illustration of the degree to which the Zambian party system conforms to what we would expect in a disciplined two-party system (Figure 8.2).

Majoritarian electoral institutions, like those in all three of our cases, would presumably drive voters toward mainstream party candidates and away from the candidates of smaller parties, who are unlikely to win. In disciplined first-past-the-post (FPTP) systems, we would therefore expect constituency-level fragmentation to resemble the curve traced in the 1991 graph in Figure 8.2. As the vote for either the main opposition party or the ruling party approaches 100 percent in a single constituency, the ENEP score approaches 1.0. In 1991,

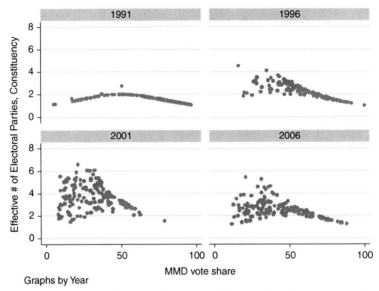

Fig. 8.2. Fragmentation of the Parliamentary Vote at the Constituency Level in Zambia, 1991–2006

constituency-level fragmentation was minimal, as the two main parties monopolized the vote. Subsequently, however, the opposition vote began to fragment, generating the patterns that we see in the later years. 2001 is an outlier both for the disorganization of the overall vote, with large numbers of constituencies at or above 5.0, and for the small number of constituencies in which the MMD scored over 50 percent of the vote.

Since constituencies are more ethnically homogenous than the country as a whole, increasing levels of vote fragmentation at the constituency level likely suggest that voters within a given ethnic group were divided, especially in 2001, over which party and which candidates best represented their interests. It is important not to overstate the conclusions we can draw from this trend toward vote fragmentation at the local level. Aggregate election results cannot tell us how the individuals of a particular group distributed their votes, nor have I examined how differences in the ethnic diversity of constituencies affected levels of vote fragmentation. The pattern of increasing vote fragmentation is suggestive, however, of an inability of parties to coordinate and discipline voters' choices over multiple election rounds. It may be that defections and party splitting rendered party cues less clear-cut or legible in 2001 and 2006 than they had been in 1991 and 1996. More likely, the fragmentation at the constituency level suggests that voters placed little stock in party labels, instead choosing candidates on the basis of personal concerns or local conflicts. This is consistent with the story told above of MMD party erosion at the local level.

Between the 2001 and 2006 elections, there was some reconsolidation of the MMD's support, and several MPs that had previously defected reaffiliated with the party. The MMD gained back seven parliamentary seats in 2002 and 2003 when MPs crossed back to the party from the Heritage Party (HP) and from the United Party for National Development (UPND).[42] After the Supreme Court nullified the original 2001 results in four constituencies, the results of these by-elections also signaled the reconsolidation of the MMD. In three of these cases, the MMD retained the seats with candidates who had contested in 2001 on either HP or Forum for Democracy and Development (FDD) tickets.[43] During this period, grassroots organizers for the UPND and other opposition parties also reaffiliated with the MMD, as did a number of party officials who had resigned in 2001 and 2002.[44] These developments may have laid the groundwork for a reconsolidation of the MMD and of the party landscape in future election rounds. But the MMD's attempts to rebuild party structures and strengthen central control may have had more mixed results. In 2002 and 2003, a large number of local party organizers were expelled from the party, particularly in Copperbelt and Lusaka provinces, for a variety of infractions and perceived "disloyalty" to the sitting MMD NEC.[45] The concentration of MMD disciplinary actions in particular areas seems to have shifted the base of party support, and it may have opened up space for the reactivation of social networks that had lain dormant.

My final comments on Zambia will reflect, briefly and speculatively, on whether corporatism and the strong mobilizing structures of organized labor have had lasting effects on Zambian party development. In the pages above, I argued that the MMD's own decisions isolated the party from its grassroots and contributed to the erosion of the organizational resources on which it had previously relied. I remarked on the diminution of the ZCTU as a potential coordinator of protest, and I stressed that the MMD established only weak party structures and poor disincentives to candidate defection. Despite this, the MMD retains some of its "focal point" qualities: this is particularly

---

[42] Two opposition parties, the UPND and the FDD, expelled a number of their MPs after the MPs had accepted ministerial positions in President Levy Mwanawasa's administration. *Times of Zambia*, March 27, 2003. These MPs retained their seats on MMD tickets by overwhelming margins. *Times of Zambia*, February 13, 2003.

[43] Electoral Commission of Zambia, "Constituencies where by-elections have taken place after the 2001 Tripartite Elections," mimeo, May 3, 2004. The MMD picked up another opposition seat after Enoch Kavindele dissolved his party in order to join the MMD. *Times of Zambia*, July 28, 2003.

[44] Interview with Vernon Mwaanga, July 21, 2003; also, *The Post*, July 14, 2003, and August 24, 2002.

[45] See, for instance, *Times of Zambia*, March 13 and June 15, 2002; *The Post*, January 25, 2003.

suggested by the ability of the party to woo back several of the MPs who had
defected in 2001 and by the partial reconsolidation of the party's base in 2006.

More interesting is the question of organized labor. The MMD once had its
strongest support in urban areas and the Copperbelt province, where
organized labor and the ZCTU had their greatest reach and influence. The
MMD lost in these areas to one of its splinters, the Patriotic Front (PF), in the
2006 elections and in a 2008 presidential by-election that had been occasioned
by the death in office of President Levy Mwanawasa. The rise of the PF was
particularly rapid. In the 2001 elections, the party received roughly 3 percent
of the presidential and parliamentary votes. In 2006, however, the PF's
charismatic presidential candidate, Michael Sata, finished in second place
with 29 percent of the vote, and its parliamentary candidates won nearly 30
percent of the seats in parliament. In a persuasive article, Larmer and Fraser
suggest that the PF capitalized on pre-existing associational networks to
mobilize party support (Larmer and Fraser 2007). More specifically, the
party drew on unions and old branch structures of the MMD (which had
defected or been ejected from the party), and it used populist rhetoric and a
staunch opposition to economic liberalization. This appealed to the coalition
between workers and the urban poor that had formed the heart of the ZCTU's
support base in the 1980s. Though the PF won most of its seats in the three
Bemba-speaking provinces, it also did well in ethnically and linguistically
mixed constituencies in Lusaka, where it won seven of twelve parliamentary
seats. In the 2008 presidential election, Cheeseman and Hinfelaar again note
the mixed ethnic and cross-ethnic – especially populist – appeals deployed by
the PF (Cheeseman and Hinfelaar 2010). Sata, once again the PF candidate,
swept all urban constituencies in the country, and he won a plurality of the
vote in approximately half the medium-density constituencies outside of the
PF's Bemba heartland.

Once again, these results suggest that the appeals used by parties – and the
ability of parties to tap into pre-existing social networks – affect how voters
choose candidates. The MMD effectively undercut the influence and negotiating power of organized labor over the course of the 1990s, but these actions
did not translate into stable control over the constituencies with the strongest
links to organized labor. The formal organizational power of the ZCTU may
have declined over the 1990s and 2000s, especially as structural adjustment
and economic decline shrunk the size of the unionized labor force. But the
networks and mobilizing structures that corporatism built may have retained
some of their mobilizing potential. It is unclear whether a reconsolidation of
the party landscape is underway in Zambia, but both the MMD's resilience
and the rise of the PF differ sharply from the patterns of party erosion and
formation that we will examine in Kenya. To a large extent, party organizations in Kenya play much weaker roles in structuring the choices of politicians
and voters, as we will see.

KENYA

The Founding Elections

As in Zambia, opposition parties in Kenya had little time in which to build party structures or establish internal decision-making procedures prior to the 1992 elections. The first major opposition party of the multi-party era, the Forum for the Restoration of Democracy (FORD), was launched as a pressure group in August 1991. The ruling party was under pressure due to domestic protests, but international donors were likely more influential in pushing the government of President Daniel arap Moi in the direction of political opening (Grosh and Orvis 1996; Brown 2001; Roessler 2005). In late 1991, several bilateral aid packages were either canceled or suspended, and the IMF and World Bank also suspended all new development aid to Kenya (Brown 2007: 309–13). In addition to the government's lack of progress on a number of economic goals, notably reductions in the size of the state, donors demanded an end to single-party rule and stricter action against corruption. Less than a month after the IMF suspension, the ruling Kenya African National Union (KANU) amended the constitution to repeal the ban on other political parties. FORD was registered as a political party in January 1992, and multiparty elections were held in December of that same year. If donors had hoped for a speedy electoral turnover, as they had recently witnessed in Zambia, they were disappointed. KANU's governing coalition was fragile, but the parliamentary and presidential elections occurred in a context of significant opposition fragmentation. In early months of 1992, FORD split on ethnic lines, and another opposition party, the Democratic Party (DP), was launched by disgruntled KANU politicians. Due to the fragmentation of the opposition vote across these and other parties, KANU candidates won re-election with fairly small pluralities of the vote in December. Moi retained the presidency with only 36 percent of the vote, and KANU candidates held half the seats in Parliament, though the party won less than 30 percent of the parliamentary vote.

The victory of the ruling party in the 1992 elections was partly due to the lack of a level playing field and the disruption of opposition party campaigns by state-sponsored violence (Barkan 1993; Fox 1996; Harbeson 1998; Throup and Hornsby 1998). The KANU state retained the use of several legal instruments that were used to block the access of opposition parties to Kenyan voters. The ruling party's control over the electoral commission and over the review and reform of electoral law created obstacles that even a united opposition would have struggled to overcome. Biased demarcation of parliamentary constituencies generated strong disproportionalities across districts and diluted the votes of opposition supporters. In the 1992 elections, 70

percent of the Kenyan electorate was concentrated in high-density constituencies that were allocated just over 50 percent of parliamentary seats, while
the lowest density constituencies, those that represented only 7.5 percent
of the electorate, were assigned 16 percent of parliamentary seats (Ndegwa
1998: 208). In both 1992 and 1997, Nairobi received one half the seats that it
would have received under a more population-equitable redistricting exercise
(Harbeson 1998: 169; also, Barkan et al. 2006). In 1997, this pattern of
malapportionment continued. Though the Kenyan constitution requires constituencies to be of roughly equal size, the twenty-two new constituencies
created in 1996 were not allocated to correct existing disproportionalities
(Ndegwa 1998: 207–8; Aywa and Grignon 2001: 106–16). Instead, the demarcation exercise was used, as it had been previously, to achieve partisan ends.
Had the 1997 demarcation exercise been guided by proportionality and the
number of voters registered in existing constituencies, eighteen of the twenty-
two new constituencies would have been apportioned to areas of opposition
support (Aywa and Grignon 2001: 111); instead, sixteen of these constituencies were placed in areas where KANU had won elections in 1992.

In addition to the manipulation of constituency demarcation, KANU passed
new regulations prior to the 1992 elections that changed the requirements for
electoral victory in presidential elections. Presidential candidates were now
required to win 25 percent of votes in five of Kenya's eight provinces – in
addition to a plurality of total votes – in order to form a government.[46] The
failure of the winning candidate to achieve this regional distribution would
trigger a run-off election. This change assured that an opposition candidate
could not win unless backed by a strong, cross-ethnic coalition. The ruling
party, on the other hand, has been on more solid ground in terms of meeting
this threshold due to its access to patronage. These new restrictions also preclud-
ed the formation of coalition governments, meaning that ministerial appointments could not be distributed to parties other than the president's own (Throup
and Hornsby 1998: 249). This deprived opposition party leaders of a tool that
theoretically could have been used to forge election pacts between parties.

There were also more overt restrictions on opposition parties. Under public
order laws, many of which were inherited from the colonial period, local state
officials – both traditional chiefs and District Administrators – had significant
latitude in interpreting what constituted legal political activity. As chiefs were
appointed by the President, both these officials and District Administrators
were strongly linked to the ruling party and enforced regulations on a partisan
basis, and they were also implicated in the organization of tribal clashes
(Klopp 2001). In terms of the law, meetings could be banned and their

---

[46] The language of the Act is unclear, raising some ambiguity regarding implementation
should a winning presidential candidate fail the 25 percent rule. *East African*, December 30,
1997, Throup and Hornsby (1998: 249).

organizers could be indefinitely detained on grounds of national security, and "seditious activity" laws allowed the state to censor and restrict political activity and media coverage (Ndegwa 1998). Finally, the Special Districts (Administration) Act allowed the state to restrict movement and political activity in "security zones." During the 1992 campaign, this law was used to ban opposition parties from areas affected by ethnic clashes and from large areas of the Rift, which MPs and other ruling party officials had deemed "KANU zones." This level of intimidation affected the ability of opposition parties to campaign and run candidates in areas of the country that experienced the highest levels of violence. For instance, in Rift Valley province, eighteen of forty-four KANU candidates were returned unopposed due to intimidation and state harassment of opposition parties (Nasong'o 2007; also, HRW 1993). These patterns of harassment spilled over to affect associational life independent of parties. In a survey in 2001, 56 percent of rural NGO activists and employees reported interference and harassment by local authorities, which was particularly common in areas of opposition support (Orvis 2003: 58).

Given the scale of political violence, and the electoral purposes to which it has been put, might violence explain opposition party weakness? From 1991 to 1997, ethnic clashes took over 1,500 lives and left 300,000 internally displaced persons, many of whom have yet to be resettled.[47] As others have pointed out, ethnic clashes capitalized on local grievances, particularly land hunger (Kahl 2006: ch. 4). Perpetrators were often recruited via ethnic networks, and they were dressed as traditional warriors and, often, armed with traditional weapons.[48] They were paid by politicians for the destruction of property and the displacement or killing of members of particular targeted groups; in some cases, they were promised land (Republic of Kenya 1992; HRW 1993; KHRC 1997; Republic of Kenya 1999). The clashes served very specific political purposes: they were used to remove likely opposition voters from areas, thereby advancing both the agendas of local elites and the overall electoral aims of KANU (Republic of Kenya 1992; HRW 1993; KHRC 1997; KHRC 1998; Republic of Kenya 1999). Because evictions were organized on an ethnic basis, violence reinforced ethnicity as the salient political identity in Kenya. It created intergroup animosity, particularly between the small tribes of the KANU coalition and the ethnic groups that tended to support opposition parties.

But conflict did not create opposition unity. Though Luo, Luhya, and Kikuyu composed the bulk of victims of the clashes, the political loyalties of these groups remained split across multiple opposition parties. Overall, the

---

[47] The death toll from these clashes is only marginally higher than the number killed during the January–February 2008 post-election violence in Kenya. Though I do not discuss the 2008 violence here, its scale supports my argument about the broader institutionalization of violence into party competition in Kenya.

[48] Klopp notes that many of those dressed as traditional warriors in Narok North were actually police and army personnel (Klopp 2001: 496).

most lasting effect of the ethnic clashes was the normalization of violence into periods of electoral competition. Gradually, political elites lost control over the networks of "violence specialists" that they had helped produce, and violence ceased to produce the same clear-cut electoral dividends for the ruling party (Anderson 2002; Kagwanja 2003; Mueller 2008). Rather than producing the party-building polarization that resulted in Zimbabwe, state-sponsored violence reinforced the salience of local ethnic animosities rather than national partisan ones. It did little to prevent the splintering of either KANU or opposition support at the local level. To this extent, violence undermined the development of strong, cross-ethnic opposition party organizations, as it reinforced ethnicity as the axis of political mobilization in Kenya. Overall, repression, violence, and electoral manipulation do not provide satisfying explanations for opposition fragmentation. Parliamentary disportionality made it more difficult for opposition parties to take a majority of parliamentary seats, but any effect on party organization or cohesion would have been indirect. Restrictions on political space complicated the mobilization of opposition voters, but 65 percent of Kenyan voters were not dissuaded from voting for opposition candidates by state repression, ethnic violence, or the partisan cast of the news media.

The failure of opposition parties to coordinate voters requires a different explanation. As suggested above and in Chapter 6, patterns of party-building in Kenya channeled party-building in the direction of ethnic mobilization. The tendency toward ethnicized party-building was evident during the earliest stages of opposition mobilization. In December 1991, a month before FORD's registration as a party, rumors of a potential split began to circulate. Some of the disagreement centered on the solicitation and misuse of party funds by members of the interim executive, but the underlying issue was the distribution of authority within the organization (Throup and Hornsby 1998: 78–9).[49] There was already an ethnic cast to party divisions, as party founder Martin Shikuku complained about the increasing influence of Kikuyu activists and defectors from KANU (Throup and Hornsby 1998: 93). Disagreements over the size of the steering committee and the form of internal party elections escalated to larger intra-party conflicts. Within a month of the party's registration, ethnic rivals Oginga Odinga and Paul Muite announced that they would pursue the party's presidency, and party structures began to split on factional and ethnic lines (Throup and Hornsby 1998: esp. 106–15, 130–51). By June, violence between supporters of different factions had become common at FORD rallies (Mwagiru et al. 2002: 7–8).[50] In September, Odinga was suspended from the party. FORD was subsequently re-registered as two

---

[49] See also *Daily Nation*, December 6, 1991; *Sunday Nation*, December 8, 1991; *Kenya Times*, December 8, 1991.
[50] *Daily Nation*, June 29, 1992; July 20 and 27, 1992.

separate parties, FORD-Kenya, Odinga's vehicle for mobilizing the Luo vote, and FORD-Asili, which drew on both Kikuyu and Luhya support. Even within ethnic blocks, however, parties were not capable of coordinating opposition to KANU. Several Kikuyu politicians, including a number of ministers, defected from KANU in 1992. Rather than joining FORD-Asili, these individuals formed the DP and selected Mwai Kibaki as their presidential candidate.

From 1992 onward, the party landscape became significantly more fractured, driven in large part by defections and party splitting at the elite level, as well as parties' general inability to forge durable ties to constituencies at the grassroots level. The general features of organizational fragmentation can be summarized quite simply: intra-party discussions focused almost entirely on the composition of parties' main offices, and losers of these battles defected to form new parties. By 1997, this process of leadership-led splitting had generated three branches of FORD and another two splinter parties, each of which was united behind a single prominent personality and drew on a distinctly ethnic constituency. These opposition parties held national congresses, but these functioned as "a mere showcase or coronation of the party leader" (Oloo 2007: 106). The processes used to select candidates for parliamentary and local offices were, across opposition parties, opaque. Even before nominations turned violent, as they did in the late 1990s, corruption and imposition of candidates led to the continual production of party splinters and defections.

Despite high levels of disorganization within parties, which will be discussed further below, opposition party leaders were still able to cobble together substantial ethnic vote bases. For instance, after the death of Luo political leader Oginga Odinga, his son was passed over for the vice-chairmanship of FORD-K in favor of another Luo. This son, Raila Odinga, left FORD-K and took over a previously insignificant party, the National Democratic Party (NDP), which had the advantage of already being registered as a party. In an example that well illustrates the role that party leadership plays in harmonizing the ethnic vote, the Luo constituencies in Nyanza that had voted overwhelmingly for FORD-K in 1992 swung their support behind the NDP. Of the thirty seats in Nyanza that the NDP contested, it won more than 70 percent of the vote in fourteen and more than 50 percent in an additional five. Other ethnic parties had similar ethnic bases, though their support was marginally more diverse. Voting patterns for the NDP also demonstrate another trend that came to the fore in 1997, which was the virtual cantonment of most opposition parties. In 1992, the major opposition parties (FORD-K, DP, and FORD-A) ran candidates in most constituencies across provinces, but they largely abandoned this strategy in 1997. In 1997, the NDP nominated candidates in only seven of twenty-nine constituencies in Central Province, fourteen of forty-nine constituencies in Rift Valley, and eight of twenty-four constituencies in Western. Only one of these candidates won election to a seat, and only five others won more than 10 percent of the vote in their constituencies.[51] The FORD parties showed similar patterns. In 1997, FORD-Kenya ran large numbers of candidates in Nyanza, Rift Valley, and Western but ran only two candidates in Central Province. FORD-People ran seven candidates in Rift Valley and fourteen in Central but ran virtually no candidates in other provinces.

In 1992, election results were sharply structured by ethnicity, so Odinga won nearly 75 percent of the vote in the Luo Nyanza province, while the DP and FORD-K candidates drew largely on Central and Eastern voters and Central and Western province voters, respectively. Foeken and Dietz point out that a similar pattern of ethnic mobilization in parliamentary contests yielded a Parliament in which ethnicity and party affiliation largely overlapped:

> 67% of FORD-Asili members [of Parliament] were Kikuyu, 61 percent of FORD-Kenya Luo and 52 percent of the DP again Kikuyu. In KANU, however, not a single Luo or Kikuyu won a seat. Among the KANU members of parliament, we find all Kalenjin representatives, 12 out of 17 elected Kamba from the southeast, 9 out of 10 elected Somali from the northeast, all 6 elected Maasai, 6 out of 9 elected Gusii, as well as representatives from all the smaller ethnic groups. (Foeken and Dietz 2000: 126–7)

In 1992 and in subsequent years, party leaders devoted little attention to constructing linkages across ethnic groups or regions, and attempts to forge cross-ethnic coalitions, much less strong cross-ethnic parties, were notably half-hearted.[52] The political fortunes of any individual politician were tied to the strength of his relationship with an ethnic base and the credibility of promises to distribute patronage to that base. As Oyugi points out, even if the rival ethnic elites within FORD had wanted to compromise, they were "prisoners of their own ethnic constituencies," all of whom wished their own leaders to ascend to the presidency (Oyugi 1997: 56). Ethnicity remains the strongest predictor of presidential vote choice in Kenya (Bratton and Kimenyi 2008). In terms of parliamentary elections, however, the weakness of party organization has fostered different voting patterns over multiple election rounds. Specifically, Kenya is characterized by increasing party system disorder. Not even politicized ethnicity, stronger in Kenya than in most other African countries, provides a constraint on vote fragmentation.

---

[51] In other provinces, NDP candidates fared even worse: in Northeast Province, all eight of the NDP's candidates won less than 1 percent of the vote, and in Western, seven of the party's eight candidates won less than 10 percent of the vote.

[52] For instance, efforts by the Kenyan churches and influential civic activist Wangari Maathai to forge an opposition coalition prior to the 1992 elections met with little success.

The Internal Organization of Parties

To a greater extent than in Zambia, Kenyan opposition parties lack both party structures and organizational durability. Of the parties that contested the 1992 elections, only the ruling party at the time, KANU, currently bears any resemblance to its original form, though it has shifted in terms of its constituency base. Of the other parties, major opposition parties have fragmented, changed leadership and constituency base, and, most obviously, altered their names several times. This organizational fluidity has had a pronounced impact on party structure and representation in Kenya. Some Kenyans navigate the fluid terrain of party politics with ease. For instance, many residents of Kisumu and Nyanza, the ethnic heartland of the Luo, refer to the multitude of Odinga-led parties they have supported by a single name, "Chama" (the party). For most Kenyans, however, the constant switching of party labels, repeated defections of candidates from one party to the next, and the lack of solid party roots to grassroots constituencies have led to distrust and dissatisfaction with parties and political elites. Since 1992, parties have become increasingly fragmented, and violence has been institutionalized into all aspects of party organization and campaigning.

Despite changes in the parties themselves since 1992, however, there are consistent tendencies in Kenyan party organization that span electoral rounds. In addition to a rich secondary literature, my conclusions rely on a set of twelve focus groups conducted in three Kenyan cities in May–June 2008. These focus groups took place long after the original FORD had disintegrated and been reconstituted into an array of successor parties, but respondents consistently drew a line between modern party organization and party organization before 1992 (i.e., "in KANU times," "back when KANU was here," "when KANU was the party"). They suggested that, in the multiparty period, there is a common party form that has characterized opposition and ruling parties alike.[53] Most importantly, Kenyan political parties are built around ethnicity. Secondly, because party leaders can rely on fairly stable ethnic vote blocks in presidential elections, where their attentions are typically fixed, there is little investment in party structures. This means that parties have little control or influence over those who contest parliamentary and local elections. Finally, even though Kenyan parties are multi-ethnic coalitions at the national level, the alliances that underlay these coalitions are driven by a complicated calculus of ethnic power-seeking, which has typically hinged on small numbers of ethnic leaders at any one time. Thus, if one speaks of party mobilization among the Luo,

---

[53] Respondents came from a variety of ethnic and partisan backgrounds, and they were mixed in terms of social background as well. It is important to underline that this is not a representative sample of Kenyans: there are significant differences between the political attitudes of urban dwellers and their rural counterparts (Logan et al. 2007).

238 *From Protest to Parties*

the focus immediately falls on Raila Odinga (and only marginally James Orengo); if one turns to the Luhya, it is Martin Shikuku and Kijana Wamalwa; for the Kikuyu, it was Kenneth Matiba, is now Mwai Kibaki, and may perhaps become Uhuru Kenyatta. Remarkably, conflict and violence between ethnic groups does not preclude elite alliances. Thus, even though earlier ethnic clashes often involved Kalenjin attacks on Luo and other "non-indigenous" groups in the Rift Valley and elsewhere, Kalenjin leader William Ruto – who was implicated in these clashes – became a prominent member of the Orange Democratic Movement (ODM) led by Odinga, a Luo, in 2005. These shifting elite alliances are demonstrative of the underlying disconnect between party elites and grassroots constituencies.

Some saw the elections of 2002, in which the ruling KANU was defeated by an opposition coalition, as a watershed. But the formation of this coalition, which contested the elections as the National Rainbow Coalition (NARC), did not mark a significant departure from the patterns of party organization of previous election rounds. Opposition leaders agreed to back a common NARC presidential candidate, and they agreed to forward a common slate of parliamentary candidates. Because the NARC vote coordinated a large proportion of opposition voters, especially at the presidential level, it won the presidency and half of the seats in Parliament. But NARC did not signal a new commitment to party-building or to strengthening lengths between party organizations and mass constituencies. As Anderson points out, the success of the opposition coalition was partly due to the collapse of KANU at both the elite level and in terms of grassroots party structures (Anderson 2003: 331–4). As in Zambia in 2001, a succession struggle had split the ruling party and triggered a large number of defections (Kagwanja 2005). The NARC coalition benefited from KANU's fragmentation, and there was a wave of defections to NARC by those who saw that the political tide had shifted. In addition to several KANU MPs, KANU and other unaffiliated parties' branch structures defected to NARC, the Liberal Democratic Party (LDP), or other coalition partners.[54] NARC's "borrowing" of the organizational capacity of its partners lent the coalition a geographical reach and support base that the opposition had never before been able to assemble. It did not, however, create anything that looks like a party organization. In 2004, when divisions emerged within NARC over constitutional reform and other issues, NARC split cleanly into its constituent parts. These splinters then reconstituted themselves into new alliances prior to the 2007 elections. The basic point is that the ability to force an electoral turnover does not necessarily imply strong party organization. In Kenya, political elites lack the party structures that allow them to discipline voters and reduce party system fragmentation. NARC's speedy rise and fall merely illustrates this fact. Figure 8.3 graphically demonstrates how vote fragmentation has been a consistent feature of parlimentary elections in Kenya.

---

[54] *Daily Nation*, October 17, 24, and 28, 2002; November 5, 2002.

At the popular level, Kenyan parties are characterized by very weak ties to popular constituencies (Widner 1997; Wanjohi 2003; Oloo 2007). From the late 1990s to the present, pervasive vote-buying and the use of youths have further undermined ties of accountability between voters and their representatives (Oloo 2007; Kramon 2009). In nearly all focus groups, Kenyans described parties as weak or absent. In order to support this assertion, they consistently mentioned two features of party behavior that they described as unique to the multiparty period. First of all, both KANU and opposition parties did not maintain an office or other presence in local areas in the periods between elections. This, coupled with the tendency of parties to rename themselves and change their party colors from election to election, led several individuals to conclude that parties did not matter and were not concerned with representation.[55] Though respondents were able to name individuals who had been active in party campaigns, many mentioned that these individuals had personal ties to party leaders and were not involved in community activities outside of election periods.[56] Party structures were either considered non-existent or they were seen as shifting along with the defections of party leaders, which respondents viewed as evidence of party weakness.[57] The tendency of candidates to defect from one party to another, particularly after primary losses, reinforced the perception of party disorganization at the local level.

In Kenya, both party primaries and general elections have become increasingly characterized by the "buying" of offices and the use of paid youths to disrupt or manipulate polling.[58] The high level of violence associated with party primaries has often been neglected by analysts of political violence in Kenya. In 1997, there had been several occasions on which primaries were manipulated or canceled due to violence.[59] By 2002, however, violence,

---

[55] The issue of permanent party offices seemed particularly emotional and triggered some degree of nostalgia, especially among the less politically engaged and less educated respondents. For instance, at a focus group for market women, which was conducted in Swahili, there was a lively discussion about where exactly the KANU party office was once located and at what hours you could find a party official inside. Focus group, Kawangware, June 2, 2008. Similar sentiments about the availability of KANU during the single-party period were expressed by respondents in Kangemi, May 29, 2008.

[56] Focus groups, Kibera, May 29, 2008, and April 21, 2009; Huruma (II), June 3, 2008.

[57] Focus groups, Changamwe, June 13, 2008; Kisumu (I), June 5, 2008; Huruma (II), June 3, 2008. At a focus group composed of ODM activists in Kibera, accounts all suggested that party officials had been recruited through personal networks or because they were from the home area of party leader Raila Odinga. Activists also confirmed that party labels were inconsequential, as they [activists] would "always follow Raila." Focus group, Kibera, May 25, 2008.

[58] Interviews with Oleng Sana, July 18, 2006; Musambayi Katumanga, July 21, 2006. Also, focus groups, Kisumu (III), June 6, 2008; Mukuru, May 30, 2008; Huruma (I), June 3, 2008; University of Nairobi, May 28, 2008.

[59] The KANU nominations seemed particularly prone to violence and disorganization. *Daily Nation*, November 26 and December 1, 1997. For more on the nominations problems of the opposition, see *Daily Nation*, December 8, 1997.

vote-buying, and imposition of candidates had become systematic across parties.[60] In 2007, the level of violence in party primaries escalated to a point that *The Standard* newspaper termed the results "*rungu* [cudgel] democracy." One youth in Huruma, a slum in Nairobi, described the mix of vote-buying and violence that characterizes elections as "women for votes, youths for fracas."[61] Newspaper reports during the 2002 and 2007 pre-election periods suggest that vote-buying, violence, and imposition of candidates were not merely urban phenomena.[62] Low levels of party institutionalization – and increasing apathy among voters – make violence and vote-buying effective tools for winning elections. However, in contrast to the strong links between party organizations and the perpetrators of violence in Zimbabwe, Kenya's violence "specialists" belonged to autonomous bodies that were never incorporated into party or state structures (Kagwanja 2001; Anderson 2002; Atemi 2002; Kagwanja 2003; Maupeu 2008: esp. 29–31; Mueller 2008). These specialists included not only the youths that were informally recruited by individual candidates but also organized militia, who had become visible political actors by the early 2000s. Over the course of the last decade, political elites have lost control over these groups, which have formed links with criminal economies and learned to sustain themselves during the periods between elections (Mwagiru et al. 2002; Katumanga 2005; Mueller 2008). The creeping institutionalization of violence into all realms of electoral competition has directly undermined formal party organization and electoral processes, and it has made the overall political context increasingly unstable and violent. This trend was evident well before the 2008 post-election violence. In the next section, we will look at increasing vote fragmentation over parliamentary rounds. I would argue that this is a result of the weakness of party organization in Kenya and the increasingly resource-driven aspects of candidates' campaigns.

Patterns of Electoral Support

The 1992 elections centered on the battle for the presidency, with the bulk of the votes splitting across the four main candidates on roughly ethnic lines. The Kikuyu vote was split between two candidates, the DP's Kibaki and FORD-Asili's candidate Kenneth Matiba. Within ethnic blocks, coordination was marginally stronger for presidential candidates than in parliamentary races, and minor party candidates received less than 1 percent of the vote.

---

[60] *Daily Nation*, November 21 and 24, 2002, and November 17, 2007; *The Standard*, November 20 and 21, 2002, and November 17, 2007.

[61] Focus group, Huruma (II), June 3, 2008. There were similar patterns of electoral manipulation in 2007 in the Nairobi locations of Mukuru, Kibera, Kayole, and Westlands, as well as in Kisumu. Field notes, December 2007.

[62] Also, focus group, University of Nairobi, May 28, 2008.

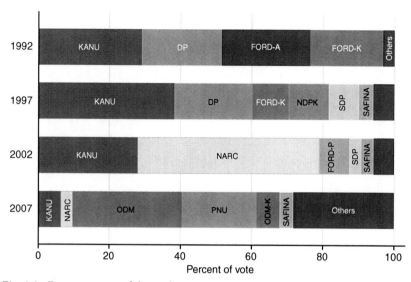

Fig. 8.3. Fragmentation of the Parliamentary Vote in Kenya, 1992–2007

Parliamentary election results are more closely related to the issues of party organization and vote coordination that interest us here, but these show only slightly higher levels of fragmentation in 1992 than in the presidential results. Over subsequent election rounds, however, individual opposition parties were unable to hold together vote blocks that had been relatively cohesive in the first multiparty elections. This led to an increasing fragmentation of the party landscape.

The dominance of ethnic mobilization in 1992 structured opposition party organization, but presidential candidates quickly lost their ability to deliver parliamentary seats to their chosen candidates within different ethnic zones. None of the opposition parties significantly invested in party structures, nor did parties maintain contacts or presence in local areas during inter-electoral periods. Even within a particular party's ethnic heartland, voters were increasingly willing to defect to smaller parties' candidates in parliamentary and local elections, or they voted for politicians who had failed to win their favored party's nomination in party primaries. Kanyinga suggests that this pattern of "mix-and-match" voting was already in place in the 1997 elections (Kanyinga 2001). The trend intensified in subsequent election rounds. Parliamentary vote coordination became increasingly weak even within ethnic zones, outside of some portions of Nyanza province. As in Zambia, Kenyan politicians' lack of investment in party structures meant that party support was vulnerable to swings in popular sentiment or to other candidates' deployment of material resources in a particular constituency. Nor did voters, chastened by backing

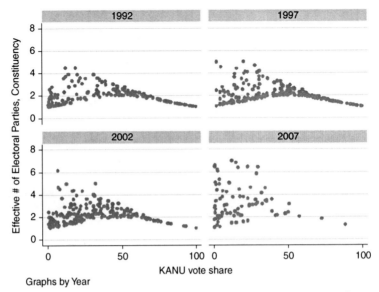

Fig. 8.4. Fragmentation of the Parliamentary Vote at the Constituency Level in Kenya, 1992–2007

Note: For the 2007 plot, two constituencies with very high levels of fragmentation have been excluded.

unsuccessful candidates in 1997 or 2002, return to mainstream parties in later elections. The 2007 elections, often depicted as a highly disciplined and polarized contest between the ODM and the Party of National Unity (PNU), marked a new high in terms of vote fragmentation. In Figure 8.3, readers will note the increasing proportion of the vote captured by parties that individually received less than 3 percent of total votes, a category represented on the far right in the figure as "others." In all prior contests, these small parties had accounted for less than 6 percent of the total vote; however, in 2007, candidates of these parties received over 28 percent of the total vote.

If we look at constituency-level fragmentation of the popular vote, we find even stronger evidence that the major parties have been unable to hold together electoral constituencies. Again, since constituencies tend to be more ethnically homogenous than either provinces or the country as a whole, we would generally expect fragmentation to be lower in constituencies, especially where parties are strongly associated with a particular ethnic group or groups, as they are in Kenya. Figure 8.4 presents the effective number of parties at the constituency level against the proportion of the vote won by the parties in control of the executive at the time of the election. Since KANU's vote share and electoral reach withered considerably after its defeat in the 2002 elections, the plot for 2007 presents the constituency-level fragmentation against the proportion of the parliamentary vote received by the PNU, then the ruling party. Even though FPTP electoral institutions in Kenya, like those in Zambia, penalize voters who do not align behind likely winners, we observe very high levels of constituency-level fragmentation.

In terms of voting within constituencies, 2007 again marks a sharp escalation of fragmentation over earlier election rounds. In 1997, only one constituency scored an ENEP score of more than 5: Kamukunji, a Nairobi high-density constituency that includes both the Kamukunji and Eastleigh slums. In 2002, there were only two. In 2007, thirty-one constituencies had ENEP scores of 5 or greater. If we lower the bar to constituency-level ENEP scores of 3.5 or lower, we observe an equally significant trend. In 1997, fourteen constituencies had ENEP scores of 3.5 or greater, almost all of which were urban constituencies. In 2002, there was only a slight increase to seventeen constituencies, reflecting NARC's role in constraining fragmentation. In 2007, however, a staggering sixty-nine constituencies were characterized by fragmentation scores of 3.5 or higher. A similar story is told with the number of candidates contesting Kenya's 210 parliamentary seats, which rose from 1,093 in 1997 to 1,243 in 2002 to 2,725 in 2007. Even though the Zambian party system demonstrated a similar increase in fragmentation following splits in the MMD prior to the 2002 elections, there were a lower number of candidates and parties over which votes were split. Overall, however, both Zambia and Kenya would seem to suggest that vote coordination fails when parties are organizationally weak and lack strong connections to voters.

CONCLUSIONS

As in many other countries in Africa, Kenyan and Zambian parties are multi-ethnic coalitions in which ethnic mobilization at the local level coexists with a national-level politics that is focused on knitting together a more diverse set of voters (e.g., Cheeseman and Ford 2007). In both countries, ethnic or ethno-regional appeals play a role in local contests. But it would be a mistake to reduce party organization, campaigns, and variation in support to the size of ethnic groups in Zambia and Kenya. Instead, what patterns of fragmentation suggest is that the strength or weakness of party organization plays an important mediating role in vote choice. Where party leaders invest in building structures and local presence, they are better able to discipline candidates, since party affiliation provides valuable information to voters, and they are better able to coordinate constituencies. This has been the case in Zimbabwe. Where political mobilization relies largely on patronage or on personal networks, candidates may defect without facing electoral penalty. If party labels are less important than other factors in shaping vote choice, politicians have few incentives to remain within parties that block upward mobility or allow little space for dissent. Just as these incentives erode the ties between candidates and party organizations, party weakness prevents the emergence of strong, durable ties between parties and constituencies.

In contrast to Zimbabwe, party supporters in both Zambia and Kenya are weakly attached to party labels, as patterns of increasing vote fragmentation suggest. The frequency with which defections occur makes the construction and maintenance of party boundaries difficult. Indeed, what is most remarkable is the fluidity with which electoral coalitions are formed and then dissolved. In 1991 and 1996, for instance, the MMD drew its strongest support from the Copperbelt and Northwest provinces, and it was often viewed as being a party of the Bemba, the ethnic group that is predominant in those provinces. In the 2006 elections, as mentioned above, a new party swept the MMD's former strongholds in the Copperbelt and Lusaka. The MMD's own support, meanwhile, shifted toward regions in which it had previously had weaker support, including the former UNIP stronghold of Eastern province. In Kenya, we observe a similar renegotiation of how particular cleavages are connected to coalition-building. For instance, at one point in time, we might observe political alliances that unite Kalenjins and Luos against Kikuyus (e.g., 2008), while at others, Kikuyus and Luos unite against Kalenjins (e.g., 2002 and 2010). The important point is that the fluidity of parties and of parties' associations with voters prevents the institutionalization of parties and the emergence of stable reference points for voters.

How does this relate to the general arguments of the book? First of all, I have argued that party organization in Zambia and Kenya was shaped by the choices of party leaders, particularly the choice not to invest in party structures or in the strengthening of ties to grassroots constituencies. In both countries, party leaders neglected party organization, and electoral battles were largely determined by the resources and appeals of local candidates themselves. In this context, defections and party-splitting are likely. Choices matter, but party-building also operates within the constraints imposed by history. In earlier chapters, I emphasized how differences in authoritarian rule created very different protest landscapes: in Zambia, the trade unions provided a cross-ethnic mobilizing structure that allowed for the coordination of political opposition; in Kenya, the lack of weak ties across ethnic and geographic lines made the coordination of protest and campaigns difficult. In Kenya, therefore, parties' reliance on ethnic networks was, in many ways, not a choice. Party elites did not have access to mobilizing structures that reached across ethnic and regional lines. The ethnicization of politics in the authoritarian period has shaped patterns of party-building after transition, just as the presence of cross-ethnic mobilizing structures in Zambia may have provided a long-run constraint on party system fragmentation. In the conclusion, I will comment further on the relative weight of legacy versus choice.

Conclusions

Party-Building and the Prospects for Democracy

This book started with a simple puzzle. Why do we find strong, cross-ethnic opposition parties in some democratizing countries, while opposition parties tend toward organizational weakness and fragmentation in others? As I started to unpack the dynamics of opposition party formation in Kenya, Zambia, and Zimbabwe, questions multiplied. How do institutions that start as tools of state control transform themselves into staging grounds for opposition? How do new opposition parties maintain the commitment of activists and discipline the behavior of candidates, especially when they have few resources? To what extent can the choices of elites overcome the obstacles presented by history – or, alternatively, squander the advantages that history has provided?

The preceding pages have examined these questions and others, but, overall, my arguments repeatedly return to a single theme. The creation and evolution of any institution – a trade union congress, a party organization, or elections themselves – is a result of both context and choice. Both the legacies of authoritarian rule and the choices and differential skill of opposition parties shape party development during democratization. In terms of the question of authoritarian legacies, there has been a tendency to neglect variation across African regimes and to view African authoritarianism as having somewhat uniform effects on associational life and political space. As the pages above have pointed out, there was real variation across African authoritarian regimes, notably in terms of the treatment of corporate actors like organized labor. Clientelism and concentration of power were characteristic of most African states, but political leaders pursued different means of linking state and society (Collier 1982; Jackson and Rosberg 1982). In terms of the role of party strategy in fostering democratization, I emphasize the utility of polarizing or confrontational tactics in building party cohesion and partisan identity. The study of earlier Third Wave transitions has led us to place negotiation and consent at the center of democratic transition. This book has instead suggested that democracy and competitive party systems require strong opposition parties, but these are most likely to be built with strategies that increase incumbent threat. Democratization in today's hybrid regimes, therefore, is likely to be marked as much by conflict as it is by negotiation.

The book's first core argument is that differences in authoritarian rule left in place institutional structures that made effective political opposition more or less likely. In countries like Zimbabwe and Zambia, where post-independence states built strong, centralized labor movements, opposition parties were able to draw upon the cross-ethnic mobilizing structures provided by labor. In contrast, in countries like Kenya, authoritarian states relied on patronage and networks of ethnic brokerage in order to rule. In these contexts, it was more difficult to coordinate protest across different social boundaries, and opposition parties were prone to fragmentation on ethnic lines. The book's second main argument is that parties are more cohesive and more successful at sustaining grassroots commitment where they choose strategies that intensify polarization on party lines. These strategies carry risks as well as organizational benefits. Where opposition parties use confrontational or polarizing strategies, they build walls around their organizations, making defection and fragmentation less likely. But a cohesive and confrontational opposition also increases incumbents' perception of threat, increasing the likelihood of violence and authoritarian retrenchment. This paradox lies at the heart of the book's conception of democratization. Strong opposition parties are required to push hybrid regimes toward democracy, but they also have the potential to trigger conflict and de-democratization. Historical legacies strongly shape opposition party formation, but they are not the sole determinants of party strength. Party development is also affected by the choices that parties make and the reactions of the rivals they confront.

An attention to history, therefore, does not preclude a significant scope for contingency and the expression of agency by political actors. The institutions and patterns established by states or by parties at any particular point often seem "sticky," or resistant to change, but they do not always generate the increasing returns that are associated with true path dependence (Pierson 2000; also, Thelen 2004). Following Collier and Collier, critical junctures – like the one that I argue occurred in the immediate post-independence period in sub-Saharan Africa – shape the political arena. The choices states make during these junctures set countries on different trajectories, but legacies retain their power only where there exist continuing "mechanisms of production" (Collier and Collier 1991: esp. ch. 8). Without periodic reinforcement, the choices made and institutions established at earlier points have ever-diminishing effects on actor behavior. Collier and Collier find mechanisms of legacy production and maintenance in the kinds of relationships between actors that emerge in the wake of critical junctures. Where labor mobilization was weaker, for instance, Latin American labor movements allied with more marginal political parties, which Collier and Collier suggest led to the radicalization of labor and of party systems in countries where this occurred.

Relational processes play a similarly prominent role in explaining opposition party strength and durability in late Third Wave democratizers. Polarizing appeals and confrontational strategies can boost activist commitment and organizational cohesion, even when opposition parties lack more tangible resources. Where parties do not attempt to construct and reinforce party-based social boundaries via conflict or polarization, the mobilizing structures that parties inherit may slowly erode. Similar opposition parties can make different choices in this respect. In Zimbabwe and Zambia, for instance, opposition parties both drew on the mobilizing structures of organized labor, but the fates of these two labor-based parties took different paths. This was partly due to the strength of the incumbent parties that these challengers faced and each party's need for sustained mobilization. In Zimbabwe, where the opposition faced a strong and cohesive incumbent party, mobilization remained an important priority for the party. Party leaders devoted significant resources to maintaining connections with grassroots constituencies and building a party-based identity. In Zambia, on the other hand, the ruling party splintered, and elite defections fueled opposition party formation to a greater extent. The opposition party won the founding elections overwhelmingly, and party leaders quickly lost interest in mobilization. The point here is simple: both mobilization and organizational investments are costly, and we should only expect them to occur in environments where party competition is high. I will return to the contributions of polarization to party-building below. In the next sections, I briefly review how the book's main arguments work, and I point out some of the ways that the book's findings might inform theories of democratization and party development. I then conclude with a brief discussion of the book's implications for real-world policies of democracy promotion.

OPPOSITION PARTIES AS LEGACY AND CHOICE

One of the major differences between opposition parties concerns the scope and the durability of their mobilizational reach. Some opposition parties are able to coordinate protest voters across the lines of ethnicity and geography, and they are able to build a strong base of activists and party workers that serve as the conduit between local and the national party structures. These parties serve as focal points for anti-incumbent voters, but they also create more rooted party structures and more stable levels of party support over time. Other opposition parties depend more heavily on candidates' personal ties and loyalties, and party structures remain underdeveloped. This book argues that this variation is due to two factors: past patterns of authoritarian rule, and the differential success of parties in polarizing the political landscape. In terms of the first of these, past patterns of authoritarian rule create the landscape in which protest movements and their party successors maneuver. Across the three countries considered in this book, historical legacies left opposition with different challenges and opportunities. But legacy was not fate: the choices made by new opposition parties, particularly regarding internal party organization and governance, shaped party development to as great an extent as did the resources parties inherited from past periods of authoritarian rule.

In Zimbabwe and Zambia, leftist governments supported the expansion and centralization of trade union structures in the immediate post-independence period. The centralized architecture of labor relations in these countries resembled the corporatist arrangements that were characteristic of some authoritarian regimes in Latin America and elsewhere. Near-compulsory membership for formal sector workers created unions with extensive – if still somewhat thin – geographical reach. The alliances between these states and organized labor occurred in such a way as to produce centralized trade unions that were well resourced and institutionally autonomous from ruling parties and governments. These unions had established structures linking labor leaders and rank-and-file membership, and, to some degree, they produced a notion of shared identity among union members. As government–labor alliances frayed, labor movements came to serve as focal points for protest and as mobilizing structures for newly formed opposition parties in both countries. In contrast, in countries where authoritarianism discouraged the construction of cross-ethnic networks and national or "peak" organizations, opposition parties inherited weaker mobilizing structures. In Kenya, for instance, authoritarian rule was built on ethnic brokerage rather than alliances with organized labor or other corporate actors. The Kenyan state's attitude toward organized labor alternated between repression, neglect, and political manipulation. In stark contrast to the expansive and hierarchical labor structures in Zimbabwe and Zambia, union-based networks in Kenya were internally fragmented and limited in geographical reach. Consequently, new opposition parties lacked the mobilizing structures that labor movements provided in the other cases. These parties instead remained reliant on ethnic mobilization and the clientelistic networks that individual politicians were able to construct. The resulting party organizations were weakly rooted, highly personalized, and more volatile than those in Zimbabwe and Zambia.

Where governments adopted corporatist policies that strengthened organized labor, they did not intend for unions to be critical of government policy or politically active. Zimbabwean and Zambian government policies toward labor were envisioned as a form of state–labor alliance, which was in accord with the leftist orientations of ruling parties in these countries. Labor was expected to deliver wage restraint and to dampen strike activity. In exchange, the government subsidized food and social services, and it adopted legislation that furthered the corporate and organizational interests of unions.

State–labor alliances provided organized labor with concrete resources: political visibility, funds and organizational structures, a substantial membership base, and a scope for criticism of government policy that was not accorded to other actors. In both Zimbabwe and Zambia, trade union congresses gradually built larger and more autonomous organizational structures, and rank-and-file members elected increasingly radical and confrontational leaders. The implementation of structural adjustment programs broke the remaining links between governments and trade union centers, and these reforms brought workers and the urban poor into direct confrontation with the state. Economic protests built solidarity and a sense of common purpose among organized labor's natural constituencies. In addition to these affective ties, the mobilizing structures of labor movements played an important role in conveying information and coordinating action across space and across social cleavages. In Kenya, on the other hand, popular protests were weak and uncoordinated, both before and after the first movements in the direction of democratization. Organized labor played no role in voicing grievances or building coalitions for political change. As political protest turned to party competition, Kenyan political elites looked out across a fairly flat associational landscape. Rather than drawing on national cross-ethnic mobilizing structures, as labor movements had allowed opposition parties to do in Zimbabwe and Zambia, Kenyan opposition parties were organized on the lines of more fragmented ethnic and personal networks.

Early organizational advantages allow labor-based opposition parties to quickly coordinate protest, but they do not automatically yield strong party organizations. Party cohesion remains a constant challenge, even in those contexts where opposition parties benefit from institutional structures that facilitate large-scale collective action. In Africa and other late Third Wave transitions, pro-democracy movements begin as unruly alliances of groups, which have divergent interests and little notion of a common identity. As movements become parties, these divisions and tendencies toward fragmentation are exacerbated: policies must be formulated, offices have to be allocated, elections must be won, and choices about party structure must be made. Since new parties typically lack institutionalized procedures for the resolution of conflict, they rarely have the ability to process competing demands and formulate clear and consistent policies. Intra-organizational conflict leads to the centralization of decision-making, the defection of candidates and local political elites, and an increasing disconnection between national leadership and grassroots constituencies. In order to live long enough to build strong party organizations, newly formed opposition parties must find means of holding together their fractious coalitions.

How do parties prevent fragmentation? A substantial literature suggests that extra-organizational institutions, notably electoral rules, affect the structure of parties and party leaders' control over candidates (e.g., Ames 1995;

Morgenstern 2001; Samuels 2002; Desposato 2004). Other scholars have suggested that parties might themselves be structured in ways that shift individuals' evaluations of the likelihood of future rewards. For instance, where parties institute internally competitive systems of nominations and advancement, aspirants are more likely to invest in party structures than to defect (Chandra 2004). Party cohesion may be strengthened through the provision of side benefits to activists and potential defectors (Panebianco 1988; James 2005). In sub-Saharan Africa, the factors that promote party cohesion elsewhere seem to have less traction. Where floor-crossing rules exist, they have weak effects on candidate behavior. Opposition parties lack the resources to provide even minimal support to candidate campaigns. Finally, African opposition parties contest elections on playing fields that are heavily tilted toward incumbent success, and opposition politicians regularly face harassment, imprisonment, and even physical attack. Calculations of long-run gain are, therefore, unlikely to sway the decisions of activists and aspirants to office. Material incentives for party loyalty are thin, while those fueling defection and organizational fragmentation are more substantial. The formation of opposition party splinters can yield concrete benefits, either through increased access to patronage or via direct co-optation by the ruling party. It is therefore unsurprising that we find high levels of organizational fragmentation and volatility in many new party systems, particularly those where incumbents retain significant patronage resources or internal organizational cohesion.

The cards are stacked against durable opposition party organizations, yet we see variation in terms of how well opposition parties are able to prevent elite defections and retain the loyalty of mass constituencies. This variation is evident in the three countries that compose the empirical base of this book. At one end of the spectrum lies Kenya, where party splitting began almost immediately upon the formation of opposition parties in 1991. In recent years, the increasing disorder of the electoral landscape has shifted the balance of power further toward individual candidates, resulting in what seems an endless churn of party launches and dissolutions. In Zimbabwe and Zambia, the presence of strong, cross-ethnic mobilizing structures provided an initial guard against party fragmentation. But opposition party development in the two countries soon diverged. In Zambia, following success in the first multiparty elections, the opposition Movement for Multiparty Democracy (MMD) entered a period of defection-fueled fragmentation and decline. It has only now begun to reconstitute itself, though it has done so around very different constituencies. In Zimbabwe, the Movement for Democratic Change (MDC) consistently retained some degree of organizational cohesion, even after the formation of two factions in 2005. It also increased its share of the popular vote, eating into the ruling party's core constituencies even as MDC politicians and supporters continued to face violent repression. In order to understand why vote fragmentation and candidate defection has not occurred in Zimbabwe, it is useful to look to the strategies implemented by the MDC and by the ruling party. Perhaps somewhat controversially, I argue that the country's high level of party polarization served as a bulwark against party fragmentation and mobilizational decline. Though the MDC had a strong social movement character at its launch, its use of polarizing and confrontational identity appeals helps explain how it has been able to hold together in highly adverse political conditions.

This book argues that party cohesion and grassroots commitment are most likely to be maintained where party-building elites consciously intensify conflict with party rivals. Through confrontational and polarizing strategies, opposition parties build walls around their organizations and around their constituencies. Defection becomes unlikely. Where strategies are mirrored by incumbent parties, and where these incumbents retain some degree of support, party-based polarization results. Polarization reinforces party cohesion through a number of mechanisms. First of all, in highly polarized contexts, party activists place greater importance on solidarity, identity appeals, and policing of inter-party boundaries. As polarization increases, social contact across party boundaries becomes less prevalent, and those who participate in political action are more likely to be incorporated and socialized into tightly knit activist networks that share a strong ideological commitment to confrontation and high-risk activism. McAdam well describes this circular process of recruitment, socialization, and increasing ideological commitment in his examination of high-risk activism in the context of the American civil rights movement (McAdam 1986).

Secondly, where they are effective, polarizing and confrontational strategies change parties' internal dynamics. Polarization makes candidate defection and the formation of third parties more difficult, as it empties out the middle ground in which candidates and parties might otherwise position themselves. In Zimbabwe, for instance, where opposition party office-holders left or were ejected from parties, they were termed "sell-outs" or "traitors." If these politicians stood again in elections, they typically lost by large margins. Finally, because the threat of splintering is lessened, opposition parties in sharply polarized settings may be able to tolerate much higher levels of participation and disagreement in party decision-making. It may be that the deployment of identity appeals and us–them distinctions foster a particular kind of party-building – based to a large extent on mobilization, creation of consensus, and institutionalized decision-making processes that link central party organs to grassroots and local branches. Where this kind of mobilization is exclusionary, it may stoke ethnic or religious violence. But where parties mobilize diverse constituencies, conflict can yield the kind of rooted organizations that are necessary for democratic consolidation.

To summarize, history provides opposition parties with resources and, occasionally, focal points around which protest can coalesce. But the ability to capitalize on pre-existing mobilizing structures does not release opposition elites from the hard tasks of party-building, nor does it ensure that party organizations will become well governed and deeply rooted. One of the arguments made in this book concerns the role of conflict in forging stronger and more responsive party organizations. By placing party conflict and relational processes like polarization at the heart of institution-building, the book suggests that democratic institution-building is a much more contingent and contested process than it has been depicted elsewhere. In the next section, I suggest some ways in which this approach challenges our more mainstream models of democratic transition.

IMPLICATIONS FOR THE STUDY OF DEMOCRATIZATION

In standard accounts of democratization, regime change is divided into three periods: political opening, the transition itself (or "breakthrough"), and democratic consolidation. The transition period is dominated by negotiations and the forging of pacts between elites within and outside the state. It is presumed to be of relatively short duration and to end with all actors' acceptance of a new institutional framework and agreement on the rules of the game. This sharp-edged periodization is primarily associated with a group of scholars who developed the agent-centered theories of democratic transitions that have dominated the literature for the past two decades (e.g., O'Donnell and Schmitter 1986; Higley and Burton 1989; Di Palma 1990; Przeworski 1991; Przeworski et al. 2000). But even in the Latin American countries where these kinds of negotiated transitions took the smoothest and most speedy paths, regime transition did not immediately dismantle "reserve realms" of authoritarian control, nor did it establish ties of accountability between elites and constituents.

The tendency of this work to present democratization as a fairly speedy, consensual process has already been widely criticized. Those most associated with the school have themselves pointed out that democratic transition and the deeper process of consolidation are distinct, and the first need not lead to the second (e.g., Linz and Stepan 1996; O'Donnell 1996). Others have criticized models of pacted transition for their "excessive voluntarism" and failure to take into account the effects of institutional context, economic conditions, and historical constraints (Karl 1990; Bratton and Van de Walle 1997; Haggard and Kaufman 1997; Geddes 1999; Mahoney and Snyder 1999). Further realms in which consensus has broken down include the contributions of civil society to democratization (e.g., Foley and Edwards 1996; Berman 1997; Encarnacion 2000; Hearn 2000; Wiktorowicz 2000;

Dicklitch and Lwanga 2003), the proper sequencing of elections and the utility of election observation (Beaulieu and Hyde 2009; Kelley 2009),[1] and the advantages of governments of national unity (Rothchild and Roeder 2005; Tull and Mehler 2005; Kirschke 2007; Gates and Strom, forthcoming).

Despite this body of criticism, empirical work on democratic transitions still tends to depict transition as a demarcated decision point. The tendency has been reinforced by recent formal work on democratization, notably Acemoglu's and Robinson's prize-winning *The Economic Origins of Dictatorship and Democracy* (2005; see also, Zielinski 1999; Boix 2003; Wantchekon 2004). This research depicts democratization as a one-shot – or, at the very least, a fairly compressed – game, in which political actors bargain over whether to choose democracy or the authoritarian status quo. The tendency to abbreviate democratization's timeline may be due to the ease with which functional yet flawed democracy seemed to be established in many of the countries that composed the first half of the Third Wave (e.g. Latin America, southern Europe). But the experience of early Third Wave democratizers, many having prior experience of democracy, may be misleading. If we look to another set of countries, democratization was more protracted and conflictual than negotiation-based theories of democratization would suggest. I do not have in mind today's hybrid regimes in Southeast Asia, the Middle East, and Africa, which many scholars are reluctant to label "democratizing".

If we instead turn our attention to the democratizers of the First Wave, we find patterns of democratization that depart significantly from the experiences of Latin America or Eastern Europe. Transitions toward representative government in Western Europe were characterized by often violent negotiations over boundaries of citizenship, acceptable limits of state power, and permissible bounds of popular mobilization (Tilly 2004a; Mann 2005; Ziblatt 2006). These countries, like today's hybrid regimes, often lingered in the intermediate ground of semi-democracy for long periods of time. Even in tranquil Switzerland, the state-society bargaining that preceded democracy was as consumed with the often authoritarian process of state-building as it was with the expansion of consultation (Tilly 2004a: 197–8). Early repertoires of contention often displayed tendencies toward violence (Thompson 1964, 1971; Snyder and Tilly 1972; Tilly 1995; Randall 2006). Episodes of violence remained a fairly typical aspect of elections throughout the nineteenth century, including in the US, and well into the twentieth in Western Europe (e.g., Tarrow 1989). In much of Western Europe, battles over boundaries of belonging and limits of state authority sparked inter-communal violence, government repression,

---

[1] There is, of course, another debate over a much larger sequencing problem: whether democratization should be pursued in contexts where institutions are poorly developed. For a policy take on this debate, see especially Rose and Shin (2001); Carothers (2007); and the response in Mansfield and Snyder (2007).

and, occasionally, war (Marx 2003; Mann 2005; also, Nexon 2009). Violence is simply more likely in contexts where state- or institution-building occurs in tandem with the expansion of participation. This is not to suggest that political opening and democratization should be postponed in countries lacking strong states and strong institutions. Instead, scholars should reassess the ways in which we conceptualize steps towards democracy, and devote greater attention to how democratization, popular mobilization, and violence interact.

We have typically assumed that it is the weakness of institutions that leads to higher levels of violence and instability in newly democratizing countries, and advice has often focused on reducing conflict in order to allow institutions to be strengthened. But what if conflict is generative? What if the intensification of conflict often accompanies – or may even be necessary for – democratic institution-building? Historically, it has been elite stalemate and the threat of undisciplined mobilization from below that has driven political elites to adapt political systems, expand suffrage, and build the kind of rooted and responsive parties that are now considered characteristic of democracy. On the other hand, where authoritarian elites retain sufficient resources to "buy off" their opposition challengers, political reforms have generally remained superficial. Thus, where electoral competition is structured around competition for patronage, pressures for substantive reform have been equally weak (Lust 2009). Conflict is lower in these systems, but they also lack the competition and confrontation that build stronger parties and place pressure on reluctant democratizers.

As I have argued above, strong opposition parties generate the pressure that is needed to drive forward democratization. In order to play this role, they must find means of boosting grassroots mobilization and maintaining opposition cohesion. Often, they accomplish these and other tasks through the intensification – not the moderation – of conflict with incumbent parties. By formulating frames that magnify the distance between themselves and incumbents, parties build the kind of oppositional identity and values that sustain mobilization. By refusing accommodation or negotiation with the ruling party, parties prevent the selective co-optation that often leads to party and vote fragmentation. Where they increase party-based polarization, opposition parties improve their ability to recruit activists, mobilize mass constituencies, and prevent the splintering of their vote bases.

The escalation of conflict has party-building advantages, but confrontational strategies also increase incumbents' perception of threat. Thus, the tools used to produce strong and cohesive opposition parties can trigger conflict, violence, and de-democratization. In polarized settings, as in Zimbabwe, hardliners on either side of the political divide become more central figures in organizational decision-making. Parties may form specialized party security structures that increase the chances of inter-party and intra-party clashes. In my account, it is not the weakness of institutions that allows for violence to occur. Nor is violence the result of intense attachments to ethnic and communal identities, which aspirant politicians attempt to activate. The choice of repression by ruling parties is not intended only to intimidate opposition voters or shift individuals' assessment of the likelihood of opposition success. Often, ruling parties are worried about the defection of particular politicians and constituencies. Confrontational and polarizing strategies are chosen becausethey are the most effective means of holding together politicians' *own* political coalitions. These organizational strategies have ambiguous effects on democratization. On the one hand, polarization may forge more competitive party systems; on the other, it may provoke violence and authoritarian retrenchment. At the very least, because confrontational strategies are effective means of party-building, conflict and violence may be more standard elements of the democratization process than is sometimes recognized.

IMPLICATIONS FOR THE STUDY OF PARTY FORMATION

Stepping back from the larger questions of democratization and political outcomes, the book makes a more direct contribution to our understandings of party development. To this point, much of the empirical work on party organization has been based on the more established democracies of Western Europe and Latin America. More recently, there has been a good deal of work on parties and party substitutes in Eastern Europe and the former Soviet Union (Moser 1999; Stoner-Weiss 2001; Grzymala-Busse 2003; O'Dwyer 2004; Hale 2005; Tavits 2005). In sub-Saharan Africa, however, parties have not yet attracted significant scholarly attention, and very little research has looked at party organization and party campaigns. As discussed in Chapter 1, African parties are often characterized as underdeveloped and formless. This generalization obscures variation in party forms and strategy across the continent. It also masks the ways in which study of African party organizations might enrich theories of party development.

What do the divergent trajectories of opposition party development in Zimbabwe, Zambia, and Kenya tell us about our general theories of party formation and organizational development? First of all, in terms of party formation, my account does not differ markedly from those of scholars working in very different contexts. We find a similar repurposing of existing institutions to serve very new roles. For instance, in Western Europe, Christian Democratic parties were built atop Catholic mass organizations, which had in turn been created by the Church in order to retain influence in the political sphere. Importantly, the formal church hierarchy did not intend for these structures to become independent political forces; indeed, the church had intended "to keep Catholic mass organizations under its strict control and depoliticize them after this struggle ended" (Kalyvas 1996: 23). These organizations, however, quickly slipped out of the control of political elites and were used as grassroots mobilizing structures. In similar fashion, centralized labor movements in Zimbabwe and Zambia were created to expand state control over the formal sector workforce. But, like Kalyvas's Catholic lay organizations, trade unions slowly took on a character of their own, and labor leaders built patterns of linkage and identity mobilization that were eventually used to subvert ruling party control. The privileging of labor in my account echoes accounts of democratization in other contexts. Trade unions and the mobilization of the working class play similarly prominent roles in explanations of democratization in Latin America and Western Europe (Collier and Collier 1991; Keck 1992; Rueschemeyer et al. 1992; Collier 1999).

Secondly, this book has borrowed from social movement theory as well as the existing parties literature in order to explain the variable strength of new parties during democratization. In hybrid regimes in Africa and elsewhere, opposition parties face particular obstacles. Popular mobilization and protest are likely to be more central party activities than they would be in established democracies. The classic literature on party organization suggests the erosion over time of the links between party leaders and the popular constituencies they ostensibly represent. Michels, for instance, argues that parties start down the slow road to oligarchy as soon as they begin to build structures and institutionalize decision-making (Michels 1962). Others maintain that parties must distance themselves from their core constituencies and from their activist pasts in order to pursue larger, more diverse electoral constituencies (Przeworski and Sprague 1986). Some social movement scholars see a similar process at work when social movements professionalize and become involved in institutional politics (Piven and Cloward 1977; Hipsher 1996). In hybrid regimes, mobilization remains an important task for opposition parties even after the first political reforms are instituted and the first multi-party elections held. Incumbents maintain control over the extent of political change, as they can use an array of tools – electoral fraud, violence, the misuse of state resources – to win elections. Opposition parties only level the playing field when they can credibly threaten electoral turnover or large-scale protest. For these reasons, opposition parties have incentives to structure their organizations in ways that preserve mobilizing reach and the involvement of activists. Strong opposition parties are likely both to begin as strong social movements and to retain their social movement attributes for extended periods of time.

Party development in democratizing Africa therefore both resembles and differs from party development in other settings. Like party formation in Western Europe and in Latin America, party organizations build upon and transform pre-existing institutional structures in order to mobilize constituencies. Unlike some accounts of party formation and institutionalization, this book argues that continued mobilization and the constant reinvention of grassroots linkages are important for maintaining party strength over time. Scholars have long suggested that adaptability is a key feature of durable party organizations (e.g., Levitsky, 2003a, 2003b). This account differs in the importance I assign to the construction of polarization – the deliberate intensification of party-based conflict – and the role that this process plays in strengthening activist commitment to parties.

IMPLICATIONS FOR POLICY-MAKING

Party development has rarely been prioritized by policy-makers, though there has been greater attention devoted to parties recently (e.g., Carothers 2006). Organizations like the Friedrich Ebert Stiftung, the National Democratic Institute, and the International Republic Institute all have established programs for political parties in emerging democracies. A large proportion of democracy and governance funding from the United States and other donors, however, remains devoted to civic education programs and to budget and program support for civil society organizations. In sub-Saharan Africa, organizations in the human rights sector have been particular beneficiaries. These are important programs. There is evidence that civic education initiatives can dampen electoral violence (Collier and Vicente 2008) and undermine voters' susceptibility to clientelistic appeals (Wantchekon 2008). Urban-based non-governmental organizations (NGOs) provide important documentation services to victims, upon which court cases and legal challenges are often based. Civic education campaigns, the actions of NGOs, and a responsible independent press can gradually shift public attitudes in the direction of greater support for democracy and human rights. Civil society played this kind of facilitative role, for instance, in Zimbabwe. In most cases, however, citizen attitudes are not the main obstacle to democratic deepening and consolidation. As scholars associated with the Afrobarometer have exhaustively documented, Africans express high levels of support for democracy, individual rights, and accountability (e.g., Bratton and Mattes 2001; Bratton et al. 2005). Both the demand and the understanding of democracy exist. What remain lacking are the mechanisms by which citizens can hold their elected representatives accountable. Civil society is important for several reasons, but the aggregation and communication of political demands should not be left to civil society. For these purposes, democracy requires strong political parties that can serve as stable referents for voters.

In addition to civil society development, the policy-making community has shown enthusiasm for coalition governments and other power-sharing arrangements. In some contexts, notably in post-war settings, these policies can provide substantial benefits. Where all parties to a conflict agree to power-sharing, agreements often ensure a level of political stability. The benefits of power-sharing may keep potential spoilers within governing coalitions. Cooperation between rivals can facilitate the rebuilding of institutions and state capacity after civil war. As a tool of democratization, however, these arrangements have several flaws. I have argued elsewhere that the institution of power-sharing in semi-democracies fosters elite collusion rather than competition, with predictable effects on corruption and government accountability (Cheeseman and LeBas 2010). Other scholars have made similar points about the connection between anemic party competition and robust government spending. For instance, in an examination of party strategies in Eastern Europe, O'Dwyer finds an association between more institutionalized party systems and more constrained growth in the size of state bureaucracies (O'Dwyer 2004). In coalitional or power-sharing governments, the constraints on budget expansion and corruption are doubly removed: all parties have access to patronage resources, and no parties have an electoral incentive to police corruption or budget sustainability. In Kenya, a coalition government inaugurated following the 2008 post-election violence has led to greater state spending and larger cabinets. The popular perception of increased corruption during the coalition period has intensified political alienation and the distrust of established parties. In this context, it seems possible that the 2012 elections in Kenya will yield even higher levels of party fragmentation.

Setting aside the potential effect of power-sharing on corruption and government consumption, these arrangements are also unlikely to facilitate democratization in the long run. Power-sharing arrangements may sometimes dampen violence or tensions between groups, but they do little to strengthen accountability, government responsiveness, or the development of strong, rooted party organizations. And the stability-boosting effects of coalition governments are by no means assured. In the worst cases, as in Zimbabwe, coalition agreements can be violated without sanction, and opposition parties have little capacity to restrain the authoritarian excesses of their ruling party partners. Following the signing of a coalition agreement between the ruling party and the two factions of the MDC in 2008, the ruling party in Zimbabwe continued its violent repression of opposition and civil society activists. Farm invasions also continued, and there has been some evidence of an increased militarization of government decision-making (ICG 2010). Beyond Zimbabwe and Kenya, the overall record of power-sharing arrangements in sub-Saharan Africa is decidedly mixed (Sawyer 2004; Tull and Mehler 2005; Lemarchand 2007; Mehler 2009). We should therefore exercise caution in urging competing parties into governments of national unity, even in the wake of significant electoral fraud or episodes of political violence.

If neither civil society development nor coalitional arrangements promote party-building, what concrete policy interventions might facilitate the formation of strong opposition parties? This book has argued that opposition parties are most effective where they capitalize on existing networks of "weak ties," which allow for the spread of information across diverse groups of people (Granovetter 1973). One might also conceive of pre-existing institutional structures of this kind as powerful means of voter coordination. Focal points of this kind allow for the signaling of "each person's expectation of what the other expects him to expect to be expected to do" (Schelling 1960: 57). Labor movements in Zimbabwe and Zambia were especially effective as focal points because authoritarian rule had left in place so few rivals in terms of national visibility. Associational life in corporatist states was not richer or more free than in divided or ethnicized countries like Kenya. It was, however, organized in a way that made focal point opposition parties more likely. The structure of associational life was hierarchical, and it de-emphasized smaller communities like locality or ethnicity as the locus for collective action. Most importantly, networks of trade unions were effective in conveying a single message to diverse constituencies. In Zimbabwe and Zambia, those opposed to the ruling party were able to reasonably expect that many other protest voters would support labor-backed candidates, even if they had little contact or knowledge of voters in other parts of the country. In contrast, in countries lacking these "focal point" opposition parties, coordination was unlikely to occur. The failure of opposition parties in Kenya during the first decade of multiparty elections is a case in point. How do focal points emerge? Are there ways that United States foreign policy – or, more importantly, the choices of local actors – could facilitate the emergence of these kinds of cross-ethnic focal point parties?

There are ways that policy might be adjusted to strengthen the ties between parties and grassroots contituencies. First of all, as currently conceived, donor interventions intended to strengthen civil society do not have substantial effects on party development. The organizations that coordinate human rights and civic education programs are rarely membership-based. Their contacts with grassroots constituencies are sporadic and cannot produce the bonds of loyalty and identification that underlay, for instance, the mobilizing capacity of labor movements in Zimbabwe and Zambia. Policies might instead focus on strengthening organizations that provide concrete benefits to particular groups across the lines of ethnicity, region, or religion. These organizations need not have any tie to politics. Indeed, associational networks organized around livelihood typically prove more durable and more cohesive than those based on principle. In the developing world, trade unions are not likely to play in future the role that they have in my account. Most countries have now adopted labor legislation that ensures freedom of association and decentralization of collective bargaining to the firm level. These reforms expand workers' choices regarding whether and which union they wish to join, but they also mean that trade unions now struggle to retain members and prevent the formation of splinter unions. Across Africa, the negotiating power of labor has been sharply diminished by these changes. Individual affiliate unions have occasionally been able to coordinate effective strikes, but the ability of labor movements to coordinate national actions, or to mobilize large-scale national protest, has been sharply curtailed. Organized labor is unlikely to serve as the primary base of opposition party mobilization, nor will it unite workers across geographic distances the way it did when labor movements were more centralized.

Labor is not the only means of building effective opposition parties, nor are opposition parties doomed to weakness in hybrid regimes where authoritarian states did not encourage the building of strong, centralized corporate actors. In the developing world, there are a variety of other networks that might serve as the base for future opposition parties: churches, agricultural cooperatives, savings circles, residents' associations, and so on. If the arguments in this book are correct, policy would be particularly effective where it is aimed at organizations that provide grassroots constituencies with concrete benefits (higher earnings, transport or inputs for crops, etc). The most promising organizations are likely to be membership-based, and they would be those that link the members of one local network to those elsewhere. This might occur through training workshops or other events held at the national or regional level, or organizations might be structured in ways that encourage cooperation across the lines of region or ethnicity. In his classic *The Logic of Collective Action*, Mancur Olson described how powerful agricultural lobbies in the United States relied on agricultural extension as a means of enforcing contribution from all beneficiaries (Olson 1965). By paying for extension, farmers funded their lobbies, and extension agents also served as networks that allowed for the spread of information. Olson describes how the farm lobby went into decline soon after agricultural extension began to be provided by the government at no cost.

This book has offered few solutions for those who seek speedy and cost-less tools of democracy promotion. This section has sketched two ways in which policy might facilitate democratization in the long run. First, targeted funding might "nudge" countries toward the more centralized associational landscapes that facilitate large-scale collective action. Support to non-political organizations with rooted yet national networks is most likely to be effective. Secondly, policy-makers should devote more attention to strengthening the competitiveness of party systems. Free and fair elections are important, but competition can emerge even in flawed electoral environments. In these settings, power-sharing will not encourage further democratization, and opposition election boycotts are ineffective means of placing pressure on incumbents. In these settings, outsiders' best policy may be a variety of benign neglect. Where international policy attempts to place pressure on reluctant democratizers through sanctions, it often inadvertently strengthens incumbents.

In Zimbabwe, for instance, targeted sanctions and travel restrictions were used for propaganda purposes; more importantly, these policies unified a heavily divided ruling party. By tarring all ZANU-PF politicians with the same brush, American and British foreign policy reinforced the impossibility of defection. Though polarization can assist in party-building, as suggested above, it can also trigger authoritarian retrenchment. Policies aimed at reducing the degree of conflict or competition in elections, or forcing incumbents toward accommodation with rivals, are unlikely to yield the desired effects.

THE WAY FORWARD

The hybrid regimes of the late Third Wave of democracy present new terrain for the study of party development and institution-building. Democratization in these regimes is likely to be both more protracted and more conflictual than the pacted transitions that characterized early Third Wave democratizers in Latin America and Southern Europe. We should, therefore, be cautious about putting too much faith in the ability of repeated elections and "liberalizing electoral outcomes" to produce democracy (e.g., Lindberg 2006; Morje Howard and Roessler 2006). In sub-Saharan Africa, the sunny haze that has accompanied founding elections and electoral turnovers has often lifted to reveal relatively little change in the status quo.

A small group of countries have consistently improved the quality and extent of competition over election rounds, with accountability and citizen satisfaction with democracy improving as well. Ghana is a case in point. Elections have grown more competitive over time, without a corresponding increase in party system volatility, and 2008 marked the country's third electoral turnover since the return to multiparty rule in 1992. Respect for human rights and indicators of the quality of governance have shown improvement over time, which we might attribute to the peaceful alteration in power between the country's two main political parties. The country has often been used as an example of democratic progress in Africa. For instance, in his analysis of how repeated rounds of elections produce greater democracy, Lindberg (2006) repeatedly returned to the case of Ghana. For each Ghana, however, there is a Senegal. After the opposition first won election in 2000, defeating one of Africa's longest serving and most rooted ruling parties, many expected significant democratic gains. In subsequent years, however, former opposition leader Abdoulaye Wade pursued increasingly authoritarian policies, leading to an opposition boycott of the postponed parliamentary elections of 2007. Senegal remains the only African regime that Freedom House has downgraded from free to partly free, but newly elected governments in Ethiopia, Kenya, Rwanda, and Zambia all generated similar cycles of optimism and disillusionment. Turnovers can refresh popular belief in democracy and electoral competition (Moehler and Lindberg 2009), but they do not necessarily generate substantive changes in governance and accountability.

Some decades ago, V.O. Key eloquently described how the absence of vibrant party competition allowed for corruption, poor-quality representation, and enclaves of authoritarianism in the American South (Key 1977). The factionalized and weakly rooted parties that Key found in southern states have eerie similarities to the party organizations that we find in many hybrid regimes today. Political change is unlikely to occur as rapidly in Africa as it did in Virginia or Florida, but the mechanisms that drive forward change are likely to be the same. The development of competitive, institutionalized party systems is the best means of encouraging political elites to respond to the demands of their constituents. In the South, the civil rights movement played a vital role in opening up the political space that was required for competition to emerge. Without the extension of full citizenship and voting rights to African Americans, competitive party systems would not have emerged. In hybrid regimes in Africa and beyond, democratization will be most likely where we find similar combinations of popular mobilization and strong party competition. I have argued that strong opposition parties are able to make use of both electoral and social movement strategies. Their facility at these strategies is based both upon the resources they inherit from past state choices and upon the choices that opposition parties make themselves. Overall, however, it is confrontation and competition that forges stronger and more rooted party organizations. By placing party conflict and relational processes like polarization at the heart of institution-building, the book suggests that democratic institution-building is a much more contingent and contested process than it has been depicted elsewhere. Political actors are unlikely to form the institutions required for representation and accountability unless they are pushed to do so. The greatest risk to democratization is therefore not the presence of conflict but its absence.

Bibliography

Newspapers

Business Day (Johannesburg, South Africa)
The Changing Times (MDC, Harare, Zimbabwe)
Chronicle (Bulawayo, Zimbabwe)
Daily Mail (Lusaka, Zambia)
Daily News (Harare, Zimbabwe)
Daily Nation (Nairobi, Kenya)
East African (Nairobi, Kenya)
The Farmer (Harare, Zimbabwe)
Financial Gazette (Harare, Zimbabwe)
Financial Review (Nairobi, Kenya)
Herald (Harare, Zimbabwe)
Horizon (Harare, Zimbabwe)
Kenya Times (Nairobi, Kenya)
Mail & Guardian (Johannesburg, South Africa)
Moto (Harare, Zimbabwe)
National Mirror (Lusaka, Zambia)
People's Voice (ZANU-PF, Harare, Zimbabwe)
The Post (Lusaka, Zambia)
The Standard (Harare, Zimbabwe)
The Standard (Lusaka, Zambia)
Times of Zambia (Ndola, Zambia)
Weekly Review (Nairobi, Kenya)
The Worker (ZCTU, Harare, Zimbabwe)
Workers' Challenge (Kitwe, Zambia)
The Zimbabwe Independent (Harare, Zimbabwe)

Periodic Reports

Media Monitoring Project of Zimbabwe (MMPZ). 2001–8. Weekly media updates.
Solidarity Peace Trust. 2008. Election Update Reports.
Zimbabwe Human Rights NGO Forum. 2002–6. Political Violence Reports, monthly.
Zimbabwe Parliamentary Debates. 1980–2004. Hansard, Parliament of Zimbabwe.
Zimbabwe Peace Project. 2005–8. Monthly Monitoring Reports.

Government Documents, Published Reports and Other Primary Materials[1]

Amani Trust. 1998. *A Consolidated Report on the Food Riots, 19–23 January, 1998.* Harare: Zimbabwe Human Rights NGO Forum.

——. 2002. *Organised Violence and Torture in the June 2000 General Election in Zimbabwe.* Harare: Amani Trust.

CCJP. 1999. *Breaking the Silence, Building True Peace: A Report on the Disturbances in Matabeleland and the Midlands, 1980 to 1988.* Harare: Catholic Commission for Justice & Peace and Legal Resources Foundation.

Crisis in Zimbabwe. 2005. *Things Fall Apart: The 2005 Parliamentary Elections.* Harare: Crisis in Zimbabwe Coalition.

FODEP. 1996. *Interim Statement of the Foundation for Democratic Process on the 18 November 1996 Presidential and Parliamentary Elections.* Lusaka: Foundation for Democratic Process.

Freedom House. 2008. *Annual Survey of Freedom House Country Scores, 1972–73 to 2007–08.* Available at http://www.freedomhouse.org

Human Rights Watch. 1993. *Divide and Rule: State-sponsored Ethnic Violence in Kenya.* New York: Human Rights Watch.

——. 1996. *Zambia: Elections and Human Rights in the Third Republic.* New York: Human Rights Watch.

——. 2002. *Fast Track Land Reform in Zimbabwe.* New York: Human Rights Watch.

——. 2003a. *Not Eligible: The Politicization of Food in Zimbabwe.* New York: Human Rights Watch.

——. 2003b. *Under a Shadow: Civil and Political Rights in Zimbabwe: Background Briefing.* New York: Human Rights Watch.

——. 2005. *Zimbabwe Evicted and Forsaken: Internally Displaced Persons in the Aftermath of Operation Murambatsvina.* New York: Human Rights Watch.

——. 2008. *'Bullets for Each of You': State-sponsored Violence since Zimbabwe's March 29 Elections.* New York: Human Rights Watch.

——. 2009. *Lethal Force: Police Violence and Public Security in Rio de Janeiro and São Paulo.* New York: Human Rights Watch.

International Crisis Group. 2002. *Zimbabwe: What Next?* Johannesburg/Brussels: International Crisis Group.

——. 2010. *Zimbabwe: Political and Security Challenges to the Transition.* Africa Briefing No. 10. Washington, DC. International Crisis Group.

IJR and SPZ. 2006. *Policing the State: An Evaluation of Political Arrests in Zimbabwe, 2000–2005.* Johannesburg: Institute of Justice and Reconciliation & Solidarity Peace Trust.

Kenya Human Rights Commission. 1997. *Kayas of Deprivation, Kayas of Blood: Violence, Ethnicity, and the State in Coastal Kenya.* Nairobi: Kenya Human Rights Commission.

——. 1998. *Killing the Vote: State Sponsored Violence and Flawed Elections in Kenya.* Nairobi: Kenya Human Rights Commission.

MDC. 2005. *How the Elections were Rigged: MDC Report on the March 2005 Parliamentary Elections.* Harare: Movement for Democratic Change.

NCA. 1998. *National Constitutional Assembly Annual Report 1998.* Harare: National Constitutional Assembly.

---

[1] Press releases mimeos, and unpublished reports are often cited in footnotes. Please contact the author for further information on obtaining unpublished reports and documents.

——. 2000. *National Constitutional Assembly Annual Report 2000*. Harare: National Constitutional Assembly.

NDI and the Carter Center. 1992. *The October 31, 1991 National Elections in Zambia*. Washington, DC: National Democratic Institute for International Affairs.

ORAP (Zimbabwe). 1987. *Fieldwork Report, 1986–1987*. Typeset mimeo, provided to me by David McDermott Hughes. Zimbabwe: Organisation of Rural Associations for Progress..

Republic of Kenya. 1992. *Report of the Parliamentary Select Committee to Investigate Ethnic Clashes in Western and Other Parts of Kenya*. Nairobi: Government Printers.

——. 1999. *Report of the Judicial Commission Appointed to Inquire into Tribal Clashes in Kenya (Akiwumi Report)*. Nairobi: Government Printers.

Republic of Zimbabwe. 1982. *Transitional National Development Plan: 1982/1983– 1984/1985, Volume One*. Harare: Government Printers.

——. 1984. *Labour and Economy: Report of the National Trade Unions Survey*. Harare: Ministry of Labour, Manpower Planning and Social Welfare.

——. 1986. *First Five-year National Development Plan: 1986–1990, Volume I*. Harare: Government Printers.

——. 1998. *Poverty in Zimbabwe*. Harare: Central Statistical Office.

Silveira House. 1978. *What about effective Trade Unionism in Zimbabwe? Findings of Zimbabwe Trade Union Leaders on Programme and Action*. Harare: Silveira House.

Solidarity Peace Trust. 2008. *Punishing Dissent, Silencing Citizens. The Zimbabwe Election 2008*. Harare: Solidarity Peace Trust of Zimbabwe.

UN-HABITAT. 2005. *Report of the Fact-Finding Mission to Zimbabwe to Assess the Scope and Impact of Operation Murambatsvina by the UN Special Envoy on Human Settlements Issues in Zimbabwe, Mr.s Anna Kajumula Tibaijuka*. New York: United Nations Human Settlements Program.

ZCTU (Zambia). 1988. *A Review of the Zambian Economy 1980–1987: A ZCTU Perspective*. Kitwe: Zambia Congress of Trade Unions/ICFTU.

ZCTU (Zimbabwe). 1993a. *Structural Adjustment and its Impact on Workers: Research Project with ZTWU/NUCI Union Shopstewards*. Mimeo. Harare: Zimbabwe Congress of Trade Unions.

——. 1993b. *Workers' Participation and Development: A Manual for Workers Education*. Harare: Zimbabwe Congress of Trade Unions.

——. 1996. *Beyond ESAP: Framework for a Long-term Development Strategy in Zimbabwe Beyond the Economic Structural Adjustment Program*. Harare: Zimbabwe Congress of Trade Unions.

——. 2000. *The Worker's Driven and Peoples Centered Development Process for Zimbabwe, June 1996 to February 2000*. Harare: Zimbabwe Congress of Trade Unions.

ZESN. 2005. *Report on Zimbabwe's 2005 General Elections*. Harare: Zimbabwe Election Support Network.

ZHRNF. 2001. *Politically Motivated Violence in Zimbabwe, 2000–2001*. Harare: Zimbabwe Human Rights NGO Forum.

——. 2002. *Human Rights and Zimbabwe's Presidential Election: March 2002*. Harare: Zimbabwe Human Rights NGO Forum.

ZIMT. 1992. *Fair Play for a Better Tomorrow: Election Report 1991*. Lusaka, Zambia: Zambia Independent Monitoring Team.

Academic Articles and Books

Abbink, Jon. 2006. "Discomfiture of Democracy: The 2005 Election Crisis in Ethiopia and its Aftermath." *African Affairs* 105:419, 173–99.

Acemoglu, Daron, and James Robinson. 2005. *Economic Origins of Dictatorship and Democracy*. Cambridge: Cambridge University Press.

Adar, Korwa, and Isaac Munyae. 2001. "Human Rights Abuses in Kenya under Daniel arap Moi, 1978–2001." *African Studies Quarterly* 5:1.

Adler, Glenn, and Eddie Webster. 1995. "Challenging Transition Theory: The Labor Movement, Radical Reform and Transition to Democracy in South Africa." *Politics and Society* 23. 1, 75–106.

Agbese, Pita Ogaba. 1999. "Party Registration and the Subversion of Democracy in Nigeria." *Issue: A Journal of Opinion* 27:1, 63–5.

Ake, Claude. 1994. "The Democratisation of Disempowerment in Africa." In Jochen Hippler, ed., *Democratisation of Disempowerment: The Problem of Democracy in the Third World*. London: Pluto Press.

Akwetey, Emmanuel. 1994. "Trade Unions and Democratisation: A Comparative Study of Zambia and Ghana." Ph.D. Dissertation, Stockholm University.

Aldrich, John. 1995. *Why Parties? The Origin and Transformation of Party Politics in America*. Chicago: University of Chicago Press.

Alexander, Jocelyn. 1998. "Dissident Perspectives on Zimbabwe's Post-independence War." *Africa* 68:2, 151–82.

Alexander, Jocelyn, and Joann McGregor. 2001. "Elections, Land, and the Politics of Opposition in Matabeleland." *Journal of Agrarian Change* 1:4, 510–33.

Alexander, Jocelyn, and Blessing-Miles Tendi. 2008. "A Tale of Two Elections: Zimbabwe at the Polls in 2008." *Bulletin of Concerned Africa Scholars*, 80.

Alexander, Peter. 2000. "Zimbabwean Workers, the MDC, and the 2000 Election." *Review of African Political Economy* 85, 385–406.

Alves, Maria Helena Moreira. 1984. "Grassroots Organizations, Trade Unions, and the Church: A Challenge to the Controlled Abertura in Brazil." *Latin American Perspectives* 11:1, 73–102.

Ames, Barry. 1995. "Electoral Strategy under Open-List Proportional Representation." *American Journal of Political Science* 39:2, 406–33.

Anderson, David. 2002. "Vigilantes, Violence and the Politics of Public Order in Kenya." *African Affairs* 101, 531–55.

——. 2003. "Briefing: Kenya's Elections 2002 – The Dawning of a New Era?" *African Affairs* 407, 331–42.

——. 2005. " 'Yours in Struggle for Majimbo'. Nationalism and the Party Politics of Decolonization in Kenya, 1955–64." *Journal of Contemporary History* 40:3, 547–64.

Andreassen, Bard-Anders, Gisela Geisler, and Arne Tostensen. 1992. "Setting a Standard for Africa? Lessons from the 1991 Zambian Elections." CMI Report R1992 No. 5. Bergen, Norway: Chr. Michelsen Institute.

Anyang' Nyong'o, Peter. 1989. "State and Society in Kenya: The Disintegration of the Nationalist Coalitions and the Rise of Presidential Authoritarianism, 1963–1978." *African Affairs* 88:351, 229–51.

Apter, David. 1955. *The Gold Coast in Transition*. Princeton, NJ: Princeton University Press.

——. 1962. "Some Reflections on the Role of a Political Opposition in New Nations." *Comparative Studies in Society and History* 4:2, 154–68.

Arrighi, Giovanni, and John Saul. 1968. "Socialism and Economic Development in Tropical frica." *Journal of Modern African Studies* 6:2, 141–69.

Ashford, Douglas. 1965. "The Elusiveness of Power: The African Single Party State." Cornell Research Papers in International Studies, No. 3. Ithaca, NY: Cornell University.

Atemi, Caleb. 2002. "Academic Suicide." Nairobi: Citizens against Violence (CAVi) & Friedrich Ebert Stiftung.

Auret, Diana. 1992. *Reaching for Justice: The Catholic Commission for Justice and Peace Looks Back at the Past Twenty Years, 1972–1992.* Gweru, Zimbabwe: Mambo Press/CCJP.

Auret, Michael. 1994. *Churu Farm: A Chronicle of Despair.* Harare: Catholic Commission for Justice and Peace.

Aywa, Francis Ang'ila, and Francois Grignon. 2001. "As Biased as Ever? The Electoral Commission's Performance prior to Polling Day." In Marcel Rutten, Alamin Mazrui, and Francois Grignon, eds., *Out for the Count: The 1997 General Elections and Prospects for Democracy in Kenya.* Kampala, Uganda: Fountain Press.

Azarya, Victor. 1988. "Reordering State-Society Relations: Incorporation and Disengagement." In Don Rothchild and Naomi Chazan, eds., *The Precarious Balance: State and Society in Africa.* Boulder, CO: Westview Press.

Banda, Darlington Amos. 1997a. *The Trade Union Situation in Zambia: An Overview of the Law, Practice and the Way Forward.* Lusaka: Friedrich Ebert Stiftung.

Banda, Fackson. 1997b. *Elections and the Press in Zambia.* Lusaka: Zambia Independent Media Association.

Barkan, Joel. 1976. "Further Reassessment of 'Conventional Wisdom': Political Knowledge and Voting Behavior in Rural Kenya." *American Political Science Review* 70:2, 452–5.

——. 1979. "Legislators, Elections and Political Linkage." In Joel Barkan and John Okumu, eds., *Politics and Public Policy in Kenya and Tanzania.* New York: Praeger.

——. 1993. "Kenya: Lessons from a Flawed Election." *Journal of Democracy* 4:3, 85–99.

Barkan, Joel, and Michael Chege. 1989. "Decentralising the State: District Focus and the Politics of Reallocation in Kenya." *Journal of Modern African Studies* 27:3, 431–53.

Barkan, Joel, Paul Densham, and Gerard Rushton. 2006. "Space Matters: Designing Better Electoral Systems for Emerging Democracies." *American Journal of Political Science* 50:4, 926–39.

Bartlett, David. 2000. "Civil Society and Democracy: A Zambian Case Study." *Journal of Southern African Studies* 26:3, 429–46.

Bates, Robert. 1971. *Unions, Parties and Political Development: A Study of Mineworkers in Zambia.* New Haven: Yale University Press.

——. 1976. *Rural Responses to Industrialization: A Study of Rural Zambia.* New Haven: Yale University Press.

——. 1981. *Markets and States in Tropical Africa: The Political Basis of Agricultural Policies.* Berkeley, CA: University of California Press.

Bates, Robert, and Paul Collier. 1993. "The Politics and Economics of Policy Reform in Zambia." In Robert Bates and Anne Kreuger, eds., *Political and Economic Interactions in Economic Policy Reform: Evidence from Eight Countries.* Cambridge, MA: Blackwell.

Bauer, Gretchen. 2004. "'The Hand that Stirs the Pot Can Also Run the Country': Electing Women to Parliament in Namibia." *Journal of Modern African Studies* 42:4, 479–509.

Bayart, Jean-Francois. 1986. "Civil Society in Africa." In Patrick Chabal, ed., *Political Domination in Africa: Reflections on the Limits of Power.* Cambridge: Cambridge University Press.

——. 1993. *The State in Africa: The Politics of the Belly.* London: Longman.

Baylies, Carolyn, and Morris Szeftel. 1992. "The Fall and Rise of Multi-Party Politics in Zambia." *Review of African Political Economy* 54, 75–91.

Baylies, Carolyn, and Morris Szeftel. 1999. "Democratisation and the 1991 Elections in Zambia." In John Daniel, Roger Southall, and Morris Szeftel, eds., *Voting for Democracy: Watershed Elections in Contemporary Anglophone Africa*. Brookfield, VT: Ashgate.

Beaulieu, Emily, and Susan D. Hyde. 2009. "In the Shadow of Democracy Promotion: Strategic Manipulation, International Observers, and Election Boycotts." *Comparative Political Studies* 42:3, 392–415.

Bellin, Eva. 2000. "Contingent Democrats: Industrialists, Labor and Democratization in Late-Developing Countries." *World Politics* 52:2, 175–205.

——. 2002. *Stalled Democracy: Capital, Labor and the Paradox of State-Sponsored Development*. Ithaca, NY: Cornell University Press.

Berman, Sheri. 1997. "Civil Society and the Collapse of the Weimar Republic." *World Politics* 49:3, 401–29.

Bermeo, Nancy. 1997. "Myths of Moderation: Confrontation and Conflict during Democratic Transitions." *Comparative Politics* 29:3, 305–22.

Bianchi, Robert. 1989. *Unruly Corporatism: Associational Life in Twentieth-century Egypt*. New York: Oxford University Press.

Bienefeld, M.A. 1979. "Trade Unions, the Labour Process, and the Tanzanian State." *Journal of Modern African Studies* 17:4, 553–93.

Bienen, Henry. 1967. *Tanzania: Party Transformation and Economic Development*. Princeton, NJ: Princeton University Press.

Bienen, Henry, and Mark Gersovitz. 1986. "Consumer Subsidy Cuts, Violence, and Political Stability." *Comparative Politics* 19:1, 25–44.

Birch, Sarah. 2005. "Single-member District Electoral Systems and Democratic Transition." *Electoral Studies* 24:2, 281–301.

Bjornlund, Eric, Michael Bratton, and Clark Gibson. 1992. "Observing Multiparty Elections in Africa: Lessons from Zambia." *African Affairs* 91:364, 405–31.

Bogaards, Matthijs. 2004. "Counting Parties and Identifying Dominant Party Systems in Africa." *European Journal of Political Research* 43:2, 173–97.

——. 2008. "Dominant Party Systems and Electoral Volatility in Africa." *Party Politics* 14:1, 113–30.

Boix, Carles. 2003. *Democracy and Redistribution*. New York: Cambridge University Press.

——. 2007. "The Emergence of Parties and Party Systems." In Carles Boix and Susan Stokes, eds., *The Oxford Handbook of Comparative Politics*. New York: Oxford University Press:

Bond, Patrick. 2001. "Radical Rhetoric and the Working Class during Zimbabwean Nationalism's Dying Days." In Brian Raftopoulos and Lloyd Sachikonye, eds., *Striking Back: The Labour Movement and the Post-Colonial State in Zimbabwe*. Harare: Weaver Press.

Brambor, Thomas, William Roberts Clark, and Matt Golder. 2007. "Are African Party Systems Different?" *Electoral Studies* 26, 315–23.

Branch, Daniel. 2006. "Loyalists, Mau Mau, and Elections in Kenya: The First Triumph of the System, 1957–1958." *Africa Today* 53:2, 27–50.

Branch, Daniel, and Nicholas Cheeseman. 2006. "The Politics of Control in Kenya: Understanding the Bureaucratic-Executive State, 1952–78." *Review of African Political Economy* 33:107, 11–31.

Brand, C. 1971. "Politics and African Trade Unionism in Rhodesia since Federation." *Rhodesian History* 2, 89–110.

Brass, Paul. 1997. *Theft of an Idol: Text and Context in the Representation of Collective Violence*. Princeton, NJ: Princeton University Press.

Bratton, Michael. 1980. *The Local Politics of Rural Development: Peasant and Party-State in Zambia*. Hanover, NH: University Press of New England.

——. 1987. "The Comrades and the Countryside: The Politics of Agricultural Policy in Zimbabwe." *World Politics*, 174–202.

——. 1989a. "The Politics of Government–NGO Relations in Africa." *World Development* 17:4, 568–87.

——. 1989b. "Beyond the State: Civil Society and Associational Life in Africa." *World Politics* 41:3, 407–30.

——. 1992. "Zambia Starts Over." *Journal of Democracy* 3:2, 81–94.

——. 1994a. "Economic Crisis and Political Realignment in Zambia." In Jennifer Widner, ed., *Economic Change and Political Liberalization in Sub-Saharan Africa*. Baltimore, MD: Johns Hopkins University Press.

——. 1994b. "Micro-democracy? The Merger of Farmer Unions in Zimbabwe." *African Studies Review* 37:1, 9–37.

——. 2008. "Vote Buying and Violence in Nigerian Election Campaigns." *Electoral Studies* 27; 621–32.

Bratton, Michael, and Mwangi Kimenyi. 2008. "Voting in Kenya: Putting Ethnicity in Perspective." *Journal of Eastern African Studies* 2:2, 272–89.

Bratton, Michael, and Bernice Liatto-Katundu. 1994. "A Focus Group Assessment of Political Attitudes in Zambia." *African Affairs* 93:373, 535–63.

Bratton, Michael, and Eldred Masunungure. 2007. "Popular Reactions to State Repression: Operation Murambatsvina in Zimbabwe." *African Affairs* 106:422, 21–45.

Bratton, Michael, Robert Mattes, and E. Gyimah-Boadi. 2005. *Public Opinion, Democracy, and Market Reform in Africa*. Cambridge: Cambridge University Press.

Bratton, Michael, and Robert Mattes. 2001. "Africans' Surprising Universalism." *Journal of Democracy* 12:1, 107–21.

——. 2009. "Neither Consolidating nor Fully Democratic: The Evolution of African Political Regimes, 1999–2008." Afrobarometer Briefing Paper No. 67. East Lansing, MI.

Bratton, Michael, and Daniel Posner. 1999. "A First Look at Second Elections in Africa, with Illustrations from Zambia." In Richard Joseph, ed., *State, Conflict and Democracy in Africa*. Boulder, CO: Lynne Rienner.

Bratton, Michael, and Nicolas Van de Walle. 1992. "Popular Protest and Political Reform in Africa." *Comparative Politics* 24:4, 419–42.

——. 1997. *Democratic Experiments in Africa: Regime Transitions in Comparative Perspective*. Cambridge: Cambridge University Press.

Brittain, Julie, and Brian Raftopoulos. 1997. "The Labour Movement in Zimbabwe: 1965–1980." In Brian Raftopoulos and Lloyd Sachikonye, eds., *Keep on Knocking: A History of the Labour Movement in Zimbabwe, 1900–1997*. Harare: Baobab Books.

Brown, Stephen. 2001. "Authoritarian Leaders and Multiparty Elections in Africa: How Foreign Donors Help to Keep Kenya's Daniel arap Moi in Power." *Third World Quarterly* 22:5, 725–40.

——. 2007. "From Demiurge to Midwife: Changing Donor Roles in Kenya's Democratisation Process." In Godwin Murunga and Shadrack Nasong'o, eds., *Kenya: The Struggle for Democracy*. Dakar, Senegal: CODESRIA.

Brownlee, Jason. 2007. *Authoritarianism in an Age of Democratization*. Cambridge: Cambridge University Press.

Bunce, Valerie. 2003. "Rethinking Recent Democratization: Lessons from the Post-communist Experience." *World Politics* 55:2, 167–92.

Burawoy, Michael. 1976. "Consciousness and Contradiction: A Study of Student Protest in Zambia." *British Journal of Sociology* 27:1, 78–98.

——. 1982. "The Hidden Abode of Underdevelopment: Labor Process and the State in Zambia." *Politics and Society*, 123–66.

Burdick, John. 1993. *Looking for God in Brazil: The Progressive Catholic Church in Urban Brazil's Religious Arena.* Berkeley, CA: University of California Press.

Burgess, Stephen. 1997. "Smallholder Voice and Rural Transformation: Zimbabwe and Kenya Compared." *Comparative Politics* 29:2, 127–49.

Burgess, Katrina. 1999. "Loyalty Dilemmas and Market Reform: Party-Union Alliances under Stress in Mexico, Spain and Venezuela." *World Politics* 52, 105–34.

Burnell, Peter. 1995. "The Politics of Poverty and the Poverty of Politics in Zambia's Third Republic." *Third World Quarterly* 16:4, 675–90.

——. 2001. "The Party System and Party Politics in Zambia: Continuities Past, Present and Future." *African Affairs* 100, 239–63.

Caillaud, Bernard, and Jean Tirole. 2002. "Parties as Political Intermediaries." *Quarterly Journal of Economics* 117:4, 1453–89.

Canin, Eric. 1997. "'Work, a Roof, and Bread for the Poor': Managua's Christian Base Communities in the Nicaraguan Revolution from Below." *Latin American Perspectives* 24:2, 80–101.

Caramani, Daniele. 2004. *The Nationalization of Politics: The Formation of National Electorates and Party Systems in Western Europe.* Cambridge: Cambridge University Press.

Carmody, Padraig. 1998. "Neoclassical Practice and the Collapse of Industry in Zimbabwe: The Cases of Textiles, Clothing and Footware." *Economic Geography* 74:4, 319–43.

Carothers, Thomas. 2006. *Confronting the Weakest Link: Aiding Political Parties in New Democracies.* Washington, DC: Carnegie Endowment for International Peace.

——. 2007. "The "Sequencing" Fallacy." *Journal of Democracy* 18:1, 12–27.

Centola, Damon, and Michael Macy. 2007. "Complex Contagions and the Weakness of Long Ties." *American Journal of Sociology* 113:3, 702–34.

Chabal, Patrick, and Jean-Pascal Daloz. 1999. *Africa Works: Disorder as Political Instrument.* Bloomington: Indiana University Press.

Chandra, Kanchan. 2001. "Symposium: Cumulative Findings in the Study of Ethnic Politics." *APSA-CP* 12:Winter, 7–11.

——. 2004. *Why Ethnic Parties Succeed: Patronage and Ethnic Headcounts in India.* Cambridge: Cambridge University Press.

——. 2005. "Ethnic Parties and Democratic Stability." *Perspectives on Politics* 3:2, 235–52.

Cheater, Angela. 1986. *The Politics of Factory Organization.* Harare: Mambo.

Cheeseman, Nic. 2006. "Introduction: Political Linkage and Political Space in the Era of Decolonization." *Africa Today* 53:2, 2–24.

Cheeseman, Nic, and Robert Ford. 2007. "Ethnicity as a Political Cleavage." Afrobarometer Working Paper No. 83. East Lansing, MI.

Cheeseman, Nic, and Marja Hinfelaar. 2010. "Parties, Platforms, and Political Mobilization: The Zambian Presidential Election of 2008." *African Affairs* 109:434, 51–76.

Cheeseman, Nic, and Adrienne LeBas. 2010. "The Costs of Coalition Government: Lessons from Zimbabwe and Kenya." Unpublished manuscript.

Chege, Michael. 1987. "The State and Labour in Kenya." In Peter Anyang' Nyong'o, ed., *Popular Struggles for Democracy in Africa*. London: Zed Books/United Nations University.

Chhibber, Pradeep. 1999. *Democracy without Associations: Transformation of the Party System and Social Cleavages in India*. Ann Arbor, MI: University of Michigan Press.

Chhibber, Pradeep, and Irfan Nooruddin. 2004. "Do Party Systems Count?: The Number of Parties and Government Performance in the Indian States." *Comparative Political Studies* 37:2, 152–87.

Chhibber, Pradeep, and Ken Kollman. 1998. "Party Aggregation and the Number of Parties in India and the United States." *American Political Science Review* 92:2, 329–42.

Chikhi, Said. 1995. "The Working Class, the Social Nexus and Democracy in Algeria." In Mahmood Mamdani and Ernest Wamba-dia-Wamba, eds., *African Studies in Social Movements and Democracy*. Dakar, Senegal: CODESRIA.

Chikulo, Bornwell. 1996. "Parliamentary By-elections in Zambia: Implications for the 1996 Poll." *Review of African Political Economy* 23:69, 447–53.

Chikwanha, Annie, Tulani Sithole, and Michael Bratton. 2004. "The Power of Propaganda: Public Opinion in Zimbabwe, 2004." Afrobarometer Working Paper No. 42. East Lansing, MI.

Chisala, Beatwell. 1991. *Lt. Luchembe Coup Attempt*. Lusaka: Multimedia Zambia.

Chitekwe, Beth, and Diana Mitlin. 2001. "The Urban Poor under Threat and in Struggle: Options for Urban Development in Zimbabwe, 1995–2000." *Environment and Urbanization* 13:2, 85–102.

Chitiga, R. 1996. "The Role of NGOs in Poverty Reduction at Different Levels in Zimbabwe: Historical Overview, Policy Networks and Resource Allocation." IDS Policy Dialogue Working Paper. Harare: University of Zimbabwe.

Clayton, Anthony, and Donald Savage. 1974. *Government and Labour in Kenya, 1895–1963*. London: Frank Cass and Company.

Cohen, John. 1993. "Importance of Public Service Reform: The Case of Kenya." *Journal of Modern African Studies* 31:3, 449–76.

Coleman, James. 1954. "Nationalism in Tropical Africa." *American Political Science Review* 48:2.

——. 1996. "Party Organizational Strength and Public Support for Parties." *American Journal of Political Science* 40:3, 805–24.

Collier, Paul, and Deepak Lal. 1986. *Labour and Poverty in Kenya, 1900–1980*. Oxford: Oxford University Press.

Collier, Paul, and Pedro Vicente. 2008. "Votes and Violence: Evidence from a Field Experiment in Nigeria." Working Paper, *CSAE WPS/2008-16*. Oxford: Centre for the Study of African Economies.

Collier, Ruth Berins. 1982. *Regimes in Tropical Africa: Changing Forms of Supremacy, 1945–1975*. Berkeley, CA: University of California Press.

——. 1999. *Paths toward Democracy: The Working Class and Elites in Western Europe and South America, Cambridge Studies in Comparative Politics*. Cambridge: Cambridge University Press.

Collier, Ruth Berins and David Collier. 1979. "Inducements versus Constraints: Disaggregating Corporatism." *American Political Science Review* 73:4, 967–86.

Collier, Ruth Berins. 1991. *Shaping the Political Arena: Critical Junctures, the Labor Movement and Regime Dynamics in Latin America*. Princeton, NJ: Princeton University Press.

Collier, Ruth Berins, and James Mahoney. 1997. "Adding Collective Actors to Collective Outcomes: Labor and Recent Democratization in Latin American and Southern Europe." *Comparative Politics* 29:3, 285–303.

Cooper, Frederick. 1987. *On the African Waterfront: Urban Disorder and the Transformation of Work in Colonial Mombasa*. New Haven: Yale University Press.

Coppedge, Michael. 1993. "Parties and Society in Mexico and Venezuela: Why Competition Matters." *Comparative Politics* 25:3, 253–74.

——. 1994. *Strong Parties and Lame Ducks: Presidential Partyarchy and Factionalism in Venezuela*. Stanford, CA: Stanford University Press.

Corrales, Javier. 2001. "Strong Societies, Weak Parties: Regime Change in Cuba and Venezuela in the 1950s and Today." *Latin American Politics and Society* 43:2, 81–113.

Cox, Gary. 1996. *Making Votes Count: Strategic Coordination in the World's Electoral Systems*. Cambridge: Cambridge University Press.

Crisp, Jeff. 1984. *The Story of an African Working Class: Ghanaian Miners' Struggles, 1870–1980*. London: Zed Books.

Dahl, Robert. 1971. *Polyarchy: Participation and Opposition*. New Haven: Yale University Press.

Dansereau, Suzanne. 1997. "Rebirth of Resistance: Labour and Structural Adjustment in Zimbabwe." *Labour, Capital and Society* 30:1, 90–122.

Dashwood, Hevina. 2000. *Zimbabwe: The Political Economy of Transformation*. Toronto: University of Toronto Press.

Davenport, Christian. 2004. "The Promise of Democratic Pacification: An Empirical Assessment." *International Studies Quarterly* 48:3, 539–60

Davenport, Christian, and David A. Armstrong. 2004. "Democracy and the Violation of Human Rights: A Statistical Analysis from 1976 to 1996." *American Journal of Political Science* 48:3, 538–54.

David, Paul. 1985. "Clio and the Economics of QWERTY." *American Economic Review* 75, 332–7.

Dawson, Michael. 1994. *Behind the Mule: Race and Class in African-American Politics*. Princeton, NJ: Princeton University Press.

Decalo, Samuel. 1992. "The Process, Prospects and Constraints of Democratization in Africa." *African Affairs* 91, 7–35.

De Nevers, Renee. 1993. "Democratization and Ethnic Conflict." In Michael Brown, ed., *Ethnic Conflict and International Security*. Princeton, NJ: Princeton University Press.

Desposato, Scott. 2004. "The Impact of Federalism on National Party Cohesion in Brazil." *Legislative Studies Quarterly* 29, 259–85.

——. 2006. "Parties for Rent? Ambition, Ideology, and Party Switching in Brazil's Chamber of Deputies." *American Journal of Political Science* 50:1, 62–80.

Dhlakama, L.G., and Lloyd Sachikonye. 1994. "Collective Bargaining in Zimbabwe: Procedures and Problems." In ILO, ed., *Political Transformation, Structural Adjustment and Industrial Relations in Africa*. Geneva: ILO.

Diamond, Larry. 2002. "Thinking about Hybrid Regimes." *Journal of Democracy* 13:2, 21–35.

Diani, Mario. 2003. "'Leaders' or Brokers? Positions and Influence in Social Movement Networks." In Mario Diani and Doug McAdam, eds., *Social Movements and Networks: Relational Approaches to Collective Action*. Oxford: Oxford University Press.

Dicklitch, Susan, and Doreen Lwanga. 2003. "The Politics of Being Non-political: Human Rights Organizations and the Creation of a Positive Human Rights Culture in Uganda." *Human Rights Quarterly* 25:2, 482–509.

Diouf, Mamadou. 1998. *Political Liberalization or Democratic Transition: African Perspectives*. Dakar, Senegal: CODESRIA.

Di Palma, Giuseppe. 1990. *To Craft Democracies: An Essay on Democratic Transitions*. Berkeley, CA: University of California Press.

Dix, Robert. 1992. "Democratization and the Institutionalization of Latin American Political Parties." *Comparative Political Studies* 24:4, 488–511.

Downs, Anthony. 1957. *An Economic Theory of Democracy*. New York: Harper and Row.

Dunning, Thad, and Lauren Harrison. 2010. "Cross-cutting Cleavages and Ethnic Voting: An Experimental Study of Cousinage in Mali." *American Political Science Review* 104:1, 21–39.

Du Toit, Pierre. 1999. "Bridge or Bridgehead? Comparing the Party Systems of Botswana, Namibia, Zimbabwe, Zambia and Malawi." In Hermann Giliomee and Charles Simkins, eds., *The Awkward Embrace: One Party Domination and Democracy*. Cape Town: Tafelberg Publishers.

Duverger, Maurice. 1964. *Political Parties*. London: Methuen.

Ekiert, Grzegeorz, and Jan Kubik. 1999. *Rebellious Civil Society: Popular Protest and Democratic Consolidation in Poland, 1989–1993*. Ann Arbor, MI: University of Michigan Press.

——. 1998. "Contentious Politics in New Democracies: East Germany, Hungary, Poland, and Slovakia, 1989–93." *World Politics* 50:4, 547–81.

Encarnacion, Omar. 2000. "Tocqueville's Missionaries: Civil Society Advocacy and the Promotion of Democracy." *World Policy Journal* 17:1, 9–18.

——. 2005. "Do Political Pacts Freeze Democracy? Spanish and South American Lessons." *West European Politics* 28:1, 182–203.

Engedayehu, Walle. 1993. "Ethiopia: Democracy and the Politics of Ethnicity." *Africa Today* 40:2, 29–52.

Epstein, A. L. 1958. *Politics in an Urban African Community*. Lusaka: Institute for African Studies.

Erdmann, Gero. 2007. "Party Research: Western European Bias and the 'African Labyrinth'." In Matthias Basedau, Gero Erdmann, and Andreas Mehler, eds., *Votes, Money and Violence: Political Parties and Elections in Sub-Saharan Africa*. Uppsala: Nordiska Afrikainstitutet.

Fawcus, Susan, and Michael Mbizvo. 1996. "A Community-based Investigation of Avoidable Factors for Maternal Mortality in Zimbabwe." *Studies in Family Planning* 27:6.

Fearon, James, and David Laitin. 1996. "Explaining Interethnic Cooperation." *American Political Science Review* 90:4, 715–35.

Fein, Helen. 1995. "More Murder in the Middle: Life-Integrity Violations and Democracy in the World, 1987." *Human Rights Quarterly* 17:1, 170–91.

Feltoe, Geoff. 2002. *A Guide to Media Law in Zimbabwe*. Harare: Legal Resources Foundation.

Ferguson, James. 1994. *The Anti-politics Machine: "Development," Depoliticization, and Bureaucratic Power in Lesotho*. Minneapolis: University of Minnesota Press.

——. 1999. *Expectations of Modernity: Myths and Meanings of Urban Life on the Zambian Copperbelt*. Berkeley: University of California Press.

Foeken, D., and T. Dietz. 2000. "Of Ethnicity, Manipulation and Observation: The 1992 and 1997 Elections in Kenya." In Jon Abbink and Gerti Hesseling, eds., *Electoral Observation and Democratization in Africa*. New York: Palgrave Macmillan.

Foley, Michael, and Bob Edwards. 1996. "The Paradox of Civil Society." *Journal of Democracy* 7:3, 38–52.

Fox, Roddy. 1996. "Bleak Future for Multi-party Elections in Kenya." *Journal of Modern African Studies* 34:4, 597–607.

Fraser, Alastair, and John Lungu. 2009. "Six Problems: Privatisation and the Zambian Copper Mines." *African Analyst Quarterly* 4:1.

Fujii, Lee Ann. 2009. *Killing Neighbors: Webs of Violence in Rwanda*. Ithaca and London: Cornell University Press.

Gamson, William. 1991. "Commitment and Agency in Social Movements." *Sociological Forum* 6:1, 27–50.

——. 1995. "Constructing Social Protest." In H. Johnston and B. Klandermans, eds., *Social Movements and Culture*. Minneapolis: University of Minnesota Press.

Geddes, Barbara. 1999. "What do we Know about Democratization after Twenty Years?" *Annual Review of Political Science* 2:1, 115–44.

Geisler, Gisela. 1987. "Sisters under the Skin: Women and the Women's League in Zambia." *Journal of Modern African Studies* 25:1, 43–66.

——. 1992. "Who is Losing out? Structural Adjustment, Gender, and the Agricultural Sector in Zambia." *Journal of Modern African Studies* 30:1, 113–39.

——. 2000. "'Parliament is another Terrain of Struggle': Women, Men, & Politics in South Africa." *Journal of Modern African Studies* 38, 605–30.

Gertzel, Cherry. 1975. "Labour and the State: The Case of Zambia's Mineworkers Union." *Journal of Commonwealth and Comparative Politics* 13, 290–304.

——. 1979. "Industrial Relations in Zambia in 1975." In U.G. Damachi and H. Seibel, eds., *Industrial Relations in Africa*. New York: Macmillan Press.

Gibbon, Peter. 1995. "Introduction." In Peter Gibbon, ed., *Structural Adjustment and the Working Poor in Zimbabwe: Studies on Labour, Women, Informal Sector Workers, and Health*. Uppsala: Noriska Afrikainstitutet.

Gills, Barry, Joel Rocamora, and Richard Wilson, eds. 1993. *Low Intensity Democracy: Political Power in the New World Order*. London: Pluto Press.

Gitari, David. 1991. "Church and Politics in Kenya." *Transformation: An International Journal of Holistic Mission Studies* 8:3, 7–17.

Gledhill, John. 2005. "States of Contention: State-led Political Violence in Postsocialist Romania." *East European Politics and Societies* 19:1, 76–104.

Goldstone, Jack. 1994. "Is Revolution Individually Rational? Groups and Individuals in Revolutionary Collective Action." *Rationality and Society* 6:1, 139–66.

Goldsworthy, David. 1982. "Ethnicity and Leadership in Africa: The 'Untypical' Case of Tom Mboya." *Journal of Modern African Studies* 20:1, 107–26.

Good, Kenneth. 1974. "Settler Colonialism in Rhodesia." *African Affairs* 73:290, 10–36.

——. 1989. "Debt and the One-Party State in Zambia." *Journal of Modern African Studies* 27:2, 297–313.

Goodman, Stephen. 1969. "Trade Unions and Political Parties: The Case of East Africa." *Economic Development and Cultural Change* 17:3, 338–45.

Gould, Jeremy. 2002. "Contesting Democracy: The 1996 Elections in Zambia." In Michael Cowen and Lise Laakso, eds., *Multi-party Elections in Africa*. Oxford: James Currey.

Gould, Roger. 1991. "Multiple Networks and Mobilization in the Paris Commune, 1871." *American Sociological Review* 56:6, 716–29.

——. 1993. "Collective Action and Network Structure." *American Sociological Review* 58:2, 182–96.

——. 1995. *Insurgent Identities: Class, Community and Protest in Paris from 1948 to the Commune.* Chicago: University of Chicago Press.

Granovetter, Mark. 1973. "The Strength of Weak Ties." *American Journal of Sociology* 78:6, 1360–80.

Green, W. John. 2005. "Guerrillas, Soldiers, Paramilitaries, Assassins, Narcos, and Gringos: The Unhappy Prospects for Peace and Democracy in Colombia." *Latin American Research Review* 40:2, 137–49.

Grosh, Barbara, and Stephen Orvis. 1996. "Democracy, Confusion, or Chaos: Political Conditionality in Kenya." *Studies in Comparative International Development* 31:4, 46–65.

Grzymala-Busse, Anna. 2003. "Political Competition and the Politicization of the State in East Central Europe." *Comparative Political Studies* 36:10, 1123–47.

Gupta, Anirudha. 1974. "Trade Unionism and Politics on the Copperbelt." In William Tordoff, ed., *Politics in Zambia.* Manchester: Manchester University Press.

Gwisai, Munyaradzi. 2002. "Revolutionaries, Resistance, and Crisis in Zimbabwe." *Links* 22:September–December.

Gyimah-Boadi, E., ed. 2004. *Democratic Reform in Africa: The Quality of Progress.* Boulder, CO: Lynne Rienner.

Haggard, Stephan, and Robert Kaufman. 1997. "The Political Economy of Democratic Transitions." *Comparative Politics* 29:3, 263–83.

Hagopian, Frances. 1990. "'Democracy by Undemocratic Means?' Elites, Political Pacts and Regime Transition in Brazil." *Comparative Political Studies* 23:2, 147–70.

Hale, Henry. 2005. "Why Not Parties? Electoral Markets, Party Substitutes, and Stalled Democratization in Russia." *Comparative Politics* 37:2, 147–66.

Hammar, Amanda. 2003. "The Making and Unma(s)king of Local Government in Zimbabwe." In Amanda Hammar, Brian Raftopoulos, and Stig Jensen, eds., *Zimbabwe's Unfinished Business: Rethinking Land, State and Nation in the Context of Crisis.* Harare: Weaver Press.

Harbeson, John. 1998. "Political Crisis and Renewal in Kenya: Prospects for Democratic Consolidation." *Africa Today* 45:2, 161–83.

Harries-Jones, Peter. 1975. *Freedom and Labour: Mobilization and Political Control on the Zambian Copperbelt.* Oxford: Basil Blackwell.

Harris, Peter. 1972. "Economic Incentives and European Immigrants in Rhodesia." *Rhodesian Journal of Economics* (September).

——. 1975. "Industrial Workers in Rhodesia, 1946–1972: Working Class Elites or Lumpenproletariat?" *Journal of Southern African Studies* April, 139–61.

Haugerud, Angelique. 1993. *The Culture of Politics in Modern Kenya.* Cambridge: Cambridge University Press.

Hearn, Julie. 2000. "Aiding Democracy? Donors and Civil Society in South Africa." *Third World Quarterly* 21:5, 815–30.

Hedstrom, Peter, Rickard Sandell, and Charlotta Stern. 2000. "Mesolevel Networks and the Diffusion of Social Movements: The Case of the Swedish Social Democratic Party." *American Journal of Sociology* 106:1, 145–72.

Heisler, Helmuth. 1971. "The Creation of a Stabilized Urban Society: A Turning Point in the Development of Northern Rhodesia/Zambia." *African Affairs* 70:279, 125–45.

Helmke, Gretchen, and Steven Levitsky. 2004. "Informal Institutions and Comparative Politics: A Research Agenda." *Perspectives on Politics* 2:4, 725–40.

Henley, John. 1978. "Pluralism, Underdevelopment and Trade Union Power: Evidence from Kenya." *British Journal of Industrial Relations* 16:2, 224–42.

Herbst, Jeffrey. 1990. *State Politics in Zimbabwe*. Berkeley, CA: University of California Press.

Herbst, Jeffrey. 2000. *States and Power in Africa: Comparative Lessons in Authority and Control*. Princeton, NJ: Princeton University Press.

Higley, John, and Michael Burton. 1989. "The Elite Variable in Democratic Transitions and Breakdowns." *American Sociological Review* 54:1, 17–32.

Hinfelaar, Hugo. 2004. *History of the Catholic Church in Zambia*. Lusaka: Bookworld Publishers/Missionaries of Africa.

Hipsher, Patricia. 1996. "Democratization and the Decline of Urban Social Movements in Chile and Spain." *Comparative Politics* 28:3, 273–97.

Holmquist, Frank. 1984. "Self-help: The State and Peasant Leverage in Kenya." *Africa: Journal of the International African Institute* 54:3, 72–91.

Holmquist, Frank, and Michael Ford. 1992. "Kenya: Slouching Toward Democracy." *Africa Today* 39:3, 97–111.

——. 1994. "Kenya: State and Civil Society the First Year after the Election." *Africa Today* 41:4, 5–25.

Horowitz, Donald. 1985. *Ethnic Groups in Conflict*. Berkeley, CA: University of California Press.

Hudson, John. 1999. *A Time to Mourn: A Personal Account of the 1964 Lumpa Church Revole in Zambia*. Lusaka: Bookworld Publishers.

Hughes, David. 1989. "Non-government Developmental Organizations and Peasant Political History in Zimbabwe." B.A. Thesis, Princeton University.

Hunt, Scott, Robert Benford, and David Snow. 1994. "Identity Fields: Framing Processes and the Social Construction of Movement Identities." In E. Larana, H. Johnston, and J. Gusfield, eds., *New Social Movements*. Philadelphia: Temple University Press.

Huntington, Samuel. 1968. *Political Order in Changing Societies*. New Haven: Yale University Press.

——. 1991. "How Countries Democratize." *Political Science Quarterly* 106:4, 579–616.

Hyde, David. 2000. "Plantation Struggles in Kenya: Trade Unionism on the Land, 1947–1963." Ph.D. Dissertation, School of Oriental and African Studies, University of London, London.

Ibrahim, Jibrin. 2007. "Nigeria's 2007 Elections: The Fitful Path to Democratic Citizenship." Special Report No. 182. Washington, DC: United States Institute of Peace.

Ihonvbere, Julius. 1995a. "From Movement to Government: The Movement for Multiparty Democracy and the Crisis of Democratic Consolidation in Zambia." *Canadian Journal of African Studies* 29:1, 1–25.

——. 1995b. "The 'Zero Option' Controversy in Zambia: Western Double Standards versus Safeguarding Security?" *Africa Spectrum* 30:1, 93–104.

Jackson, Robert, and Carl Rosberg. 1982. "Why Africa's Weak States Persist: The Empirical and the Juridical in Statehood." *World Politics* 35:1, 1–24.

——. 1982. *Personal Rule in Black Africa: Prince, Autocrat, Prophet, Tyrant*. Berkeley, CA: University of California Press.

James, Scott. 2005. "Patronage Regimes and American Party Development from 'The Age of Jackson' to the Progressive Era." *British Journal of Political Science* 36, 39–60.

Jeffries, Richard. 1978. *Class, Ideology and Power in Africa: The Railwaymen of Sekondi.* Cambridge: Cambridge University Press.

Joireman, Sandra. 1997. "Opposition Politics and Ethnicityin Ethiopia: We Will All GoDown Together." *Journal of Modern African Studies* 35:3, 387–403.

Jones Luong, Pauline. 2002. *Institutional Change and Political Continuity in Post-Soviet Central Asia.* Cambridge: Cambridge University Press.

Joseph, Richard. 1992. "Zambia: A Model for Democratic Change." *Current History* May, 199–201.

——. 1997. "Democratization in Africa after 1989: Comparative and Theoretical Reflections." *Comparative Politics* 29:3, 363–82.

——. 1999. "The Reconfiguration of Power in Late Twentieth-Century Africa." In Richard Joseph, ed., *State, Conflict and Democracy in Africa.* Boulder, CO: Lynne Rienner.

Kaarsholm, Preben. 1999. "Si ye pambili – Which Way Forward? Urban Development, Culture and Politics in Bulawayo." In Brian Raftopoulos and Tsuneo Yoshikuni, eds., *Sites of Struggle: Essays in Zimbabwe's Urban History.* Harare: Weaver Press.

Kagwanja, Peter. 2001. "Politics of Marionettes: Extra-legal Violence and the 1997 Elections in Kenya." In Marcel Rutten, Alamin Mazrui, and Francois Grignon, eds., *Out for the Count: The 1997 General Elections and Prospects for Democracy in Kenya.* Kampala: Fountain Publishers.

——. 2003. "Facing Mount Kenya or Facing Mecca? The Mungiki, Ethnic Violence and the Politics of the Moi Succession in Kenya, 1987–2002." *African Affairs* 102, 25–49.

——. 2005. "'Power to Uhuru': Youth Identity and Generational Politics in Kenya's 2002 Elections." *African Affairs* 105:418, 51–75.

Kahl, Colin. 2006. *States, Scarcity, and Civil Strife in the Developing World.* Princeton, NJ: Princeton University Press.

Kalyvas, Stathis. 1996. *The Rise of Christian Democracy in Europe.* Ithaca, NY: Cornell University Press.

——. 1998. "From Pulpit to Party: Party Formation and the Christian Democratic Phenomenon." *Comparative Politics* 30:3, 293–312.

Kanyinga, Karuti. 2001. "'Mix-and-Match Parties and Persons': The 1997 General Elections in the Meru and Embu Regions of Kenya." In Marcel Rutten, Alamin Mazrui, and Francois Grignon, eds., *Out for the Count: The 1997 General Elections and Prospects for Democracy in Kenya.* Kampala: Fountain Publishers.

Kapferer, Bruce. 1969. "Norms and Manipulation of Relationships in a Work Context." In J. C. Mitchell, ed., *Social Networks in Urban Situations: Analyses of Personal Relationships in Central African Towns.* Manchester: Manchester University Press.

Karatnycky, Adrian, and Peter Ackerman. 2005. *How Freedom is Won: From Civic Struggle to Durable Democracy.* New York: Freedom House.

Karl, Terry Lynn. 1986. "Petroleum and Political Pacts: The Transition to Democracy in Venezuela." In Guillermo O'Donnell, Philippe Schmitter, and Laurence Whitehead, eds., *Transitions from Authoritarian Rule: Latin America.* Baltimore, MD: Johns Hopkins University Press.

——. 1990. "Dilemmas of Democratization in Latin America." *Comparative Politics* 23:1, 1–21.

Kasfir, Nelson. 1974. "Departicipation and Political Development in Black African Politics." *Studies in Comparative International Development* 9:3, 3–25.

Kaspin, Deborah. 1995. "The Politics of Ethnicity in Malawi's Democratic Transition." *Journal of Modern African Studies* 33:4, 595–620.

Kato, Junko. 1998. "When the Party Breaks Up: Exit and Voice among Japanese Legislators." *American Political Science Review* 92:4, 857–70.

Katumanga, Musambayi. 2005. "A City under Siege: Banditry & Modes of Accumulation in Nairobi, 1991–2004." *Review of African Political Economy* 32:106, 505–20.

Keck, Margaret. 1992. *The Workers' Party and Democratization in Brazil*. New Haven: Yale University Press.

Keefer, Phillip. 2010. "The Ethnicity Distraction? Political Credibility and Partisan Preferences in Africa." Afrobarometer Working Paper No. 118. East Lansing, MI.

Kees van Donge, Jan. 1998. "Reflections on Donors, Opposition and Popular Will in the 1996 Zambian General Elections." *Journal of Modern African Studies* 36:1, 71–99.

Kelley, Judith. 2009. "D-Minus Elections: The Politics and Norms of International Election Observation." *International Organization* 63:4, 765–87.

Key, V.O. 1977. *Southern Politics in State and Nation*. Knoxville: University of Tennessee Press.

Kibble, Steve. 1992. "Zambia: Problems for the MMD." *Review of African Political Economy* 53, 104–8.

Kirschke, Linda. 2000. "Informal Repression, Zero Sum Politics and Late Third Wave Transitions." *Journal of Modern African Studies* 38:3, 383–405.

——. 2007. "Semipresidentialism and the Perils of Power-Sharing in Neopatrimonial States." *Comparative Political Studies* 40:11, 1372–94.

Kitschelt, Herbert. 2000. "Linkages between Citizens and Politicians in Democratic Polities." *Comparative Political Studies* 33:6/7, 845–79.

Kitschelt, Herbert, and Steven Wilkinson. 2006. "Citizen-Politician Linkages: An Introduction." In Herbert Kitschelt and Steven Wilkinson, eds., *Patrons, Clients and Policies: Patterns of Democratic Accountability and Political Competition*. Cambridge: Cambridge University Press.

Klopp, Jacqueline. 2000. "Pilfering the Public: The Problem of Land Grabbing in Contemporary Kenya." *Africa Today* 47:1, 7–26.

——. 2001. "'Ethnic Clashes' and Winning Elections: The Case of Kenya's Electoral Despotism." *Canadian Journal of African Studies* 35:3, 473–517.

——. 2002. "Can Moral Ethnicity Trump Political Tribalism? The Struggle for Land and Nation in Kenya." *African Studies* 61:2, 269–94.

Klopp, Jacqueline, and Elke Zuern. 2007. "The Politics of Violence in Democratization: Lessons from Kenya and South Africa." *Comparative Politics* 39:2, 127–46.

Komakoma, Joe, ed. 2003. *The Social Teaching of the Catholic Bishops and other Christian Leaders in Zambia: Major Pastoral Letters and Statements, 1953–2001*. Ndola, Zambia: Mission Press.

Kramon, Eric. 2009. "Vote-Buying and Political Behavior: Estimating and Explaining Vote-Buying's Effect on Turnout in Kenya." Afrobarometer Working Paper No. 114. East Lansing, MI.

Kriger, Norma. 1992. *Zimbabwe's Guerilla War: Peasant Voices*. Cambridge: Cambridge University Press.

——. 2003. *Guerrilla Violence in Post-war Zimbabwe: Symbolic and Violent Politics, 1980–1987*. Cambridge: Cambridge University Press.

——. 2005. "ZANU (PF) Strategies in General Elections, 1980–2000: Discourse and Coercion." *African Affairs* 104:414, 1–34.

Kuenzi, Michelle, and Gina Lambright. 2001. "Party System Institutionalization in 30 African Countries." *Party Politics* 7:4, 437–68.

——. 2005. "Party Systems and Democratic Consolidation in Africa's Electoral Regimes." *Party Politics* 11:4, 423–46.

Kuperus, Tracy. 1999. "Building Democracy: An Examination of Religious Associations in South Africa and Zimbabwe." *Journal of Modern African Studies* 37:4, 643–68.

Kydd, Jonathan. 1988. "Coffee after Copper? Structural Adjustment, Liberalisation, and Agriculture in Zambia." *The Journal of Modern African Studies* 26:2, 227–51.

Laakso, Lise. 2002. "The Politics of International Election Observation: The Case of Zimbabwe in 2000." *Journal of Modern African Studies* 40:3, 437–64.

Laakso, Markku, and Rein Taagepera. 1979. "'Effective' Number of Parties: A Measure with Application to West Europe." *Comparative Political Studies* 12:1, 3–27.

Laitin, David. 1986. *Hegemony and Culture: Power and Religious Change among the Yoruba*. Chicago: University of Chicago Press.

——. 1998. *Identity in Formation: The Russian-Speaking Populations in the Near Abroad*. Ithaca, NY: Cornell University Press.

Larmer, Miles. 2005. "Reaction & Resistance to Neo-liberalism in Zambia." *Review of African Political Economy* 32:103, 29–45.

——. 2006. "'A Little Bit Like a Volcano.' The United Progressive Party and Resistance to One Party Rule in Zambia, 1964–1980." *International Journal of African Historical Studies* 39:1, 49–83.

——. 2007. *Mineworkers in Zambia: Labour and Political Change in Post-colonial Africa*. London: Tauris.

Larmer, Miles, and Alastair Fraser. 2007. "Of cabbages and King Cobra: Populist politics and Zambia's 2006 election." *African Affairs* 106:425, 611–37.

LeBas, Adrienne. 2006. "Polarization as Craft: Explaining Party Formation and State Violence in Zimbabwe." *Comparative Politics* 38:4, 419–38.

——. 2007. "The Politics of Institutional Subversion: Organized Labor and Resistance in Zambia." In John Chalcraft and Yaseen Noorani, eds., *Counterhegemony in the Colony and Postcolony*. New York: Palgrave Macmillan.

——. 2010. "Party Organization and the Evolution of Party Systems in Africa." Paper presented at the Princeton Workshop on Political Parties in the Developing World. April 30–May 1, Princeton, NJ.

Lehoucq, Fabrice, and Ivan Molina. 2002. *Stuffing the Ballot Box: Fraud, Electoral Reform, and Democratization in Costa Rica*. New York: Cambridge University Press.

Lemarchand, Rene. 2007. "Consociationalism and Power Sharing in Africa: Rwanda, Burundi, and the Democratic Republic of Congo." *African Affairs* 106:422, 1–20.

Levine, Daniel H. 1988. "Assessing the Impacts of Liberation Theology in Latin America." *The Review of Politics* 50:2, 241–63.

Levine, Daniel H., and Scott Mainwaring. 1989. "Religion and Popular Protest in Latin America: Contrasting Experiences." In Susan Eckstein, ed., *Power and Popular Protest: Latin American Social Movements*. Berkeley, CA: University of California Press.

Levitsky, Steven. 2003a. *Tranforming Labor-based Parties in Latin America: Argentine Personism in Comparative Perspective*. New York: Cambridge University Press.

——. 2003b. "From Labor Politics to Machine Politics: The Transformation of Party-Union Linkages in Argentine Peronism, 1983–1999." *Latin American Research Review* 38:3, 3–36.

Levitsky, Steven, and Maxwell Cameron. 2003. "Democracy without Parties? Political Parties and Regime Change in Fujimori's Peru." *Latin American Politics and Society* 45:3, 1–33.

Levitsky, Steven, and Lucian Way. 2002. "The Rise of Competitive Authoritarianism." *Journal of Democracy* 13:2, 51–65.

——. 2010. *Competitive Authoritarianism: Hybrid Regimes After the Cold War*. New York: Cambridge University Press.

Liatto, Bernice. 1989. *Organised Labour and the State in Zambia*. Ph. D. Dissertation, University of Leeds.

Lindberg, Staffan. 2003. "It's Our Time to 'Chop:' Do Elections in Africa Feed Neopatrimonialism Rather than Counter-Act It?" *Democratization* 10:2, 121–40.

——. 2006. *Democracy and Elections in Africa*. Baltimore, MD: Johns Hopkins University Press.

——. 2007. "Institutionalization of Party Systems? Stability and Fluidity among Legislative Parties in Africa's Democracies." *Government and Opposition* 42:2, 215–41.

Linz, Juan and Alfred Stepan. 1996. *Problems of Democratic Transition and Consolidation: Southern Europe, South America and Post-Communist Europe*. Baltimore, MD: Johns Hopkins University Press.

Linz, Juan, and Arturo Valenzuela, eds. 1994. *The Failure of Presidential Democracy: The Case of Latin America*. Baltimore, MD: Johns Hopkins University Press.

Lipset, Seymour, and Stein Rokkan. 1967. *Party Systems and Voter Alignments*. New York: The Free Press.

Lofchie, Michael F. 1975. "Political and Economic Origins of African Hunger." *Journal of Modern African Studies* 13:4, 551–67.

Logan, Carolyn. 2008. "Rejecting the Disloyal Opposition? The Trust Gap in Mass Attitudes toward Ruling and Opposition Parties." Afrobarometer Working Paper No. 94. East Lansing, MI.

Logan, Carolyn, Thomas Wolf, and Robert Sentamu. 2007. "Kenyans and Democracy: What do they Really Want from it, Anyway?" Afrobarometer Working Paper No. 70. East Lansing, MI.

Lohmann, Susanne. 1994. "The Dynamics of Informational Cascades: The Monday Demonstrations in Leipzig, East Germany, 1989–91." *World Politics* 47:1, 42–101.

Lombard, C. Stephen. 1972. "Farming Co-operatives in the Development of Zambian Agriculture." *Journal of Modern African Studies* 10:2, 294–9.

Loxley, John. 1990. "Structural Adjustment in Africa: Reflections on Ghana and Zambia." *Review of African Political Economy* 47, 8–27.

Ludwig, Kimberley. 2001. "Prospects for Pluralism: Economic Interest Groups and Dual Transition in Zambia's Third Republic." Ph.D. Dissertation, Michigan State University.

Lungu, Gatian. 1997. "Some Bizarre Clauses in a Noble Document: Critical Observations on the Constitution of Zambia (Amendment) Act No. 18 of 1996." *ZANGO, the University of Zambia Journal of Contemporary Issues* 21:11, 20–30.

Lunn, Jon. 1999. "The meaning of the 1948 General Strike in colonial Zimbabwe." In Brian Raftopoulos and Tsuneo Yoshikuni, eds., *Sites of Struggle: Essays in Zimbabwe's Urban History.* Harare: Weaver Press.

Lust-Okar, Ellen. 2004. "Divided They Rule: The Management and Manipulation of Political Opposition." *Comparative Politics* 36:2, 159–79.

——. 2009. "Competitive Clientelism in the Middle East." *Journal of Democracy* 20:3, 122–35.

Lyons, Terrence. 1996. "Closing the Transition: The May 1995 Elections in Ethiopia." *Journal of Modern African Studies* 34:1, 121–42.

MacGarry, Brian. 1993. *Growth? Without Equity? The Zimbabwe Economy and the Economic Structural Adjustment Programme.* Gweru: Mambo Press and Silveira House.

Madrid, Raul. 2005. "Indigenous Voters and Party System Fragmentation in Latin America." *Electoral Studies* 24:4, 689–707.

Mahoney, James. 2000. "Path dependence in historical sociology." *Theory and Society* 29, 507–48.

——. 2004. "Comparative-Historical Methodology." *Annual Review of Sociology* 30, 81–101.

Mahoney, James, and Richard Snyder. 1999. "Rethinking Agency and Structure in the Study of Regime Change." *Studies in Comparative International Development* 34:2, 3–32.

Mainwaring, Scott. 1987. *The Catholic Church and Politics in Brazil, 1916–1985.* Stanford, CA: Stanford University Press.

——. 1988. "Political Parties and Democratization in Brazil and the Southern Cone." *Comparative Politics* 21:1, 91–120.

——. 1999. *Rethinking Party Systems in the Third Wave of Democratization: The Case of Brazil.* Stanford, CA: Stanford University Press.

Mainwaring, Scott, and Timothy Scully, eds. 1995a. *Building Democratic Institutions: Party Systems in Latin America.* Stanford, CA: Stanford University Press.

——. 1995b. "Introduction: Party Systems in Latin America." In Scott Mainwaring and Timothy Scully, eds., *Building Democratic Institutions: Party Systems in Latin America.* Stanford, CA: Stanford University Press.

Makumbe, John, and Daniel Compagnon. 2000. *Behind the Smokescreen: The Politics of Zimbabwe's 1995 General Elections.* Harare: University of Zimbabwe Publications.

Malkki, Liisa. 1995. *Purity and Exile: Violence, Memory, and National Cosmology among Hutu Refugees in Tanzania.* Chicago: University of Chicago Press.

Mamdani, Mahmood. 1996. *Citizen and Subject: Contemporary Africa and the Legacy of Late Colonialism.* Princeton, NJ: Princeton University Press.

Mamdani, Mahmood, and Ernest Wamba-dia-Wamba, eds. 1995. *African Studies in Social Movements and Democracy.* Dakar, Senegal: CODESRIA.

Manase, Wilson. 1992. "Grassroots Education in Zimbabwe: Successes and Problems Encountered in Implementation by the Legal Resources Foundation of Zimbabwe." *Journal of African Law* 36:1, 11–18.

Mann, Michael. 2005. *The Dark Side of Democracy: Explaining Ethnic Cleansing.* Cambridge: Cambridge University Press.

Manning, Carrie. 2005. "Assessing African Party Systems after the Third Wave." *Party Politics* 11:6, 707–27.

Mansfield, Edward, and Jack Snyder. 2007. "The Sequencing 'Fallacy'." *Journal of Democracy* 18:3, 5–10.

Maphosa, G.J. 1992. "Industrial Democracy in Zimbabwe?" In Angela Cheater, ed., *Industrial Sociology in the First Decade of Zimbabwean Independence.* Harare: University of Zimbabwe.

Marongwe, Nelson. 2003. "Farm Occupations and Occupiers in the New Politics of Land in Zimbabwe." In Amanda Hammar, Brian Raftopoulos, and Stig Jenson, eds., *Zimbabwe's Unfinished Business: Rethinking Land, the State and Nation in the Context of Crisis.* Harare: Weaver Press.

Marx, Anthony. 2003. *Faith in Nation: Exclusionary Origins of Nationalism.* New York: Oxford University Press.

Mattes, Robert, and Carlos Shenga. 2007. "'Uncritical Citizenship' in a 'Low-Information' Society: Mozambicans in Comparative Perspective." Afrobarometer Working Paper No. 91.

Maupeu, Hervé. 2008. "Retour sur les violences." In J. Lafarge, ed., *Les élections générales de 2007 au Kenya.* Paris: Karthala.

Maxwell, David. 1995. "The Church and Democratisation in Africa: The Case of Zimbabwe." In Paul Gifford, ed., *The Christian Churches and the Democratisation of Africa.* Leiden: EJ Brill.

Mbeki, Govan. 1984. *South Africa: The Peasants' Revolt.* London: International Defence and Aid Fund for Southern Africa.

Mboya, Tom. 1956. "Kenyan Trade Unions Fight for Freedom." *Africa Today* 3:2, 2–5.

McAdam, Doug. 1982. *Political Process and the Development of Black Insurgency, 1930–1970.* Chicago: University of Chicago Press.

McAdam, Doug. 1986. "Recruitment to High-Risk Activism: The Case of Freedom Summer." *American Journal of Sociology* 92:1, 64–90.

McAdam, Doug, Sidney Tarrow, and Charles Tilly. 2001. *Dynamics of Contention.* New York: Cambridge University Press.

McFaul, Michael. 2002. "The Fourth Wave of Democracy and Dictatorship: Noncooperative Transitions in the Postcommunist World." *World Politics* 54:2, 212–44.

McGregor, Joann. 2002. "The Politics of Disruption: War Veterans and the Local State in Zimbabwe." *African Affairs* 402, 9–38.

McGuire, James. 1997. *Peronism without Peron: Unions, Parties and Democracy in Argentina.* Stanford, CA: Stanford University Press.

Meebelo, Henry. 1986. *African Proletarians and Colonial Capitalism: The Origins, Growth and Struggles of the Zambian Labour Movement to 1964.* Lusaka: Kenneth Kaunda Foundation.

Mehler, Andreas. 2009. "Peace and Power Sharing in Africa: A Not so Obvious Relationship." *African Affairs* 108:432, 453–73.

Meijer, Fons. 1990. "Structural Adjustment and Diversification in Zambia." *Development and Change* 21:4, 657–92.

Melson, Robert. 1971. "Ideology and Inconsistency: The "Cross-Pressured" Nigerian Worker." *American Political Science Review* 65:1, 161–71.

Mendelberg, Tali. 2001. *The Race Card: Campaign Strategy, Implicit Messages, and the Norm of Equality.* Princeton, NJ: Princeton University Press.

Menthong, Hélène-Laure. 1998. "Vote et communautarisme au Cameroun: un vote de coeur, de sang et de raison'." *Politique Africaine* 69, 40–51.

Michels, Robert. 1962. *Political Parties: A Sociological Study of the Oligarchical Tendencies of Modern Democracy.* New York: Macmillan.

Miguel, Edward. 2004. "Tribe or Nation? Nation Building and Public Goods in Kenya versus Tanzania." *World Politics* 56:3, 327–62.

Mitchell, J. Clyde. 1956. *The Kalela Dance: Aspects of Social Relations among Urban African in Northern Rhodesia.* Manchester: Rhodes-Livingstone Institute.

Moehler, Devra, and Staffan Lindberg. 2009. "Narrowing the Legitimacy Gap: Turnovers as a Cause of Democratic Consolidation." *Journal of Politics* 71:4, 1448–66.

Molinar, Juan. 1991. "Counting the Number of Parties: An Alternative Index." *American Political Science Review* 85:4, 1383–91.

Momba, Jotham. 2003. "Democratic Transition and the Crises of an African Nationalist Party: UNIP, Zambia." In M. Mohamed Salih, ed., *African Political Parties: Evolution, Institutionalisation and Governance.* London: Pluto Press.

Monroe, Kristen Renwick. 2001. "Morality and a Sense of Self: The Importance of Identity and Categorization for Moral Action." *American Journal of Political Science* 45:3, 491–507.

——. 2004. *The Hand of Compassion: Portraits of Moral Choice during the Holocaust.* Princeton, NJ: Princeton University Press.

Morgenstern, Scott. 2001. "Organized Factions and Disorganized Parties: Electoral Incentives in Uruguay." *Party Politics* 7:2, 235–56.

Morgenthau, Ruth Schacter. 1964. *Political Parties in French-Speaking West Africa.* Oxford, England: Clarendon Press.

Morje Howard, Marc, and Philip Roessler. 2006. "Liberalizing Electoral Outcomes in Competitive Authoritarian Regimes." *American Journal of Political Science* 50:2, 365–81.

Morlino, Leonardo. 2005. "Anchors and Democratic Change." *Comparative Political Studies* 38:7, 743–70.

Morrison, Minion K.C., and Jae Woo Hong. 2006. "Ghana's political parties: How Ethno/Regional Variations sustain the National Two-Party System." *Journal of Modern African Studies* 44:4, 623–47.

Moser, Robert. 1999. "Independents and Party Formation: Elite Partisanship as an Intervening Variable in Russian Politics." *Comparative Politics* 31:2, 147–65.

Mosley, Paul. 1986. "The Politics of Economic Liberalization: USAID and the World Bank in Kenya, 1980–84." *African Affairs* 85:338, 107–19.

Moyo, Sam. 1991. "NGO Advocacy in Zimbabwe: Systematising an Old Function or Inventing a New Role?" Working Paper No. 1. Harare: Zimbabwe Environmental Regional Organisation.

——. 2001. "The Land Occupation Movement and Democratisation in Zimbabwe: Contradictions of Neoliberalism." *Millennium* 30:2, 311–30.

Moyo, Sam, John Makumbe, and Brian Raftopoulos, eds. 2000. *NGOs, the State and Politics in Zimbabwe.* Harare: SAPES Trust.

Mozaffar, Shaheen. 1989. "Clarifying Some Analytical Issues in Corporatism." In Julius Nyang'oro and Timothy Shaw, eds., *Corporatism in Africa: Comparative Analysis and Practice.* Boulder, CO: Westview Press.

Mozaffar, Shaheen, and James Scarritt. 2005. "The Puzzle of African Party Systems." *Party Politics* 11:4, 399–421.

Mozaffar, Shaheen, James Scarritt, and Glen Galaich. 2003. "Electoral Institutions, Ethnopolitical Cleavages, and Party Systems in Africa's Emerging Democracies." *American Political Science Review* 97:3, 379–90.

Mueller, Susanne. 2008. "The Political Economy of Kenya's Crisis." *Journal of Eastern African Studies* 2:2, 185–210.

Muir, Douglas, and John Brown. 1975. "Labour Legislation and Industrial Disputes: The Kenyan Case." *British Journal of Industrial Relations* 13:3, 334–45.

Mukui, J.T. 1983. "The Politics and Economics of the 1979 Tripartite Agreement in Kenya: A Note." *African Affairs* 82:329, 559–63.

Mukwena, Royson. 1992. "Zambia's Local Administration Act, 1980: A Critical Appraisal of the Integration Objective." *Public Administration and Development* 12, 237–47.

Mutasah, Tawanda. 2001. "The founding of the National Constitutional Assembly in Zimbabwe: Why, How, and Where?" Manuscript provided by the author.

Mutizwa-Mangiza, Dorothy. 1992. "An Evaluation of Workers' Real Participation in Decision-making at Enterprise Level." In Angela Cheater, ed., *Industrial Sociology in the First Decade of Zimbabwean Independence*. Harare: University of Zimbabwe.

Mutua, Makau. 2001. "Justice under Siege: The Rule of Law and Judicial Subservience in Kenya." *Human Rights Quarterly* 23:1, 96–118.

Mwagiru, Makumi, Oleng Sana, and Kenneth Njau. 2002. *Facts about Majeshi ya Wazee*. Nairobi: Centre for Conflict Research & Friedrich Ebert Stiftung.

Mwanakatwe, John. 2003. *Teacher, Politician, Lawyer: My Autobiography*. Lusaka: Bookworld Publishers.

Mylonas, Harris, and Nasos Roussias. 2008. "When Do Votes Count? Regime Type, Electoral Conduct, and Political Competition in Africa." *Comparative Political Studies* 41:11, 1466–91.

Nasong'o, Shadrack. 2007. "Political Transition without Transformation: The Dialectic of Liberalization without Democratization in Kenya and Zambia." *African Studies Review* 50:1, 83–107.

Ndegwa, Stephen. 1997. "Citizenship and Ethnicity: An Examination of Two Transition Moments in Kenyan Politics." *American Political Science Review* 91:3, 599–616.

——. 1998. "The Incomplete Transition: The Constitutional and Electoral Context in Kenya." *Africa Today* 45:2, 193–211.

Ndhlovu, Aaron. 1978. *The Role of the Trade Union Movement in the Armed Revolutionary Struggle and its Task after the Struggle*. Lusaka: ZAPU.

Nelson, Joan. 1979. *Access to Power: Politics and the Urban Poor in Developing Nations*. Princeton, NJ: Princeton University Press.

Neto, Octavio Amorim, and Gary Cox. 1997. "Electoral Institutions, Cleavage Structures, and the Number of Parties." *American Journal of Political Science* 41:1, 149–74.

Nexon, Daniel. 2009. *The Struggle for Power in Early Modern Europe: Religious Conflict, Dynastic Empires, and International Change*. Princeton: Princeton University Press.

Nkiwane, Tandeka. 1998. "Opposition Politics in Zimbabwe: The Struggle within the Struggle." In Adebayo Olukoshi, ed., *The Politics of Opposition in Contemporary Africa*. Uppsala: Nordiska Afrikainstitutet.

Nordlund, Per. 1996. *Organising the Political Agora: Domination and Democratisation in Zimbabwe and Zambia.* Uppsala: Uppsala University Press.

Nyambuya, M.N. 1994. "The Social Impact of Cost Recovery Measures in Zimbabwe." *SAPEM* March, 14–15.

Nyang'oro, Julius. 1989. "State Corporatism in Tanzania." In Julius Nyang'oro and Timothy Shaw, eds., *Corporatism in Africa: Comparative Analysis and Practice.* Boulder, Co: Westview Press.

Nyoni, Sithembiso. 1987. "Indigenous NGOs: Liberation, Self-Reliance and Development." *World Development* 15, 51–6.

Ochieng', William, and Robert Maxon. 1992. *An Economic History of Kenya.* Nairobi, Kenya: East African Educational Publishers.

O'Donnell, Guillermo. 1996. "Illusions about Consolidation." *Journal of Democracy* 7:2, 34–51.

O'Donnell, Guillermo, and Philippe Schmitter. 1986. *Transitions from Authoritarian Rule: Tentative Conclusions about Uncertain Democracies.* Baltimore, MD: Johns Hopkins University Press.

O'Dwyer, Conor. 2004. "Runaway State Building: How Political Parties Shape States in Postcommunist Eastern Europe." *World Politics* 56:4, 520–53.

Oloo, Adams. 2007. "The Contemporary Opposition in Kenya: Between Internal Traits and State Manipulation." In Godwin Murunga and Shadrack Nasong'o, eds., *Kenya: The Struggle for Democracy.* Dakar, Senegal: CODESRIA.

Olson, Mancur. 1965 (1971). *The Logic of Collective Action: Public Goods and the Theory of Groups.* Cambridge, MA: Harvard University Press.

Olukoshi, Adebayo, ed. 1998. *The Politics of Opposition in Contemporary Africa.* Uppsala: Nordiska Afrikainstitutet.

Ordeshook, Peter, and Olga Shvetsova. 1994. "Ethnic Heterogeneity, District Magnitude and Number of Parties." *American Journal of Political Science* 38:1, 100–23.

Orvis, Stephen. 2003. "Kenyan Civil Society: Bridging the Urban–Rural Divide?" *Journal of Modern African Studies* 41:2, 247–68.

——. 2006. "Bringing Institutions Back into the Study of Kenya and Africa." *Africa Today* 53:2, 95–110.

Osa, Maryjane. 2003. "Networks in Opposition: Linking Organizations through Activists in the Polish People's Republic." In Mario Diani and Doug McAdam, eds., *Social Movements and Networks: Relational Approaches to Collective Action.* Oxford: Oxford University Press.

Ottaway, Marina. 2003. *Democracy Challenged: The Rise of Semi-Authoritarianism.* Washington, DC: Carnegie Endowment for International Peace.

Oyugi, Walter. 1997. "Ethnicity in the Electoral Process: The 1992 General Elections in Kenya." *African Journal of Political Science* 2:1, 41–69.

Panebianco, Angelo. 1988. *Political Parties: Organization and Power.* New York: Cambridge University Press.

Pedersen, Mogens. 1980. "On Measuring Party System Change: A Methodological Critique and a Suggestion." *Comparative Political Studies* 12:4, 387–403.

Phimister, Ian. 1988. *An Economic and Social History of Zimbabwe, 1890–1948: Capital Accumulation and Class Struggle.* New York: Longman.

Phiri, Isaac. 1999. "Why African Churches Preach Politics: The Case of Zambia." *Journal of Church and State* 41:2, 323–47.

Pierson, Paul. 2000. "Increasing Returns, Path Dependence and the Study of Politics." *American Political Science Review* 94, 251–67.

——. 2004. *Politics in Time: History, Institutions, and Social Analysis.* Princeton, NJ: Princeton University Press.

Piven, Frances Fox, and Richard Cloward. 1977. *Poor People's Movements: Why They Succeed, Why They Fail.* New York: Pantheon Books.

Pletcher, James R. 1986. "The Political Uses of Agricultural Markets in Zambia." *Journal of Modern African Studies* 24:4, 603–17.

Poletta, Francesca. 2006. *It Was Like a Fever: Storytelling in Protest and Politics.* Chicago: University of Chicago Press.

Poletta, Francesca, and James Jasper. 2001. "Collective Identity in Social Movements." *Annual Review of Sociology* 27, 283–305.

Polhemus, James. 1997. "Democracy Betrayed: Zambia's Third Republic." Paper presented at the Annual Meeting of the African Studies Association of Australia and the Pacific, September 25–27, 1997. Furnished to me by USAID Zambia.

Posner, Daniel. 2003. "The Colonial Origins of Ethnic Cleavages: The Case of Linguistic Divisions in Zambia." *Comparative Politics* 35:2, 127–46.

——. 2004a. "Measuring Ethnic Fractionalization in Africa." *American Journal of Political Science* 48:4, 849–63.

——. 2004b. "The Political Salience of Cultural Difference: Why Chewas and Tumbukas are Allies in Zambia and Adversaries in Malawi." *American Political Science Review* 98:4, 529–45.

——. 2006. *Institutions and Ethnic Politics in Africa.* Cambridge: Cambridge University Press.

Posner, Daniel, and David Simon. 2002. "Economic Conditions and Incumbent Support in Africa's New Democracies: Evidence from Zambia." *Comparative Political Studies* 35:3, 313–36.

Press, Robert. 2004. "Establishing a Culture of Resistance: The Struggle for Human Rights in Kenya (1987–2002)." Ph.D. Dissertation, Department of Political Science, University of Florida, Gainesville, Florida.

Przeworski, Adam. 1991. *Democracy and the Market: Political and Economic Reforms in Eastern Europe and Latin America.* Cambridge: Cambridge University Press.

Przeworski, Adam, and John Sprague. 1986. *Paper Stones: A History of Electoral Socialism.* Chicago: University of Chicago Press.

Przeworski, Adam, Michael Alvarez, Jose Antonio Cheibub, and Fernando Limongi. 2000. *Democracy and Development: Political Institutions and Well-Being in the World, 1950–1990.* New York: Cambridge University Press.

Quick, Stephen A. 1977. "Bureaucracy and Rural Socialism in Zambia." *Journal of Modern African Studies* 15:3, 379–400.

Raftopoulos, Brian. 1997. "The Labour Movement in Zimbabwe: 1945–1965." In Brian Raftopoulos and Lloyd Sachikonye, eds., *Keep on Knocking: A History of the Labour Movement in Zimbabwe, 1900–1997.* Harare: Baobab Books.

Raftopoulous, Brian. 2000. "The State, NGOs and Democratisation." In Moyo, Makumbe and Raftopoulos, eds., *NGOs, the State, and Politics in Zimbabwe.* Harare: SAPES Trust.

——. 2006. "Reflections on Opposition Politics in Zimbabwe: The Politics of the Movement for Democratic Change (MDC)." In Brian Raftopoulos and Karin

Alexander, eds., *Reflections on Democratic Politics in Zimbabwe*. Cape Town: Institute for Justice and Reconciliation.

Rakner, Lise. 1994. *Trade Unions in Processes of Democratisation: A Study of Party Labour Relations in Zambia*. Bergen, Norway: Chr. Michelson Institute.

———. 2001. "The Pluralist Paradox: The Decline of Economic Interst Groups in Zambia in the 1990s." *Development and Change* 32, 521–43.

———. 2003. *Political and Economic Liberalisation in Zambia, 1991–2001*. Uppsala: Nordiska Afrikainstitutet.

Rakodi, Carole. 1988. "The Local State and Urban Local Government in Zambia." *Public Administration and Development* 8:1, 27–46.

Randall, Adrian. 2006. *Riotous Assemblies: Popular Protest in Hanoverian England*. Oxford: Oxford University Press.

Ranger, Terence. 1983. "The Invention of Tradition in Colonial Africa." In E. Hobsbawm and T. Ranger, eds., *The Invention of Tradition*. New York: Cambridge University Press.

———. 2004. "Nationalist Historiography, Patriotic History and the History of the Nation: The Struggle over the Past in Zimbabwe." *Journal of Southern African Studies* 30:2, 215–34.

Reeler, Anthony. 2003. *The Role of Militia Groups in Maintaining ZANU-PF's Political Power*. Unpublished manuscript, available at www.kubatana.net, Harare.

Regan, Patrick, and Errol Henderson. 2002. "Democracy, Threats and Political Repression in Developing Countries: Are Democracies Internally Less Violent?" *Third World Quarterly* 23:1, 119–36.

Reilly, Benjamin. 2001. *Democracy in Divided Societies: Electoral Engineering for Conflict Management*. Cambridge: Cambridge University Press.

Renfrew, Anne. 1992. *ESAP and Health: The Effects of the Economic Structural Adjustment Programme on the Health of the People of Zimbabwe*. Gweru: Mambo Press/Silveira House.

Reynolds, Andrew. 1999. *Electoral Systems and Democratization in Southern Africa*. Oxford: Oxford University Press.

Rich Dorman, Sara. 2001. "Inclusion and Exclusion: NGOs and Politics in Zimbabwe." D.Phil. Thesis, University of Oxford, UK.

———. 2002. "'Rocking the Boat?': Church-NGOs and Democratization in Zimbabwe." *African Affairs* 101:402, 75–92.

———. 2003. "NGOs and the Constitutional Debate in Zimbabwe: From Inclusion to Exclusion." *Journal of Southern African Studies* 29:4, 845–63.

Riddell, Roger. 1990. "Zimbabwe." In Roger Riddell, ed., *Manufacturing Africa*. London: James Currey.

Roessler, Philip. 2005. "Donor-Induced Democratization and Privatization of State Violence in Kenya and Rwanda." *Comparative Politics* 37:2, 207–28.

Rose, Richard, and Doh Chull Shin. 2001. "Democratization Backwards: The Problem of Third-Wave Democracies." *British Journal of Political Science* 31, 331–54.

Ross, Stanley. 1992. "The Rule of Law and Lawyers in Kenya." *Journal of Modern African Studies* 30:3, 421–42.

Rothchild, Donald. 1971. "The Beginning of Student Unrest in Zambia." *Transition* 40: December, 65–74.

Rothchild, Donald, and Philip Roeder. 2005. "Power Sharing as an Impediment to Peace and Democracy." In Donald Rothchild and Philip Roeder, eds., *Sustainable Peace: Power and Democracy after Civil War*. Ithaca, NY: Cornell University Press.

Rueschemeyer, Dietrich, Evelyn Huber Stephens, and John Stephens. 1992. *Capitalist Development and Democracy*. Chicago: University of Chicago Press.

Rustow, Dankwart. 1970. "Transitions to Democracy: Toward a Dynamic Model." *Comparative Politics* 2:3, 337–63.

Rutherford, Blair. 2001a. "Farm Workers and Trade Unions in Hurungwe District in Post-Colonial Zimbabwe." In Brian Raftopoulos and Lloyd Sachikonye, eds., *Striking Back: The Labour Movement and the Post-Colonial State in Zimbabwe*. Harare: Weaver Press.

——. 2001b. *Working on the Margins: Black Workers, White Farmers in Postcolonial Zimbabwe*. Harare: Weaver Press.

——. 2008. "Conditional Belonging: Farm Workers and the Cultural Politics of Recognition in Zimbabwe." *Development and Change* 39:1, 73–99.

Sabar-Friedman, Galia. 1997. "Church and State in Kenya, 1986–1992: The Churches' Involvement in the 'Game of Change'." *African Affairs* 96:382, 25–52.

Sachikonye, Lloyd. 1986. "State, Capital and Trade Unions." In I. Mandaza, ed., *Zimbabwe: The Political Economy of Transition*. Dakar, Senegal: CODESRIA.

——. 1993. "Bearing the Brunt: Labor and Structural Adjustment in Zimbabwe." *Southern Africa Report* 8:5.

——. 2001. "The State and the Union Movement in Zimbabwe: Co-optation, Conflict and Accommodation." In Bjorn Beckman and Lloyd Sachikonye, eds., *Labour Regimes and Liberalization: The Restructuring of State–Society Relations in Africa*.

Samuels, David. 2000. "Ambition and Competition: Explaining Legislative Turnover in Brazil." *Legislative Studies Quarterly* 25:3, 481–97.

——. 2002. "Presidentialized Parties: The Separation of Powers and Party Organization and Behavior." *Comparative Political Studies* 35:4, 461–83.

Sandbrook, Richard. 1972. "Patrons, Clients and Unions: The Labour Movement and Political Conflict in Kenya." *Journal of Commonwealth Political Studies* 10, 3–25.

——. 1977. "The Political Potential of African Urban Workers." *Canadian Journal of African Studies* 11:3, 411–33.

Sartori, Giovanni. 1976. *Parties and Party Systems*. Cambridge: Cambridge University Press.

Saunders, Richard. 1995. "Civics in Zimbabwe: Are They Making a Difference?" *Southern Africa Report* 10:3.

——. 1996. "Zimbabwe: ESAP's Fables." *Southern Africa Report* 11:2.

——. 2000. *Never the Same Again: Zimbabwe's Growth toward Democracy, 1980–2000*. Harare: Strand Multiprint (Pvt) Limited.

——. 2001. "Striking Ahead: Industrial Action and Labour Movement Development in Zimbabwe." In Lloyd Sachikonye and Brian Raftopoulos, eds., *Striking Back: The Labour Movement and the Post-Colonial State in Zimbabwe, 1980–2000*. Harare: Weaver Press.

Sawyer, Amos. 2004. "Violent Conflicts and Governance Challenges in West Africa: The Case of the Mano River Basin Area." *Journal of Modern African Studies* 42:3 437–63.

Scarritt, James R. 2006. "The Strategic Choice of Multiethnic Parties in Zambia's Dominant and Personalist Party System." *Commonwealth & Comparative Politics* 44:2, 234–56.

Schachter, Ruth. 1961. "Single-Party Systems in West Africa." *American Political Science Review* 55:2, 294–307.

Schaffer, Frederic, and Andreas Schedler. 2007. "What is Vote Buying?" In Frederic Shaffer, ed., *Elections for Sale: The Causes and Consequences of Vote Buying.* Boulder, CO: Lynne Rienner.

Schattschneider, E.E. 1942. *Party Government.* New York: Holt, Rinehart & Wilson.

Schedler, Andreas, ed. 2006. *Electoral Authoritarianism: The Dynamics of Unfree Competition.* Boulder, CO: Lynne Rienner.

——. 2002a. "The Menu of Manipulation." *Journal of Democracy* 13:2, 36–50.

——. 2002b. "The Nested Game of Democratization by Elections." *International Political Science Review* 23:1, 103–22.

Schelling, Thomas. 1960. *The Strategy of Conflict.* Cambridge, MA: Harvard University Press.

Schiphorst, Friedrich. 2001. *Strength & Weakness: The Rise of the Zimbabwe Congress of Trade Unions and the Development of Labour Relations, 1980-1995.* Ph. D. Dissertation, University of Leiden. Leiden, The Netherlands.

Schmitter, Philippe. 1974. "Still the Century of Corporatism?" *Review of Politics* 36:1, 85–131.

Schonfeld, William. 1983. "Political Parties: The Functional Approach and the Structural Alternative." *Comparative Politics* 15:4, 477–99.

Schumpeter, Joseph. 1976. *Capitalism, Socialism and Democracy.* New York: HarperCollins.

Scott, Ian. 1978. "Middle Class Politics in Zambia." *African Affairs* 77:308, 321–34.

Scott, James. 1969. "Corruption, Machine Politics, and Political Change." *The American Political Science Review* 63:4, 1142–58.

Shabad, Goldie, and Kazimierz Slomczynski. 2004. "Inter-party Mobility among Parliamentary Candidates in Post-Communist East Central Europe." *Party Politics* 10:2, 151–76.

Shaw, Timothy. 1982. "Beyond Neo-colonialism: Varieties of Corporatism in Africa." *Journal of Modern African Studies* 20:June, 239–61.

Shefter, Martin. 1994. *Political Parties and the State: The American Historical Experience.* Princeton, NJ: Princeton University Press.

Sibanda, Arnold. 2002. "Voicing a Peasant Alternative: The Organisation of Rural Associations for Progress (ORAP) in Zimbabwe." In Ben Romdhane and Sam Moyo, eds., *Peasant Organisations and the Democratisation Process in Africa.* Dakar, Senegal: CODESRIA.

Simon, David. 2002. "Can Democracy Consolidate in Africa amidst Poverty? Economic Influences upon Political Participation in Zambia." *Commonwealth & Comparative Politics* 40:1, 23–42.

Simutanyi, Neo. 1987. "Political Economy of Workers' Participation: The Role of Trade Unions in Promoting Industrial Democracy in Zambia." M.A. Thesis, University of Zambia.

——. 1996a. "Organised Labour, Economic Crisis, and Structural Adjustment in Africa: The Case of Zambia." In Bornwell Chikulo and Owen Sichone, eds., *Democracy in Zambia: Challenges for the Third Republic.* Harare: SAPES Trust.

——. 1996b. "The Politics of Structural Adjustment in Zambia." *Third World Quarterly* 17:4, 825–39.

Singh, Makhan. 1969. *History of Kenya's Trade Union Movement to 1952.* Nairobi: East African Publishing House.

Sithole, Masipula. 1997. "Zimbabwe's Eroding Authoritarianism." *Journal of Democracy* 8:1, 127–41.

Sithole, Masipula, and John Makumbe. 1997. "Elections in Zimbabwe: The ZANU(PF) Hegemony and its Incipient Decline." *African Journal of Political Science* 2:1, 122–39.

Skalnes, Tor. 1993. "The State, Interest Groups and Structural Adjustment in Zimbabwe." *Journal of Development Studies* 29:April.

Smith, Benjamin. 2005. "Life of the Party: The Origins of Regime Breakdown and Persistence under Single-Party Rule." *World Politics* 57, 421–51.

Smith, R. Drew. 1999. "Missionaries, Church Movements, and the Shifting Religious Significance of the State in Zambia." *Journal of Church and State* 41:3, 525–50.

Snyder, David, and Charles Tilly. 1972. "Hardship and Collective Violence in France, 1830 to 1960." *American Sociological Review* 37:5, 520–32.

Snyder, Jack. 2000. *From Voting to Violence: Democratization and Nationalist Conflict.* New York: W.W. Norton.

Snyder, Jack, and Karen Ballentine. 1996. "Nationalism and the Marketplace of Ideas." *International Security* 21:2, 5–40.

Southall, Roger, and Roddy Fox. 1999. "Lesotho's general election of 1998: Rigged or de rigeur?" *Journal of Modern African Studies* 37:4, 669–96.

Southall, Roger, and Geoffrey Wood. 1996. "Local Government and the Return to Multi-partyism in Kenya." *African Affairs* 95:381, 501–27.

Stephan, Maria, and Erica Chenoweth. 2008. "Why Civil Resistance Works: The Strategic Logic of Nonviolent Conflict." *International Security* 33:1, 7–44.

Stokes, Susan. 2005. "Perverse Accountability: A Formal Model of Machine Politics with Evidence from Argentina." *American Political Science Review* 99:3, 315–25.

Stoner-Weiss, Kathryn. 2001. "The Limited Reach of Russia's Party System: Under-institutionalization in Dual Transitions." *Politics and Society* 29:3, 385–414.

Strom, Kaare. 1990. "A Behavioral Theory of Competitive Political Parties." *American Journal of Political Science* 34:2, 565–98.

Sylvester, Christine. 1995. "Whither Opposition in Zimbabwe?" *Journal of Modern African Studies* 33:3, 403–23.

Szeftel, Morris. 2000. "'Eat with Us': Managing Corruption and Patronage under Zambia's Three Republics, 1964–1999." *Journal of Contemporary African Studies* 18:2, 207–24.

Taagepera, Rein, and Matthew Soberg Shugart. 1989. *Seats and Votes: The Effects and Determinants of Electoral Systems.* New Haven: Yale University Press.

Takougang, Joseph. 2003. "The 2002 Legislative Election in Cameroon: A Retrospective on Cameroon's Stalled Democracy Movement." *Journal of Modern African Studies* 41:3, 421–35.

Tarrow, Sidney. 1989. *Democracy and Disorder: Protest and Politics in Italy, 1965–1975.* Oxford: Oxford University Press.

——. 1994. *Power in Movement: Social Movements, Collective Action, and Politics.* New York: Cambridge University Press.

Tavits, Margit. 2005. "The Development of Stable Party Support: Electoral Dynamics in Post-Communist Europe." *American Journal of Political Science* 49:2, 283–98.

Taylor, Scott. 1999. "Race, Class and Neopatrimonialism in Zimbabwe." In Richard Joseph, ed., *State, Conflict and Democracy in Africa.* Boulder, CO: Lynne Rienner.

Tembo, T.Z. 1996. *The Road to Multiparty Democracy in Zambia and its Conse-quences.* Livingstone, Zambia: Sanisani Chemist.

Thelen, Kathleen. 2004. *How Institutions Evolve: The Political Economy of Skills in Germany, Britain, the United States and Japan.* Cambridge: Cambridge University Press.

Thompson, E.P. 1964. *The Making of the English Working Class.* New York: Pantheon.

——. 1971. "The Moral Economy of the English Crowd in the Eighteenth Century." *Past and Present* 50:1, 76–136.

Throup, David, and Charles Hornsby. 1998. *Multi-party Politics in Kenya: The Kenyatta and Moi States and the Triumph of the System in the 1992 Election.* Athens, OH: Ohio University Press.

Tibbetts, Alexandra. 1994. "Mamas Fighting for Freedom in Kenya." *Africa Today* 41:4, 27–48.

Tilly, Charles. 1978. *From Mobilization to Revolution.* Reading, MA: Addison-Wesley.

——. 1995. *Popular Contention in Great Britain, 1758–1834.* Cambridge, MA: Harvard University Press.

——. 2003a. *Stories, Identities and Political Change.* Lanham, MD: Rowman & Littlefield.

——. 2003b. *The Politics of Collective Violence.* Cambridge: Cambridge University Press.

——. 2004a. *Contention and Democracy in Europe, 1650–2000.* New York: Cambridge University Press.

——. 2004b. "Social Boundary Mechanisms." *Philosophy of the Social Sciences* 34:2, 211–36.

Touwen, Anne. 1990. "Socio-economic Development of Women in Zambia: An Analysis of Two Women's Organisations." Research Report, No. 42. Leiden, The Netherlands: African Studies Centre.

Tripp, Aili. 2004. "The Changing Face of Authoritarianism in Africa: The Case of Uganda." *Africa Today* 50:3, 3–26.

Tronvoll, Kjetil. 2001. "Voting, Violence and Violations: Peasant Voice on the Flawed Elections in Hadiya, Southern Ethiopia." *Journal of Modern African Studies* 39:4, 697–716.

Tull, Denis M., and Andreas Mehler. 2005. "The Hidden Costs of Power-Sharing: Reproducing Insurgent Violence in Africa." *African Affairs* 104:416, 375–98.

Valenzuela, J. Samuel. 1989. "Labor Movements in Transitions to Democracy: A Framework for Democracy." *Comparative Politics* 21:July, 445–72.

Vambe, Maurice Taonezvi. 2000. "Popular Songs and Social Realities in Post-Independence Zimbabwe." *African Studies Review* 43:2, 73–86.

Van Binsbergen, Wim. 1976. "Religious Innovation and Political Conflict in Zambia: A Contribution to the Interpretation of the Lumpa Rising." *African Perspectives* 2, 101–35.

Van de Walle, Nicolas. 2002. "Africa's Range of Regimes." *Journal of Democracy* 13:2, 66–80.

——. 2003. "Presidentialism and Clientalism in Africa's Emerging Party Systems." *Journal of Modern African Studies* 41:2, 297–322.

Van de Walle, Nicholas, and Kimberly Smiddy Butler. 1999. "Political Parties and Party Systems in Africa's Illiberal Democracies." *Cambridge Review of International Affairs* 13:1, 14–28.

Van Donge, Jan Kees. 2009. "The Plundering of Zambian resources by Frederick Chiluba and his Friends: A Case Study of the Interaction between National Politics and the International Drive towards Good Governance." *African Affairs* 108:430, 69–90.

Van der Plaetse, B., G. Hlatiwayo, L. Van Eygen, B. Meessen, and B. Criel. 2005. "Costs and Revenue of Health Care in a Rural Zimbabwean District." *Health Policy and Planning* 20:4, 243–51.

Varshney, Ashutosh. 2003. *Ethnic Conflict and Civic Life: Hindus and Muslims in India*. New Haven: Yale University Press.

Vickery, Kenneth. 1998. "The Rhodesia Railways African Strike of 1945, Part I: A Narrative Account." *Journal of Southern African Studies* 24:3, 545–60.

Villarreal, Andres. 2002. "Political Competition and Violence in Mexico: Hierarchical Social Control in Local Patronage Structures." *American Sociological Review* 67:4, 477–98.

VonDoepp, Peter. 1996. "Political Transition and Civil Society: The Cases of Kenya and Zambia." *Studies in Comparative International Development* 31:1, 24–47.

——. 2005. "Party Cohesion and Fractionalization in New African Democracies: Lessons from Struggles over Third-term Amendments." *Studies in Comparative International Development* 40:3, 65–87.

Wallerstein, Immanuel. 1966. "The Decline of the Party in Single-Party African States." In Joseph LaPalombara and Myron Weiner, eds., *Political Parties and Political Development*. Princeton, NJ: Princeton University Press.

Wanjohi, Nick. 2003. "The Sustainability of Political Parties in Kenya." In M. Mohamed Salih, ed., *African Political Parties: Evolution, Institutionalisation and Governance*. London: Pluto Press.

Wantchekon, Leonard. 2003. "Clientalism and Voting Behavior: Evidence from a Field Experiment in Benin." *World Politics* 55, 399–422.

——. 2004. "The Paradox of 'Warlord' Democracy: A Theoretical Investigation." *American Political Science Review* 98:1, 17–33.

——. 2008. "Expert Information, Public Deliberation and Electoral Support for Good Governance: Experimental Evidence from Benin." Working Paper. New York University.

Watts, Duncan. 1999. "Networks, Dynamics, and the Small-World Phenomenon." *American Journal of Sociology* 105:2, 493–527.

Way, Lucan. 2005. "Authoritarian State Building and the Sources of Regime Competitiveness in the Fourth Wave: The Cases of Belarus, Moldova, Russia, and Ukraine." *World Politics* 57:2, 231–61.

Widner, Jennifer. 1991. "Interest Group Structure and Organization in Kenya's Informal Sector: Cultural Despair or a Politics of Multiple Allegiances?" *Comparative Political Studies* 24:1, 31–55.

——. 1992. *The Rise of the Party-State in Kenya: From Nyayo to Harambee*. Berkeley, CA: University of California Press.

——. 1997. "Political Parties and Civil Societies in sub-Saharan Africa." In Marina Ottaway, ed., *Democracy in Africa: The Hard Road Ahead*. Boulder, CO: Lynne Rienner.

Wiseman, John. 1986. "Urban Riots in West Africa, 1977 to 1985." *Journal of Modern African Studies* 24:3, 509–18.

Wiktorowicz, Quintan. 2000. "Civil Society as Social Control: State Power in Jordan." *Comparative Political Studies* 33:1, 43–61.

Wood, Brian. 1988. "Trade-Union Organisation and the Working Class." In Colin Stoneman, ed., *Zimbabwe's Prospects: Issues of Race, Class, State and Capital in Southern Africa*. London: Macmillan.

Wood, Elisabeth. 2000. *Forging Democracy from Below: Insurgent Transitions in South Africa and El Salvador, Cambridge Studies in Comparative Politics*. Cambridge: Cambridge University Press.

Young, Crawford, and Thomas Turner. 1985. *The Rise and Decline of the Zairian State*. Madison: University of Wisconsin Press.

Zakaria, Fareed. 1997. "The Rise of Illiberal Democracy." *Foreign Affairs* 76: November, 22–43.

Zaller, John. 1992. *The Nature and Origins of Mass Opinion*. Cambridge: Cambridge University Press.

Zelniker, Shimshon. 1971. "Changing Patterns of Trade Unionism: The Zambian Case." Ph.D. Dissertation, University of California Los Angeles.

Ziblatt, Daniel. 2006. "How did Europe Democratize? A Review Article." *World Politics* 58: January, 311–38.

Zielinski, Jakub. 1999. "Transitions from Authoritarian Rule and the Problem of Violence." *Journal of Conflict Resolution* 43:2, 213–28.

Zolberg, Aristide. 1966. *Creating Political Order: The Party-States of West Africa*. Chicago: University of Chicago Press.

Zukas, Simon. 2002. *Into Exile and Back*. Lusaka: Bookworld Publishers.

Index

Lightning Source UK Ltd.
Milton Keynes UK
UKOW030625160513

210752UK00001B/2/P